# Military Medals
## of
## America

**Colonel Frank C. Foster**

First Edition

**Published by MOA Press**
**Medals of America Press**
114 Southchase Blvd.
Fountain Inn, SC 29644
www.moapress.com
www.usmedals.com

## Dedicated to

# LONNY BORTS

**Lawrence "Lonny" Borts** developed a lifelong interest in military awards as a boy in New York City during World War II. After graduating from the New York University College of Engineering, he spent most of his professional life with the Grumman Corporation, retiring in 1992 as an Engineering Specialist in Airborne Surveillance Systems. He maintained one of the largest collections of military ribbons in the world and was consultant to several U.S. Armed Forces directorates and medals research societies. He realized every collector's dream when he participated in the design of the Coast Guard "E" Ribbon and the Kosovo Campaign Medal. Lonny was the author of *United Nations Medals and Missions*, the most comprehensive reference work on the subject and co author of eight editions of *Military Medals of the United States* the fore-runner of this book. He passed away in 2017 and will be sorely missed by the author, his many friends, family and Beverly, his bride of over 60 years.

Hardcover Edition ISBN — 978-1-884452-71-0
Softcover Edition ISBN — 978-1-884452-72-7
Library of Congress Control Number: 2018908760

### Copyright © 2018 by MOA Press

All rights reserved. No part of this publication may be reproduced, stored in retrieval systems or transmitted by any means, electronic, mechanical or by photocopying, recording or by any information storage and retrieval system without permission from the publishers, except for the inclusion of brief quotations in a review.

Edited by Mrs. Linda Brailsford Foster

Proudly printed in the United States of America
by RR Donnelly, Williamston, South Carolina 29697
Mr. Eric Steadman-Lead Pressman

### Published by MOA Press (Medals of America Press)
114 Southchase Blvd.
Fountain Inn, SC 29644
www.moapress.com
www.usmedals.com

# Military Medals of America

| | |
|---|---|
| Introduction | 5 |
| The Beginning of Military Awards | 6 |
| History of United States Military Awards | 10 |
| Types of Military Medals, Ribbons & Devices | 36 |
| How to Determine Veteran's Military Medals | 38 |
| Issue of U.S. Medals to Veterans, Retirees and Their Families | 40 |
| Displaying Military Awards for all Services | 51 |
| Wear of Medals, Insignia and the Uniform by Veterans, Retirees and Former Service Member | 94 |
| Wearing Ribbons and Medals | 96 |
| Presentation Guide to Decorations, Medals, Unit Awards & Service Ribbons | 100 |
| Armed Forces Ribbon Chart Displays | 102 |
| USN, USMC, USCG, Right Breast Displays on the Full Dress Uniform | 114 |
| UN and Merchant Marine Ribbons | 115 |
| Armed Forces Attachments and Devices | 116 |
| Early U.S. Military Medals 1782 to 1939 | 124 |
| U.S. Military Awards 1939 to Present | 131 |
| The Pyramid of Honor | 132 |
| The Medals of Honor | 134 |
| Medals, Unit Awards and Ribbon Descriptions | 144 |
| Foreign Military Decorations | 216 |
| United Nations and NATO medals | 220 |
| Foreign Service Medals | 223 |
| USN and USCG Marksmanship awards | 226 |
| Bibliography | 230 |
| Index | 230 |

## About the Author

### COLONEL FRANK FOSTER

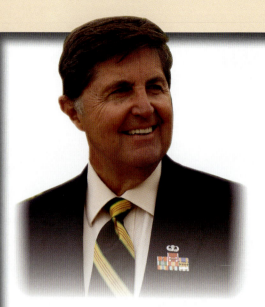

COL. FRANK C. FOSTER ( Ret.), obtained his BS from The Citadel, MBA from the University of Georgia and is a graduate of the Army's Command and General Staff College and War College. He saw service as a Battery Commander in Germany and served in Vietnam with the 173rd Airborne Brigade and USARV General Staff. In the Adjutant General's Corps, he served as the Adjutant General of the Central Army Group, the 4th Infantry Division and was the Commandant and Chief of the Army's Adjutant General's Corps from 1986 to 1990. His military service provided him a unique understanding of the Armed Forces Awards System. He currently operates Medals of America Press and is the author of the *The Decorations, Medals, Badges and Insignia of the United States Army*, *The Medals and Ribbons of the United States Air Force* and coauthor of *The Decorations and Medals of the Republic of Vietnam* and *Marine Awards and Insignia* along with numerous other publications. He and his wife Linda, who was decorated with the Army Commander's Medal in 1990 for service to the Army, live in Greenville, South Carolina.

## Grateful Acknowledgements

The author wish to express his deepest appreciation to the following individuals for their invaluable contributions. Without their unselfish efforts, this book would have ended as an unfilled dream.

- The entire Medals of America team with special thanks to: Mrs. Linda Foster for the splendid job in editing this book, Mrs. Lois Owens for custom mounting, Mr. Kirk Stotzer Art Director and Ms. "Buz" Buswell - Pre Press.
- The Medals of America review team of Master Chief (Ret.) Jerry Dantzler and First Sgt. (Ret.) Keith Taylor.
- Col. (Ret.) Charles Mugno, Director of the Institute of Heraldry.
- COL. (Ret.) F. P. Anthony and Mrs. Charlene Rose formerly of the U.S. Marine Corps Military Awards Branch.
- Ms. Phyllis Dula, U.S. Coast Guard Military Personnel Management Specialist and her predecessor, Ms. Diane E. Porter.
- Mr. James "Jim" Thompson for Marine guidance.
- Mr. John Sylvester, for Vietnamese awards.
- Major Peter Morgan for great insignia advice.
- Dr. Steve Hines and Mrs. Terri Hines for their techinical assistance in getting the book on different production platforms.
- Mr. Bryan Scott Johnson for his references on Medals of the Revolution and readiness to lend a helping hand.
- CDR Jerome Mahar (USN Ret.) - Awards Policy J1 (Personnel) DOD Joint Staff.
- Mr. Clinton Foster for the generous use of his fine photographs of early numbered U.S. Military Medals.
- Mr. Augusto Meneses, Design Director of ADDMedia Creatives for his most excellent work in preparing this book.

# Introduction

Twenty plus years ago, Lonny Borts and I sat down at a table in Red Top Plantation, Fountain Inn, South Carolina to draft the first edition of our *Complete Guide to United States Military Medals*. After eight editions and 200,000 copies it is time to replace and expand the book. If any justification is required, you need only to note that the United States Armed Forces have produced over 100 new military awards in 70 plus years since the unification of the Armed Forces in 1947, or an average of over one new award per year. What is also remarkable since 1947 the majority of the new awards have been ribbon only awards, especially in the Air Force and Coast Guard. To put it in prospective of the 106 new military awards since 1947, 57 of them have been ribbon only awards. While the establishment of so many awards is a clear indication of the many missions and roles thrust upon the Armed Forces since the United States assumed its mantle of world leadership it also reflects the importance of medals and ribbons to an all volunteer force.

This book is enlarged by over 30 pages and encompasses not only the award changes made over the past 20 years, but now covers all significant military medals back to the start of the Republic in 1776. As before, it is designed to be a definitive illustrated reference and guide covering United States decorations, medals and ribbons for veterans, their families, active duty and reserve personnel. It is also meant as a single source for the military decorations and medals of each service. Some of the material is derived from the latest military awards and uniform manuals and other authoritative sources, although my personal opinions usually slip in from time to time.

Owing to the complimentary reviews enjoyed by earlier books, I expanded the original format and substantially upgraded readability (hopefully). There are new sections on the history of military medals, how to determine a veteran's medals and how to display veterans medals and ribbons so as to make the subject a little clearer.

The book also tries to reflect the growing appreciation throughout our country for the sacrifice and effort our veterans have endured to earn these awards. This awareness is coupled with the desire of families and veterans to display the honors their grateful country has awarded them. I have kept the best of the earlier editions and enhanced them with new material on the wear, display and variations of our military awards. I hope that you will be pleased by the level of detail and features in this book that cover the entire spectrum of United States Military awards. Some of the new sections are:

A. The color device and ribbon attachment pages that reflect a complete history and their correct wear.
B. Complete order of precedence charts for the wear of multi-service ribbons developed in response to veterans who have served in more than one Service branch.
C. Detailed ribbon charts which show award precedence for each of the five Services spanning the period from World War II to the Global War on Terrorism.

Finally, in what has become a trademark, the new *Inherent Resolve Campaign Medal* is presented on page 199.

And then there's that ugly word; MISTEAKS. Every book in print, probably dating back to the Gutenberg Bible, no matter how often edited, brilliantly-conceived or well-intentioned, is bound to possess its share of errors and mispelled words. We have worked hard to make this an error free book. If any errors are detected, please accept my apologies, let me know through our publisher and be assured they will be corrected in future editions. In this spirit, I will start the ball rolling by pointing out that the words "MISTEAKS" and "mispelled" in the second sentence of this paragraph are both misspelled.

As the famous Charleston artist John Doyle once said: 'It takes two people to paint a picture, one to paint and one to tell the painter when to stop." This book may have gotten a little carried away in some areas but hopefully not. I hope that this new edition will provide you the insights and information to honor the veteran in your family.

Your suggestions to improve future editions are always appreciated. Cheers!

**Col. Frank C. Foster**
*(USA, Ret.)*
*Greenville, SC*

# The Beginning of Military Awards

There is an old saying that you have to know where you have been before you know where you are going. That's true in understanding military decorations, awards and insignia. The ancient Egyptians as early as a thousand B. C. awarded military decorations such as golden bees or golden flies to outstanding warriors. Tomb writings for example refer to three massive golden bees linked by a golden chain that were thought to be a decoration of recognition for distinguished service at El-Kab for a certain Aahmes. Remarkable tomb pictures describe the ceremony of the award of golden bracelets, necklaces, golden flies and lions. Didu, a standard bearer under pharaoh Amenhotep III, was awarded a necklace with golden flies and a golden lion. His cousin, Nebkemi who had the same rank, received a golden bracelet. Women, too, might be honored. Queen Ahhotep received three golden flies for her role in the struggle against the Hyksos (foreign invaders).

While the beginning of military awards can be traced to the ancient Egyptians and the Greeks it was the Roman Legions who first organized an award system honoring their soldiers for bravery and service. Once recognized, Roman soldiers wore these decorations in battle, parades and displayed them in their homes after their military service. If an entire Roman legion was cited for valor a decoration was added to the Legion's eagle standard.

Two thousand years ago the Greek historian Polybius wrote: "If there was any fight, and some soldiers distinguish themselves by bravery, the legion commander would bring his troops together and call forward those to be decorated. The Roman commander would call out the merits, deeds and heroic actions for which the Roman soldier was to be decorated and present the legionnaire with a necklace, armbands or set of disks. During the ceremony the commander would often tie the item to Legionnaires armor." (Just as a commander pins a military medal on the chest of a soldier today.)

During the time of the Roman Empire, the Roman army established a series of decorations for military bravery. The most common decoration for bravery was a golden circle necklet called a Torques.

Torques were worn around the necks of Celtic Warriors, and their award originally represented the defeat of an enemy in single combat. Over time the Torques became an award for bravery. A second type of valor award for all ranks were embossed or plain armbands called Armillae. Another highly coveted award was an embossed disc called a Phalerae which were sometimes awarded in sets and worn on a leather harness over the legionnaire's armor. These discs were presented in bronze, silver and gold and there was no limit to the number a soldier could be awarded.

Above these three awards the Romans, following the Greeks, presented various crowns such as the Corona Aurea (Golden Crown) presented to Centurions for victorious personal combat and the Corona Vallaris (Fortification) crown awarded to the first legionaries or centurion over the walls of an enemy fortification.

A very high honor was the Corona Civia, a crown of Oak leaves for saving the life of a fellow Roman citizen during battle. Eventually, the Corona Civia allowed recipients to serve as Senators in the Roman Senate. The one distinction between Roman army awards and today is the Romans only decorated living soldiers. There were no posthumous honors for the fallen.

The most valuable and prestigious awards were not reserved for the rich and powerful but in theory at least a foot soldier was eligible for major awards the same as the commander, the centurion or general. Bravery awards were made according to bravery and merit. "Virtue atque opera in ea pugna" (His valor and his deeds in battle) and "virtutis causa" (Because of his valor). A parallel between Roman and modern American military awards is that the highest Roman awards such as the" corona civica" which brought many social privileges in the soldier's lifetime and the American Medal of Honor is that both can be earned by privates, sailors, marines or airmen as well as generals.

After the fall of Rome, the custom of awarding medals for military service probably owes its origin to the badges used within the armies of England after the decline of armor and before the introduction of distinctive uniforms. The badges themselves of course grew out of the coats of arms which emblazon retainer's liveries. There are a number of instances of record where commanders rewarded men on the battlefield by giving them badges struck in some valuable metal or perhaps embossed with precious stones. Heroes, who were decorated in this way remove the ordinary metal insignia from their coats or hats and worn instead the much prize emblem. This was probably the beginning of medal granting and wearing as it is in the Armed Forces of today.

U.S. Air Force Combat Action Medal

The symbols from the Roman standard pictured above can be seen in the decorations and awards of Napoleon, United States Army insignia as early as 1812 and the Third Reich to name a few. So as we begin the history of United States decorations and awards it is clear our early designs of the eagle, lightning, victory wreaths of laurel and oak came from ancient Roman Legions.

It was Queen Elizabeth I who introduced the custom of bestowing medals as rewards for naval and military service based on her fleet's defeat of the Spanish Armada in 1588. The most famous is known as the **Armada Medal** medal and bore profile of Queen Elizabeth in an elaborate quilted dress with neck ruff and diadem. The reverse of the medal shows a tiny island surrounded by a storm beaten sea while a bay tree stands unaffected by the wind. The inscription in Latin translates," Not even in danger affect it". The design provided is with a loop for suspension around the wear's neck and influenced medals for the coming centuries.

*Set of Roman Phalerae found in Germany and displayed in the Lauersfort Phalera, Burg Linn Museum Center, Krefeld, Germany.*

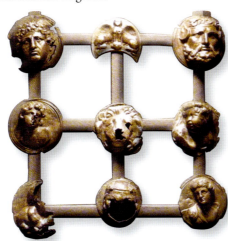

While Queen Elizabeth was the first to award an English war medal she presented them sparingly and only to naval personnel. Charles I instituted **The Forlorn Hope Medal** in 1643 which was to be awarded to soldiers who distinguished themselves in battle but there are no records of it being awarded. You could say it was the earliest forerunner of the **Victoria Cross**.

Medals of America 7

The first military medal that could be really designated as the earliest campaign medal where the entire army received the medal was awarded by Oliver Cromwell to commemorate the **Battle of Dunbar** in 1650. The medal was struck in two sizes, a small gold medal for officers and a large silver one for the ranks. Both had Cromwell's profile on the front with the battle scene in the background and on the reverse was a rather curious perspective view of Parliament.

**The Battle of Culloden** medal was the earliest to be provided with a ribbon of special pattern in 1746. What is interesting about the Battle of Culloden medal is it was an engraved oval designed to be worn around the neck of officers by means of a Crimson ribbon having a green border. Probably the first award to be issued with a specific ribbon. The medal was struck in gold, silver and perhaps bronze and was given to commanders only not to the rank-and-file. While the first campaign medal was the Dunbar award it was almost 2 centuries later that the English similarly recognized their soldiers and that was for the victory at Waterloo.

I think it's worth noting here that both the United Kingdom and United States, once they instituted the practice of campaign medals and decorations had a fairly common practice of presenting these awards to their recipients two to three years later. This is especially noteworthy in the United States when many of the campaign medals were not struck until several years after the conflict, World War II being the a large scale example and the Civil War over 40 years later.

During the several centuries that medals were being granted in the England and France, a wide range of metals were used, generally silver, gold and bronze were by far the most usual with various shapes in the early days favoring an oval but circular pieces such as this French Medal of Constantine the Great on horseback generally found the greatest favor by 1650.

Across the channel the French had developed their own series of awards with perhaps the most famous being the order of St. Louis which was after the Revolutionary war probably the origin for the design of the American Society Order of Cincinnatus. The Royal and Military Order of Saint Louis Ordre Royal et Militaire de Saint-Louis is a dynastic order of chivalry founded in 1693 by King Louis XIV , named after Saint Louis (King Louis IX of France). It was intended as a reward for exceptional officers, notable as the first decoration that could be granted to non-nobles.

So as we enter the period of the American Revolution in 1776 we can say the European model for military awards at that time, with rare exception, was to award gold and silver medals from the King to the commander of his victorious forces. The founders of United States did not look favorably upon anything that reflected government by a monarch. The Constitution provides that, " no title of nobility shall be granted by the United States; and no person holding any office of profit or trust under them shall, without the consent of Congress, accept any present, or emolument, office or title of any kind whatever from any King, Prince or foreign state." Following this early mandate the United States forbid any officer or enlisted man to wear any medal or decoration granted by any foreign state or ruler.

The Continental Congress while refuting all the trappings of a monarch and sovereign did copy the practice of awarding special commemorative gold medals to victorious commanders on land and sea. Under the initial supervision of Benjamin Franklin and Thomas Jefferson, Congress commissioned the finest French royal engravers to prepare the medals. The task of designing, approving and manufacturing the medals meant it was several years between the victory and the actual presentation to the recipient.

Mr. Jefferson had a more democratic and promotional idea to spread the impact of these awards throughout the country and even abroad. He was so proud of the United States great victories that these Congressional medals represented and their exquisite artistic design that he wanted to have a set issued to every college in United States and a set of the medals presented to heads of state, and foreign dignitaries. Jefferson clearly saw the medals as the best way to preserve the memory, valor and distinction of American soldiers and sailors.

Athena (Minerva) holding Victory 297-281 B. C.

Minerva defending a young America 1781 A.D..

Minerva on the first Medals of Honor 1861 A.D..

The medallion above was struck about 297-281 B. C. and shows Athena (Minerva) holding Victory (Nike). Athena was the ancient Greek goddess of wisdom and warfare, who was later syncretized with the Roman goddess Minerva. Minerva was the Roman goddess of wisdom and strategic warfare. Almost 2000 years later, when designing America's famous Victory Medal of Independence, French engraver Augustin Dupré made sure that France (in the form of Athena) was seen as the protector of the young American republic (shown as an infant holding two snakes) by fighting off the British Lion who is leaping at the child. Minerva's shield is decked with the lilies of France. The final latin inscription reads" The courageous child was aided by the gods" and dated October 1777/1781.

Less than a 100 years later in 1861 the Navy Medal of Honor reflects the same design elements using Minerva, the Roman goddess of war and adding an owl perched on her helmet to represent wisdom. In the Roman tradition, her left hand holds rods and an ax blade, symbolic of authority. In her right hand is the shield of the Union of States. A man clutching snakes in his hands, representing Discord, recoils from Minerva.

The head of Minerva is the focal point of the Army Medal of Honor while the wreath of green leaves is the laurel wreath, the first known symbol of honor from the ancient days of Greece and Rome. The military symbols of honor, valor and merit have a long history of thousands of years.

John Paul Jone's Medal in Bronze and Gold.

John Paul Jone's Medal dies and a gold medal struck from them.

*In a letter Thomas Jefferson wrote to M. Dupre, Engraver of Medals and Medallist of the French Royal Academy of Painting and Sculpture, dated Feb. 13, 1789, he sends the "devices" (designs) "for the medals for General Morgan and Rear-Admiral Paul Jones..." to Dupre for "the success of the dies up to the striking of three hundred and fifty of each medal in gold, silver or bronze... The hand engraved dies of medal by the French medalist Augustin Dupré as well as gold and bronze examples are shown above.*

**Medals of America** 9

*"Few inventions could be more happily calculated to diffuse the knowledge and preserve the memory of illustrious characters and splendid events, than medals." wrote Col David Humpreys in 1787 while corresponding for Gen. Washington at Mount Vernon.*

*Benjamin Franklin, the U.S. Ambassador to France commissioned Benjamin Duvivier, Chief Engraver of the Paris Mint to produced the first medal in 1781 to honor General Washington for the Seige of Boston.*

# A Brief History of United States Military Awards

**Revolutionary War 1775-1782.** "Few inventions could be more happily calculated to diffuse the knowledge and preserve the memory of illustrious characters and splendid events, than medals." These words written in 1787 expressed the feelings of the Continental Congress in March 1776 when they instituted the tradition of awarding medals as the highest distinction of national appreciation for our military heroes.

General Washington's success in driving the British from Boston in 1776, General Horatio Gates' victory at Saratoga in 1777, the storming of the British Forts at Stony Point and Paulus Hook in 1779, and General Greene's Southern victories in 1781 all led to the final British surrender at Yorktown in 1781. These were great milestones in the United States' War of Independence. The people and Congress were very proud of their heroes and wished to bestow a sign of national recognition especially upon those officers who had distinguished themselves in battle.

As a result, Congress voted to award gold medals to outstanding military leaders. The first approved medal honored George Washington and similar medals were bestowed upon other victors such as General Horatio Gates and Captain John Paul Jones for his naval victory over the HMS Serapis in 1779.

Since Benjamin Franklin, the U.S. Ambassador to France at the time, had access to the best of the French Royal engravers, it was only natural for this country to turn to France for help in the actual production of our first military medals. Under Franklin's leadership the Chief Engraver of the Paris Mint produced the first medal in 1784. However, following Franklin's departure from France, the development of the other medals for American heroes was extremely slow until Col. David Humphreys and, later, Thomas Jefferson became involved. It was not until March, 1790, that President Washington received his gold medal and silver copies of all the medals approved by Congress over 10 years earlier.

While these large table top presentation medals were not designed to be worn on the military uniform many thought otherwise since General Horatio Gates' portrait shows his medal hanging from a neck ribbon. Thomas Jefferson wanted these medals, of which he was very proud, to be known and preserved throughout the world. He planned to present sets of these medals to heads of state, foreign dignitaries and every college in the United States. Jefferson clearly saw medals as the best way to preserve the memory, valor and distinction of America's soldiers and sailors.

*President Thomas Jefferson clearly saw medals as the best way to preserve the memory, valor and distinction of America's soldiers and sailors.*

10 **Military Medals of America**

## The Continental Congress issued 11 medals for 7 battles:

The Siege of Boston, March 1776 (one medal)

The Battle of Saratoga in October 1777 (one medal)

The Battle of Stony Point in July 1779 (three medals)

The Battle of Paulus Hook August 1779 (one medal)

The Battle of Flamborough Head September 1779 (one medal)

The Battle of Cowpens January 1781 (three medals)

The Battle of the Eutaw Springs September 1781 (one medal)

*Gold medal struck to honor George Washington for his service in driving the British from Boston in 1776.*

These battles are significant enough to American military history and American military awards to go into some detail since they are rarely seen and appreciated today.

### The Siege of Boston

In the wake of the battles of Lexington and Concord on 19 April 1775, American colonial forces closed in on the city of Boston. They were initially guided by Brig. Gen. William Heath of the Massachusetts militia; however, he later passed command to Gen. Artemas Ward. Over the next several days, patriot forces were augmented by new arrivals from Connecticut, Rhode Island and New Hampshire. Within the city, the British commander, Lieut. Gen. Thomas Gage was surprised by the size and the perseverance of the American forces. He began to fortify parts of the city against attack, consolidating his forces in the city proper and erecting defenses across the Boston neck. The British were deprived of access to the surrounding countryside, but the harbor remained open and ships of the Royal Navy, under Vice Admiral Samuel Graves, were able to supply the British troops in the city. Lacking artillery to break the stalemate, Massachusetts Provincial Congress dispatched Col. Benedict Arnold to seize the guns at Fort Ticonderoga. Joining with Col. Ethan Allen's Green Mountain boys, Arnold captured the fort on 10 May.

On 25 May, HMS Cerberus arrived in Boston carrying Major Generals William Howell, Henry Clinton and John Burgoyne. The newly arrived officers and their troops advocated for breaking out of the city and seizing Bunker Hill, above Charlestown, and Dorchester Heights south of the city. Learning of the British plans on 15 June, the Americans moved quickly to occupy both locations. On Charlestown peninsula, Colonel William Prescott had 1200 men erect a fortified line on Breed's Hill during the night of the 16th. Spotting the Americans works the next morning, General Howel led British forces over to Charlestown and attacked on 17 June.

Repelling the large British assaults, Prescott's men stood firm and were only forced to retreat when they ran out of ammunition. In the fighting, Howe's troops suffered over 1000 casualties while the Americans sustained around 450. The high cost of victory at the Battle of Bunker Hill would influence British command decisions for the remainder of the campaign. Having taken the Heights, the British began work to fortify the Charlestown neck to prevent another American incursion.

Colonel, later General Henry Knox

General George Washington, as Commander in Chief of the Army, received the first Gold Medal awarded by Congress from Thomas Jefferson on 17 March, 1790, 14 years after liberating Boston on 17 March, 1776.

While events were unfolding in Boston, the Continental Congress in Philadelphia created the Continental Army on June 14 and appointed George Washington as commander in chief the following day. Riding north to take command, Washington arrived outside of Boston on three July. He established his headquarters in Cambridge and started molding the masses of colonial troops into an army.

In November, Henry Knox presented a plan to Washington for transporting Ticonderoga's cannons to Boston. Impressed, he appointed Knox as a Colonel and sent him to Fort Ticonderoga. In late November, an armed American ship succeeded in capturing the British Brigantine Nancy outside of Boston Harbor. Loaded with munitions, it provided Washington with much needed gun powder and arms. In Boston, the situation for the British changed when Gen. Gage was relieved in favor of Gen. Howe. Though reinforced to about 11,000 men, the British were chronically short on supplies. As winter set in, Washington's army was reduced to about 9000 men through desertion's and expiring enlistments. His situation improved in January 1776, when Col. Knox arrived in Cambridge with 59 cannons from Ticonderoga. In February, Washington proposed a plan to drive the British from the city by placing guns on Dorchester Heights. Assigning several of Knox's guns to Cambridge and Rocksberry, Washington began a diversionary bombardment of the British lines overnight the 4th of March. Early in the morning of 5 March, American troops moved cannons to Dorchester Heights where they could strike the city and British ships in the harbor. Seeing the American fortifications on the Heights in the morning, Howe initially planned to assault the position but was prevented by a snow storm late in the day. On 8 March, Gen. Washington received word that the British intended to evacuate and would not burn the city if allowed to leave unmolested. Gen. Washington did not formally respond, but agreed to the terms and the British began embarking along with numerous Boston loyalists. On 17 March, the British departed for Halifax, Nova Scotia and the American forces entered the city. Having been taken after an 11 months siege, Boston remained in American hands for the remainder of the war.

Congress voted to present to Gen. Washington a Gold Medal for his victory over the British in Boston. Benjamin Franklin while in Paris commissioned Benjamin Duvivier, Chief Engraver of the Paris Mint to sculptor the medal. Shown to the left are both sides of America's first military medal. The front is inscribed in Latin with the translation reading, "The American Congress to George Washington, Commander in Chief of the Army, the assertor of liberty". An undraped bust of Gen. Washington is facing the right. The reversal of the medal, again in Latin, translates to read, "the enemy put to flight for the first time" and shows Gen. Washington on horseback, surrounded by his staff, pointing towards the British fleet, which is leaving Boston. The American army in battle array stands front of its entrenchment ready to occupy the city. Underneath in Latin it reads, "Boston retaken, March 17, 1776"

# The Battle of Saratoga

During the summer of 1776, a powerful army under British Gen. Sir William Howell invaded the area around New York City. Professional British troops defeated and outmaneuvered Gen. George Washington's ill trained forces in one battle after another. As 1776 ended, the cause for American independence seem all but lost. Washington's successful gambles at the battle of Trenton and Princeton kept hope alive, but the British were still holding New York and intermediate vicinity, Newport, Rhode Island and Canada. In hopes of crushing the American rebellion before foreign powers might intervene, the British devised a plan to invade New York from their base in Canada in 1777. Control of the Hudson river valley would cut off new England, the hot bed of the rebellion in the north, from the rest of the colonies.

The architect of the plan, Maj. Gen. John Burgoyne, commanded the main thrust through the Lake Champlain Valley and had initial success with the capture of Fort Ticonderoga. But the British advance was slow. With his plans unraveling, Burgoyne refused to change his advance towards Albany, New York. However, the British delays gave the Americans time to re-organize and reinforce their army. On 19 September, the British fought with part of Gen. Gates's army and were driven from the battlefield with heavy casualties with Gates' army still blocking their move to Albany. Gen. Burgoyne elected to move into a fortified encampment, counting on assistance from the British troops in New York. On October 7, with supplies running dangerously low and options running out, he attempted to outmaneuver the Americans. In fierce fighting the British and their allies were routed and driven back to their outer fortifications where they were overwhelmed by attacking Americans and had to withdraw into their inner works near the river. The following day the British tried to retreat northward toward safety. Hampered by bad roads, the British retreat made only 8 miles in two days and stopped near the small village of Saratoga. Gates's army followed and surrounded Burgoyne's army. With no other option Burgoyne surrendered on 17 October 1777. The American victory at Saratoga was a major turning point in the war for American Independence, raising the spirits of the patriots and convincing France to intervene in the war as an ally of the new republic. It would be French military assistance that would keep the rebel cause from collapsing and tip the balance at Yorktown, Virginia in 1781– Winning America its ultimate victory as a free and independent nation.

Horatio Gates' medal was awarded for the victory of the Battles of Saratoga. While Gates was technically in command of the 12,000 continental troops who stopped General Burgoyne's advancing invasion into Saratoga from Vermont the actual Battles of Saratoga were won by the leadership of General Philip Schuyler and his aggressive field commanders including Benedict Arnold, Daniel Morgan and John Stark. However, as the designated Commander, General Gates received credit and a medal for the victories.

Major Gen. Horatio Gates

Reverse of General Gates's Gold Medal. Note the ring attached at the top so the General could wear the medal

*The Congress awarded a gold medal to Major Gen. Horatio Gates for his victory at Saratoga. The front of the Gates' medal is inscribed In Latin and reads: "The American Congress to Horatio Gates, a valiant General." On the front a bust of General Gates in uniform faces to the left. The French engraver was Nicolas-Marie Gautteaux, who was the French graveur des médailles du Roi. The reverse of the medal shows Lieut. Gen. Burgoyne surrendering his sword to Gen. Gates. In the background, the vanquished troops of Great Britain are grounding their arms and standards. On the right is a victorious American army, in order of battle with colors flying. The Latin inscription reads: "The safety of The northern regions. The enemy surrendered at Saratoga on 17 October, 1777."*

**Medals of America** 13

# The Battle of Stony Point

In the wake of the battle of Monmouth in June 1778, British forces under Lieut. Gen. Sir Henry Clinton largely remained idle in New York city. As the 1779 campaigning season began, Clinton sought to lure Washington out of the mountains and into a general engagement. To accomplish this he dispatched about 8000 men up the Hudson river. As part of the movement, the British seized the American fort at Stony Point on the eastern bank of the Hudson as well as Verplank's Point on the opposite shore in late May and began fortifying them against attack. The loss of these positions deprived the Americans of using King's Ferry, a key river crossing over the Hudson. When the main British force withdrew to New York after having failed to force a major battle, a garrison of between 600 and 700 man was left at Stony Point. To recapture the positions, Gen. Washington decided to attack utilizing the Continental Army's Corps of Light Infantry, commanded by Brig. Gen. Anthony Wayne who had proven his military prowess earlier in the war. On 15 July, Wayne's men began their advance on Stony Point using only bayonets in a surprise attack shortly before midnight benefiting from limited moonlight. As Wayne's men crept near the fort from the south they found their approach flooded with several feet of water. Wading forward they created enough noise to alert the British. As the alarm was raised, the Americans began their attack with the first to enter the innermost British defense being Lieut. Col. De Fluery who personally cut down the British flag. He was followed closely by Maj. John Stewart's troops from the north. With the American forces forming in his rear, the British commander was ultimately compelled to surrender after 30 minutes of fighting. Gerald Wayne sent a dispatch to Gen. Washington informing him, "The Fort and Garrison are ours. Our officers and men behaved like men who are determined to be free." It was a stunning victory for Gen. Wayne with over 500 British soldiers captured. The Battle of Stony Point proved a big boost to American morale and one of the final battles of the war for American independence in the north.

For their actions at Stony Point Brig. Gen. Anthony Wayne received a gold medal engraved by Nicolas-Marie Gatteaux in 1789. An earlier medal was created by Benjamin Duvivier at the request of Benjamin Franklin, but was merely a duplicate of Lt. Col. de Fleury medal with the original text scratched out and re-engraved. The Gatteaux medal depicts America, personified as an Indian queen, standing and having at her feet a bow, an alligator and the American shield, presenting General Wayne a Laurel and mural crown and the reverse pictures the Battle of Stony Point.

Lieutenant Colonel De Fleury was a former French officer chosen by General Wayne to lead one of two columns in the Assault on Stony Point. The Frenchman was the first over the wall, leading his men with only bayonets, and personally cut down the British colors. His unfailing courage and brilliant execution of General Wayne's orders earned him a silver Congressional medal. Colonel De Fleury's actions at Stony Point are memorialized on his medal.

Major Stewart was awarded a silver medal by the Continental Congress for his gallantry and courage. The medal by Royal engraver Gatteaux shows America, as an Indian queen awarding him a palm branch. The reverse of the medal shows Major Stewart at the head of his men crossing an abatis of trees and pursuit of the defeated enemy; in the background American troops are mounting the assault of Stony Point.

*The Anthony Wayne medal celebrates his leadership assaulting Stony Point (July 15 1779). He personally led his men, under cover of night, in an attack which lasted only thirty minutes and produced 550 captured British soldiers.*

*Lt. Col. Louis De Fleury's silver medal reads: "A memorial and reward of courage and boldness", and the back:"The American republic presented this gift to D. De Fleury, a French Knight, the first to mount the wall".*

*Major John Stewart's extreme courage and vigor during the 1779 Assault on Stony Point earned a Congressional silver medal. He commanded the left advancing party, whose path included the virtually vertical ascent toward the fort. Major Stewart was already famous in the Continental Army for his heroic actions under General Sullivan and at the assault on Staten Island.*

## The Battle of Paulus Hook

Congress awarded Maj. Henry (Light Horse) Harry Lee a gold medal for his victory at Paulus Hook. The medal is inscribed :" The American Congress to Henry Lee, Major of Cavalry. The back of the medal reads: "In spite of rivers and fortifications, he vanquished the enemy through skill and military bravery with a handful of men, and he conquered through humane conduct those who had been subdued by the sword. In commemoration of the Battle of Paulus Hook, August 19, 1779."

## The Battle of Flamborough Head

On 23 September 1779, off the east coast of England, a four ship Continental Navy squadron comprising the 40 gun ship USS Bonhomme Richard, a 36 gun and 32 gun frigate, and a 12 gun Brig, encountered a 41 British merchant ship convoy arriving from the Baltics laden with precious commodities. The merchants were guarded by two British warships, HMS Serapis of 44 guns and a smaller ship of 20 guns. At the conclusion of the battle both British ships struck their colors.

The stories of the battle are as important as the actually event. The battle saw Captain John Paul Jones in command of USS Bonhomme Richard, a French merchant ship refitted for battle. Jones locked his ship on the HMS Serapis since his ship was no match for the 50 gun British frigate. Pounded by the heavier British frigate and with his ship taking on water, burning, and despite heavy casualties the legend of Captain Jones yelling out "I have not yet begun to fight," to his sailors and "I will sink before I strike," to the British Captain set the tone and standard for American Naval valor. While a bloody and mutually destructive fight, the victory of the USS Bonhomme Richard against the powerful Royal Navy gave the United States Navy its earliest traditions of heroism and victory.

*Lee was the only recipient of a Congressional Gold medal for actions in the American Revolution who ranked below a General. Lee was awarded his medal both for his success in leading the raid, but also his immensely humane treatment of prisoners.*

*The gold medal was awarded to Capt. John Paul Jones for his capture of the HMS Serapis.*

*The gold medal was awarded to Capt. John Paul Jones for his capture of the HMS Serapis. The front of the meal reads:" The American Congress to John Paul Jones, Captain of the Navy". The medal was designed by the French medalist Augustin Dupré. The back of the medal shows naval action between the USS Bonhomme Richard, 40 guns and the British HMS Serapis of 50 guns. Both vessels are grappled, lying head to stern. The Bonhomme Richard is on fire, and her crew are boarding the HMS Serapis to the left, with a third vessel as shown. Latin at the top reads "The enemies vessels taken or put to flight". "Off the coast of Scotland, September 23, 1779".*

Medals of America

*The medal designed by Augustin Dupre is considered the finest artistic creation of the entire series of 11 medals. The front shows an Indian Princess placing a crown on General Daniel Morgan. The back captures the powerful motion of Gen. Morgan on horseback leading his troops in the attack on the British forces. The Latin translates: "Victory, the vindicator of liberty" at the top and on the bottom "The enemy put to flight, taken, or slain at the Cowpens, January 17, 1781.*

With the war in the north grinding towards a stalemate the British decided on a new Southern strategy. In 1780 the British decided to turn their war efforts to the south with their major focus on South Carolina. This led to more revolutionary war battles in the state of South Carolina than any other state.

## The Battle of Cowpens

1781 was a decisive first step by American forces in reclaiming South Carolina from the British and alternately turning the tide of the Revolutionary war. The victory at the Battle of Cowpens convinced many doubtful Americans that the war could actually be won. The patriot forces composed of continental regiments and militia units were led by Brig. Gen. Daniel Morgan. Knowing that American militia units were not always reliable in battle, Morgan placed them in the middle of the line with the Continental Army behind them. He ask his militia to fire two shots before retreating to the rear and reforming. His battle plan worked to perfection. The British forces confidently attacked straight on. They were met by militia which performed exactly as ordered. They fired two volleys before retreating. The British, knowing the reputation of the militia to run felt confident that victory was at hand and advanced full force to destroy the American troops. Instead of finding retreating militiamen they were met by the Continental infantry, Continental sharpshooters, militia and cavalry led by Lt. Colonels William Washington and John Howard who drove in from both flanks. At the end of the battle over 100 British soldiers and loyalists were killed and 600 captured. Had Gen. Morgan and his Continental forces lost the battle of Cowpens, it is likely that General Cornwallis would have been successful in crushing the rebellion in South Carolina and making his move to North Carolina. The victory at Cowpens gave the militia and the patriots a renewed sense of optimism that the war for independence could be won.

*The Silver medal awarded Lt. Colonel Washington, who commanded the cavalry, shows him leading his men in pursuit of the enemy cavalry with a winged victory hovering over him holding a crown of laurel. He was 29 years old. Like Howard, Washington's medal was engraved by Benjamin Duvivier.*

*The Silver medal awarded Lt. Colonel John Edgar Howard, who commanded a regiment of infantry, shows him in pursuit of an enemy soldier carrying away a flag. A winged victory hovers over him holding a crown of laurel and a palm branch. He also was 29 years old at the time of the battle and suffered seven sword wounds in the battle. The inscription on the back states: " Because in vigorously pursuing the enemy with a handful of soldiers he gave a noble example of innate courage at the battle of the Cowpens, January 17,1781". Benjamin Duvivier, Chief Engraver of the Paris Mint prepared the dies but they are not of his normal high quality.*

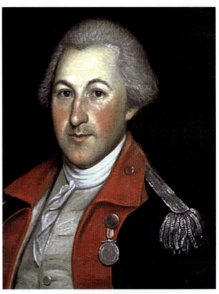

*Lt. Colonel John Edgar Howard*

## The Battle of Eutaw Springs

By 1781, General Nathanael Greene had begun a steady push to drive the British out of the south. After a series of battles, General Greene's troops attacked the British at their camp at Eutaw Springs. While both sides claimed victory it was the final battle for the British in the Carolinas. General Greene's leadership was inspirational for six years of continuous fighting during which he did not take a day of leave and his actions inspired the patriot forces in the Carolinas.

His gold medal reads:" The American Congress to Nathaniel Greene, a distinguished general. The back of the medal reads: "The safety of the southern regions" and "The enemy vanquished at Eutaw on the 8th of September, 1781."

The back of the medal shows winged Victory holding a crown of laurel in her right hand and a palm branch in her left: one foot is resting on a trophy of arms and flags of conquered enemies. The medal is by the French medalist Augustin Dupré. In 1787 the medal was finally presented to Greene's widow, the General having died in 1786.

*General Nathanael Greene's Gold Medal for Eutaw Springs.*

## Benjamin Franklin's Famous Victory Medal - Libertas Americana

*Head of Liberty*

*Benjamin Franklin*

*France personified as Athena (Minerva) acting as Americas nurse and mentor.*

While stationed in France during the American Revolutionary War, Benjamin Franklin was sent a detailed after action report of the Yorktown victory and asked to establish a monument in its honor. Instead he proposed a medal, depicting the United States as the infant Hercules in cradle, strangling the two serpent sent by Hera (the snakes representing the Battle of Saratoga and the Siege of Yorktown). Above him France personified as Athena (Minerva) would act as his nurse and mentor. The design on the medal's reverse was co developed by the French painter Esprit-Antoine Gibelin and engraver Augustin Dupré, who made sure that France would be seen as the protector of the infant by fighting the British Lion who is pouncing at the child. Minerva's shield is decked with the lilies of France. The final Latin inscription reads" The courageous child was aided by the gods". and dated October 1777/1781.

The front of the medal shows the Head of Liberty with flowing hair as if she is running to announce America's victories to the entire world. A spear of liberty surmounted by the Phrygian cap rest on her right shoulder with the date 4 July 1776. Records indicated 300 medals were struck in gold, silver and bronze, many of which were personally presented by Franklin to celebrate the new Republic. The first 2 gold medals were presented by Franklin to the King and Queen of France.

This was indeed the most famous of the Revolutionary War medals and when time came to design the Medal of Honor in 1861 it is clear where the designers went for inspiration. Minerva holding a shield banishes Discord (the south) who holds two snakes. Even today's Army Medal of Honor features the head of Minerva, Goddess of War.

Medals of America 17

# The "Andre" Medal

Patriots John Paulding, Isaac Van Wart and David Williams were the recipients of the Andre medal

The "Andre" medal broke the custom of restricting the award of medals to successful senior officers and is doubly unique in that it was designed for wear around the neck. The medal was presented by Congress in 1780 to the three enlisted men who captured British Major John Andre with the plans of the West Point fortifications in his boot. Patriots John Paulding, Isaac Van Wart and David Williams were the recipients of the Andre medal and as time passed were additionally authorized a lifetime pension. Major Andre, the captured British officer, was hung as a spy.

In August 1782, George Washington established the Badge of Military Merit, the first U.S. decoration which had general application to all enlisted men and one which he hoped would inaugurate a permanent awards system. At the same time, he expressed his fundamental awards philosophy when he issued an order from his headquarters at Newburgh, New York, which read:

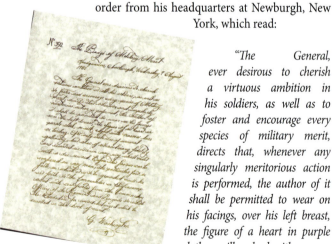

"The General, ever desirous to cherish a virtuous ambition in his soldiers, as well as to foster and encourage every species of military merit, directs that, whenever any singularly meritorious action is performed, the author of it shall be permitted to wear on his facings, over his left breast, the figure of a heart in purple cloth or silk, edged with narrow lace or binding. Not only instances of unusual gallantry, but also of extraordinary fidelity, and essential service in any way, shall meet with a due reward...the road to glory in a patriot army and a free country is thus opened to all. This order is also to have retrospect to the earliest days of the war, and to be considered a permanent one."

Although special and commemorative medals had been awarded previously, until this point no decoration had been established which honored the private soldier with a reward for special merit. The wording of the order is worth careful study. The object was "to cherish a virtuous ambition" and "to foster and encourage every species of military merit." Note also, that Washington appreciated that every kind of service was important by proposing to reward, "not only instances of unusual gallantry, but also of extraordinary fidelity and essential service in any way." And finally, the wonderfully democratic sentence, "the road to glory in a patriotic army and free country is thus opened to all."

Coming as it did, almost a year after Cornwallis' surrender at Yorktown, the message was never given widespread distribution and, as a result, there were only three known recipients of this badge, Sergeants Elijah Churchill, William Brown and Daniel Bissell. Unfortunately, after the Revolution, the award fell into disuse and disappeared for 150 years.

1782 Badge of Military Merit

However, it did not die, primarily due to the efforts of the Army's then Chief of Staff, General Douglas MacArthur, (and, by no accident, one of its first recipients). On the 200th anniversary of Washington's birth, February 22, 1932, the War Department announced that:

*"By order of the President of the United States, the Purple Heart, established by Gen. George Washington at Newburgh, New York ....is hereby revived out of respect to his memory and military achievements."*

Washington's "figure of a heart in purple" was retained as the medal's central theme and embellished with Washington's likeness and his coat of arms. The words "For Military Merit" appear on the reverse as a respectful reference to its worthy predecessor. In effect this makes the Purple Heart the oldest military medal in the United States

Towards the end of the war or immediately after, General Washington also authorized a stripe to be sewn on the sleeve of outstanding noncommissioned officers to honor three years of exemplary service or those with six years wore two stripes. These exemplary service or good conduct stripes disappeared after the Revolutionary War along with the original Badge of Military Merit.

However, while Congress would not approve medals for the Revolutionary soldiers, the Continental Army officers banded together with their French counterparts and created the Order of the Cincinnati with a very distinctive medal to wear. In the years after the revolution, membership grew and members served in all the major offices of the United States Government as well as many state and local governments. Some, including Thomas Jefferson, were alarmed at the apparent creation of an elite order that excluded enlisted men and in most cases militia officers. However, over time, the order has evolved into a patriotic society and its first members set tradition by establishing commemorative decorations or medals when none were authorized by Congress.

**The Republic 1783-1811.** While the need for national defense began almost at once to suppress internal rebellions such as Shays' Rebellion (1786-1787), the Whiskey Tax Rebellion in 1794 and a Pennsylvania protest against war taxes called Fries' Rebellion in 1799, the country relied almost exclusively on volunteer or militia forces. The idea of a standing Army seemed a real threat to the civilian government. Minuteman volunteer militias seemed to be the American way besides which it was much more economical than paying for a standing army.

During this first thirty plus years of our new nation, regular and volunteer Army and Navy Commanders were honored for their service with large medallions authorized by Congress (as described earlier) or with special commemorative swords often paid for by public subscription from a patriotic and grateful community. Enlisted soldiers and sailors were rewarded in various monetary ways with naval prize money or land grants for soldiers in the newly-acquired territories.

With the exception of Congressionally-awarded medals, the Congress rejected the use of military decorations, orders and medals as being in the image of royalty and aristocracy. It was an attitude that lasted almost 100 years until the Army and Navy began to reflect the Republic's rise as a world power at the beginning of the twentieth century. The development of America's pyramid of military honors reflected the nation's ascendancy as a world power beginning with the War with Spain, through its significant role in World War I and finally emerging as leader of the Free World in World War II.

Badge of Military Merit.

The Purple Heart Medal of 1932

Order of the Cincinnati

# The War of 1812 (1812-1815)

During the first 50 years of the United States, Military Awards and Decorations were extremely few compared to today. Generally only high ranking officer were honored for heroic efforts and victory. Congress had 3 ceremonial accolades reserved for senior officers of victorious battles. All of these awards had to approved by congress. The most prestigious award was a "Congressional Gold Medal" minted and engraved for a specific action or event. Next, was the "Ceremonial Sword," custom made to recognize a spectacular achievement. However, the most common reward for a highly distinguished officer was a "Letter of Thanks" from the congress.

British impressment of American sailors into the Royal Navy, interception of neutral ships and blockades of the United States during British hostilities with France led the United States to declare war against Great Britain in 1812. The War of 1812 saw widespread introduction of the American bald eagle as the national symbol on flags, hats, breastplates and belt buckles. The Congress retained the custom of commissioning large presentation medals to victorious commanding officers managing to more than double the Gold Medals from 11 during the Revolution to 14 for Naval Officers and 13 for Army Generals in the much shorter war of 1812.

As an example, shown to the left, is a medal presented to Major General Alexander Macomb for his victory at the Battle of Plattsburgh in 1814.

A number of naval officers were voted medals, swords and other honors by Congress for victories against such British ships as the HMS Guerriere in 1812, HMS Detroit and Caledonia on the Niagara River in October 1812 and later the HMS Frolic, HMS Java and numerous other men of war.

**Nation Building 1816-1843** – In Florida the Army fought the Spanish often taking areas like Pensacola but returning them in later negotiations until Florida became a U.S. territory in 1821. The Army also fought a series of wars with the Seminole Indians, the Blackhawks and the Creeks through 1842. By 1823 the Army was ordered across the Mississippi to begin action against the western indians. Engagements between pirates and American ships occurred repeatedly around Cuba, Puerto Rico, Santo Domingo and Yucatan. Over three thousand pirate attacks on merchantmen were reported between 1815 and 1823. In 1815 the Second Barbary War was declared against the United States by the Barbary States, but not reciprocated by the United States Congress. However, Congress did authorize a large fleet under Captain Stephen Decatur to attack Algiers and obtain indemnities. Here as in the past victories were noted by congressional or by local medallions or commemorative swords.

Ceremonial Sword

*Major General Alexander Macomb. In recognition of the "gallantry and good conduct" of Major General Alexander Macomb, and the officers and men under his command, in defeating a veteran British Army at Plattsburg on September 11, 1814.*

*Captain Oliver Hazard Perry and Captain Jesse D. Elliott. In recognition of the "decisive and glorious victory gained on Lake Erie" by Captain Oliver Hazard Perry and Captain Jesse D. Elliott, on September 10, 1813. Approved January 6, 1814*

*First of two Congressional Gold Medal presented to Major General Winfield Scott for his victory over the British troops in 1814 during the War of 1812.*

See next page for his second award.

# The Mexican War (1844-1848) and the Beginning of Change

During the time of the Mexican War and thereafter the Federal Government still showed a great reluctance to strike medals for soldiers and sailors but continued the award of Congressional Gold Medals. However, various states such as South Carolina and New York showed no such resistance. For example, the state of South Carolina struck 1000 silver medals for members of the Volunteer Palmetto Regiment who served in the Mexican War. Each large silver medal was engraved with the name of the soldier and individually presented to the soldier or next of kin. Officers received Gold Medals. Some cities such as Charleston, South Carolina also commissioned medals specifically for their local company. It is interesting to note that the South Carolina medals were designed for table top display but veterans immediately took to drilling small holes in the top of the medal and wearing them as watch fobs or hanging them from their coat lapel on patriotic occasions.

This was the turning point where Congressional Gold Medals no longer became the only military award for valor and victorious service but focused on persons who performed an achievement which had an impact on America history long after the achievement. So here we leave Congressional Medals and begin focus on military medals as we know them today.

After the war Regular Army officers who served in the Mexican War formed the Aztec Club of 1847 and struck a distinctive medal for their members which later was authorized by Congress to wear on their uniform. This tradition of forming military societies with special medals continued throughout the China Relief campaign and the Philippine Insurrection. Congress later approved these medals for wear on the uniform.

Aztec Club Medal

The Certificate of Merit was established by the Army in 1847 to reward soldiers who distinguished themselves in battle, but this was not translated into a medal until 1905.

Although the United States was growing a professional army and navy, the Congress showed no desire to award them military medals. The wearing of military medals was still associated with European royalty and was, therefore, generally unpopular with elected officials. However, in the great American tradition of not waiting for Congressional action, local authorities often struck medals to honor the service of their particular volunteer units. And, as noted above, regular army officers formed their own association and designed their own medal to wear.

*Very large (3 1/2 inches wide) Congressional Gold medal with General Scott's bust facing left under banner marked "Major General Winfield Scott." Fifteen raised stars on either side, and "Resolution of Congress March 9, 1848" presented to Winfield Scott for his service as the Army Commander in Chief during the Mexican War of 1847.*

*General Scott exerted great influence on the United States Army during its first 100 years of existence. Nicknamed "Old Fuss and Feathers" for his attention to detail and taste for gaudy uniforms, he fought in the War of 1812, the Blackhawk War, the Seminole Wars, the Mexican-American War, and the Civil War. As of today four people had been awarded more than one gold medal: Winfield Scott (1814 for War of 1812 and 1848 for Mexican–American War), Zachary Taylor (1846, 1847, and 1848 for Mexican-American War), Lincoln Ellsworth (1928 and 1936 for polar exploration), and Hyman G. Rickover (1958 for the "Nuclear Navy" and 1982 for his entire career).*

Gold and Silver Palmetto Regiment Medals

Army  Navy

Civil War Medals of Honor

Butler medal for colored troops in the Battle of Newmarket Heights in 1864.

Army and Navy Civil War Campaign Medals

Civil War Campaign Medal reverses

# Civil War (1861-1865)

The Civil War saw the first United States military decorations. The Navy Medal of Honor arose from a public resolution signed into law by President Lincoln on 21 December 1861. It authorized the preparation of 200 medals of honor to promote the efficiency of the Navy. It was followed by a joint resolution of Congress on the same day which approved the design and defined requirement eligibility of the potential recipients. The Army Medal of Honor was established by a joint resolution of Congress, July 12, 1862 with an effective date; of April 15, 1861. The Medal of Honor was originally only to be presented to enlisted men for heroic service in the United States Army. However, as the war continued the award of a Medal of Honor was extended to include Army officers.

Union Officers began creating unit medals as early as 1862 when the officers of General Kearny's division ordered a gold medal after the General's death to commemorate serving under his command. The next Division commander ordered a bronze cross for award to enlisted men of the division. Other private medals were the Gilmore Medal struck by General Gilmore for his troops around Charleston, SC and the Butler Medal for colored troops in the Battle of Newmarket Heights in 1864. Most of these were paid for by the commanders and had limited use.

Following the Civil War, there was an absolute explosion of veterans commemorative medals, reunion medals and badges. The Grand Army of the Republic reunion medals began to so closely resemble the Medal of Honor that Congress was eventually forced to change the Medal of Honor and to patent its new design. (See page 24 for example.)

In 1905 President Roosevelt authorized campaign medals retroactive to the Civil War. The Civil War Campaign Medal (Army) was issued for any federal army service between April 15, 1861 an April 9, 1865 (with extended service in the state of Texas through August 20, 1866). The Navy and Marine Corps were also authorized Civil War Campaign Medals, with each service having a different design on the reverse of the medal. The original Army campaign medal had a red, white and blue ribbon which was changed in 1913 to match the Navy and Marine Corps Civil War Medal blue and gray ribbon design.

The Civil War Campaign Medal is considered the first campaign service medal of the United States Armed Forces. The decoration is now authorized members of the United States and the Confederate States Armed Forces who had served in the American Civil War between 1861 and 1865. The blue and gray ribbon denotes the respective uniform colors of the U.S. and Confederate troops. See page 125.

# Confederate Medals

There were no Confederate States medals. Prior to the 1905 United States Civil War medal Confederate soldiers only received recognition from the hands of the United Daughters of the Confederacy (UDC) who designed and struck a handsome Southern Cross of Honor. The design is a Maltese Cross with the battle flag of the Confederate forces on the face, surrounded by a reef of laurel with the inscription, "United Daughters of the Confederacy to the U.C.V." The reverse of the cross has the Latin motto of the Confederate States' "Deo Vindice" (God our Vindicator) with the dates 1861-1865. On the four arms of the cross are the words "Southern Cross of Honor". Beginning in 1900 approximately 80,000 crosses were awarded, with the last Cross of Honor presented posthumously in 1959 to Confederate Rear Admiral and Brigadier General Raphael Semmes.

A Commemorative Stonewall Brigade Medal was commissioned in Paris, France in 1863 and sent back to the south through the Federal blockade. However, the medals never left the warehouse and were never presented to the Brigade soldiers. Today they are used by a Georgia Chapter of the United Daughters of the Confederacy as special gifts.

Southern Cross of Honor

The Stonewall Jackson Medal

# The Indian Campaign Medal (1865-1891)

Between 1865 and 1891 the United States Army conducted a series of running battles against the Indians in the Western portion of the United States. The Indian Campaign Medal was established by War Department General Orders on 21 January, 1907 and was authorized for military service in any campaign against any tribe during certain periods and locations. In 1918 the Indian Campaign Medal was retroactively authorized a small five pointed silver star, 3/16 of an inch in diameter for gallantry in action during the Indian Wars. These rarely awarded stars were referred to as Citation Stars and were attached to the center of the medal's ribbon.

Indian Campaign Medal

# The Navy Good Conduct Badge of 1869

The Navy Good Conduct Medal dating back to 1869 is the third-oldest continuously presented award after the Army Medal of Honor and the Navy Medal of Honor. While there have been four versions of the Navy Good Conduct Medal, the first was issued from 1870 to 1884. The medal was not worn on the uniform but presented as a badge during discharge. This of course makes the Navy Good Conduct Medal the earliest of any of the Services' Good Conduct Medals. The Marine Corps issued their Good Conduct Medal in 1896, the Coast Guard in 1923 and the Army in 1941.

The 1869 medal was a Maltese cross made of nickel, with the words "FIDELITY - ZEAL - OBEDIENCE" in a circle and "U.S.N." in the center of the disc. The reverse was blank except for the engraved name of the recipient. The cross hung from a small one-half inch wide red, white, and blue ribbon. Sailors called it the "Nickel Cross". It was redesigned in 1880 along the lines of the current medallion.

Marine Corps Good Conduct Medal of 1896

Navy Good Conduct Badge of 1869

Medals of America 23

# Military Society Medals (1865-1913)

Up until the Spanish American War no Army or Navy in the world was so little decorated as the United States. The simplicity of uniforms were set off by no medals or ribbons. After the Civil War, Congress under pressure from veteran's organizations permitted officers and enlisted men to wear their Corps and Division badge. For nearly twenty years, the Medal of Honor remained the sole American military award of any kind. Although the Navy had authorized the first Good Conduct Badge in 1869, clearly the officers and enlisted personnel of the Army and Navy wanted to have medals like their counterparts around the world.

Their solution was to have Congress approve the wearing of the military society medals such as The Aztec club which consisted of officers who served in Mexico in 1847, the Grand Army of the Republic, the Loyal Legion, Army and Navy Union of the United States of America, and the Military Order of the Dragon, commemorating the China relief expedition were just a few. The point was the professional officer corps wanted an awards system to recognize service and if the government was not going to create one they would. The post civil war Congress contained a large number of veterans so approval to wear these society medals on uniforms was not difficult. In regard to Military Society medals a subject that often comes up is a question of wearing certain military society medals on military uniforms. Title X of United States code, section 1123 (a) states:

> "A member of the Army, Navy, Air Force or Marine Corps who is a member of a military society originally composed of men who served in the Armed Forces of the United States during the Revolutionary War, the War of 1812, the Mexican War, the Civil War, the Spanish-American War, the Philippine Insurrection, or the Chinese Relief Expedition may wear, on certain occasions of ceremony, the distinctive badges adopted by that society."

Basically this can be interpreted that a member of the Armed Forces who is a member of one of the societies listed below can wear these medals on their uniform. The Society of the Cincinnatus, the General Society of the War of 1812, the Aztec Club, the Military Order of the Loyola Legion of the United States, the Naval order of the United States and the medals of the Veterans of Foreign Wars since the original founders of the VFW were veterans of the Spanish American war, the Philippine Insurrection and the Chinese Relief Expedition of 1900.

While there may be an occasion when one would wear Society medals or ribbons on their active duty uniform it is seldom to my knowledge actually done. However, the occasion does occur, that veterans wearing miniature medals on formal occasions could wear their society medals after (at the end) of their military decorations and service medals.

The demand for a national military awards system was there and support slowly gained ground. The election of President Roosevelt opened the flood gates.

*Colonel Charles C. Warren wearing the Aztec Club and other Society medals on his uniform for an official portrait.*

*Veteran's Medals such as this jeweled Grand Army of the Republic Society Medal could equal the jeweled orders of Europe.*

Society of the Cincinnatus

Aztec Club of 1847

General Society of the War of 1812

Grand Army of the Republic Society medal

Military Order of the Loyal Legion

Military Order of the Dragon 1900

# Spanish American War (1898 -1899)

It was not until the turn of the 20th Century that a host of medals were authorized to commemorate the events surrounding the Spanish-American War. This was future President Theodore Roosevelt's "Bully Little War" that produced seven distinct medals for only four months of military action. Supply had finally caught up with demand.

The first of these was the medal to commemorate the victory of the naval forces under the command of Commodore Dewey over the Spanish fleet at Manila Bay. This award was notable as it was the first such medal in U.S. history to be awarded to all officers and enlisted personnel present during a specific military expedition. It is also one of the handsomest American medals ever designed.

When Roosevelt, an ardent supporter of the military, ultimately reached the White House, he took it upon himself to legislate for the creation of medals to honor all those who had served in America's previous conflicts. Thus, by 1908 the U.S. had authorized campaign medals, some retroactive, for the Civil War, Indian Wars, War with Spain, Philippine Insurrection and China Relief Expedition of 1900-01. While the Army, Navy and Marines used the same ribbons, different medals were struck. Concurrently the custom of wearing service ribbons on the tunic was adopted during this same time frame (using different orders of precedence for each service). Thus, the different Armed Services managed to establish the principle of independence in the creation and wearing of awards that is virtually unchanged today.

*Admiral Dewey wearing his campaign Medal known as the Manila Bay ("Dewey") Medal.*

West Indies Naval Campaign (Sampson) Medal (Navy)

Spanish Campaign Medal Army

Spanish Campaign Medal Navy, Marines

West Indies Campaign Medal Navy and Marines

Spanish War Service Medal Army

Cuban Occupation Medal Army

# Philippines, China and Central America (1900-1917)

By the time the final peace treaty with Spain was ratified in March 1899, the Philippine Insurrection had already broken out and the majority of regular army and volunteer troops were in the Philippines fighting against insurrectionists, Philippine nationalists and Muslim fundamentalists, a conflict which was to rage from 1899 to 1913. Between 1900 and the 1930s, American soldiers, sailors and marines were dispatched to such areas as China in 1900, Cuba in 1906, Mexico in 1911, Nicaragua in 1912, Haiti in 1915, and the Dominican Republic in 1916, to quell rebellions and deal with civil unrest. As was their earlier custom, the Army and the Navy designed and authorized their own medals to commemorate these events. The Marine Corps, although under the overall command of the Navy, preserved their uniqueness by using the Navy medals with the special Marine Corps design on the reverse.

In 1905, the Army's Philippine Campaign Medal was issued followed in 1908 by a Navy version. The silver Citation Star was retroactively authorized in 1918 for wear on the medal for Army personnel who had performed feats of heroism or bravery. The Navy's version of the Philippine Campaign Medal was issued with no devices authorized and was originally suspended from a red and yellow ribbon but on August 12, 1913, the Navy changed the ribbon color to match the Army's version of the award.

Soon after the Spanish-American War and the Philippine Campaign, the Army grew from 64,000 to well over 120,000 regular and volunteer troops spread halfway around the world. The Navy was also covering the West Indies, Caribbean and projecting its power as far as China. In 1900, when fanatical Chinese called "Boxers", a rough English translation of the "Righteous Fists of Fire Society," attacked American nationals and other foreigners in the International Legations in Peking, China, the United States sent more than 5,000 soldiers and a battalion of Marines to join a multinational relief force.

The final action just prior to World War I was the Mexican Campaign which took place between the years 1911 and 1917. Once again, civil disobedience, this time in the form of large-scale military activities by well-armed revolutionaries, caused the United States to mount a Punitive Expedition into Mexico to bring peace to the region. Also, in the largest naval activity since the Spanish-American War, Navy and Marine Corps personnel took part in major battles along Mexico's Caribbean coast. In the aftermath of the conflict, the Army Mexican Service Medal was awarded to approximately 15,000 soldiers and the Navy version was awarded to 16,000 sailors and 2,500 marines. As was common practice by now, the medal designs were all different, but the ribbons were identical. For those Army members who had been cited for gallantry in combat, the Citation Star was retroactively authorized in 1918 as a device to the Mexican Service Medal but no devices were authorized for the Navy's medal. Early versions of the Campaign medals of this period were issued with serial numbers stamped on the bottom rim of the medal or engraved on the reverse side with the date of service. This practice was discontinued on later replacement medals.

Spanish Campaign Medal, 1898, 1st Ribbon (Army)

Spanish Campaign Medal, 1898, 2d Ribbon (Marines)

Mexican Service Medal, 1914-1919, (Army)

# Certificate of Merit (1905)

Certificate of Merit Medal (Army)

The Certificate of Merit was authorized by Congress in 1847 as a paper certificate that could be awarded to any private soldier during the Mexican War who distinguished himself by "gallantry performed in the presence of the enemy". In 1854 it was approved for award to noncommissioned officers as well as privates and after a brief period of disuse, it was reinstituted in 1874. In 1892 it was authorized to be awarded for distinguished service other than gallantry in the presence of the enemy and in 1905 a medal was authorized for all Certificate of Merit holders. Just over 1200 Certificates of Merit were awarded. In 1918 the award was disestablished as it had become obsolete with the authorization of the Distinguished Service Cross. During the time in which it was in existence, its order of precedence was just after the Medal of Honor. Under Public Law 193 of July 9, 1918 which established the Distinguished Service Cross and Distinguished Service Medal, the Certificate of Merit could be exchanged for a Distinguished Service Medal. On March 5, 1934, under Public Law 114, a change was made by which all Distinguished Service Medals awarded to previous Certificate of Merit holders were to be surrendered and automatically replaced by the Distinguished Service Cross.

# Bringing Order to U.S. Awards Design with the Institute of Heraldry 1918

Heraldry is a simple yet practical art and science dating back to the 12th century that uses symbols, metals (gold & silver) and colors to identify a position, organization, or individual. Heraldic symbols have been used by the United States military since the late 18th century, but its origin as a European custom associated with royalty discouraged widespread use. The spirit of democracy that dominated our first hundred years rejected such symbols. Consequently, there was no formal use or acceptance of heraldry in the early history of the United States.

On 17 June 1918, however, President Woodrow Wilson wrote the Secretary of War Newton Baker, suggesting that the design of military medals be "artistically reconsidered by the official art commission." As a result of this correspondence, a Heraldic Program Office was created within the War Department General Staff to take responsibility for the coordination and approval of coats of arms, decorations and other insignia for Army organizations. In 1924, formal staff responsibility for specific military designs was delegated to the Quartermaster General.

As the need for symbolism expanded, the scope of heraldic services evolved into a sizable program. World War II significantly contributed to the growth of the program. In 1949 the Army was directed provide heraldic services to all military departments and expanded in 1957 through the enactment of Public Law 85-263, authorizing the Secretary of the Army to furnish heraldic services to the military departments and other branches of the federal government.

In 1960 "The Institute of Heraldry" was established under the Quartermaster General as the only federal government organization devoted to the art and science of military heraldry and official symbolism. Upon the reorganization of the Army in 1962, the Heraldic Program was assigned to the Adjutant General's Office and in 2004 moved from the Adjutant General to the Administrative Assistant to the Secretary of the Army. The Institute celebrated its 50th anniversary in August 2010.

The Institute of Heraldry furnishs heraldic services to the Executive Office of the President, the Department of Defense, and all other Federal agencies. This encompasses research, design, development, standardization, quality control, and other services which are fundamental to the creation and custody of official heraldic items. Such items include coats of arms, decorations, flags, streamers, agency seals, badges, and other types of insignia that are approved for use and/or display. The Institute of Heraldry also provides the general public with limited research and information services concerning heraldic insignia.

The Institute of Heraldry and the Commission of Fine Arts share a long and illustrious relationship in the design of official government insignia and military medals. The Commission of Fine Arts, upon request of the Institute of Heraldry, advises upon the merits of proposed designs for medals, insignia, seals and other significant emblems for the United States Government. The Institute of Heraldry is a national treasure and their website is an amazing source of information on military awards and insignia for all Americans.

# World War I (1917-1918)

At the time of the U.S. entry into World War I, the Medal of Honor, Certificate of Merit and Navy/Marine Corps Good Conduct Medals still represented America's entire inventory of personal decorations. This presented the twin dangers that the Medal of Honor might be cheapened by being awarded too often and that other deeds of valor might go unrecognized. By 1918, popular agitation forced the authorization of two new awards, the Army's Distinguished Service Cross and Distinguished Service Medal, created by Executive Order in 1918. In the same year, the traditional U.S. refusal to permit the armed forces to accept foreign decorations was rescinded, allowing military personnel to accept awards from the grateful Allied governments. In 1919, the Navy created the Navy Cross and its own Distinguished Service Medal for Navy and Marine Corps personnel.

The issuance of the World War I Victory Medal established another precedent, that of wearing clasps with the names of individual battles on the suspension ribbon of a general campaign medal. This was an ongoing practice in many countries, most notably Britain and France, since the 19th Century. When the ribbon bar alone was worn, each clasp was represented by a small (3/16" diameter) bronze star. Fourteen such clasps were adopted along with five clasps to denote service in specific countries. However, the latter were issued only if no campaign clasp was earned. Only one service clasp could be issued to any individual and they were not represented by a small bronze star on the ribbon bar. It is a final irony that the British, who were the greatest proponents of the practice, never issued a single bar with their own version of the Victory Medal.

During this period, the Army introduced the Citation Star which was established by Congress on July 9, 1918. This award, a 3/16 inch diameter silver star device, was originally authorized to be worn on the World War I Victory Medal to denote those who had been cited for extreme heroism or valor. The device, which evolved into the Silver Star Medal in 1932, was soon made retroactive as an attachment to the Army service medals for the Civil War, Indian, Spanish, China and Mexican Campaigns. Although the Citation Star was strictly a U.S. Army device, an identical ribbon attachment designated the Navy Commendation Star, was authorized for wear on the World War I Victory Medal by Navy and Marine Corps personnel who had received a Letter of Commendation from the Secretary of the Navy. However, the two awards were not considered equivalent and the Navy version was not upgradable in subsequent years to the Silver Star Medal. Bronze oak leaf clusters were also introduced to indicate a second award of the Medal of Honor or other decoration in lieu of a second medal.

| Army World War I Campaign Clasps | Navy World War I Service Clasps |
|---|---|
| Cambrai | Overseas |
| Somme Defensive | Armed Guard |
| Lys | Atlantic Fleet |
| Aisne | Aviation |
| Montdidier-Noyon | Destroyer |
| Champagne-Marne | Escort |
| Aisne-Marne | Grand Fleet |
| Somme Offensive | Mine Laying |
| Oise-Aisne | Mine Sweeping |
| Ypres-Lys | Mobile Base |
| St. Mihiel | Naval Battery |
| Meuse-Argonne | Subchaser |
| Vittorio-Veneto | Submarine |
| Defensive Sector | Salvage |
| Army Service Clasps | Transport |
| France | Patrol |
| Italy | West Indies |
| Siberia | White Sea |
| Russia | Asiatic |
| England | |

*Army Distinguished Service Cross First Version*

*Navy Cross*

*World War I Victory Medal with Campaign Clasps*

*With Silver Star*

28  Military Medals of America

This 16 foot stainglass window at the Army War College displays all of the Army fighting Division Patches (Marine Regiments servred in the Army's 2d Infantry Division).

# World War I Commemorative Medals

Upon the return of troops to the United States after World War I, many county, state and federal organizations rushed to produce Commemorative medals to honor their returning soldiers. The quality of medal design and strike was quite good and the local commemorative medals were highly prized by veterans and their families. Almost a thousand different WW I Commemorative Medals were presented to their returning veterans by city, county, state and fraternal organizations A beautiful example is South Carolina's Greenville County medal shown directly below with other examples.

WW I, Greenville, S.C. Commemorative

Medals of America 29

# World War II (1941-1945)

On September 8, 1939, in response to the growing threat of involvement in World War II, the President proclaimed a National Emergency in order to increase the size of U.S. military forces. For the first time, a peacetime service award, the American Defense Service Medal, was authorized for wear by those personnel who served during this period of National Emergency prior to the attack on Pearl Harbor on December 7, 1941.

America's participation in World War II saw a significant increase in both personal decorations and campaign medals. Since U.S. forces were serving all over the world, a campaign medal was designed for each major (and carefully defined) area. The three medals for the American, Asiatic-Pacific and European-African-Middle Eastern Campaigns encompassed the globe. However, the World War I practice of using campaign bars was discarded in favor of 3/16" bronze stars that could denote each designated military campaign from a major invasion to a submarine war patrol.

World War II also introduced the first (and only!) service medal unique to female military personnel. Known as the Women's Army Corps Service Medal, it was authorized for service in both the W.A.C. and its predecessor, the Women's Army Auxiliary Corps. The war also saw the large scale award of foreign medals and decorations to American servicemen. The Philippine Government, for one, authorized awards to commemorate the Defense and Liberation of their island country. The first foreign award designed strictly for units, the Philippine Presidential Unit Citation, patterned after a similar American award, was also approved for wear by American forces. In the European Theater, France and Belgium made many presentations of their War Crosses (Croix de Guerre) to U.S. military personnel.

The end of World War II saw the introduction of two counterparts of previous World War I awards, the Victory and Occupation Medals. This time, no bars or clasps were authorized for the Victory Medal, but bars were issued with the Occupation Medal to denote the recipient's area of service. The Prisoner of War Medal and the Philippine Independence Medal are other examples of medals approved after the war.

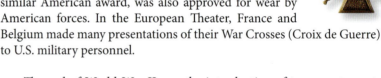

Army Occupation Medal

Navy Occupation Service Medal

Prisoner of War Medal

Philippine Defense Medal

Philippine Liberation Medal

Philippine Independence Medal

## But where were the World War II Veterans's Medals?

During World War II generally only decorations such as the Distinguished Service Cross, Silver Star, Distinguished Flying Cross and Purple Heart were manufactured. Brass was restricted to the manufacture of munitions so campaign medals were mainly issued as ribbon bars and soldiers, sailors, marines and airmen were not given medals but only ribbon bars to pin on their uniforms. In fact most of the campaign medals were unavailable to veterans until several years after the war. By then most service personnel had been discharged from the Armed Forces and returned to civilian life.

The photograph to the right is a good example of what was available for veterans to wear home. His two campaign ribbons (European-African-Middle Eastern and Asiatic Pacfic Campaigns) are 1/2 inch high old style ribbons missing his campaign stars while his Victory ribbon and Good Conduct Medal are the standard 3/8 inch height of the Army and Air Force World War II ribbons. Unless the veteran went through the process of writing the government and asking for their medals, World War II veterans never received their actual campaign or Victory medals. In fact a number of World War II awards were not approved until several years after the war. The approval of the Bronze Star Medal for meritorious service to combat infantrymen and combat medics was not authorized until almost the end of 1947. The Victory and Occupation Medals were not manufactured until mid 1946 by which time many of the personnel authorized them had long since left the Armed Forces.

That is the reason you seldom see WW II veterans wearing their medals or displaying them. Not that they weren't proud of their service for they were very, but you can't wear medals you did not have.

## The Cold War (1945 -1991)

The Cold War lasted over 40 years with conflict, tension, and competition beginning in 1946 between the Western World under the leadership of the United States and the Soviet Union and its satellites. From the mid-1940s to the early 1990s, both sides tried to gain advantage using weapons development, military coalitions, espionage, invasions, propaganda and competitive technology, including the famous space race. The Cold War produced massive defense spending on conventional forces and nuclear arms and multiple proxy wars but no actual combat between the USA and USSR. Millions of Americans served in the Armed Forces often in tense and dangerous situations during this period.

In 1998, Congress authorized the Secretary of Defense to award a Cold War Victory Medal to all veterans of the Cold War. However, to date the Secretary of Defense has only authorized a Cold War Recognition Certificate to all members of the armed forces and qualified federal government civilian personnel who served during the Cold War, 2 September, 1945 to 26 December, 1991. The Department of Defense has stated that it will not create a Cold War Service medal nor authorize any commemorative medals made by private vendors for wear on the military uniform. The DOD position is that manufacturing the medal would be too expensive, a surprising position, since processing and mailing the certificate cost about the same as supplying a medal. However, Cold War Victory

Commemorative Medals are perhaps one of the most popular and frequently purchased military medals today. They are not official nor can they be worn on active duty uniforms but they continue the tradition going back to the Revolution of veterans filling their own needs.

The Army runs the Cold War Recognition Certificate program and Cold War veterans can write to the address below for a certificate. Response can be over a month. Write:

**U.S. Army Human Resources Cmd**
**Cold War Recognition Program**
**ATTN: AHRC-PDP-A Dept 480**
**1600 Spearhead Division Ave.**
**Fort Knox, Ky 40122-5408**

National Defense Service Medal | US Korean Service Medal | Korea Defense Service Medal | UN Korean Service Medal | ROK War Service Medal | Korean Presidential Unit Citation

# Korea (1950-1954)

The Korean Conflict, fought under the United Nations banner, saw the creation of two new medals for service. The first was the Korean Service Medal, which continued the practice of using 3/16" bronze stars on the ribbon to denote major campaigns. The second, the National Defense Service Medal, was established to recognize the contribution of all military personnel to national defense during a period of armed hostility. Some outstanding units were also awarded the Republic of Korea Presidential Unit Citation and all participants were awarded the United Nations Service Medal. By order of the Korean government, the award was also retroactively authorized to every unit of the United States Army which had deployed to Korea between 1950 and 1954. It was also awarded to the Commander and U.S. Marine Corps Forces Korea for service between 09 December 1999 to 24 April 2002.

In the 1950s, the Republic of Korea (ROK) asked the United States Government for approval to present the Korean War Service Medal to the U.S. troops who served in the Korean conflict, but the award was turned down by the U.S. Government. However as the fiftieth Anniversary of the Korean War approached, veterans groups placed more and more pressure on their congressional representatives and in 1999 the medal was approved for Korean War veterans. The late approval results in the Korean War Service Medal's order of precedence being after the Kuwait Liberation Medal instead of the normal chronological order for foreign awards.

The Korea Defense Service Medal (KDSM) was instituted in 2003 and made retroactive to 1954. The medal is awarded to members of the Armed Forces who have served in the Republic of Korea or adjacent waters since the Korean War to uphold the armistice between South and North Korea. A service member must have at least thirty consecutive days service in the Korean theater to qualify for the KDSM. The medal is also granted for 60 non-consecutive days of service for reservists on annual training in Korea. All Korean War veterans who served 30 days in Korea after 27 July 1954 are eligible for Korea Defense Service Medal. The Korea Defense Service Medal is retroactive to the end of the Korean War and is granted to any service performed after July 28, 1954.

In addition to campaign and service medals normally awarded to a veteran of the Korean War, most Services approved the award of the Good Conduct Medal for a period of one year when service was in Korea. During the Korean War, the Air Force, a separate service since 1947, still used many Army awards. As a results Air Force veterans who earned the Good Conduct Medal during the conflict were awarded the Army Good Conduct Medal.

The period of the Korean War saw the standardization of service ribbons for the Navy and Marine Corps to a smaller size of 3/8 inch high by 1 3/8 inch wide. This had long been the service ribbons size used by the Army and the Air Force. Prior to the standardization the Navy and Marine Corps used ribbons 1/2 inch high by 1 3/8 inches wide.

National Defense Service Medal

Armed Forces Expeditionary Medal

U.S. Vietnam Service Medal

RVN Campaign Medal

RVN Gallantry Cross Unit Citation

# Vietnam (1961-1973)

The first American advisors in the Republic of South Vietnam were awarded the new Armed Forces Expeditionary Medal which was created in 1961 to cover campaigns for which no specific medal was instituted. However, as the U.S. involvement in the Vietnamese conflict grew, a unique award, the Vietnam Service Medal was authorized, thus giving previous recipients of the Expeditionary Medal the option of which medal to accept. The Government also authorized the acceptance of the Republic of Vietnam Campaign Medal by all who served for six months in-country, or in the surrounding waters or the air after 1960. Towards the end of the war a blanket general order authorized the RVN Gallantry Cross Unit Citation for all those who served in Vietnam.

The most notable change in medal policy occurred during the Vietnam War when the Department of Defense authorized the large scale acceptance of South Vietnamese awards. The South Vietnamese Armed Forces had a comprehensive awards system built to reflect their past as a former French colony. Since a large number of American military advisors and special forces worked with the South Vietnamese Armed Forces for over 15 years, (many serving multiple tours) numerous medals for valor and service were presented to U.S. personnel. Some of the most awarded were the Vietnamese Cross of Gallantry (for valor), the Civil Actions Medal and the Armed Forces Honor Medal (meritorious service). The last two medals are unusual since they were in two different degrees; first class for officers and second class for enlisted personnel. All foreign medals awarded to members of the U.S. Armed Forces were either furnished by the foreign government or purchased by the recipient since the United States government does not provide foreign medals to members of the Armed Forces.

After Vietnam, many new decorations, medals and ribbons came into being as the Department of Defense and the individual Services developed a complete structure to reward performance from the newest enlistee to the most senior Joint Staff officer. Some of the awards, such as the Army Service Ribbon and the Air Force Training Ribbon have no medal but reward the young recruits for successfully completing their transition from civilian to a ready member of the Armed Forces. Achievement and Commendation Medals provide a powerful means for a field commander to recognize younger individuals for outstanding performance.

Vietnamese Cross of Gallantry (for valor)

Armed Forces Honor Medal

Civil Actions Medal (Foreign Decoration)

National Defense Service Medal

Southwest Asia Service Medal

Saudi Arabian Medal for the Liberation of Kuwait

Kuwait Medal for the Liberation of Kuwait.

Former Yugoslavia

NATO Medal (Kosovo)

NATO Article 5 Medal

NATO Article 5 medal

NATO Non Article 5 Medal

NATO ISAF Medal

## Gulf War (1991-1995)

The conflict in the Persian Gulf, as previously noted, saw the reinstitution of the National Defense Service Medal (this time it also covered the Reserves) and the creation of the Southwest Asia Service Medal for the personnel in Iraq, Kuwait, Saudi Arabia, Oman, Bahrain, Qatar and United Arab Emirates. Between January 17, 1991 and November 30, 1995, service members who performed duty "in support of" the Persian Gulf War are eligible to receive the Southwest Asia Service Medal if duty was performed in either Israel, Egypt, Turkey, Syria or Jordan. The Southwest Asia Service Medal is authorized four campaign stars for service, but only a maximum of three campaign stars can be awarded with the medal. Each recipient of the medal must wear at least one campaign star.

The Department of Defense also approved the wear of the Saudi Arabian Medal for the Liberation of Kuwait, which probably wins the award as the "Most Colorful Medal" authorized American military personnel. Later the Department of Defense also authorized the Kuwait Medal for the Liberation of Kuwait.

## NATO Medals (1998 to Present)

In 1998 the North Atlantic Treaty Organization began authorizing medals for NATO specific service. The NATO Kosovo Campaign Medal was issued by the United States armed forces for participation in the Kosovo operations. For U.S. Forces, the Non-Article 5 Medal for Balkan Service replaced the NATO Kosovo Medal effective 1 January 2003. NATO also created an Article 5 Medal, a Non-Article 5 Medal and a NATO Meritorious Service Medal.

The idea is some what similar to the U.S. Joint Service awards which are used to reward joint staff service outside of a service members normal branch of service (i.e. Army, Navy, Air Force, Marines or Coast Guard). For U.S. Forces, service stars indicate additional awards to the NATO Medal. In the USA, NATO medals authorized for wear include the NATO Medal for Former Yugoslavia, the NATO Medal for Kosovo Service, both of the Article 5 Medals, the Non-Article 5 medals for the Balkans and Afghanistan International Security and Assistance Force (ISAF), The NATO Meritorious Service Medal and the Macedonia NATO Medal and the Non-Article 5 Medal for service in Iraq.

Afghanistan Campaign Medal

Iraq Campaign Medal

Global War on Terrorism Expeditionary Medal

Global War on Terrorism Service Medal

## The Global War on Terrorism and The Liberation of Afghanistan and Iraq *(2001 to Present)*

The cruel and cowardly terrorist hijacking and attack on the World Trade Center led to a vigorous series of counter attacks on terrorists and their supporters. To recognize these efforts, the National Defense Service Medal was reauthorized in 2001 and two new awards, the Global War on Terrorism Expeditionary and Service Medals were authorized. A White House spokesman said the medals recognize the "sacrifices and contributions" military members make in the global war on terror.

Following the liberation of Afghanistan, an Afghanistan Campaign Medal was created on November 29, 2004 retroactive to October 24, 2001 to acknowledge service there. A similar medal, known as the Iraq Campaign Medal was authorized for service during the same period within the borders of Iraq and is retroactive to March 19, 2003. The two medals may be awarded with the Army's Arrowhead device for assault/parachute landings and with the Marine combat operation insignia for qualified Naval personnel assigned to Marine Corps units. These medals replace the Global War on Terrorism Expeditionary Medal for service in Afghanistan and Iraq and military personnel can not receive both for the same period of service. In 2016 a new medal, the Inherent Resolve Campaign Medal, was added for continued conflict in the middle east.

All decorations, service medals and ribbons provide a unique and handsome way for the nation to honor her veterans for valor and faithful service but also have another important purpose. The display on a serviceman's chest can tell a commander, fellow members of the Armed Forces and veterans the level of experience and performance of the wearer. When a commander reviews his officers and noncommissioned officers, it only takes a minute to recognize their backgrounds and performance from their ribbons. From the individual service members viewpoint, military awards recognize devotion to duty, performance, valor and service in a way no other manner can accomplish. These medals and ribbons reflect how our country recognizes hundreds of years of unbroken dedicated service and valor by members of our Armed Forces going back to the birth of the Republic. I hope this book provides you a good understanding of the evolution, meaning and importance of American military awards and their history up to the present.

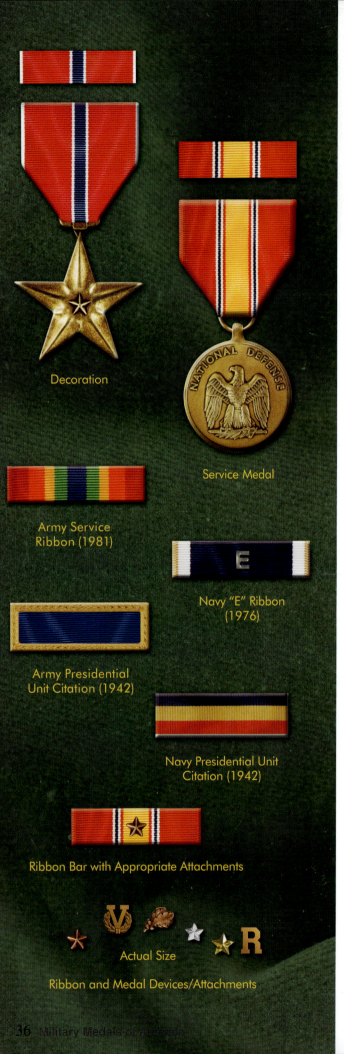

# Types of Military Medals, Ribbons and Devices

There are two general categories of medals awarded by the United States to its military personnel, namely, decorations and service medals.

**Decorations.** Since the establishment of our first awards, decorations for valorous or meritorious actions have traditionally been in the shape of a star, cross, hexagon or similar heraldic configuration. Although a small number of decorations are round, (e.g., Navy Distinguished Service Medal, Airman's Medal, Coast Guard Achievement Medal, etc.)

**Service Medals.** The circular shape has been used almost exclusively for service medals. These can be awarded for good conduct, participation in a particular campaign, expedition or service on foreign soil. Generally full size medals are restricted for wear on full dress uniforms, the miniature medals for wear on mess dress or evening dress uniforms and ribbon bars for everyday service uniforms. On civilian clothing, wearing miniature medals or an enameled lapel pin, in the colors of a specific ribbon, have been in vogue since the early part of the 20th Century. Additionally, since World War II, the enamel hat pin in the form of the appropriate medal has found favor with veterans' organizations for unofficial wear on their organizational hats.

**Ribbon Only Awards.** Ribbon only awards may be personal decorations (such as the Navy Marine Corps Combat Action Ribbon or the U.S. Coast Guard's Commandant's Letter of Commendation Ribbon), unit awards or individual service awards. The use of ribbon only awards begin during World War II. Some ribbon only awards have later been converted to full-size medals. Today all five of the military Services use ribbon only awards especially as individual service awards.

**Unit Citations.** The use of unit citations to recognize outstanding performance by a military unit or ship really came into play during World War II. The War Department decided the best way to recognize individual members of a unit or a ship for outstanding performance in combat or in support should be the use of a ribbon only award. The Army and Navy Presidential Unit Citations are the organizational equivalent of an individual award of The Army Distinguished Service Cross or the Navy Cross. Since the establishment of the Presidential Unit Citation, a number of additional unit citations as well as foreign unit citations have appeared. Army personnel may wear the unit citations of the unit to which they are assigned but must remove them when they leave the unit unless they served in the unit at the time the citation was earned. U.S. Army unit citations and some U.S. Air Force unit citations are unique in that they are mounted within a gold frame whereas the Coast Guard may or may not have a gold frame.

**Attachments or Appurtenances.** Small metal devices are worn on the ribbon bar or the medal's suspension ribbon to denote additional awards, campaigns, additional honors or subsequent service. These attachments come in the form of stars, oak leaf clusters, numerals, arrowheads, etc. and are another means to indicate the level and extent of the medal holder's service to his country. The attachments and the manner of their placement are shown in detail in subsequent pages as well as the ribbon displays prescribed by the individual Armed Services.

# Actual Size Military Medal Variations

Decorations are announced in official military orders. The orders are filed in an individual's military record jacket and retired to a records holding area when the individual is discharged or retired. A decoration usually comes with a citation, certificate and boxed medal with ribbon and lapel pin.

Authorization for service medals are noted in an individual's official military records. They are generally issued in a small cardboard box. Ribbon-only awards and unit citations are sometimes issued but generally the individual has to purchase them. Foreign medals, such as the Republic of Vietnam Campaign Medal are generally required to be purchased by individual service members.

Announcement of the decoration is published in official orders.

Republic of Vietnam's Gallantry Cross Award Certificate and Orders.

Medals of America 37

# How to Determine a Veteran's Military Medals

Many veterans and their families are unsure of which military medals they were awarded and often for good reasons. Twenty-five, thirty, even fifty years after military service, it is often difficult to remember or clearly identify the awards a veteran may have earned the right to wear or display. Thousands of veterans have been heard to say "I don't want any awards I'm not authorized, but I want everything I am authorized." So the question is, "What are the medals authorized the veteran for his military service during each conflict?"

There are a number of reasons besides the passage of time that veterans are not always sure of their military awards. At the end of World War II many campaign medals had not yet been struck and were only issued as ribbons due to the restriction on brass and other metals for the war effort. Many unit awards had not yet been authorized and on the whole, most soldiers, sailors, marines and airmen were more interested in going home than they were in their military records. Other changes such as Congress' decision in the 1947s to authorize a Bronze Star Medal for meritorious service to all recipients of the Combat Infantryman and Combat Medical Badge was not well known. Many veterans never realized that they had earned a Bronze Star Medal. Perhaps the most striking example is the recently-approved Republic of Korea War Service Medal. The Republic of Korea offered the medal to all U.S. Korean War veterans but it was not accepted by our government until 1999. In other cases, veterans came home and stuffed their medals and awards into a cigar box which usually found its way into the hands of children and these magnificent symbols of valor and service from a grateful nation simply disappeared over time.

Today there is a wonderfully renewed interest in wearing and displaying United States military medals, both to honor veterans' patriotic service and to display a family's pride in military service. World War II, Korea and Vietnam veterans now wear their medals at formal social and patriotic events and a display of military medals and insignia is often in the family home place of honor.

As mentioned earlier, military medals are divided into two categories: Decorations awarded for valor or meritorious service and Campaign and Service medals awarded for a particular service or event. Additionally there are Unit Awards which are for unit valor and meritorious service and ribbon-only awards presented for completing special training or recognizing certain service.

Decorations are individual awards which are of such singular significance that most veterans and their family will remember when such awards have been presented. Decorations are noted on a veteran's official discharge papers (called a DD Form 214) as well as published in official unit orders. However there are exceptions, such as the Bronze Star Medal issued for meritorious service after World War II and in some cases Purple Heart medals that were never officially presented. Someone who is unsure if they received a decoration can request the National Records Center in St. Louis or other veterans records holding areas to check their records. Home of Heroes at www.homeofheroes.com list all Medal of Honor, Service Crosses and most Silver Star awardees. Bronze Star, Air Medal, Purple Heart, Commendation and Achievement medals are announced in unit orders which are normally found in the individual's military service record.

Campaign and service medals, unit awards and ribbon-only awards are more clearly identifiable. The Army for example, has a campaign register which provides a clear indication of which campaign medals, unit awards, campaign stars and foreign unit awards are authorized a particular unit during certain periods of time. To aid in identifying the campaign medals authorized veterans of different conflicts and to show how they can be displayed, United States and Allied campaign medals authorized since World War II are summarized on the next page. Exact criteria for each medal and the campaigns associated with it are shown in detail later in the book.

Basically there are several ways to identify the military medals a veteran has earned. The early medals such as the Civil War Campaign medal are easy. If an ancestors served during the Civil War then they earned it (see page 125). The other early campaign medals prior to World War I, such as the Spanish-American campaign medals were earned by both 250,000 federal and state volunteers and their records are in the National Archives on microfilm. These files can be found by going to www.familysearch.com.

World War I is fairly straight forward, with few exceptions for all of the soldiers, sailors, marines and airmen who receive the World War I Victory Medal (see page 129). Their campaign bars and any other awards are also available on the government website: www.archives.gov.

## World War II and Later

The identification of World War II and later veterans is the information most veterans and families want and that really just comes from two places. The first is the veteran's discharge certificate which has his service history. Early World War II Army versions were an AGO Form 55 which later became the Department of Defense Form 214 (DD 214). While this is the official record it is often incomplete or missing information which was not available at the time of the veteran's discharge. Which of course is the purpose of this book, to bring veterans and their families up today on their military awards. So let's start with how you obtain a copy of your DD 214 or for the veteran in your family.

All of the federal government's military records for World War II veterans are stored at the National Personnel Records Center (NPRC) in St. Louis, Missouri. The National Personnel Records Center is part of the National Archives and Records Administration.

There are specific rules for requesting a veterans records because of the privacy act. As long as the veteran is still living, he is the only one who may request his complete military records. However if the veteran is deceased, then the next of kin is entitled to the complete military file. By the next of kin the NRPC means the unmarried widow or widower, son or daughter, father or mother, brother or sister of a deceased veteran. Grandchildren, nieces or nephews are not generally included his next of kin.

So if you are not the next of kin of the deceased veteran you really must have one of the next of kin make the request for the records. One exception is the military files will be provided if you are really the only living relative of a deceased veteran. While the NPRC will provide the complete military files for the purpose of identifying the military awards you are really only interested in the DD 214 record of discharge.

Unfortunately in 1973 there was a huge fire at the NPRC that destroyed nearly 18 million official military personnel records. Eighty per cent of those records destroyed were for Army and Army Air Force personnel that had been discharged between 1912 and 1960. Approximately 75% of Air Force records for personnel who were discharged between 1947 to 1964 beginning with the last name Hubbard through Z were also destroyed. The Air Force became a separate service from the Army in 1947. Even if you're relatively sure that the veterans records may have been burned you should go ahead and send them a request because NPRC has been able to reconstruct some files.

There is a another source for locating a veteran's DD214. Surprisingly a very high percentage of all veterans recorded a copy of their DD 214 in the local county courthouse. At the time of the veterans discharge it was recommended that they do this because it was the single most important document for them to have for applying for any veteran's benefits. By having it recorded at the local County Courthouse they could always obtain a copy. If you are researching a veteran's file you might be very pleasantly surprised to find a copy on file at the county courthouse.

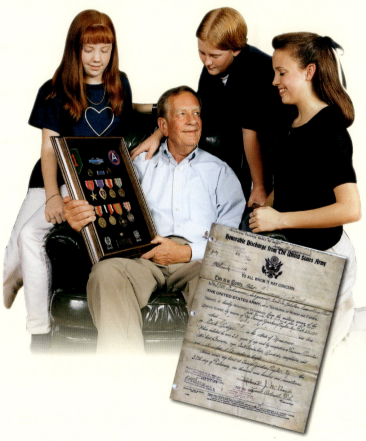

# Issue of U.S. Medals to Veterans, Retirees and Their Families

## How to Request the DD214

Veterans of any United States military service may request medals never issued (the majority of WW II veterans for example) or replacement of medals which have been lost, stolen, destroyed or rendered unfit through no fault of their own. Requests may also be filed for awards that were earned but, for any reason, were never issued to the veteran. A good example is the Korea Defense Service Medal which was recently approved and back dated to cover everyone who served in Korea after 1954. More than 2 million former service personnel are now authorized this medal. The next-of-kin of deceased veterans may also make the same request for the medals of their veteran family member.

The National Personnel Records Center, Military Personnel Records (NPRC-MPR) is the repository of millions of military personnel, health, and medical records of discharged and deceased veterans of all services during the 20th century. Information from the records is made available upon written request (with signature and date) to the extent allowed by law. Please note that NPRC holds historical Military Personnel Records of nearly 100 million veterans. The vast majority of these records are paper-based and not available on-line.

There are two ways for those seeking information regarding military personnel records stored at NPRC (MPR). If you are a veteran or next-of-kin of a deceased veteran, you may now use **vetrecs.archives.gov** to order a copy of your military records. For all others, your request is best made using a **Standard Form 180.** It includes complete instructions for preparing and submitting requests.

**Using the vetrecs.archives.gov** Requests for the issuance or replacement of military service medals, decorations, and awards should be directed to the specific branch of the military in which the veteran served. However, for Air Force (including Army Air Corps) and Army personnel, the National Personnel Records Center will verify the awards to which a veteran is entitled and forward the request with the verification to the appropriate service department for issuance of the medals.

The Standard Form (SF 180), Request Pertaining to Military Records, is recommended for requesting medals and awards. Provide as much information as possible and send the form to the appropriate address shown on the next page.

1. **How to Obtain Standard Form 180 (SF-180), Request Pertaining to Military Records**

A. Download and print a copy of the SF-180 in PDF format by going to: *http://www.archives.gov/facilities/mo/st_louis/ military_personnel_records standard_form_180.html#sf.*

B. Write to The National Personnel Records Center 9700 Page Avenue, St. Louis, Missouri 63132.

The SF 180 may be photocopied as needed. You must submit a separate SF 180 for each individual whose records are being requested.

2. **Write a Letter to Request Records**

If you are not able to obtain SF-180, you may still submit a request for military records by letter. The letter should indicate if the request is for a specific medal(s), or for all medals earned. It is also helpful to include copies of any military service documents that indicate eligibility for medals, such as military orders or the veteran's report of separation (DD Form 214 or its earlier equivalent). Federal law [5 USC 552a(b)] requires that all requests for information from official military personnel files be submitted in writing. Each request must be signed (in cursive) by the veteran or his next-of-kin indicating the relationship to the deceased and dated (within the last year). For this reason, no requests are accepted over the internet.

Requests must contain enough information to identify the record among the more than 70 million on file at NPRC (MPR). Certain basic information is needed to locate military service records. This information includes:

- The veteran's complete name used while in service, Service number or social security number
- Branch of service

If the request pertains to a record that may have been involved in the 1973 fire, also include:
- Place of discharge
- Last unit of assignment
- Place of entry into the service, if known

Submit a separate request (either SF 180 or letter) for each veteran whose records are being requested. Response times for records requested from the (NPRC) vary greatly depending on the nature of the request. For example, the NPRC Military Records Facility can run a backlog of 180,000 requests and receives approximately 5,000 requests per day. The Center may have a difficult time locating records since millions of records were lost in a fire in 1973. Although the requested medals can often be issued on the basis of alternate records, the documents sent in with the request are sometimes the only means of determining proper eligibility.

Finally, you should exercise extreme patience. It may take several months or, in some cases, a year to determine eligibility and dispatch the appropriate medals. The Center asks that you not send a follow-up request for 90 days. Because of these delays, many veterans simply purchase their medals from a supplier such as *www.usmedals.com*.

Generally, there is no charge for medal or award replacements from the government. The length of time to receive a response or your medals and awards varies depending upon the branch of service sending the medals.

# Cold War Recognition Certificate

In accordance with section 1084 of the Fiscal Year 1998 National Defense Authorization Act, the Secretary of Defense approved awarding Cold War Recognition Certificates to all members of the armed forces and qualified federal government civilian personnel who faithfully served the United States during the Cold War era, from Sept. 2, 1945 to Dec. 26, 1991. The application for the certificate is best obtained by doing an internet search for Cold War Recognition Certificate since the site location has changed several times.

| | ARMY | |
|---|---|---|
| If the person served in the Army, the request should be sent to: | **National Personnel Records Center**<br>1 Archives Drive<br>St. Louis, MO 63138 | In case of a problem or an appeal write to:<br>**U.S. Army Human Resources Cmd**<br>Awards Division<br>Attn: AHRC-PDP-A<br>1600 Spearhead Ave.<br>Fort Knox, KY 40122-5408 |
| | AIR FORCE | |
| The Air Force processes requests for medals through the National Personnel Records Center, which determines eligibility through the information in the veteran's records. Once verified, a notification of entitlement is forwarded to Randolph Air Force Base, Texas, from which the medals are mailed to the requestor. To request medals earned while in the Air Force or its predecessors, the Army Air Corps or Army Air Force veterans or their next-of-kin should write to: | **National Personnel Records Center**<br>1 Archives Drive<br>St. Louis, MO 63138 | In case of a problem or an appeal write to:<br>**Headquarters Air Force Personnel Ctr**<br>**AFPC/DPPPR**<br>550 C Street West, Suite 12<br>Randolph AFB, TX 78150-4714 |
| | NAVY | |
| If the person served in the Navy, the request should be sent to: | **National Personnel Records Center**<br>1 Archives Drive<br>St. Louis, MO 63138 | In case of a problem or an appeal write to:<br>**Department of the Navy**<br>**Chief of Naval Operations (DNS-35)**<br>2000 Navy Pentagon<br>Washington, DC 20350-2000 |
| | MARINE CORPS | |
| If the person served in the Marine Corps, the request should be sent to: | **National Personnel Records Center**<br>1 Archives Drive<br>St. Louis, MO 63138 | In case of a problem or an appeal write to:<br>**Commandant of the Marine Corps**<br>**Military Awards Branch (MMMA)**<br>2008 Elliot Road<br>Quantico, VA 22134 |
| | COAST GUARD | |
| If the person served in the Coast Guard, the request should be sent to: | **Coast Guard Personnel Center**<br>4200 Wilson Blvd, Suite 900<br>(PSC-PSD-MA) STOP 7200<br>Arlington, VA 20598-7200 | In case of a problem or an appeal write to:<br>**Commandant U.S. Coast Guard**<br>**Medals and Awards Branch (PMP-4)**<br>Washington, DC 20593-0001 |

# World War II Military Medals Records

Many readers of earlier editions ask for detail information about determining a veterans military awards. As mentioned on the previous pages the veterans DD214 or equivalent is the key. Shown below is a typical World War II DD214 with the individuals name removed. It is also a good example of the need to be able to translate the military abbreviations of that period and figure out what may be missing. In this case can you find the clue that tells you the soldier became authorized the Bronze Star medal in 1947, two years after his discharge in 1945 ? The key is award of the Combat Medical Badge (Med Badge).

Navy, Marine and Coast Discharges are similiar to the ones shown for World War II Army and Army Air Force.

ENLISTED RECORD AND REPORT OF SEPARATION
HONORABLE DISCHARGE

177-92

1. LAST NAME - FIRST NAME - MIDDLE INITIAL: veteran's name
2. ARMY SERIAL NO.: 37 611 552
3. GRADE: Pfc
4. ARM OR SERVICE: MD
5. COMPONENT: AUS
6. ORGANIZATION: Med Det 194th Gli Inf
7. DATE OF SEPARATION: 16 Nov 45
8. PLACE OF SEPARATION: Separation Center Jefferson Barracks Mo.
9. PERMANENT ADDRESS FOR MAILING PURPOSES: 1844 So 12th St St Louis Mo.
10. DATE OF BIRTH: 16 Jul 1943
11. PLACE OF BIRTH: Elvins Mo.
12. ADDRESS FROM WHICH EMPLOYMENT WILL BE SOUGHT: See #9
13. COLOR EYES: Brown
14. COLOR HAIR: Brown
15. HEIGHT: 6'
16. WEIGHT: 161 lbs.
17. NO. DEPEND.: 1
18. RACE: WHITE X
19. MARITAL STATUS: SINGLE X
20. U.S. CITIZEN: YES X
21. CIVILIAN OCCUPATION AND NO.: Painter Helper 9-32.21

MILITARY HISTORY

22. DATE OF INDUCTION: 12 Apr 1943
23. DATE OF ENLISTMENT: -----
24. DATE OF ENTRY INTO ACTIVE SERVICE: 19 Apr 1943
25. PLACE OF ENTRY INTO SERVICE: Jefferson Barracks Mo.
SELECTIVE SERVICE DATA — 26. REGISTERED: YES X
27. LOCAL S.S. BOARD NO.: #1
28. COUNTY AND STATE: Farmington Mo.
29. HOME ADDRESS AT TIME OF ENTRY INTO SERVICE: Flat River Mo.
30. MILITARY OCCUPATIONAL SPECIALTY AND NO.: Truck driver light 345
31. MILITARY QUALIFICATION AND DATE (i.e., infantry, aviation and marksmanship badges, etc.): Parachutist GO#138 Hq 17th AB 27 Jul44
32. BATTLES AND CAMPAIGNS: Rhineland, Ardennes, Central Europe.
33. DECORATIONS AND CITATIONS: Awarded 3 bronze stars for the above Campaign GO 33-40 1945 Good Conduct Medal. Med badge GO#49 Hq 194th Gli Inf 20 May 45. Glider badge GO#59 Hq 194th Gli Inf 26 Jul 44
34. WOUNDS RECEIVED IN ACTION: None
35. LATEST IMMUNIZATION DATES: SMALLPOX 20Apr43 30Jul45; TYPHOID 20Apr43 4May43; TETANUS 20Apr43 1June43; OTHER (specify) BT/A
36. SERVICE OUTSIDE CONTINENTAL U.S. AND RETURN: DATE OF DEPARTURE 20 Aug 44, 19 Aug 45; DESTINATION ETO, USA; DATE OF ARRIVAL 28 Aug 41, 29 Aug45
37. TOTAL LENGTH OF SERVICE: CONTINENTAL SERVICE 1 yrs 6 mos 25 days; FOREIGN SERVICE 1 yrs 0 mos 10 days
38. HIGHEST GRADE HELD: Pfc
39. PRIOR SERVICE: None
40. REASON AND AUTHORITY FOR SEPARATION: AR 615-365 Convenience of the Govt RR 1-1 (Demobilization) 15 Dec 44
41. SERVICE SCHOOLS ATTENDED: None
42. EDUCATION (Years): Grammar 8, High School 0, College 0

PAY DATA

43. LONGEVITY FOR PAY PURPOSES: 2 years 7 months 5 days
44. MUSTERING OUT PAY: TOTAL $300, THIS PAYMENT $100
46. TRAVEL PAY: $ 4.45
47. TOTAL AMOUNT, NAME OF DISBURSING OFFICER: 206.75 J.W. MC MANUS LT COL F.D.

INSURANCE NOTICE

48. KIND OF INSURANCE: Nat. Serv. X
49. HOW PAID: Allotment X
50. Effective Date of Allotment Discontinuance: 31 Oct 45
51. Date of Next Premium Due: 30 Nov 45
52. PREMIUM DUE EACH MONTH: $6.50
53. INTENTION OF VETERAN TO: Continue Only X

55. REMARKS (This space for completion of above items or entry of other items specified in W. D. Directives): No time lost under AW 107. Lapel button issued. Entitled to wear the Amer Theatre Campaign Ribbon. European-African-Middle Eastern Theatre Campaign Ribbon, 2 overseas bars. Victory Ribbon. Inactive ERC service from the 12 Apr 43 to 19 Apr 43. ASR score 55 (2 Sep 45)

57. PERSONNEL OFFICER: T. J. DOWNIE 1st LT, SIG., C.

APPLICATION FOR READJUSTMENT ALLOWANCE MADE THROUGH STATE OF MISSOURI

FORREST ROBINSON, ST. FRANCOIS CO., MO.

WD AGO Form 53-55, 1 November 1944

This form supersedes all previous editions of WD AGO Forms 53 and 55 for enlisted persons entitled to an Honorable Discharge, which will not be used after receipt of this revision.

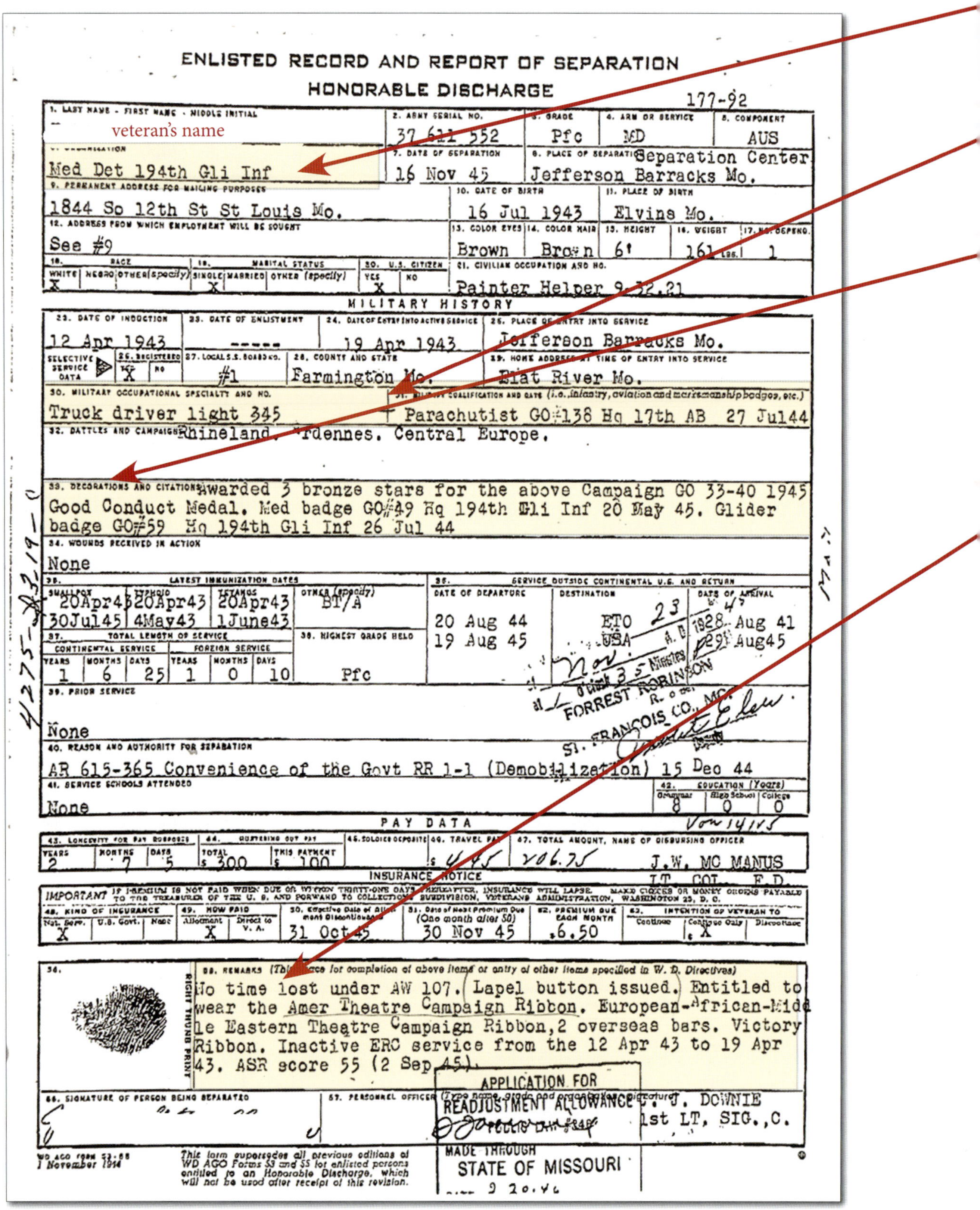

# Interperting the DD 214 for Awards
## World War II Military Medals

Just below where the veteran's name is in the upper left-hand corner you can see he was assigned to a medical detachment in the 194th Glider Infantry (An Airborne Regt, assigned to the 17th Airborne Division)

Box 30 indicates he was a truck driver (ambulance most likely) and box 31 shows he was paratrooper qualified.

Box 32 and 33 are the ones that you will always be most interested in as they identify decorations and awards. Box 32 says he served in three campaigns, Rhineland, Ardennes and Central Europe. Box 33 indicates the three bronze stars for the above campaigns but does not identify the campaign ribbons/medals until the remarks in box 35. It does identify the award of Good Conduct Medal followed by an MED badge citing the general order by which it was awarded. It also notes the award of a glider badge in 1944.

In box 55, the remarks section it indicates he was issued the honorable discharge lapel pin (aka "The Ruptured Duck"). It also states he is authorize the American Theater Campaign ribbon, European African Middle Eastern Theater Campaign ribbon, 2 overseas bars and a Victory Ribbon. Notice there is no reference to the word medals because many of the medals such as the Victory Medal were not minted until a year or more after the war.

So when this veteran was discharged and returned to the United States in August 1945 he received 4 ribbons and an honorable discharge lapel pin. He also had earned the parachute badge, the glider badge and combat medical badge which was referred to during World War II as a Medical badge (Med. badge).

What the DD214 does not tell (and could not know) is the award of the Medical Badge (now called the Combat Medical Badge) authorized him the Bronze Star Medal as of Army General Orders in 1947. He was also authorized the American Theater Campaign Medal, the European – African – Middle Eastern Theater Campaign Medal, the Victory Medal (which was not struck until 1947) and the Army of Occupation Medal which was not available until 1947 but was authorized for all military personnel that served at least 30 days in occupied enemy territory. The 194th GIR served in the Army of Occupation of Germany from 2 May - 14 August 1945. Since Germany surrendered in May 1945 and he return home in August 1945 he is authorized the Army Occupation of Germany Medal. The DD 214 gives you all the clues but knowing the medals that pertain to the period and war fills in the complete picture of his awards.

*Paratroopers of the 17th Airborne Division to include a medic are honored after the Battle of the Bugle.*

*Ribbons he came home with in August 1945.*

*Medals he is actually authorized but probably never recieved.*

# World War II Campaign Medals

The basic medals of World War II are shown above. The Navy, Marine Corps and Coast Guard had already established Good Conduct Medals while the Army (which included the Army Air Force) established a Good Conduct Medal in 1941.

The American Defense Service Medal was authorized for the period of national emergency prior to 7 December 1941. After America declared war, the conflict was divided into (1) the American theater, (2) the European, African, Middle Eastern theater, and the (3) Asiatic Pacific Theater. Examples of the medals awarded are shown above.

American Defense was awarded for service between 1939 and 7 Dec. 1941.

American Campaign was for service in the American Theater, outside the US for 30 days or in the US for a year. Most veterans qualified for this medal.

All WW II veterans qualified for the Victory Medal.

WW II veterans who served 30 days in an occupied country qualify for an Occupation Medal.

Philippine Defense and Liberation Medals for service in the Philippines.

This soldier's DD214 types out 3 of his 5 medals. The 2 medals not shown are the Victory Medal and the 1947 retroactive award of the Bronze Star medal for his award of the Combat Infantry Badge.

The U.S. Government will not issue foreign awards and he or his family will have to purchase the Phillipine Liberation Medal.

```
26. DATE OF ENTRY ON ACTIVE DUTY    27. MILITARY OCCUPATIONAL SPECIALTY AND NO.

22 April 1944                       Tank Unit Commander  1203           RECORDED
28. BATTLES AND CAMPAIGNS
Ardennes                                                                The Adjutant General's Office
Central Europe                                                          Concord, New Hampshire
29. DECORATIONS AND CITATIONS                                                   AUG 12 1947
Purple Heart Medal            ETO Service Medal                         Date..................
World War II Victory Medal  American Theatre Service Medal
WOUNDS RECEIVED IN ACTION

Belgium  1 January 1945
```

This Army Armor Officer DD214 has a stamp showing it was registered with the New Hampshire Adjutant General's Office. He is authorized 4 medals. Armor soldiers did not qualify for the Combat Infantry Badge so he is not authorized the 1947 retroactive award of the Bronze Star medal.

The European African Middle Eastern Theater Campaign Medal is abbreviated as the ETO Service medal or sometimes the EAME. He would have 2 battle stars on his ETO medal as shown by the 2 listed campaigns.

```
NOTICE OF SEPARATION FROM U.S. NAVAL SERVICE   10296   BOOK 103 PAGE 310
NAVPERS-553 (REV. 8-45)

                                               5. PLACE OF SEPARATION
                                               USN Personnel Separation Center
                                               Lido Beach, L.I., N.Y.

806 194

14. MEANS OF ENTRY           17. DATE OF ENTRY INTO ACTIVE SERVICE   18. NET SERVICE (FOR PAY PURPOSES)
                             12-18-43                                 2-5-9
[X] ENLISTED [X] INDUCTED [ ] COMMISSIONED
DATE 12-11-43  DATE 12-11-43  DATE          19. PLACE OF ENTRY INTO ACTIVE SERVICE
                                             Buffalo, N.Y.
                                            21. RATINGS HELD                22. FOREIGN AND/OR SEA
                                            AS, F2c, F1c, WT3/c              SERVICE WORLD WAR II
Those of Rating                                                              [X] YES  [ ] NO
See Rating Description Booklet
                                            24. SERVICE (VESSELS AND STATIONS SERVED ON)
                                            AFISTA, Rochester,N.Y./NRS,Buffalo,N.Y
Recruit Trg., Sampson, N.Y.   6             NTS,Sampson,N.Y./ NTS, NorVa./
                                            USS FRYBARGER/ NTS,NorVa./
                                            USS JOSEPH E.CONNOLY/
                                            PSC Lido Beach,L.I.,N.Y.

NTS    5/46        6 46      36.10           Yes
       36.82              19.75    $100    EP O'ROURKE

American Theater Medal
European African Middle Eastern
Medal                                        F. R. Ahmuty
Asiatic Pacific Medal 1 Star                 F. R. AHMUTY, Lieut., USNR
Victory Medal                                By direction
```

This sailor's World War II discharge shows the rating he held in box 21 (WT3/c) Water Tender 3rd Class and the ships he served on. In July 1942 the Navy discontinued the procurement and issuance of Good Conduct medals for the duration of World War II to conserve metal and offset the increased clerical work. Notations of eligibility were made in service jackets for later issue however the Navy required 3 years service for a Good Conduct Medal and his discharge shows 2 years, 5 months and 9 days active service so he did not qualify for a Good Conduct Medal. However his European African Middle Eastern Theater Campaign Medal should show at least 1 battle/campaign star as you can not earn the medal without being in at least one campaign. He is authorized the 4 medals shown plus 1 star on his European African Middle Eastern Theater Campaign Medal.

Medals of America  45

# Korean Campaign Medals 1950-1954

The Armed Forces approved acceptance of the ROK War Service Medal in Oct. 1999 for all Korean War Veterans. The Korea Defense Service Medal for 30 days service in Korea after 27 July 1954 was approved in 2003.

After World War II the Navy and Marine Corps changed the ribbon drape of their Good Conduct Medals. Althought the Air Force became a separate service in 1947 it still used the Army Good Conduct Medal during the Korean War and up to 1 June 1963 when the Air Force Good Conduct Medal was authorized.

*See page 50 for abbreviation guide.*

With service in WW II and Korea this Infantry Officer's DD214 is a great example of the many abbreviations you will see. BSM/W/V means a Bronze Star Medal with Valor Device (as opposed for award for meritorious service) and 3 Oak leaf clusters to indicate he was awarded the medal 4 times. ADSM is the American Defense Service Medal; ACM is the American Campaign Medal; APCM W/2BS is the Asiatic Pacific Campaign Medal with 2 Bronze stars: PH is the Purple Heart Medal: WWII VM is the Victory Medal and the AOM (Ger) is the Army Occupation Medal with Germany Bar. His service awards in the Korean War are indicated by NDSM which is the National Defense Service Medal; the KSM W/2 Bz Strs is the Korean Service Medal with 2 Bronze Stars. PLR is the Phillipine Liberation Medal; PIR is the Philippine Independence Medal; PHIL PVC is the Philippine Presidential Unit Citation; ROKPVC is the Republic of Korea Presidential Unit Citation. The CIB is his award of the Combat Infantry Badge but does not indicate if there was a second award for Korea. 6 O/S Bars stand for 6 six months periods in combat and the ARCOM stands for award of the Army Commendation Medal. What is missing is the ROK War Service Medal which was not approved until 1999.

# Vietnam Campaign Medals 1965-1973

Good Conduct Medals (Current issue) — National Defense Service Medal — U.S. Vietnam Service Medal — Vietnam Campaign Medal — RVN Gallantry Cross Unit Citation

26. DECORATIONS, MEDALS, BADGES, COMMENDATIONS, CITATIONS AND CAMPAIGN RIBBONS AWARDED OR AUTHORIZED
Navy Achievement Medal w/"V", Combat Action Ribbon, Presidential Unit Citation w/2*, Meritorious Unit Commendation, Good Conduct Medal w/5*, National Defense Service Medal, Vietnam Service Medal w/5*, Republic of Vietnam Cross of Gallantry w/Bronze Star,

27. REMARKS
Item#26 continued: Republic of Vietnam Meritorious Unit Commendation w/palm & frame, Republic of Vietnam Meritorious Unit Commendation Civic Action Color 1st Class w/palm & frame, Republic of Vietnam Campaign Medal w/device, Rifle Expert Badge 3rd Award, Pistol Sharpshooter Badge, Letter of Commendation 1973, Certificate of Appreciation 1973, Letters of Appreciation 1973, 1974, 1975 (3). Served in Vietnam: 27 Oct 67 - 2 Nov 68. Extension of service was at the request and for the convenience of the Government.

This career Marine's discharge spells out his awards and uses the *symbol to indicate campaign and additional awards stars. Note the RVN Cross of Gallantry is listed w/ bronze Star which means it is a personal decoration from the South Vietnamese government and not a unit award.

The Vietnam Service Medal with 5* will be represented by a single silver star (in lieu of 5 bronze stars) on the medal drape. The Combat Action Ribbon is the Navy/Marine general equivalent of the Army Combat Infantry Badge.

21. HOME OF RECORD AT TIME OF ENTRY INTO ACTIVE SERVICE
WALKER ROUTE, COLEVILLE, CALIFORNIA
23a. SPECIALTY NUMBER & TITLE  b. RELATED CIVILIAN OCCUPATION AND D.O.T. NUMBER
ASM (0000/0000)  620 — MOTORIZED VEHICLE MECH.

22. STATEMENT OF SERVICE | YEARS | MONTHS | DAYS
a. CREDITABLE FOR BASIC PAY PURPOSES (1) NET SERVICE THIS PERIOD | 04 | 11 | 13
(2) OTHER SERVICE | 00 | 00 | 00
(3) TOTAL (Line (1) plus Line (2)) | 04 | 11 | 13
b. TOTAL ACTIVE SERVICE | 04 | 11 | 13
c. FOREIGN AND/OR SEA SERVICE | 02 | 02 | 17

24. DECORATIONS, MEDALS, BADGES, COMMENDATIONS, CITATIONS AND CAMPAIGN RIBBONS AWARDED OR AUTHORIZED
NATIONAL DEFENSE SERVICE MEDAL, REPUBLIC OF VIETNAM SERVICE MEDAL, VIETNAM CAMPAIGN MEDAL, NAVY UNIT COMMENDATION, MERITORIOUS UNIT COMMENDATION, VIETNAMESE CROSS OF GALLANTRY, GOOD CONDUCT (1ST) 27JUN70.

This sailor's Vietnam era discharge is missing the campaign stars for his Vietnam Service Medal and while it shows 2 years and 2 months foreign service or sea service it is difficult to tell how many campaign stars he rates on his service medal. If you know the dates of his service in Vietnam you can compute the campaign stars from the table listed on the page describing the Vietnam Service Medal. The Vietnamese Cross of Gallantry listed after the Unit Commendations has to be a unit award and not a personal decoration such as the one shown on the marine's discharge above. The clerk most likely left off the words Unit Citation since he was running out of room. Naval personnel would have recieved the RVN Navy Cross of Gallantry as a personnel decoration not an Army verison. The Vietnamese Cross of Gallantry Unit Citation was a blanket award to all Armed Forces personnel who served in Vietnam.

### CORRECTION TO DD FORM 214, CERTIFICATE OF RELEASE OR DISCHARGE FROM ACTIVE DUTY
This Report Contains Information Subject to the Privacy Act of 1974, As Amended.

| 1. NAME (Last, First, Middle) | 2. DEPARTMENT, COMPONENT AND BRANCH<br>ARMY/AUS/INF | 3. SOCIAL SECURITY NUMBER<br>(Also, Service Number if applicable) |
|---|---|---|
| 4. MAILING ADDRESS (Include ZIP Code)<br>OSHKOSH GARDEN NEBRASKA 69154 | | |

5. ORIGINAL DD FORM 214 IS CORRECTED AS INDICATED BELOW:

| ITEM NO. | CORRECTED TO READ |
|---|---|
| | SEPARATION DATE ON DD FORM 214 BEING CORRECTED: 1969/11/07 |
| 24 | DELETE: VIETNAM SERVICE MEDAL//<br>ADD: PURPLE HEART//COMBAT INFANTRYMAN BADGE//ARMY GOOD CONDUCT MEDAL//REPUBLIC OF VIETNAM MEDAL W/DEVICE (1960)//REPUBLIC OF VIETNAM GALLANTRY CROSS W/PALM UNIT CITATION//REPUBLIC OF VIETNAM CIVIL ACTIONS HONOR MEDAL FIRST CLASS UNIT CITATION//EXPERT MARKSMANSHIP QUALIFICATION BADGE W/RIFLE BAR (M-14)//SHARPSHOOTER MARKSMANSHIP QUALIFICATION BADGE W/MACHINE GUN BAR (M-60)//MARKSMAN MARKSMANSHIP QUALIFICATION BADGE W/RIFLE BAR (M-16)//VIETNAM SERVICE MEDAL W/TWO BRONZE SERVICE STARS//NOTHING FOLLOWS |

Occasionally a DD214 discharge needs to be corrected and this soldier's DD214 is a good example showing the Vietnam Service Medal was deleted and replaced with an entry at the end of the update form showing it was to have 2 campaign stars. This corrected form does an excellent job spelling out his awards and badges.

| ITEM NO | CORRECTED TO READ |
|---|---|
| | SEPARATION DATE ON DD FORM 214 BEING CORRECTED: 27 OCT 70 |
| 24 | DELETE: VSM//BSM//ARCOM<br>ADD: VIETNAM SERVICE MEDAL W/3 BRONZE SERVICE STARS//REPUBLIC OF VIETNAM GALLANTRY CROSS W/PALM UNIT CITATION BADGE//PURPLE HEART//ARMY COMMENDATION MEDAL W/"V" DEVICE//BRONZE STAR MEDAL W/"V" DEVICE AND FIRST OAK LEAF CLUSTER//NOTHING FOLLOWS |

This DD214 discharge corrections deletes the abbreviations; VSM//BSM//ARCOM and spells out full name with the appropriate devices. In this case there is a big difference between a BSM and ARCOM with no devices and the corrected verisons that show the awards were for valor as opposed for meritorious service and the that there were 2 awards of the Bronze Star Medal (Oak Leaf)

24 DECORATIONS, MEDALS, BADGES, COMMENDATIONS, CITATIONS AND CAMPAIGN RIBBONS AWARDED OR AUTHORIZED

NDSM  VCM  VSM  ARCOM  CIB  AIR MEDAL  2 O/S BARS
BSM  SPS (M-14)

This soldier's Vietnam era discharge is typical of abbreviations: NDSM is National Defense Service Medal; the VCM is the RVN Vietnam Campaign Medal; the VSM is the Vietnam Service Medal but missing the campaign stars and it is difficult to tell how many campaign stars he rates on his service medal without knowing when he was there. If you know the dates of his service in Vietnam you can compute the campaign stars from the table listed on the page describing the Vietnam Service Medal. ARCOM is the Army Commendation Medal, CIB, the Combat Infantryman Badge and Air Medal (AM) is correct. The 2 overseas service bars tell you he spent a year in Vietnam so he will have at least 2, up to 4 campaign stars depending on the period. The BSM is the Bronze Star Medal and SPS is for a Sharp Shooters badge. The Vietnamese Cross of Gallantry Unit Citation is missing.

| 19. INDOCHINA OR KOREA SERVICE SINCE AUGUST 5, 1964<br>☒ YES ☐ NO  92 DAYS THAILAND, 182 DAYS RVN | 20. HIGHEST EDUCATION LEVEL SUCCESSFULLY COMPLETED (in Yrs.)<br>SECONDARY/HIGH SCHOOL 12  COLLEGE ___ YRS | | |
|---|---|---|---|
| 21. TIME LOST (Preceding Two Yrs.)<br>NO TIME LOST | 22. DAYS ACCRUED LEAVE PAID<br>38.5 days | 23. SERVICEMEN'S GROUP LIFE INSURANCE COVERAGE<br>☐ $15,000 ☐ $35,000<br>☒ $20,000<br>☐ $10,000 ☐ NONE | 24. DISABILITY SEVERANCE PAY<br>☒ NO ☐ YES<br>AMOUNT NONE | 25. PERSONNEL SECURITY INVESTIGATION<br>a. TYPE *LNAC  b. DATE COMPLETED 22 SEP 72 |

26. DECORATIONS, MEDALS, BADGES, COMMENDATIONS, CITATIONS AND CAMPAIGN RIBBONS AWARDED OR AUTHORIZED
SS,BS(1OLC),PH,SLSM,VSM,RVCR,NDSM,AFCOM 1 JUL 72-30 JUL 75),SAEMR,AFOUA,AFM 900-3//

This Air Force Hero's Vietnam era discharge is a classic in abbreviations: SS (Silver Star Medal); BS (1OLC) is the Bronze Star Medal with an Oak Leaf Cluster; PH is the Purple Heart Medal; SLSM is the very rare Silver Life Saving Medal; the VSM is the Vietnam Service Medal but missing the campaign stars. He is authorized at least one.

The RVCR is the RVN Vietnam Campaign Medal; NDSM is National Defense Service Medal; AFCOM is the USAF Commendation Medal, the SAEMR is a Small Arms Expert Marksman ribbon and AFOUA is the AF Outstanding Unit award. The Vietnamese Cross of Gallantry Unit Citation is missing.

*See page 50 for abbreviation guide.*

# Cold War 1947-1991

Millions of Americans served in the Armed Forces during the Cold War often in dangerous and difficult places. In many cases the current Good Conduct Medals of the Army, Navy, Marines, Air Force and Coast Guard were all they were authorized.

# Southwest Asia, Bosnia/Kosovo, Afghanistan & Iraq Campaign Medals

**Southwest Asia Service Medal 1991-1995**
**Bosnia/Kosovo Campaign Medal 1999-2013**
**Afghanistan Campaign Medal 2001-To a date To Be Determined**
**Iraq Campaign Medal 2003-2011**
**Inherent Resolve Campaign Medal 2014-To a date To Be Determined**

After Vietnam the Armed Forces began a much better job desciding the decorations and awards of honorably discharged personnel. Current DD214s such as shown on the next page clearly spell all authorized awards the veteran has earned. Examples of the campaign medals for the period above are shown below and two examples of the DD214 discharges used today are shown on the next page.

Medals of America 49

**13. DECORATIONS, MEDALS, BADGES, CITATIONS AND CAMPAIGN RIBBONS AWARDED OR AUTHORIZED** (All periods of service)
PURPLE HEART (2ND AWARD)//ARMY ACHIEVEMENT MEDAL//ARMY GOOD CONDUCT MEDAL//NATIONAL DEFENSE SERVICE MEDAL//AFGHANISTAN CAMPAIGN MEDAL W/ TWO CAMPAIGN STARS//IRAQ CAMPAIGN MEDAL W/ CAMPAIGN STAR//OVERSEAS SERVICE RIBBON (2ND AWARD)//NATO MEDAL//COMBAT INFANTRYMAN BADGE//CONT IN BLOCK 18

**14. MILITARY EDUCATION** (Course title, number of weeks, and month and year completed)
AIRBORNE COURSE, 3 WEEKS, 2007//INFANTRYMAN COURSE, 8 WEEKS, 2007//WARRIOR LEADER COURSE, 2 WEEKS, 2009//NOTHING FOLLOWS

15a. COMMISSIONED THROUGH SERVICE ACADEMY — YES X NO
b. COMMISSIONED THROUGH ROTC SCHOLARSHIP (10 USC Sec. 2107b) — YES X NO
c. ENLISTED UNDER LOAN REPAYMENT PROGRAM (10 USC Chap. 109) (If Yes, years of commitment: NA ) — YES X NO

16. DAYS ACCRUED LEAVE PAID 12
17. MEMBER WAS PROVIDED COMPLETE DENTAL EXAMINATION AND ALL APPROPRIATE DENTAL SERVICES AND TREATMENT WITHIN 90 DAYS PRIOR TO SEPARATION — YES / NO X

**18. REMARKS** ////////////////////////////////////////////////////////////////////
CONTINUOUS HONORABLE ACTIVE SERVICE: 20070206-20120527//ENLISTMENT BONUS PAID: $5000.00, 20070405//SERVED IN A DESIGNATED IMMINENT DANGER PAY AREA//SERVICE IN IRAQ 20071115-20090215//SERVICE IN AFGHANISTAN 20101030-20110917//MEMBER HAS COMPLETED FIRST FULL TERM OF SERVICE//NOT ELIGIBLE FOR SEPARATION PAY; SIGNED DECLINATION FOR CONTINUED SERVICE, DA FORM 4991-R//CONT FROM BLOCK 13: //PARACHUTIST BADGE//NOTHING FOLLOWS

---

**13. DECORATIONS, MEDALS, BADGES, CITATIONS AND CAMPAIGN RIBBONS AWARDED OR AUTHORIZED** (All periods of service)
ARMY COMMENDATION MEDAL (3RD AWARD)//ARMY ACHIEVEMENT MEDAL (2ND AWARD)//ARMY SUPERIOR UNIT AWARD//ARMY GOOD CONDUCT MEDAL//ARMY RESERVE COMPONENT ACHIEVEMENT MEDAL (2ND AWARD)//NATIONAL DEFENSE SERVICE MEDAL (2ND AWARD)//GLOBAL WAR ON TERRORISM EXPEDITIONARY MEDAL//CONT IN BLOCK 18

**14. MILITARY EDUCATION** (Course title, number of weeks, and month and year completed)
NONE//NOTHING FOLLOWS

(Specify the item number of the block continued for each entry.) ////////////////////
CONT FROM BLOCK 18: PROFESSIONAL DEVELOPMENT RIBBON (2ND AWARD)//ARMY SERVICE RIBBON//OVERSEAS SERVICE RIBBON//ARMED FORCES RESERVE MEDAL W/ 10-YEAR DEVICE-BRONZE HOURGLASS//ARMED FORCES RESERVE MEDAL W/ M DEVICE//NOTHING FOLLOWS

**18. REMARKS**
SERVED IN A DESIGNATED IMMINENT DANGER PAY AREA//SERVICE IN UNITED ARAB EMIRATES 20130807-20140505//ITEM 12D ABOVE DOES NOT ACCOUNT FOR ANNUAL AND/OR WEEKEND TRAINING THIS SOLDIER MAY HAVE ACCOMPLISHED PRIOR TO DATE ENTERED IN ITEM 12A//INDIVIDUAL COMPLETED PERIOD FOR WHICH ORDERED TO ACTIVE DUTY FOR PURPOSE OF POST SERVICE BENEFITS AND ENTITLEMENTS//ORDERED TO ACTIVE DUTY IN SUPPORT OF OPERATION ENDURING FREEDOM IAW 10 USC 12302//MEMBER HAS COMPLETED FIRST FULL TERM OF SERVICE//CONT FROM BLOCK 13: //GLOBAL WAR ON TERRORISM SERVICE MEDAL//NON COMMISSIONED OFFICER//SEE ATTACHED CONTINUATION SHEET

# Abbreviations

| | | | |
|---|---|---|---|
| AM | Air Medal | JMUA | Joint Meritorious Unit Citation |
| ACM | American Campaign Medal | JSAM | Joint Service Achievement Medal |
| ADSM | American Defense Service Medal | JSCM | Joint Service Commendation Med |
| ASM | Antarctic Service Medal | KSM | Korean Service Medal |
| AFEM | Armed Forces Expeditionary Medal | KCM | Kosovo Campaign Medal |
| AFRM | Armed Forces Reserve Medal | KLM(K) | Kuwait Liberation Medal (Kuwait) |
| AFSM | Armed Forces Service Medal | KLM(SA) | Kuwait Liberation Medal (Saudi Arabia) |
| AAM | Army Achievement Medal | LM or LOM | Legion of Merit |
| ARCOM | Army Commendation Medal | M or M Dev | Letter "M" Device |
| GCM or AGCM | Army Good Conduct Medal | V or V Dev | Letter "V" Device |
| AOM | Army of Occupation Medal | MHA | Medal for Humane Action |
| ARCAM | Army Reserve Components Ach. Medal | MH or MOH | Medal of Honor |
| ARCOTR | Army Reserve Components Overseas Tng | MSM | Meritorious Service Medal |
| ASR | Army Service Ribbon | MUC | Meritorious Unit Citation |
| ASUA | Army Superior Unit Citation | NDSM | National Defense Service Medal |
| APCM | Asiatic-Pacific Campaign Medal | NPDR | NCO Professional Development Rib |
| BF | Belgian Fourragere | NOL | Netherlands Orange Lanyard |
| BA, AH or BAH | Bronze Arrowhead | OLC | Oak Leaf Cluster |
| OLC or BOLC | Bronze Oak Leaf Cluster | OSR | Overseas Service Ribbon |
| BSS or BCS | Bronze Service Star | PDR | Philippine Defense Ribbon |
| BSM | Bronze Star Medal | PIR | Philippine Independence Ribbon |
| CIB | Combat Infantryman Badge | PLR | Philippine Liberation Ribbon |
| CMB or MB | Combat Medical Badge | POW | POW Medal |
| DDSM | Defense Distinguished Service Medal | PU | Presidential Unit Citation |
| DMSM | Defense Meritorious Service Medal | PH | Purple Heart |
| DSSM | Defense Superior Service Medal | VCM | Republic of Vietnam Campaign |
| DFC | Distinguished Flying Cross | SS | Silver Star |
| DSC | Distinguished Service Cross | SM | Soldier's Medal |
| DSM | Distinguished Service Medal | SWASM | Southwest Asia Service Medal |
| EAMECM or EAME or ETO | European-African-Middle Eastern Campaign Medal | UNSM | United Nations Service Medal |
| EFMB | Expert Field Medical Badge | VUA | Valorous Unit Citation |
| EIB | Expert Infantryman Badge | VSM | Vietnam Service Medal |
| FF | French Fourragere | WACSM | Women's Army Corps Service Medal |
| HSM | Humanitarian Service Medal | WWIVM | World War I Victory Medal |

# Introduction to Awards Display Cases of the
# Army • Navy • Marines • Air Force • Coast Guard

The most appropriate use of military medals after active service is to mount the medals for permanent display in home or office. This reflects the individual's patriotism and the military service rendered to the United States.

United States decorations are usually awarded in a presentation set which normally consists of a medal, ribbon bar and lapel pin, all contained in a special case. During World War II, the name of the decoration was stamped in gold on the front of the case. However, as budget considerations assumed greater importance, this practice was gradually phased out and replaced by a standard case with "United States of America" emblazoned on the front. At the present time, the more common decorations, (e.g., Achievement and Commendation Medals), come in small plastic cases suitable only for initial presentation and storage of the medal.

The most effective method of protecting awards involves the use of a shadow box or glass front display case with at least 1/2 inch between the medals and the glass. This provides a three dimensional view and protects the medal display in a dust-free environment.

Any physical alteration destroys the integrity of the medal and the use of glue ruins the back of the ribbon and medal. The best way to mount medals is in a display case specially designed for that purpose.

The mounting board is absolutely critical. Acid-free Gator board at least 1/4 inch thick covered with a high quality velour-type material to which Velcro™ will adhere will allow the medals to be mounted using Velcro™ tape which locks the medal firmly into place without damage. The added advantage is the medals and insignia can be moved without damage.

**Medals of America** 51

# A Case in Point on How Not to Display Medals

Admiral R. A. Ofstie, a veteran of World War I and World War II.

The correct display of Admiral R. A. Ofstie's career awards. It would be even better with individual medal name plates.

Here is an example of someone who went to a lot of work to do a poor job of displaying a naval hero's medals. The display in question is of Vice Admiral R. A. Ofstie, a veteran of World War I and World War II whose final assignment was commanding the American Sixth Fleet. Admiral Ofstie was a distinguished naval commander in World War II who was awarded the Navy Cross and Silver Star for valor as well as the Navy Distinguished Service Medal and the Legion of Merit.

This haphazard public display of the Admiral's medals shown above is a perfect example of why this book goes into the detail of the order precedence of the medals and an understanding of the campaign medals that accompany military service during different conflicts. In this case someone went to a great deal of trouble to take a box of some of the admiral's medals and carefully cut out a form for each medal in a piece of styrofoam (unfortunately a very bad material to preserve the medals). The medals are displayed in such a haphazard manner that they certainly confuses Navy veterans, family members or historians who view the display.

The admiral was awarded the Navy Cross, our country second highest award for valor, but for some reason two of the medals are displayed and inserted haphazardly in the line of other medals. In actuality the admiral was awarded the Navy Cross only once as well as a Distinguished Service Medal, the Silver Star and the Legion of Merit as his prominent decorations. Two World War I Victory Medals are displayed as well as the Spanish Order of Military Merit and the Polish Cross of Military Merit but no campaign medals of World War II.

His naval aviator wings are displayed at the bottom of the case over a group of miniature medals which are mounted in reverse order showing the foreign decorations first. The display leaves out his World War II campaign medals in addition to the World War II Victory Medal and National Defense Service Medal. Based on his World War II service he would've also received the Philippine Liberation Medal.

A correctly assembled display above shows his full military honors. This is the attention to detail we owe every American veteran.

# An Easy way to Display Medals

The first six veterans I ask to read the draft of this book all made the suggestion, " Before you show examples of medal displays take a minute to show how simple it is to mount the medals correctly".

Basily you start with identifying the veteran's medals which can be done for major conflicts beginning on page 44. While it will not identify decorations for valor or merit it gives everyone a great starting point and a veterans discharge (DD214) , pictures in uniform or oral family history often fill in the rest.

In this case I prepared a display for a an enlisted Marine Korean War veteran. He was a member of the 1st Marine Division and had earned a Good Conduct Medal, National Defense Service Medal, Korean War Service Medal. UN Campaign Medal and the later approved Korean War Service Medal. As a combat marine he was authorized the Combat Action ribbon and his unit was authorized the Presidential Unit Citation and the Korean Presidential Unit Citation. he had not served in Korea after the conflict so he was not authorized the newer Korean Defense Service medal

I then selected a red background and 12 by 16 inch display with a red velcro friendly fabric. After removing the fabric covered gator board type backboard from the frame I laid the back flat on a table and decided on placement or arrangement of awards.

You then layout your medals, ribbons, badges and patches upside down, side to be taped up, on your colored back. You can then arrange them in the design that you like. Decide if you want to clip pins or tape over them with Velcro©. Prongs can be pushed into the foam core backing.

Cut Velcro tape into pieces as needed. Peel off protective paper and FIRMLY press onto back of object to be mounted. Place velcro tape at strategic points where objects make contact with the fabric backboard. All spots where Velcro is applied should be clean (no dust or fingerprints). Velcro backs can be reused indefinitely. Velcro tape can be removed from collectable items. If the sticky tape is removed from the object it is holding for any reason NEW tape should be used.

Once you have the layout you want, press the medal, patch or insignia FIRMLY into place on fabric backboard. Insert the fabric covered gator board into the frame, close it up, attach your hanger and you've done a great job. Spot something wrong or want to add something just open up the case, peel off the medals and badges and rearrange by pressing into a new postion, no glue, no mess.

The display tells the story of a member of 106th "Golden Lion" Infantry Division which was struck by the full weight of the German Winter Offensive on December 16th, 1944. A battle we all know by the name of the "The Battle of the Bulge".

## Awards Displays that Honor American Veterans!

The most positive thing a veteran or their family can do to honor and remember their service to our country is to display their military awards for future generations. Many veterans or families are not sure where to start. Sometimes there is an old uniform, a cigar box full of old insignia that children or grandchildren once played with or perhaps some old black and white photographs.

The picture above shows what this book can help you do. The old uniform carries the insignia of an infantry corporal in the 106th "Golden Lion" Infantry Division which took the full weight of Von Rundstedt's Ardennes Campaign in December of 1944. This veteran had been awarded the Combat Infantry Badge, the Bronze Star medal, the Purple Heart medal, the Good Conduct Medal, the American Campaign Medal and the European-African-Middle Eastern Campaign Medal and the World War Victory Medal.

The Division was assigned occupation duty in Bad Ems after the war which qualifies him for the World War II Occupation Medal and he has personally added the Battle of the Bulge Commemorative Medal to indicate his participation in one of most significant and difficult battles of World War II. The display tells the story of his service with his medals, division, branch insignia and qualification badges even to his World War II Honorable discharge pin. A display of service that will be admired by generations to come.

Medals of America  55

# U.S. Army Award Display World War II

- Army Rank
- Medals
- Campaign Battle Stars
- Shooting Badges
- Brass Plates
- Army Insignia
- Army Badges
- Commemorative Medals
- Honorable Discharge Pin AKA "Ruptured Duck"

**World War II (Europe)**

**Did You Know?** The soldiers of World War II did not received their campaign medals at the end of the war. They only received the ribbon bars because brass had been restricted for munitions and many of the medals had yet to be struck or approved. In fact, some medals were not approved until 1985.

The display shows the awards and insignia that tell the unique story of each veteran's service. Each medal, badge, unit insignia, rank and ribbon recalls an event in the life of the veteran it honors.

**Letters**

I was a 21 year old in college when I enlisted in 1942. After Basic training I joined the 87th Division in Camp McCain, and in March 1944 transferred into European replacement pool which departed on a troop ship with 4,000 replacements for Italian campaign casualties. After a fast Atlantic crossing, to Oran, North Africa we went to Naples, Italy and in June, near Rome, assigned to Company G, 157th Infantry Regiment, 45th Division as a 60mm mortarman. We trained for and invaded southern France. We battled through Vosges Mountains along western edge of France into Alsace. By Jan. 1945, I was one of 13 survivors from Company G.

After Germany surrendered we were alerted for the invasion of Japan. We felt the bomb saved our lives. I was home for Christmas.

56 **Military Medals of America**

# U.S. Army Award Display WW II, Europe and Pacific

### World War II (Pacific)
This veteran's case shows American and Pacific service with medals and commemoratives reflecting Combat Service, and victory over Japan. Ribbons above Medals. WW II Tech 5 rank with Honorable Discharge Button & Shooting Badges.

### World War II (Pacific)
This Staff Sgt. combat veteran case shows Pacific service in the 25th and Americal Division including the Liberation of the Phillippines, the Presidential Unit Citation, and shooting badges.

### World War II (Europe)
These displays show the awards and insignia that tell the unique story of each veteran's service.

Medals of America 57

# U.S. Army Korean War Award Display Examples (1950-53)

**Korean War -** This Corporal's display has a ribbon rack flanked by unit awards. Second row of medals are commemoratives, reflecting Combat Service, ROK Presidential unit citation, Korean & UN Service plus Honorable Service. Shooting Badges and Brass plate round out his military story.

**Korean War -** Korean War Master Sgt. has picture as focal point and gold plated medals with medal description plates. Shooting badges and ROK Presidential Unit Citation. Korean Service and United Nations Commemoratives round out a magnificent display.

**Did You Know?** Korean War veterans had to wait 46 years before the ROK War Service Medal was authorized and even longer before the Korean Defense Service medal was approved.

**Korean War -** This veteran's flag is displayed with a picture in uniform and his Bronze Star and multiply awards of the Purple Heart medal.

**Korean War -** These two displays tell the story that both men were on Japan occupation duty when the Korean War started and while each have the same medals they are displayed differently. Actually the display on the right was done by the veteran's son after his dad passed on.

58  Military Medals of America

# Cold War Veteran Displays (1947-1991)

**Letters**

I served four years with the 25th Div. at Schofield Barracks, Hawaii. We trained throughout the Pacific Theater to include missions with Fijian forces as well as Operation Team Spirit, where we were airlifted to South Korea for the annual maneuver exercise. In those four years I could feel the spirit of the Army returning after Vietnam, of course off duty in Hawaii didn't hurt morale. I was proud to have made Sgt. in 4 years.

**Cold War -**
*This Infantry Sgt. display reflects meritorious service in the Reserve Forces for over 10 years.*

**Cold War -**
*This Sgt. served in the 4th Infantry Division and in Europe as well as in the Reserve Forces.*

Medals of America 59

# U.S. Army Vietnam Display Cases

**Vietnam Insignia**
**Medals**
**Sharpshooter w/Bar**
**Brass Plates**
**Patches**
**Campaign Battle Stars**
**Commemorative Medals**
**Army Insignia**
**Display Cases**

### Vietnam 1965-1975
Over 3,403,000 Americans served in Vietnam during the 10 years of fighting. Their devotion to duty and combat record was extraordinary. Only after the US military withdrew after signing a peace accord did South Vietnam fall to the Communist who ignored the peace accord.

### Vietnam -
This II Field Force soldier pictured on the radio personalized his award display case with medallions, his unit patch, his ribbons, skill badges and rank. He added two commemorative medals to represent that he had been in combat action and one to represent his RVN Gallantry Cross Unit Citation.

### Vietnam -
This Patriotic Combat Medic Specialist served 18 months and 5 campaigns in Vietnam plus reserve service.

### Vietnam -
This Infantry CPL's handsome oak display case shows distinguished service in the First Infantry Division, the "Big Red One."

### Vietnam -
This Artillery Recon Sgt. served in MACV and ARVN units and was decorated by both. Commemorative Medals for Unit awards balance a terrific personal display.

### Vietnam -
This Patriotic Transportation Specialist served 18 months and 5 campaigns in Vietnam plus reserve service.

60 Military Medals of America

# U.S. Army Vietnam Award Displays

**Letters**

I joined the 5th Infantry "Red Diamond" Division in 67 and was alerted for Vietnam deployment March 1968. We reorganized as 1st Brigade Separate with Colonel Glikes as CO. After intensive training we loaded vehicles on railroad cars and arrived at Quang Tri, in July. August we moved into "Leatherneck Square" bordered by Con Thien, Cam Lo, Dong Ha, Gio Linh. My unit, D Co., 1-11 Inf was patrolling north of Con Thien when we ran into dug-in NVA units and got pinned down. C Company and tanks from 1-77 came charging in and we ran the NVA out of their holes. We conducted battalion-size operations all over the demilitarized zone until November when we moved to AO Marshall Mountain near Quang Tri City doing routine patrols with the 1st ARVN Division. It was a year I will never forget nor the guys I served with!

**Vietnam -**
*This Military Intelligence Specialist 5th class served in Korea, Europe and Vietnam and rounds out his decorations and service medals with a 1968 Tet Offensive commemorative medal and RVN Gallantry Cross Unit award.*

**Vietnam -**
*The First Sgt. served in the First Air Cavalry Division and the 11th Armored Cavalry Regt. in Vietnam. He has Army Aircrew wings and has been awarded the Distinguished Flying Cross.*

Medals of America 61

# U.S. Army Gulf War "Desert Storm" Displays

### Army Desert Storm
A classic configuration flanked with "Big Red One" patches and centering the Army medallion above the senior NCO's ribbons. A handsome display for a Master Sgt. and especially nice using individual name plates underneath each medal

### Liberation of Kuwait and service in Kosovo
This great young American Infantry Captain earned three foreign awards in Desert Storm and Kosovo and used the Liberation of Kuwait Commemorative Medal to round out his display.

### Army Desert Storm
Another classic configuration with the new Combat Action Badge flanked with a 3rd and 4th Infantry Division Patches and medals below. Challenge coins, skill and rank badges flank a brass plate.

### Army Desert Storm
This Reserve Sgt served in "Desert Storm" and later was also mobilized for service in Iraq as part of the Global War on Terror.

62 **Military Medals of America**

# U.S. Army Afghanistan and Iraq Display Cases

### Army "Iraqistan"
This Infantry Captain has been mobilized twice once with the 18th Airborne Corps and with the 3rd Infantry Division and displays his 13 full size medals accented with insignia and badges. The medallion makes for a great centerpiece and the unit challenge coins below show his unit pride in service. The stark black background really allows the color of the ribbons to be visually dominant. The display would be better with a brass nameplate to show dates of service since he has served in Afghanistan, Iraq and Kosov.

### Army "Iraqistan"
This former specialist to Major tells his military service with his 14 full size medals accented with insignia and badges. The hat brass makes for a great centerpiece and the coins below show his pride in rank and service. The name plates below the medals and the larger brass name plate provide details of his career as an enlisted man and officer with service in Afghanistan, Iraq, South Korea and Kosov.

### Afghanistan and Iraq service
This young Air Defense Sgt. earned 2 decorations and the Combat Action Badge in Afghanistan and Iraq during his military service. His dogtag is a nice touch.

### Afghanistan and NATO service with one mobilization with the 33rd Inf. Division
This Artillery Captain adds a non authorized Combat Artillery badge to his display.

### Afghanistan and Iraq service
This great young paratrooper Infantry Staff Sgt. with the 173rd Airborne Bde earned the CIB and 3 decorations in Afghanistan and Iraq. Ribbon only awards on bottom.

Medals of America 63

# U.S. Army Iraq Display Cases

### Iraq and Desert Storm
A truly awesome display of a paratrooper Sgt. First Class from the 82d and 173rd Airborne. The arrowhead on his Iraq Campaign medal indicates he made a combat parachute jump into Iraq with the 173rd and fought in Desert Storm with the 82d Airborne Division.

### Army Iraq
This traditional Army green shadow box features Combat Service Identification Badges in lieu of patches for a modern uniform look. This Master Sgt. has 2 Reserve awards and added unoffical combat engineer and armor badges at the bottom.

### Iraq
This Quartermaster Sgt proudly displays his Combat Action badge over his medals. His Wheel Driver qualifation badge is displayed over his Expert Rifleman's badge.

### Iraq
This Specialist 4th class displays his badges over his ribbons, unit awards and medals. In addition to his CIB he proudly displays his hard earned Expert Infantryman's badge.

# Other Army Medal, Miniature medals and Ribbon Display Cases

### Other Types of Displays
Medals mounted with certificates such as the Bronze Star and Distinguished Flying Cross are a very handsome display as well as displays featuring miniature medals mounted for wear. Ribbon and badges make a nice smaller display as well as mounting a single medal with ribbon.

# U.S. Army Multi Wars Career Display Cases

Medals of America 65

# U.S. Navy World War II Award Displays

**U.S. Navy in WW II**
WW II sailors fought in 3 theaters;
1) Defending America from U-boats.
2) Carrying the war across the Atlantic into Europe and the Mediterranean.
3) Stopping the Japanese fleet in the Pacific, liberating the Philippines and destroying the Imperial Navy.

When the most victorious Navy in the world demobilized, there were no medals to honor these great sailors, only ribbon bars to symbolize their hard earned medals.
Most World War II medals were not struck until after the war and many awards were not officially approved until years after the war.

**World War II Pacific**
The display above shows the awards and insignia that tell the unique story of a Navy veteran's service. Medals, badges, unit insignia, rank, ID tags and ribbons, each tell an event in the history and the life of the veteran it honors.

**World War II**
This Pharmacist's Mate, 1st Class is a typical USN WW II display. In addition to his Good Conduct and service medals displayed he has the American Defense Medal showing service before WW II.

**World War II**
This Seaman 1st Class did not recieve a Good Conduct Medal (one liberty too many?). However he did see service in Europe as well as the Pacific and saw occupation duty in Japan for several months after the war.

**Letters**

I joined the USS Mifflin October 1944 and we sailed to Pearl with 1000 4th Marines and then landed them at Iwo Jima. We lost almost 20 crew men before sailing for Saipan. We then carried the 2d Marines to Okinawa and back to Saipan. After a refit in San Francisco, we transported Army replacements to Manila and took on the 33rd Infantry for duty in Japan. The best was " magic carpet ride "duty taking veterans back home until 1946.

## Honor the Service... Remember the Sailor

### World War II
This Boatswain Mate, 3rd Class served on the USS Colorado. He has 4 campaign stars and in addition to his Good Conduct and service medals displays 1 commemorative medals for Combat Action.

### World War II
This Aerographer's mate, was awarded the DFC as well as the Air Medal. He has 9 campaign stars (1 silver and 4 bronze) on his Pacific Campaign Medal in addition to his Good Conduct and other service medals.

### World War II
This Boatswain Mate, 1st Class has added his ribbons over his Medals but left off his campaign stars. In addition to his Good Conduct and service medals he added a Divers badge, and modern Small craft and Surface Warfare badges.

Medals of America

# Navy Korean War Displays

**U.S. Navy Officer in Korea**
This USN Lieutenant with 3 campaign stars added a Korean Service Commemorative and Navy and Korean PUC.

**Korean War**
This Petty Officer 3rd class does not show campaign stars on the Korean Campaign medal (he would have at least one) but added the Korean Service Medal for his service after the conflict ended. He also has the Navy Combat Action Ribbon and Korean PUC.

### Letters

After high school I enlisted in 1949 and ended up as a crew man on the minesweeper USS Mockingbird (AMS - 27). We were a tight crew with a good captain. The work was cold, wet and dangerous. The mine chasing operations off of Inchon and Wonsan were really scary. I saw the sweeper Magpie go down and the Pirate and the Pledge sink from mines. After we rescued the survivors, they made us the flagship of Mine Division 31. This honor allowed us to be the first into any mine field. I was really happy to finally see our home port Yokosuka for repairs. We earned our battle stars for Korean service.

**Korean War**
This Radio Man Petty Officer's picture of the USS Missouri adds a very personal touch to a handsome display of war service. He has added numerous commemorative medals to reflect his combat service.

**Korean War**
This Navy pilot served in all 10 Korean war campaigns and earned the DFC and Air Medal. Today he would also be authorized the Offical Korean War Service medal.

# Navy Cold War Award Displays
1947-1991

**Korean War with China and Occupation Service**
*This Chief Radioman Officer's dog tags adds a very personal touch to a handsome display of war service medals.*

Cold War veteran Senior Chief has added the Navy Commemorative medal to reflect his Navy pride. The Bullion crest balances the picture in a display that proudly shows his naval service and is the pride and joy of his daughter.

**Cold War Navy**
*This Petty Officer Storekeeper served on the USS Boxer from 1961 to 1965 and in addition to his medals added the ribbons his father earned on an aircraft carrier in WW II and Korea. Dogtags and his old ID card add a personal touch.*

Medals of America 69

# U.S. Navy Vietnam Award Displays

**Vietnam**
This brave "Seabee" earned the Combat Seabee badge and a V for valor on his Commendation Medal.

**Vietnam**
This sailor mounted his ribbons and medals three abreast as for uniform wear.

**Vietnam**
This Air Crewman Petty Officer added Commemorative medals to represent his ribbon only awards.

### Letters

I will never forget the eerie feeling as the USS Coral Sea (CVA-43) aircraft carrier was joined along side by a supply ship. It seemed all to close as they shot the line across and pulled a heavier one until we were sending cargo back and forth. The ships would seem to pitch, and then the load would swing as we steamed straight ahead. It was an ammo supply replenishment and we were taking on 500 pound bombs on the line stretched between two ships. What an awesome experience to be rolling 500 pounders across the hangar bay in a hurried fashion but yet slow enough to con-trol in case the ship would shift in the waves. It's just one of the many exercises that happened and it is all too hard to describe it you have never done it. It's hard to envision; if you have done it, you'll never forget.

# U.S. Navy Desert Storm (SWA) Award Displays

**Liberation of Kuwait**

This Desert Storm veteran added a Combat Action Commemorative medal to represent his Combat Action Ribbon. Commemoratives are used to show service not recognized elsewhere. Challenge coins add another personal touch.

*This Navy veteran's display is a source of family pride.*

**Liberation of Kuwait**

### Letters

Our Aegis class cruiser USS San Jacinto fired the first Tomahawk missile on Iraq from our position in the Red Sea. I think over 100 Tomahawk missiles were fired that day from our ships. It was awesome watching missile after missile rise from the other ships. It was something to be part of the greatest Navy in the world.

Medals of America 71

# U.S. Navy Afghanistan, Iraq and War on Terror Displays

**This Iraq** veteran used his ribbons and medals to show his service in Iraq and at sea. Brass name plates help identify his medals.

**This Hospital Corpsman Petty Officer 1st Class** veteran used his ribbons and medals to show his service in Iraq and at sea. The fleet Marine Force Badge over his ribbons is awarded for service with the Marines. The Brass name plates under the medals help his family recognize the medals.

### Letters

Our A-7 and A-6 attack aircraft begin flying during the Vietnam War and were reaching the end of their useful service lives. Despite their age, they performed really well. The last two A-7 Corsair squadrons, whose deactivation was postponed for Desert Storm, did not lose a plane to enemy action. We were proud that our hard training paid off.

# U.S. Navy Afghanistan, Iraq and War on Terror Displays

**This Hospital Corpsman** veteran used his ribbons and medals to show his service in Afghanistan; Iraq and in Korea. The Fleet Marine Force Badge over his ribbons is awarded for service with the Marines. The Brass name plates under the medals help his family recognize the medals.

**This Global War on Terror** veteran used his ribbons and medals to show his service in Iraq and at sea. Brass name plates under the medals help recognize the medals while the challenge coins are unique personal items.

**This Iraq** veteran used his ribbons and medals to show his service in Iraq and at sea. Brass name plates help identify his medals and his "dogtag" and challenge coin add a nice personal touch.

**This Chief Radioman's** display reflects many years of service at sea all over the world. He has been decorated 6 times for meritorious service.

Medals of America

# U.S. Marine Corps Display Examples World War II

## World War II, Marine Corps Display Cases

- Campaign Battle Stars
- Medals
- Honorable Discharge Pin
- Shooting Badges
- Brass Plates
- Patches
- Marine Insignia
- Commemorative Medals
- Unit Awards

**This 4th Marine Division Veteran** fought in three Pacific Campaigns and added 4 Commemorative Medals to his case to show combat action and victory over Japan.

**This 5th Marine Division Veteran** was a paratrooper and wounded in the Pacific campaign and added 3 Commemorative Medals and ribbons to to show combat action and a Presidential Unit Citation.

74 Military Medals of America

**This 4th Marine Division Veteran** Placed ribbons above his medals and served in the occupation of Japan after the war. His Combat Action ribbon is above his Honorable Discharge pin.

**This Marine WW II Veteran** with the Silver Star Medal was a Japanese Prisoner of War from 1942 to 1945 (note the Phillippine Defense Medal).

## Pacific Service

Case to the right shows a 2d Marine Division private who was awarded the Purple Heart. The gold plated medals shown are: Purple Heart, Good Conduct, Asiatic-Pacific with 3 battle stars, WW II Victory and Combat Action Commemorative Medal. Other examples shown below are "mustangs" who rose throught the ranks to Captain and Major. The bottom right "mustang" served in both WW II and Korea.

**Marine WW II Veteran** "Big Jim Pierce" proudly holding his World War II medals where he rose from Private to Major..

# USMC Display Korea and Vietnam

### Korean Service
Dress Collar Insignia and the 1st Marine Division Patch are displayed above the Good Conduct, National Defense Service, Korean Service, UN Korean Service and the ROK War Service Medals. Displayed below are the Combat Action Ribbon with Navy and Korean Presidential Unit Citations above a name plate and metal collar rank.

### USMC Korean Service
The Marine Corporal served in both the 1st Marine and 3d Division and was wounded three times. This a classic Korean War display with the ribbons mounted over the medals.

### WW II & Korean Marine Pilot
This Marine Captain was awarded two DFCs and three Air Medals during his service in both World War II and Korea. He should have at least one campaign star on his Asiatic Pacific and Korean Campaign Medal.

### Marine Corps Cold War Service
Thousands of great Americans served in the Marine Corps during the Cold War (1947-1991). Their dedicated service is reflected with various awards as shown in these examples..

## Marine Corps Vietnam Service

500,000 Marines served in Vietnam from 1962 to 1975. These examples reflect 4 different display styles to include a set of mounted for wear medals.

## Vietnam Service

In this Corporal's display below his Collar and Cap Insignia are above the Purple Heart, Navy Commedation, Achievement and Good Conduct medals. After his other medals are the RVN Gallantry Cross and RVN Campaign Medals. The Combat Action Ribbon and Navy PUC are shown above a name plate with Marksmanship Badges.

The case to the right shows the career awards of a highly decorated Marine Colonel who was awarded three different times with the RVN Gallantry Cross as well as three other Vietnamese awards.

## Vietnam War

Medals of America 77

## Desert Storm
## Liberation of Kuwait

### Desert Storm
A Marine Medallion and Dress Collar Insignia are displayed above Ribbons and Medals. The Medals are: Navy Commendation, Navy Achievement, Good Conduct, National Defense Service, Southwest Asia Service and Saudi & Kuwait Liberation Medals plus two commemoratives. The Ribbon set also includes the Sea Service and Overseas Service Ribbons, which are ribbon only awards. Marksmanship badges flank the name plate.

### Marine Corps Regular Service / Cold War
Rank and Cap Insignia are over Ribbons and Medals. The Medals are: Navy Achievement, Good Conduct, National Defense Service, Armed Forces Expeditionary, Armed Forces Service, Humanitarian Service and UN Service. The Ribbon set also includes the Sea Service which is a ribbon only awards.

**78** Military Medals of America

# Afghanistan and the War on Terror

**Service in Afghanistan and the War on Terror**
This Marine with service in Afghanistan and War on Terror and is parachute and Diver qualified..

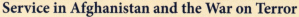

**This displays show service in Afghanistan and the War on Terror**
This case shows a Marine with prior service in the US Army in Kosovo and USMC service in Afghanistan. His USMC Good Conduct Medal goes in front of his Army Good Conduct and his Navy Achievement Medal goes before the Army Achievement Medal. He is missing campaign stars on his Afghanistan Campaign Medal. The last medal is a NATO Medal for Kosovo service.

**Liberation of Iraq**
This Marine Staff Sgt. awards show he was mobilized from the Marine Reserves for service in Iraq. In addtional to his two medals for meritorious service he was twice awarded the Outstanding Volunteer Service Medal for his work within his local community

**Special Presentation of the Purple Heart Medal**

Medals of America 79

**Liberation of Iraq**
This Marine Corporal displays his Iraq service with gold plated medals below his ribbon only awards. His last medal is the Humanitarian Service Medal.

**Afghanistan, Iraq and NATO Service**
This case shows a Marine with prior service in Kosovo and one campaign each in Afghanistan and Iraq. His Navy Achievement Medal and USMC Good Conduct Medal flank his challenge coins and ribbons. The last medal is a NATO Medal for Kosovo service.

**Master Gunnery Sergeant with 3 Mobilizations**
This senior Non commissioned officer displays his awards with over 25 years active and reserve service. His Armed Forces Reserve medal shows 20 years reserve service and 3 mobilizations..

Military Medals of America

# The Display Case tells the Story of a Veteran's Service to Our Country

What branch and unit, ship or squadron, what awards and campaigns, what skills and rank, where and when.

**Marine Insignia**

**Personal Decoration**

**Name plates to identify medals**

**Expert Shooting Badge shows skill.**

**Engraved brass plate tells who, what, when, where.**

**Marine Corps medallion serves as focal point for display**

**Ribbon rack shows individual and unit awards.**

**Good Conduct Medal**

**Campaign Battle Star** — Iraq Service Medal with 2 campaign stars.

**Golbal War on Terror Service Medal**

### Iraq Veteran's Service Display

*Each display case will be different just as each veteran's service was different and each service will have different insignia. Each case will show the honors a grateful nation has bestowed on her veterans.*

# Army Air Force Displays World War II

Patches
Medals
Honorable Discharge Pin
Shooting Badges
Brass Plates

Army AF Insignia
Campaign Battle Stars
Commemorative Medals
Army Air Force Insignia

World War II, 8th Air Force

### World War II & Reserve Service

This case is an example of a AAF Pilot who served through 5 campaigns in the Pacific and until 1974 in the in Air Force Reserve. Note the Europe and Japan Bars on his Army Occupation Medal.

## Army Air Force

Fighters, bombers & transports flew from Berlin to Burma and back. From Pearl Harbor to the Atomic bombs, no Air Force ever met such a challenge as World War II or deserves their awards more than the Army Air Corps. Their losses were second only to the Infantry.

At the end of the war their Campaign medals were not available only ribbons to show their service.

Aerial Gunner | Pilot Wings
Navigator WWII | Bombardier
Air Crew Wings | Aircraft Flight Engineer

### World War II, 14th Air Force

These two cases are good examples of adding personal items to a veteran's award display that make them truly unique. The case above features a pilot who served in China. He has added his Nationalist Chinese pilot wings and his dog tags. The next to last medal is the WW II Nationalist China Memorial Medal followed by the Air Combat Commemorative medal.

**9th Air Force** veteran to the left is one of the lucky ones. An aerial gunner shot down over Europe, he has his caterpillar pin, a handmade parachute badge and his German issued Stalag POW ID tag. You will note his POW Medal just after his Air Medal. This a good example of how you can add personal items that enhance the story of a veteran's military service.

Army AF | 1st AF | 2nd AF | 3rd AF
4th AF | 5th AF | 6th AF | 7th AF
8th AF | 9th AF | 10th AF | 11th AF
12th AF | 13th AF | 14th AF | 15th AF
18th AF | 20th AF | Far East AF

82  Military Medals of America

# Army Air Force

The Army Air Force, fighting on 3 fronts, swept the sky clear of all foes but not without sacrifice. From the beginning at Pearl Harbor to the finish of the Japanese Empire with the Atomic bombs, America's airmen were patriots with losses only second to the Infantry.

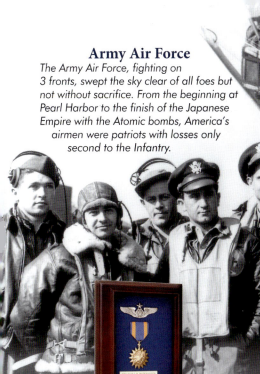

US Army Photo

AAF Pacific, POW Japan, 30 years Service

AAF Pacific, DFC, Air Medal, Service in China

AAF Pacific, 1942-1946

AAF Pacific Pilot, 10 Campaign stars

AAF Europe, POW Germany, 1943-1968 Service

AAF Pacific, 8 Campaign stars, 2 Philippine medals

AAF Pacific, Flight Engineer, 2d Air Force

Medals of America 83

# U.S. Air Force Displays, Korean War

## U.S. Air Force 1947 to Present

### Honor the Service...Remember the Airman

Korean War Display Example

### U.S. Air Force

The U.S. Air Force became a separate service from the Army in 1947. The USAF continued to use many Army medals until after the Korean War (the Army Good Conduct Medal was used until 1963).

In Korea the new USAF gained control of the sky using a combination of prop and jet aircraft. Airmen suffered in boiling summer heat and freezing winter snows to keep air superiority over the communist Chinese and North Koreans.

Most Air Force Korean War veterans have not received all of their medals. The ROK War Service Medal was not authorized until 46 years after the war and the Korean Defense Service medal even later.

### Korean War

This Airman's case reflects service in a Forward Air Evacuation Group. During the Korean War the Air Force still awarded the Army Good Conduct Medal.

### World War II & Korean War

This Major's case tells he enlisted before WW II, was wounded in Europe and a POW, received the DFC and French Cross of War and later served three campaigns in Korean. The UN Service Medal, ROK War Service medal, and ROK Presidential Unit ribbon are also displayed.

# U.S. Air Force Displays, Vietnam

**Vietnam**
This pilot has added a Vietnamese Cross of Gallantry Commemorative Medal in honor of his RVN Gallantry Unit Citation.

**Vietnam**
Airman First Class John L. Levitow was the first USAF enlisted person to receive the USAF Medal of Honor. He was awarded the MOH for saving his AC-47 gunship and crew in Vietnam. This young Airman earned the Medal of Honor and 2 RVN Gallantry Cross Medals with his Purple Heart and 8 Air Medals. An extraordinary display of valor.

**Medal of Honor Vietnam**

**Korea and Vietnam Service**

**Vietnam**
This Airman used his dogtags, 2 challenge coins and medal brass identification plates to personalize his award display case.

**World War II, Korea and Vietnam Service**
This pilot enlisted in WW II, became a pilot; earned a Silver Star and was wounded twice during his three wars (WW II, Korea and Vietnam).

# U.S. Air Force Cold War Displays

**Cold War -** The Cold War was kept cold by the enormous deterrent of SAC and our world wide airmen. Cold War Veterans number over 30 millions, servring in 70 different countries under very difficult and often dangerous circumstances with little reward or acknowledgement. Their service needs to be recognized since it was key to bringing down the USSR and its satellites. Their selfless duty deserves to be rewarded.

**Cold War Service Pacific Air Force**

**Cold War Service**

**Cold War Service**

**Cold War Service in the USAF Reserves**

86   Military Medals of America

# U.S. Air Force Southwest Asia/ Gulf War Displays

### Desert Shield / Desert Storm/ SWA
This Master Sgt. was mobilized from the Air Force Reserve to serve in the Gulf War and while his ribbons indicate 3 Campaign stars they are missing from his campaign medal. He added 4 Commemorative medals.

### Liberation of Kuwait / Desert Storm
This case displays a Command Pilot's awards from service in both the Liberation of Kuwait and Iraq as well as the Global War on Terror. Ribbon only awards are displayed below his medals. Note the multiple awards of the Air Medal are arranged vertically in the Air Force as opposed to the Army and Army Air Corps who mount them horizontally.

### Three Different Displays

While the three displays show almost the same awards each veterans has chosen a different way to display them and each added a personal touch. One young Sgt. added a Combat Service Commemorative while another added a Cold War Victory Medal. the Senior NCO chose a classic display of ribbons over medals with his special skill badge. There are as many ways to display awards as there are veterans.

### Liberation of Kuwait/Desert Storm
This USAF TSgt. has 5 awards of the Good Conduct Medal. His full set of ribbons tell he was once awarded the Coast Guard Meritorious Unit award with Operational Device.

Medals of America 87

# U.S. Air Force Afghanistan and Iraq Displays

### Gulf War, NATO and Afghanistan Service
This case displays a Command Pilot's awards from service in both the Liberation of Kuwait and Afghanistan as well as the Global War on Terror and NATO service. A very nice display reflecting a Colonel's many years of service.

### Afghanistan
This Airman served in a Joint Command during his service in Afghanistan as indicated by his Joint Service Commemmendation and Achievement Medals. Dogtags added a nice touch.

### Afghanistan and Iraq Service
This Air Force NCO displays his awards for Afghanistan and Iraq with gold plated medals which the Air Force restricts the offical wear of to Honor Guards. However, it is fine to use them in a veteran's display.

### Afghanistan
This Master Sgt.'s awards show he served in Korea during peace time and was mobilized for service in Afghanistan. Note 5 awards of the AF Reserve Meritorious Service Medal.

# U.S. Air Force Gobal War on Terror Displays

### Iraq Service
This Airman mounted a classic display and included his ribbon only awards. His Iraq campaign stars are missing.

### Iraq and Kosovo Service
A great senior NCO display with the new Combat Action Medal as well as the Kosovo, Iraq and NATO Campaign Medals.

### Gobal War on Terror
This AF Reserve Sgt. was mobilizied to serve in the War on Terror

### Gobal War on Terror
Nice display of a young Airman's service in the United States.

### Gobal War on Terror
A Senior Officer's display with service in Korea and NATO.

Medals of America 89

# U.S. Coast Guard Displays

- Photo
- Patches
- Brass Plates
- Rating
- Medals
- Campaign Battle Stars
- Commemorative Medals

SSG JOHN M. BLACK
3rd ARMY, 1ST DIV, 18TH INFANTRY
1942 - 1946

### World War II

## U.S. Coast Guard in WW II

**In** WW II the Coast Guard was part of the Navy and fought in 3 theaters;
1) Defending America from U-boats.
2) Carrying the war across the Atlantic into Europe and the Mediterranean.
3) Piloting the Marine and Army landing craft during landings in Europe and the Pacific.

When the most victorious Navy/Coast Guard in the world demobilized there were no medals to honor these great Coast Guard sailors, only ribbon bars to symbolize their hard earned medals.

Most World War II medals were not struck until after the war and many awards were not officially approved until years after the war.

### U.S. Coast Guard Service in World War II and Korea

These six displays show examples of USCG service in World War II and in the Korean War. The Coast Guard has it's own Good Conduct Medal even when assigned to the Navy during war as well as Coast Guard specific decorations.

90  Military Medals of America

*Honor the Service...
Remember the Coast Guardman.*

**Coast Guard in Vietnam**

**Coast Guard in Vietnam**

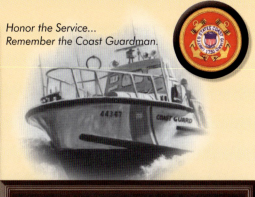

**Coast Guard in Vietnam**

Many Coast Guard men worked with the Vietnamses Navy and small boat units defending the long coast.

**Coast Guard Reserve Service**

This Senior Chief has been awarded the rare CG Silver Life Saving Medal as well as the Good Conduct Medal for active and reserve duty. Next to last two medals are for Rifle and Pistol Marksmanship.

**Cold War Veteran**

**Cold War Veteran**

**Cold War Veteran**

Medals of America 91

# United States Coast Guard

### SWA/DESERT STORM
This Chief Warrant Officer has a classic Coast Guard career display to include the 9-11 Medal, numerous multiple awards, four Good Conduct Medals and the Coast Guard Rifle Marksmanship Medal. A perfect set of mounted ribbons with attachments and rank make a special display.

USCG Officer Hat Badge

Enlisted Hat Badge

**Gobal War on Terror**

### SWA / LIBERATION OF KUWAIT
A CG Petty Officer's classic display from "Desert Shield / Desert Storm"

**Gobal War on Terror**

Senior Petty Officer Cutterman

**Gobal War on Terror**

This Chief Petty Officer War on Terror veteran displays the 9 11 Medal, Good Conduct, Reserve Good Conduct, National Defense, GWOT Service Medal, Armed Forces Service Medal, Humanitarian Service Medal, CG Reserve Medal and CG Expert Rifle & Pistol.

**Gobal War on Terror**

CG Coxswain with two Mobilizations.

# United States Merchant Marine

The Merchant Marine primarily transports cargo and passengers during peacetime but in times of war the Merchant Marine is often an auxiliary to the United States Navy, and is called upon to deliver military personnel and materiel for the armed forces. Merchant Marine officers may also be commissioned as military officers by commissioning unlimited tonnage Merchant Marine officers as Strategic Sealift Officers in the Naval Reserves.

The federal government maintains fleets of merchant ships via organizations such as Military Sealift Command (part of the US Navy) and the National Defense Reserve Fleet, which is managed by the United States Maritime Administration.

Although in World War II the Merchant Marine suffered a per capita casualty rate greater than those of the US Armed Forces, merchant mariners who served in World War II were denied such veterans recognition until 1988 when a federal court ordered active military service recognition to American merchant seamen who participated in World War II."

**MERCHANT MARINE OFFICER**
*This Officer severed 20 years in the Merchant Marine from 1942 to 1962. While his medals are not mounted in correct order of precedence they reflect his 20 years service to include two commemorative medals for Korea and WW II.*

## United States Merchant Marine Medals

Distinguished Service Medal | Meritorious Service Medal | Mariners Medal | Merchant Achievement Medal | Merchant Marine Defense Medal | Atlantic War Zone Medal | Mediterranean Middle East War Zone Medal

Pacific War Zone Medal | Victory Medal | Korean Service Medal | Vietnam service Medal | Merchant Marine Expeditionary Award | Prisoner of War Medal | Soviet Commendation Medal

 Gallant Ship Citation ribbon

 Merchant Marine Combat Bar

Medals of America 93

# Wear of Medals, Insignia and the Uniform by Veterans, Retirees and Former Service Members

## Introduction

One of the first lessons taught to new recruits is proper wear of the uniform and insignia. The same rules apply to wear of military awards by veterans and retirees on their old uniform. There are many occasions when tradition, patriotism, ceremonies and social occasions call for the wear of military awards.

## Civilian Dress

The most common manner of wearing a decoration or medal is as a lapel pin in the left lapel of a civilian suit jacket. The small enameled lapel pin represents the ribbon bar of a single decoration or medal an individual has received (usually the highest award or one having special meaning to the wearer).

Many well-known veterans such as former Senator Bob Dole, a World War II Purple Heart recipient, wear a lapel pin. Pins are available for all awards and some ribbons such as the Combat Action Ribbon or Presidential Unit Citation. Small miniature wings, parachute badges and Combat Infantry Badges are also worn in the lapel or as a tie tack.

Additionally, retirees are encouraged to wear their retired pin and World War II veterans are encouraged to wear their Honorable Discharge Pin (affectionately referred to as the "ruptured duck").

Honorably discharged and retired Armed Forces members may wear full-size or miniature medals on civilian suits on appropriate occasions such as Memorial Day and Armed Forces Day. Female members may wear full-size or miniature medals on equivalent dress. It is not considered appropriate to wear skill or qualification badges on civilian attire.

## Formal Civilian Wear

For more formal occasions, it is correct and encouraged to wear miniature decorations and medals. For a black or white tie occasion, the rule is quite simple: if the lapel is wide enough wear the miniatures on the left lapel or, in the case of a shawl lapel on a tuxedo, the miniature medals are worn over the left breast pocket. The center of the holding bar of the bottom row of medals should be parallel to the ground immediately above the pocket. Do not wear a pocket handkerchief. Miniature medals really do make a handsome statement of patriotic service at weddings and other social events.

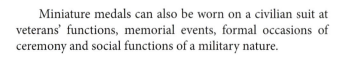

Miniature medals can also be worn on a civilian suit at veterans' functions, memorial events, formal occasions of ceremony and social functions of a military nature.

# Wear of the Uniform by Retired Personnel

On certain occasions, retired Armed Forces personnel may wear either the uniform prescribed at the date of retirement or any of the current active duty authorized uniforms. Retirees should adhere to the same grooming standards as Armed Forces active duty personnel when wearing the uniform (for example, a beard is inappropriate while in uniform). Whenever the uniform is worn, it must be done in such a manner as to reflect credit upon the individual and the service from which he/she is retired. (Do not mix uniform items.)

**The occasions for uniform wear by retirees are**

- Military ceremonies.
- Military funerals, weddings, memorial services and inaugurals.
- Patriotic parades on national holidays.
- Military parades in which active or reserve units are participating.
- Educational institutions when engaged in giving military instruction or responsible for military discipline.
- Social or other functions when the invitation has obviously been influenced by the member's earlier active service.

Honorably separated wartime veterans may wear the uniform authorized at the time of their service. The occasions are:

- Military funerals, memorial services, and inaugurals.
- Patriotic parades on national holidays.
- Any occasion authorized by law.
- Military parades in which active or reserve units are participating.

Non-wartime service personnel separated (other than retired, Army National Guard and Reserve) are not authorized to wear the uniform but may wear the medals.

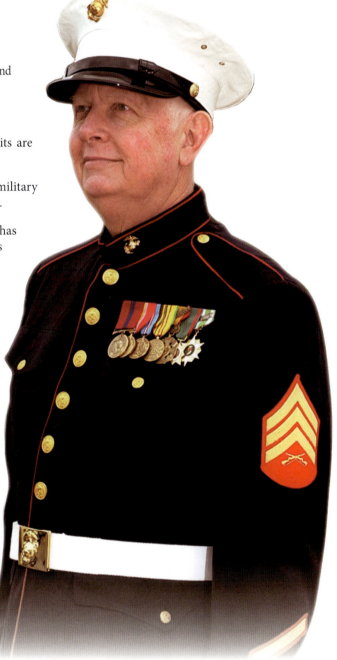

# How Army Medals Are Worn

## United States Army

Wear of Service Ribbons 1975

Wear of Service Ribbons 1945

**Wear of Service Ribbons** — Ribbons may be worn on the Army green, blue and white uniform coats. The ribbons are worn in one or more rows in order of precedence with either no space or 1/8 inch between rows, no more than four ribbons to a row. The top row is centered or aligned to left edge of the row underneath, whichever looks the best. Unit awards are centered above the right breast pocket with a maximum of three per row.

**Wear of Full Size Decorations & Service Medals** — Decorations and service medals may be worn on the Army blue or white uniform after retreat and by enlisted personnel on the dress green uniform for social functions. The medals are mounted in order of precedence, in rows with not more than four medals in a row. The top row cannot have more medals than the one below. Rows are separated by 1/8 inch. Medals may not overlap (as Navy and Marines do), so normally there are only three to a row due to the size of the coat. Unit citations are centered over the right breast pocket 1/8 inch above the top of the pocket. Service and training ribbons are not worn with full size medals.

**Wear of Miniature Decorations & Service Medals** — Miniature medals are scaled down replicas of full size medals. Only miniature medals are authorized for wear on the mess and evening uniform jackets and with the blue and white uniform after retreat on formal occasions. Miniature medals are mounted on bars with the order of precedence from the wearer's right to left. The medals are mounted side by side if there are four or less. They may be overlapped up to 50% when five, six or seven are in a row. Overlapping is equal for all medals with the right one fully displayed. When two or more rows are worn, the bottom pendants must be fully visible.

For information on uniform wear policy, consult Army Regulation 670-1, Wear and Appearance of Army Uniforms and Insignia. Uniform policy website and Point-of-Contact information is located at *http://www.armyg1.army.mil/hr/uniform/default.asp*

# How Navy & Coast Guard Medals Are Worn

Military Ribbons

## United States Navy

(The Coast Guard generally follows U.S. Navy guidelines)

**Wear of Service Ribbons** — Wear up to 3 in a row; if more than three ribbons, wear in horizontal rows of three each. The top row contains the lesser number, centered above the row below, no spaces between ribbon rows. Rows of ribbons covered by coat lapel may contain two ribbons each and be aligned. Wear ribbons with lower edge of bottom row centered 1/4 inch above left breast pocket and parallel to the deck.

Coast Guard members may either wear their senior three ribbons or all ribbons. When ribbons are covered 1/3 or more by the lapel ribbon rows can be decreased to 2 or 1 if all ribbons are worn in this situation.

**Wear of Full Size Decorations & Service Medals** — When wearing large medals on full dress uniforms align the bottom row same as ribbon bars. All rows may contain maximum of 3 medals side by side or up to 5 overlapping. Overlapping is proportional with inboard medal showing in full. Mount a second row of medals so they cover the suspension ribbon of the medals below. When large medals are worn, all unit citations and ribbons with no medal authorized are centered over the right breast pocket the bottom edge 1/8 inch above the top of the pocket.

**Wear of Miniature Medals** — Wear miniature medals with all formal and dinner dress uniforms. Place holding bar of lowest row of miniatures 3 inches below the lapel notch, centered on the lapel. Center the holding bar immediately above the left breast pocket on the blue and white service coat. You may wear up to five miniature medals in a row with no overlap on the dinner jacket, center up to 3 miniature medals on the lapel. Position 4 or more miniatures at the inner edge of the lapel extending beyond the lapel to the body of the jacket.

Military Miniature Medals

# How U.S. Marine Medals Are Worn

Military Ribbons

Military Medals

Miniatures

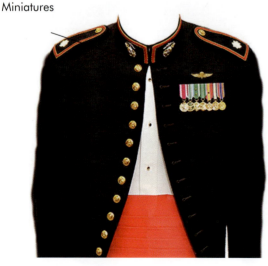

Military Miniature Medals

## United States Marine Corps

**Wear of Service Ribbons** — Ribbons are authorized on Marine dress "B", dress "A" or shirts when prescribed as an outer garment. They are normally worn in rows of 3 or rows of 4 when displaying a large number of awards. If the lapel conceals any ribbons, they may be placed in successively decreasing rows, i.e., 4, 3, 2, 1. All aligned vertically on center, except if the top row can be altered to present the neatest appearance. Ribbon rows may be spaced 1/8 inch apart or together. Ribbon bars are centered 1/8 inch above the upper left pocket. When marksmanship badges are worn, the ribbon bars are 1/8 inch above them.

**Full Size Medals** — Marines may wear up to four medals side by side on a 3 inch bar. A maximum of seven medals may be overlapped (not to exceed 50% with the right or inboard medal shown in full). Full size medals on the blue or white dress jacket are centered on the left breast pocket with the upper edge of the holding bar on line midway between the 1st and 2nd button of the jacket. When large medals are worn, all unit citations and ribbons with no medals authorized are centered over the right breast pocket the bottom edge 1/8 inch above the top of the pocket.

For men, the maximum width of the holding bar for large medals is 5-1/2 inches, and the length of the medals from top of holding bar to bottom of medallions is 3-1/4 inches. A maximum of four large medals side by side will fit on the maximum width of holding bar; however, a maximum of seven medals will fit on the holding bar if overlapped. The overlapping on each row is equal (not to exceed 50 percent). The right or inboard medal shows in full.

Women wear no more than three large medals side by side on a single holding bar not to exceed 4-1/8 inches; however, a maximum of five medals will fit on the holding bar if overlapped.

**Wear of Miniature Medals** — When miniature medals are worn, no ribbons will be worn. On evening dress jackets miniature medals will be centered on the left front jacket panel midway between the inner edge and the left armhole seam, with the top of the bar on line with the 2nd blind button hole. On mess dress and SNCO's evening and mess dress, the miniature medals are centered on the left lapel with the top of the holding bar 1 inch below the lapel notch. Maximum of 10 overlapped.

# How U.S. Air Force Medals Are Worn

## United States Air Force

**Wear of Service Ribbons** — Ribbons may be worn on service dress and blue shirt. Ribbons are normally worn in rows of three with the bottom bar centered and resting on the top edge of the pocket. Ribbons may be worn four-in-a-row with the left edge of the ribbons aligned with the left edge of the pocket to keep the lapel from covering ribbons. There is no space between rows of ribbons. Current regulations stipulate that members may choose which ribbons to wear, if any.

**Full Size Medals** — Normally worn three to a row, but may be overlapped up to five medals on a holding bar. No medal should be overlapped more than 50% and the medal nearest the lapel should be fully exposed. Six medals should be displayed in two rows, three over three. Regular size medals are worn on the service dress and ceremonial dress uniforms with the medal portion of the bottom row immediately above the top of the pocket button.

**Miniature Medals** — Miniature medals are worn on the blue mess dress or on formal dress. The miniatures are centered between lapel and arm seam and midway between top shoulder seam and top button of jacket. If more than four miniatures, the wearer has the option of mounting up to seven by overlapping or going to a second bar. Seven is the maximum on one bar, however, many in the Air Force prefer only a maximum of four to a bar.

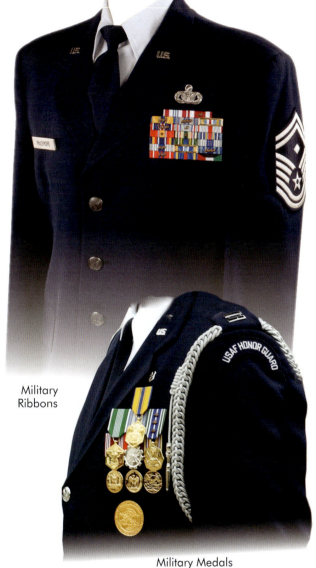

Military Ribbons

Military Medals

Korean War

Military Miniature Medals

Medals of America 99

# Presentation of U.S. Military Military Ribbons and Medals

## The Pyramid of Honor

The awards system of the United States described in the introduction, has evolved into a structured program often called the "Pyramid of Honor." The system is designed to reward services ranging from heroism on the battlefield to superior performance of noncombat duties and even includes the completion of entry level training.

Far from being disturbed by the award proliferation, the Armed Services have embraced Napoleon's concept of liberally awarding medals and ribbons to enhance morale and esprit de corps. This expanded and specifically tailored awards program is generally very popular in the all volunteer armed forces and has played a significant part in improving morale, job performance, recruitment and reenlistments amongst junior officers and enlisted personnel.

The decorations and awards which represent the rich United States military heritage from 1939 onward are presented on the following pages. These awards paint a wonderful portrait of this country's dedication to the ideals of freedom and the devotion and sacrifices required of the military to support those ideals.

Beginning on page 137 color plates picture each ribbon and medal and then identify the Service or event to which the award is authorized, the date instituted and the criteria for award along with appropriate attachments. The numbers in parentheses on the Order of precedence charts Device displays refer to the tables contained in the "Attachments and Devices" section, starting on page 116. A quick guide outline is shown below and on the facing page.

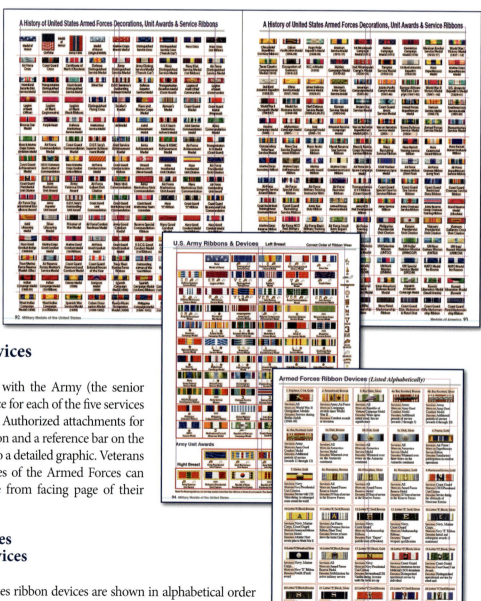

## Ribbon Chart Showing the Complete History of U.S. Awards

Starting on page 102 is a one of a kind chart which reads left to right across each page and shows the ribbon for every award since the Civil War with variations (Commonly awarded foreign, United Nations and NATO ribbons are also shown). The chart is a colorful walk through U.S. Military awards history. Merchant Marine ribbons are on page 115.

## Order of Precedence Ribbon Charts for All Services

Beginning on page 104 starting with the Army (the senior service), the correct order of precedence for each of the five services plus the Merchant Marine are shown. Authorized attachments for each ribbon are shown below the ribbon and a reference bar on the right side of the page provides guides to a detailed graphic. Veterans who have service in multiple branches of the Armed Forces can determine their order of precedence from facing page of their current service ribbon chart.

## Armed Forces Ribbon Devices (Appurtenances) for All Services

On page 116-119 all Armed Forces ribbon devices are shown in alphabetical order from the Gold Airplane to Target, Rifle and Gold. For those who desire even more detail very specific guidance is laid out beginning on page 120.

## Right Breast Ribbons on Full Dress Uniforms for Navy, Marine Corps and Coast Guard Services

Unlike the Army and the Air Force, the Navy, Marine Corps and Coast Guard authorize wear of ribbon only awards on the right breast of the uniform with full size medals. The correct order of precedence is shown on pages 114.

## Early United States Military Medals

Starting on page 124 the very first medals are described followed by the earliest campaign medals beginning with the Civil War and continuing up to the 1930s. Each campaign medal is shown with the reverse which was basically the difference between the Navy and Marine Corps medals. Key information is furnished with each medal

## United States Military Medals from World War II

Starting on page 131 the current military medals, ribbon only and unit awards are described beginning in the order of precedence with the Medal of Honors and continuing up to today. Each award is clearly illustrated and identified by service or services it applies to, with the date instituted, criteria for award and devices which apply.

## Commonly awarded Foreign, United Nations and NATO Medals Military Medals

Starting on page 216 commonly awarded foreign military decorations, unit awards and medals are displayed in precedence starting with World War I and II and continuing up to today. Each award is illustrated and identified by country which has awarded it with the date instituted, criteria for award and devices which apply.

## Examples of Military Society and Commemorative Medals

Examples of Commemorative medals which played such a part in the history and development of awards system are shown on page 28. The Grand Army of the Republic reunion medal is an excellent example of why the The Congressional Medal of Honor design was changed and patented in 1904. The Cold War Victory Commemorative Medal (page 31) is a current example of an award established privately for those dedicated service personnel who served honorably during a most dangerous period of history and were not officially rewarded by the U.S. Government for their efforts. Other examples are shown in various award display cases.

## The Stolen Valor Act

The Stolen Valor Act of 2005, signed into law by President George W. Bush, was a statute that broadened the provisions of a previous law and addressed the unauthorized wear, manufacture or sale of certain military decorations and medals. The law made it a federal misdemeanor to falsely represent oneself as having received any U.S. military decoration or medal. If convicted, defendants might have been imprisoned for up to six months, (up to one year in the case of the Medal of Honor). In United States v. Alvarez the U.S. Supreme Court ruled on June 28, 2012, that the Stolen Valor Act was too restrictive and an unconstitutional abridgment of freedom of speech under the First Amendment, striking down the law in a 6 to 3 decision. In 2012, a new bill was introduced in the House of Representatives which passed by a vote of 410-3. The sponsors argued that the bill would survive judicial review since it resolved the constitutional issues involved and targets those who falsely claim to have earned certain major military decorations or any medal signifying combat service. A companion bill, the Stolen Valor Act of 2013 was ratified by the United States Senate on May 22, 2013 and signed into law by the President on June 3, 2013.

# A History of United States Armed Forces Decorations, Unit Awards & Service Ribbons

| | | | | | | | | | |
|---|---|---|---|---|---|---|---|---|---|
| Medal of Honor | Medal of Honor Civil War | Medal of Honor Army-1896 | Medal of Honor (Original Width) | Marine Corps Brevet Medal | Distinguished Service Cross | Distinguished Service Cross ("French Cut") | Navy Cross | Navy Cross (1st Ribbon) | |
| Air Force Cross | Coast Guard Cross | Certificate of Merit (Obsolete) | Defense Distinguished Service Medal | Army Distinguished Service Medal | Army Disting. Service Medal ("French Cut") | Navy Distinguished Service Medal | Navy Dist. Service Medal (1st Ribbon) | Air Force Distinguished Service Medal | |
| Homeland Security Dist. Service Medal | Transportation Distinguished Service Medal | Coast Guard Distinguished Service Medal | Silver Star | D.O.T. Secretary's Outstanding Achievm't Medal | Defense Superior Service Medal | Transportation Guardian Medal (Coast Guard) | Legion of Merit (Chief Commander) | Legion of Merit (Commander) | |
| Legion of Merit (Officer) | Legion of Merit (Legionnaire) | Legion of Merit (Neck Ribbon) | Distinguished Flying Cross | Soldier's Medal | Navy and Marine Corps Medal | Airman's Medal | Coast Guard Medal | Coast Guard Medal (not used) | |
| Bronze Star Medal | Purple Heart | Defense Meritorious Service Medal | Meritorious Service Medal | Air Medal | Aerial Achievement Medal | D.O.T. Secy's Meritorious Achvm't Medal | Joint Service Commendation Medal | Army Commendation Medal | |
| Navy & Marine Corps Commendation Medal | Air Force Commendation Medal | Coast Guard Commendation Medal | D.O.T. Secy's Superior Achievement Medal | Joint Service Achievement Medal | Army Achievement Medal | Navy & USMC Achievement Medal | Air Force Achievement Medal | Transportation 9-11 Medal (Coast Guard) | |
| Coast Guard Achievement Medal | USCG Commandant's Letter of Commendation | Navy & Marine Corps Combat Action Ribbon | Air Force Combat Action Medal | Coast Guard Combat Action Ribbon | Wound Ribbon (1917) (Never Issued) | Army Presidential Unit Citation | Navy Presidential Unit Citation | Air Force Presidential Unit Citation | |
| Coast Guard Presidential Unit Citation | Joint Meritorious Unit Award | Army Valorous Unit Award | Air Force Gallant Unit Citation | Navy Unit Commendation | Army Meritorious Unit Commendation | Air Force Meritorious Unit Award | Navy Meritorious Unit Commendation | Air Force Outstanding Unit Award | |
| Air Force Organizational Excellence Award | Army Superior Unit Award | D.O.T. Secy's Outstanding Unit Award | Coast Guard Unit Commendation | Coast Guard Meritorious Unit Commendation | Coast Guard Meritorious Team Comndatn | Navy "E" Ribbon | Coast Guard "E" Ribbon | Coast Guard Bicentenniel Unit Commendation | |
| Gold Lifesaving Medal | Silver Lifesaving Medal | Prisoner of War Medal | Air Force Combat Readiness Medal | Army Good Conduct Medal | Reserve Special Commendation Ribbon | Navy Good Conduct Medal | Navy Good Conduct Medal (2nd Ribbon) | Navy Good Conduct Medal (1st Ribbon) | |
| Navy Good Conduct Badge (1869-84) | Marine Corps Good Conduct Medal | Marine Good Conduct Medal (1st Ribbon) | Air Force Good Conduct Medal | Coast Guard Good Conduct Medal | U.S.C.G. Good Conduct Medal (1st Ribbon) | Army Reserve Components Achvm't Medal | Naval Reserve Meritorious Service Medal | Selected Marine Corps Reserve Medal | |
| Fleet Marine Force Reserve Medal- (Obs.) | Air Reserve Forces Meritor's Service Medal | Coast Guard Reserve Good Conduct Medal | Coast Guard Enlisted Person of the Year | Navy Fleet Marine Force Ribbon | Outstanding Airman of the Year Ribbon | Air Force Recognition Ribbon | Civil War Campaign Medal (1861-65) | Civil War Campaign (1st Army Ribbon) | |
| Indian Campaign Medal (1865-91) | Indian Campaign Medal (1st Ribbon) | Dewey Medal (1898) | Sampson Medal | Spanish Campaign Medal (1898) | Spanish Campaign Medal (1st Army Ribbon) | Spanish Campaign Medal (1st Navy Ribbon) | Cardenas Medal of Honor (1898) | Specially Meritorious Medal (1898) | |
| West Indies Campaign Medal (1898) | West Indies Campaign (1st Ribbon) | Spanish War Service Medal (1898) | Cuban Occupation Medal (1898-1902) | Puerto Rican Occupation Medal (1898) | Philippine Campaign Medal (1899 - 1913) | Philippine Campaign (1st Navy Ribbon) | Philippine Congressional Medal (1899-1902) | China Campaign Medal (1900-01) | |

102  Military Medals of America

# A History of United States Armed Forces Decorations, Unit Awards & Service Ribbons

| | | | | | | | | |
|---|---|---|---|---|---|---|---|---|
| China Relief Expedition (1st Navy Ribbon) | Cuban Pacification Medal (1906-09) | Peary Polar Expedit'n Medal (1908-09) | Mexican Service Medal (1911-17) | 1st Nicaraguan Campaign Medal (1912) | Haitian Campaign Medal (1915) | Dominican Campaign Medal (1916) | Mexican Border Service Medal (1916-17) | World War I Victory Medal (1917 - 18) |
| Texas Cavalry Congressional Medal (1918) | Occupation of Germany (1918-23) | N.C.-4 Medal (1919) | Haitian Campaign Medal (1919-20) | 2nd Nicaraguan Camp'n Medal (1926-33) | Yangtze Service Medal (1926-32) | 1st Byrd Antarctic Expedit'n (1928-30) | Navy Expeditionary Medal | Marine Corps Expeditionary Medal |
| 2nd Byrd Antarctic Expedit'n (1933-35) | China Service Medal (1937, 1945) | Amer. Defense Service Medal (1939-41) | Women's Army Corps Service Medal | American Campaign Medal (1941-46) | Asiatic-Pacific Camp'n Medal (1941-46) | Europe-African-Mid East Camp'gn (1941-46) | World War II Victory Medal (1941 - 46) | U.S. Antarctic Expedit'n Medal (1939-41) |
| World War II Occupat'n Medal (1945-57) | Medal for Humane Action (1948-49) | Nat'l Defense Service Medal (1950, 61, 90, 01) | Korean Service Medal (1950-54) | Antarctica Service Medal | Coast Guard Arctic Service Medal | Armed Forces Expeditionary Medal | Vietnam Service Medal (1965-73) | Southwest Asia Service Medal (1991-95) |
| Kosovo Campaign Medal (1999- ) | Afghanistan Campaign Medal (2001- ) | Iraq Campaign Medal (2003 - 11) | Inherent Resolve Campaign Medal | War on Terrorism Expeditionary Medal (2001- ) | War on Terrorism Service Medal (2001- ) | Korea Defense Service Medal (1954- ) | Armed Forces Service Medal | Humanitarian Service Medal |
| Outstanding Volunteer Service Medal | Navy Sea Service Deployment Ribbon | Navy Arctic Service Ribbon | Naval Reserve Sea Service Ribbon | Navy & Marine Corps Overseas Service Ribbon | Navy Recruiting Service Ribbon | Navy Recruit Training Service Ribbon | Navy Ceremonial Guard Ribbon | Navy Recruit Honor Graduate Ribbon |
| Marine Corps Recruiting Ribbon | Marine Corps Drill Instructor Ribbon | Marine Security Guard Ribbon | Marine Corps Combat Instructor Ribbon | Air Force Air & Space Campaign Medal | USAF Nuclear Deterrence Opns Medal | Air Force Overseas Ribbon (Short Tour) | Air Force Overseas Ribbon (Long Tour) | Air Force Expeditionary Service Ribbon |
| Air Force Longevity Service Award Ribbon | Air Force Special Duty Ribbon | Air Force Military Training Instructor Rib'n | Air Force Recruiter Ribbon | Transportation 9-11 Ribbon (Coast Guard) | Coast Guard Special Oper'ns Service Ribbon | Coast Guard Sea Service Ribbon | Coast Guard Restricted Duty Ribbon | Coast Guard Overseas Service Ribbon |
| Coast Guard Basic Training Honor Graduate Ribbon | Coast Guard Recruiting Service Ribbon | Army Sea Duty Ribbon | Armed Forces Reserve Medal | Army NCO Prof. Development Ribbon | Army Service Ribbon | Army Overseas Service Ribbon | Army Reserve Comp. Overseas Training Ribbon | Naval Reserve Medal (Obsolete) |
| Marine Corps Reserve Ribbon (Obsolete) | Air Force NCO Prof. Military Education Grad. | Air Force Basic Military Training Honor Graduate | Air Force Small Arms Expert Marksman | Air Force Training Ribbon | Philippine Presidential Unit Citation | Korean Presidential Unit Citation | Vietnam Presidential Unit Citation | Vietnam Gallantry Cross Unit Citation |
| Vietnam Civil Actions Unit Citation | Philippine Defense Ribbon | Philippine Liberation Ribbon (1944 - 45) | Philippine Independence Ribbon (1946) | United Nations Korean Service Medal | UN Palestine Mission (UNTSO) | UN India/ Pakistan Mission (UNMOGIP) | UN New Guinea Mission (UNTEA) | UN Iraq/ Kuwait Mission (UNIKOM) |
| UN Western Sahara Mission (MINURSO) | UN Cambodia Mission 1 (UNAMIC) | UN Yugoslavia Mission (UNPROFOR) | UN Cambodia Mission 2 (UNTAC) | UN Somalia Mission (UNOSOM) | UN Haiti Mission (UNMIH) | UN Special Service Medal (UNSSM) | NATO Medal for Bosnia | NATO Medal for Kosovo |
| NATO Medal for Operation Eagle Assist | NATO Medal for Operation Active Endeavor | NATO Medal for Balkan Operations | NATO Medal for Afghanistan, Sudan, Iraq | Multinational Force & Observers Medal | Inter-American Defense Board Medal | Republic of Vietnam Campaign Medal | Kuwait Liberation Medal (Saudi Arabia) | Kuwait Liberation Medal (Kuwait) |
| Republic of Korea War Service Medal | Navy Distinguished Marksman Badge | Navy Distinguished Pistol Shot Badge | Navy Dist. Marksman & Pistol Shot | Navy Rifle Marksmanship Ribbon | Navy Pistol Marksmanship Ribbon | Coast Guard Dist. Marksman & Pistol Shot | Coast Guard Rifle Marksmanship Ribbon | Coast Guard Pistol Marksmanship Ribbon |

Medals of America 103

# U.S. Army Ribbons & Devices   Left Breast     Correct Order of Ribbon Wear

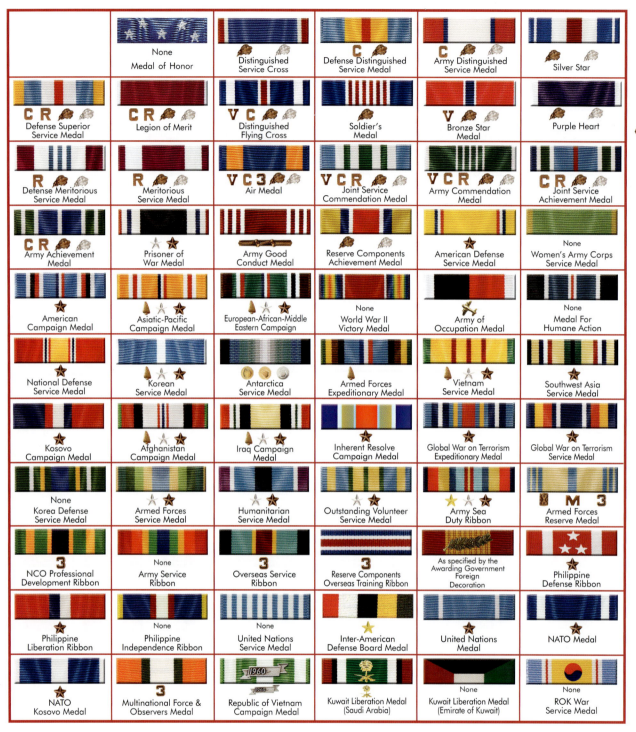

## Army Unit Awards

Note: Per Army regulations, no row may contain more than four ribbons or three (3) unit awards. The display is arranged solely to conserve space on the page.

# Correct Wear of Multi-Service Awards on the Uniform

## Army Order of Precedence *(Other Services in Italics)*

Medal of Honor (Army, Navy, Air Force)
Distinguished Service Cross
*Navy Cross*
*Air Force Cross*
*Coast Guard Cross*
Defense Distinguished Service Medal
Army Distinguished Service Medal
*Navy Distinguished Service Medal*
*Air Force Distinguished Service Medal*
Homeland Security Dist. Service Medal
*Transportation Dist. Service Medal*
*Coast Guard Distinguished Service Medal*
Silver Star
Defense Superior Service Medal
Legion of Merit
Distinguished Flying Cross
Soldier's Medal
*Navy & Marine Corps Medal*
*Airman's Medal*
*Coast Guard Medal*
Bronze Star Medal
Purple Heart
Defense Meritorious Service Medal
Meritorious Service Medal
Air Medal
*Aerial Achievement Medal*
Joint Service Commendation Medal
Army Commendation Medal
*Navy & Marine Corps Commendat'n Medal*
*Air Force Commendation Medal*
*Coast Guard Commendation Medal*
*Transportation 9-11 Medal*
Joint Service Achievement Medal
Army Achievement Medal
*Navy & Marine Corps Achievement Medal*
*Air Force Achievement Medal*
*Coast Guard Achievement Medal*
*Coast Guard Commandant's Letter of Commendation Ribbon*
*Combat Action Ribbon (Navy, Marine Corps)*
*Air Force Combat Action Medal*
*Combat Action Ribbon (Coast Guard)*

Gold Lifesaving Medal
Silver Lifesaving Medal

Prisoner of War Medal
*Air Force Combat Readiness Medal*
Army Good Conduct Medal
*Reserve Special Commendation Ribbon*
*Navy Good Conduct Medal*
*Marine Corps Good Conduct Medal*
*Air Force Good Conduct Medal*
*Coast Guard Good Conduct Medal*
Army Reserve Components Achievement Medal
*Naval Reserve Meritorious Service Medal*
*Selected Marine Corps Reserve Medal*
*Air Reserve Forces Meritorious Service Medal*
*Coast Guard Reserve Good Conduct Medal*
*Coast Guard Enlisted Person of the Year Ribbon*
*Navy Fleet Marine Force Ribbon*

*Outstanding Airman of the Year Ribbon*
*Air Force Recognition Ribbon*
*Navy Expeditionary Medal*
*Marine Corps Expeditionary Medal*
China Service Medal
American Defense Service Medal
Women's Army Corps Service Medal
American Campaign Medal
Asiatic-Pacific Campaign Medal
European-African-Middle Eastern Campaign Medal
World War II Victory Medal
Army of Occupation Medal
*Navy Occupation Service Medal*
Medal for Humane Action
National Defense Service Medal
Korean Service Medal
Antarctica Service Medal
*Coast Guard Arctic Service Medal*
Armed Forces Expeditionary Medal
Vietnam Service Medal
Southwest Asia Service Medal
Kosovo Campaign Medal
Afghanistan Campaign Medal
Iraq Campaign Medal
Inherent Resolve Campaign Medal
Global War on Terrorism Expeditionary Medal
Global War on Terrorism Service Medal
Korea Defense Service Medal
Armed Forces Service Medal
Humanitarian Service Medal
Outstanding Volunteer Service Medal
Army Sea Duty Ribbon
Armed Forces Reserve Medal
Army N.C.O. Professional Development Ribbon
Army Service Ribbon
Army Overseas Service Ribbon
Army Reserve Components Overseas Training Ribbon
*Navy Sea Service Deployment Ribbon*
*Navy Arctic Service Ribbon*
*Naval Reserve Sea Service Ribbon*
*Navy & Marine Corps Overseas Service Ribbon*
*Navy Recruiting Service Ribbon*
*Navy Recruit Training Service Ribbon*
*Navy Ceremonial Guard Ribbon*
*Navy Recruit Honor Graduate Ribbon*
*Naval Reserve Medal*
*Marine Corps Recruiting Ribbon*
*Marine Corps Drill Instructor Ribbon*
*Marine Security Guard Ribbon*
*Marine Combat Instructor Ribbon*
*Marine Corps Reserve Ribbon*
*Air Force Combat Readiness Medal*
*Air Force Air & Space Campaign Medal*
*Air Force Nuclear Deterrence Operation Medal*
*Air Force Overseas Ribbon (Short Tour)*
*Air Force Overseas Ribbon (Long Tour)*
*Air Force Expeditionary Service Ribbon*
*Air Force Military Training Instructor*

*Air Force Recruiter Ribbon*
*Air Force N.C.O. Professional Military Education Graduate Ribbon*
*Air Force Basic Military Training Honor Graduate Ribbon*
*Air Force Training Ribbon*
*Transportation 9-11 Ribbon*
*Coast Guard Special Operations Service Ribbon*
*Coast Guard Sea Service Ribbon*
*Coast Guard Restricted Duty Ribbon*
*Coast Guard Basic Training Honor Graduate Ribbon*
*Coast Guard Recruiting Service Ribbon*

Foreign Military Decorations

Philippine Defense Ribbon
Philippine Liberation Ribbon
Philippine Independence Ribbon
United Nations Korean Service Medal
Inter-American Defense Board Medal
United Nations Medal
NATO Medal for Bosnia
NATO Medal for Kosovo
NATO Article 5 & Non-Article 5 Medals
Multinational Force & Observers Medal
Republic of Vietnam Campaign Medal
Kuwait Liberation Medal (Saudi Arabia)
Kuwait Liberation Medal (Kuwait)
Korean War Service Medal

### UNIT CITATIONS (Right Breast):

Army Presidential Unit Citation
*Air Force Presidential Unit Citation*
*Navy Presidential Unit Citation*
Joint Meritorious Unit Award
Army Valorous Unit Award
*Air Force Gallant Unit Citation*
*Coast Guard Presidential Unit Citation*
Army Meritorious Unit Commendation
*Navy Unit Commendation*
*Air Force Meritorious Unit Award*
*Air Force Outstanding Unit Award*
*Air Force Organizational Excellence Award*
*D.O.T. Secretary's Outstasnding Unit Award*
*Coast Guard Unit Commendation*
Army Superior Unit Award
*Navy Meritorious Unit Commendation*
*Coast Guard Meritorious Unit Commendation*
*Coast Guard Meritorious Team Commendation*
*Navy "E" Ribbon*
*Coast Guard "E" Ribbon*
*Coast Guard Bicentennial Unit Commendation*
Philippine Presidential Unit Citation
Korean Presidential Unit Citation
Vietnam Presidential Unit Citation
Vietnam Gallantry Cross Unit Citation
Vietnam Civil Actions Unit Citation

## The following awards may not be worn on Army Uniform

Air Force Longevity Service Award Ribbon
Navy Rifle Marksmanship Ribbon
Navy Pistol Marksmanship Ribbon

Coast Guard Rifle Marksmanship Ribbon
Coast Guard Pistol Marksmanship Ribbon
Air Force Small Arms Expert Marksmanship Ribbon

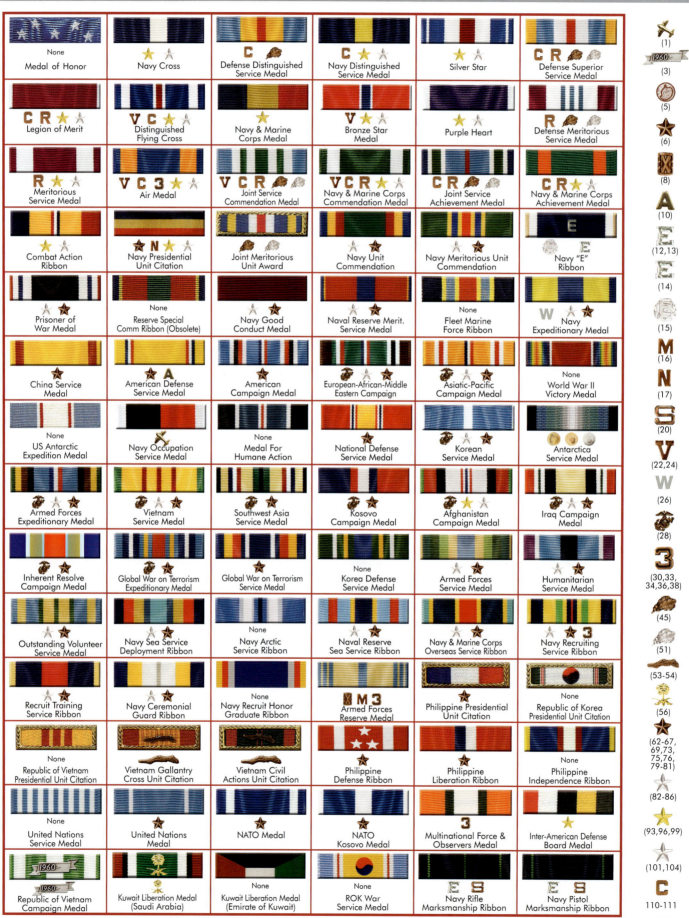

# Navy Order of Precedence *(Other Services in Italics)*

Medal of Honor (Navy, Army, Air Force)
Navy Cross
*Distinguished Service Cross*
*Air Force Cross*
*Coast Guard Cross*
Defense Distinguished Service Medal
Navy Distinguished Service Medal
*Army Distinguished Service Medal*
*Air Force Distinguished Service Medal*
Homeland Security Dist. Service Medal
*Transportation Distinguished Service Medal*
*Coast Guard Distinguished Service Medal*
Silver Star
Defense Superior Service Medal
Legion of Merit
Distinguished Flying Cross
Navy & Marine Corps Medal
*Soldier's Medal*
*Airman's Medal*
*Coast Guard Medal*
Bronze Star Medal
Purple Heart
Defense Meritorious Service Medal
Meritorious Service Medal
Air Medal
*Aerial Achievement Medal*
Joint Service Commendation Medal
Navy & Marine Corps Commendat'n Medal
*Army Commendation Medal*
*Air Force Commendation Medal*
*Coast Guard Commendation Medal*
*Transportation 9-11 Medal*
Joint Service Achievement Medal
Navy & Marine Corps Achievement Medal
*Army Achievement Medal*
*Air Force Achievement Medal*
*Coast Guard Achievement Medal*
Combat Action Ribbon (Navy, Marine Corps)
*Air Force Combat Action Medal*
*Combat Action Ribbon (Coast Guard)*

Navy Presidential Unit Citation
*Army Presidential Unit Citation*
*Air Force Presidential Unit Citation*
*Coast Guard Presidential Unit Citation*
Joint Meritorious Unit Award
*Army Valorous Unit Award*
*Air Force Gallant Unit Citation*
Navy Unit Commendation
Navy Meritorious Unit Commendation
*Army Meritorious Unit Commendation*
*Air Force Meritorious Unit Award*
*Air Force Outstanding Unit Award*
*Air Force Organizational Excellence Award*
*Army Superior Unit Award*
*D.O.T. Secretary's Outstanding Unit Award*
*Coast Guard Unit Commendation*
*Coast Guard Meritorious Unit Commendat'n*
*Coast Guard Meritorious Team Commendat'n*
Navy "E" Ribbon
*Coast Guard "E" Ribbon*
*Coast Guard Bicentennial Unit Commendat'n*

Gold Lifesaving Medal
Silver Lifesaving Medal
Prisoner of War Medal
Reserve Special Commendation Ribbon
Navy Good Conduct Medal
*Marine Corps Good Conduct Medal*
*Army Good Conduct Medal*
*Air Force Good Conduct Medal*
*Coast Guard Good Conduct Medal*
Naval Reserve Meritorious Service Medal
*Selected Marine Corps Reserve Medal*
*Army Reserve Components Achievement Medal*
*Air Reserve Forces Meritorious Service Medal*
*Coast Guard Reserve Good Conduct Medal*
*Coast Guard Enlisted Person of the Year Ribbon*
Navy Fleet Marine Force Ribbon

Navy Expeditionary Medal
*Marine Corps Expeditionary Medal*
China Service Medal
American Defense Service Medal
*Women's Army Corps Service Medal*
American Campaign Medal
European-African-Middle Eastern Campaign Medal
Asiatic-Pacific Campaign Medal
World War II Victory Medal
U.S. Antarctic Expedition Medal
Navy Occupation Service Medal
*Army of Occupation Medal*
Medal for Humane Action
National Defense Service Medal
Korean Service Medal
Antarctica Service Medal
*Coast Guard Arctic Service Medal*
Armed Forces Expeditionary Medal
Vietnam Service Medal
Southwest Asia Service Medal
Kosovo Campaign Medal
Afghanistan Campaign Medal
Iraq Campaign Medal
Inherent Resolve Campaign Medal
Global War on Terrorism Expeditionary Medal
Global War on Terrorism Service Medal
Korea Defense Service Medal
Armed Forces Service Medal
Humanitarian Service Medal
Outstanding Volunteer Service Medal
Navy Sea Service Deployment Ribbon
Navy Arctic Service Ribbon
Naval Reserve Sea Service Ribbon
Navy & Marine Corps Overseas Service Ribbon
Navy Recruiting Service Ribbon
*Marine Corps Recruiting Ribbon*
*Marine Corps Drill Instructor Ribbon*
*Marine Security Guard Ribbon*
*Marine Combat Instructor Ribbon*
Navy Recruit Training Service Ribbon
Navy Ceremonial Guard Ribbon
Navy Recruit Honor Graduate Ribbon
*Transportation 9-11 Ribbon*

*Coast Guard Special Operations Service Ribbon*
*Coast Guard Sea Service Ribbon*
*Coast Guard Restricted Duty Ribbon*
*Coast Guard Basic Training Honor Graduate Ribbon*
*Coast Guard Recruiting Service Ribbon*
*Air Force Air & Space Campaign Medal*
*Air Force Nuclear Deterrence Operation Medal*
*Air Force Overseas Ribbon (Short Tour)*
*Air Force Overseas Ribbon (Long Tour)*
*Air Force Expeditionary Service Ribbon*
*Air Force Longevity Service Award Ribbon*
*Air Force Military Training Instructor Ribbon*
*Air Force Recruiter Ribbon*
*Army Sea Duty Ribbon*
Armed Forces Reserve Medal
Naval Reserve Medal
*Marine Corps Reserve Ribbon*
*Army N.C.O. Professional Development Ribbon*
*Army Service Ribbon*
*Army Overseas Service Ribbon*
*Army Reserve Components Overseas Training Ribbon*
*Air Force N.C.O. Professional Military Education Graduate Ribbon*
*Air Force Basic Military Training Honor Graduate Ribbon*
*Air Force Small Arms Expert Marksmanship Ribbon Air Force Training Ribbon*

Foreign Military Decorations

Philippine Presidential Unit Citation
Korean Presidential Unit Citation
Vietnam Presidential Unit Citation
Vietnam Gallantry Cross Unit Citation
Vietnam Civil Actions Unit Citation

Philippine Defense Ribbon
Philippine Liberation Ribbon
Philippine Independence Ribbon
United Nations Korean Service Medal
United Nations Medal
NATO Medal for Bosnia
NATO Medal for Kosovo
NATO Article 5 & Non-Article 5 Medals
Multinational Force & Observers Medal
Inter-American Defense Board Medal
Republic of Vietnam Campaign Medal
Kuwait Liberation Medal (Saudi Arabia)
Kuwait Liberation Medal (Kuwait)
Korean War Service Medal

Navy Rifle Marksmanship Ribbon
Navy Pistol Marksmanship Ribbon
*Coast Guard Rifle Marksmanship Ribn*
*Coast Guard Pistol Marksmanship Ribbon*

# The following awards may not be worn on the Navy Uniform

Coast Guard Commandant's Letter of Commendation Ribbon
Air Force Combat Readiness Medal
Outstanding Airman of the Year Ribbon
Air Force Recognition Ribbon

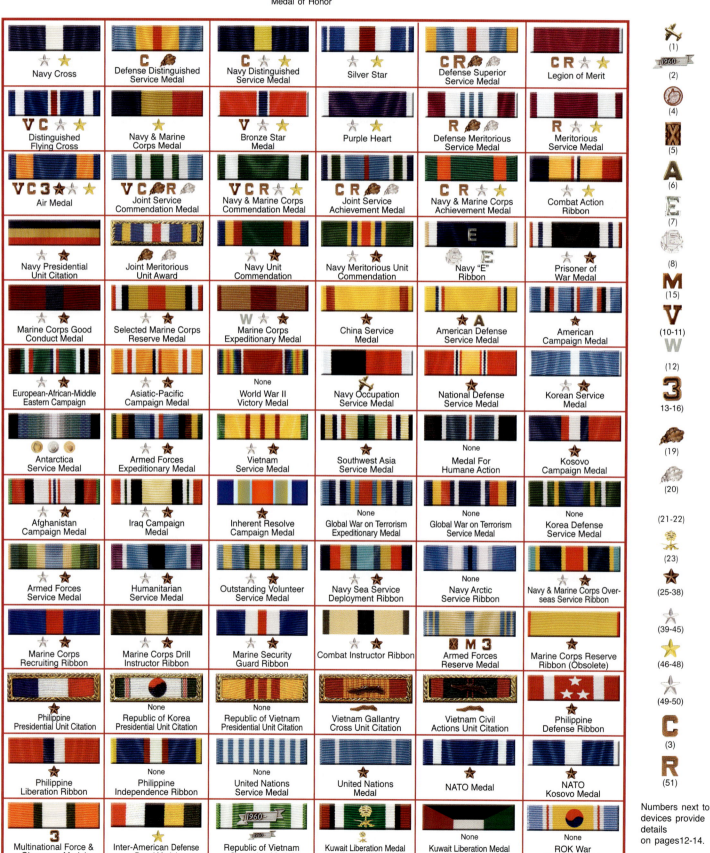

# Marine Corps Order of Precedence *(Other Services in Italics)*

Medal of Honor (Navy, Army, Air Force)
Navy Cross
*Coast Guard Cross*
*Distinguished Service Cross*
*Air Force Cross*
Defense Distinguished Service Medal
Navy Distinguished Service Medal
*Army Distinguished Service Medal*
*Air Force Distinguished Service Medal*
Homeland Security Dist. Service Medal
Transportation Distinguished Service Medal
*Coast Guard Distinguished Service Medal*
Silver Star
Defense Superior Service Medal
Legion of Merit
Distinguished Flying Cross
Navy & Marine Corps Medal
*Soldier's Medal*
*Airman's Medal*
*Coast Guard Medal*
Bronze Star Medal
Purple Heart
Defense Meritorious Service Medal
Meritorious Service Medal
Air Medal
*Aerial Achievement Medal*
Joint Service Commendation Medal
Navy & Marine Corps Commendat'n Medal
*Army Commendation Medal*
*Air Force Commendation Medal*
*Coast Guard Commendation Medal*
Transportation 9-11 Medal
Joint Service Achievement Medal
Navy & Marine Corps Achievement Medal
*Army Achievement Medal*
*Air Force Achievement Medal*
*Coast Guard Achievement Medal*
Combat Action Ribbon (Navy, Marine Corps)
*Air Force Combat Action Medal*
*Combat Action Ribbon (Coast Guard)*

Navy Presidential Unit Citation
*Army Presidential Unit Citation*
*Air Force Presidential Unit Citation*
*Coast Guard Presidential Unit Citation*
Joint Meritorious Unit Award
*Army Valorous Unit Award*
*Air Force Gallant Unit Citation*
Navy Unit Commendation
Navy Meritorious Unit Commendation
*Army Meritorious Unit Commendation*
*Air Force Meritorious Unit Award*
*Air Force Outstanding Unit Award*
*Air Force Organizational Excellence Award*
*Army Superior Unit Award*
*D.O.T. Secretary's Outstanding Unit Award*
*Coast Guard Unit Commendation*
*Coast Guard Meritorious Unit Commendat'n*

*Coast Guard Meritorious Team Commendation*
Navy "E" Ribbon
*Coast Guard "E" Ribbon*

Gold Lifesaving Medal
Silver Lifesaving Medal

Prisoner of War Medal
*Air Force Combat Readiness Medal*
*Army Good Conduct Medal*
Reserve Special Commendation Ribbon
Marine Corps Good Conduct Medal
*Navy Good Conduct Medal*
*Air Force Good Conduct Medal*
*Coast Guard Good Conduct Medal*
Selected Marine Corps Reserve Medal
*Army Reserve Components Achievement Medal*
*Naval Reserve Meritorious Service Medal*
*Air Reserve Forces Meritorious Service Medal*
*Coast Guard Reserve Good Conduct Medal*
*Coast Guard Enlisted Person of the Year Ribbon*
Navy Fleet Marine Force Ribbon
Marine Corps Expeditionary Medal
*Navy Expeditionary Medal*
China Service Medal
American Defense Service Medal
*Women's Army Corps Service Medal*
American Campaign Medal
European-African-Middle Eastern Campaign Medal
Asiatic-Pacific Campaign Medal
World War II Victory Medal
*U.S. Antarctic Expedition Medal*
Navy Occupation Service Medal
*Army of Occupation Medal*
Medal for Humane Action
National Defense Service Medal
Korean Service Medal
Antarctica Service Medal
*Coast Guard Arctic Service Medal*
Armed Forces Expeditionary Medal
Vietnam Service Medal
Southwest Asia Service Medal
Kosovo Campaign Medal
Afghanistan Campaign Medal
Iraq Campaign Medal
Inherent Resolve Campaign Medal
Global War on Terrorism Expeditionary Medal
Global War on Terrorism Service Medal
Korea Defense Service Medal
Armed Forces Service Medal

Humanitarian Service Medal
Outstanding Volunteer Service Medal
Navy Sea Service Deployment Ribbon

Navy Arctic Service Ribbon
Naval Reserve Sea Service Ribbon
Navy & Marine Corps Overseas Service Ribbon
Marine Corps Recruiting Ribbon
Marine Corps Drill Instructor Ribbon
Marine Security Guard Ribbon
Marine Combat Instructor Ribbon
*Navy Recruiting Service Ribbon*
*Navy Recruit Training Service Ribbon*
*Navy Ceremonial Guard Ribbon*
*Navy Recruit Honor Graduate Ribbon*
*Air Force Air & Space Campaign Medal*
*Air Force Nuclear Deterrence Operation Medal*
*Air Force Overseas Ribbon (Short Tour)*
*Air Force Overseas Ribbon (Long Tour)*
*Air Force Expeditionary Service Ribbon*
*Air Force Military Training Instructor Ribbon*
*Air Force Recruiter Ribbon*
*Transportation 9-11 Ribbon*
*Coast Guard Special Operations Service Ribbon*
*Coast Guard Sea Service Ribbon*
*Coast Guard Restricted Duty Ribbon*
*Coast Guard Basic Training Honor Graduate Ribbon*
*Coast Guard Recruiting Service Ribbon*
*Army Sea Duty Ribbon*
Armed Forces Reserve Medal
*Army Overseas Service Ribbon*
*Naval Reserve Medal*
Marine Corps Reserve Ribbon

Philippine Presidential Unit Citation
Korean Presidential Unit Citation
Vietnam Presidential Unit Citation
Vietnam Gallantry Cross Unit Citation
Vietnam Civil Actions Unit Citation
Philippine Defense Ribbon
Philippine Liberation Ribbon
Philippine Independence Ribbon
United Nations Korean Service Medal
United Nations Medal

Foreign Decorations

NATO Medal for Bosnia
NATO Medal for Kosovo
NATO Article 5 & Non-Article 5 Medals
Multinat'l Force & Observers Medal
Inter-American Defense Board Medal
Republic of Vietnam Campaign Medal
Kuwait Liberation Medal (Saudi Arabia)
Kuwait Liberation Medal (Kuwait)
Korean War Service Medal

# The following awards may not be worn on the Marine Corps Uniform

Coast Guard Commandant's Letter of Commendation Ribbon
Coast Guard Bicentennial Unit Commen
Army N.C.O. Professional Development Ribbon
Army Service Ribbon
Army Reserve Components Overseas Training Ribbon

Air Force Longevity Service Award Ribbon
Air Force N.C.O. Professional Military Education Graduate Ribbon
Air Force Basic Military Training Honor Graduate Ribbon
Air Force Small Arms Expert Marksmanship Ribbon

Air Force Training Ribbon
Navy Rifle Marksmanship Ribbon
Navy Pistol Marksmanship Ribbon
Coast Guard Rifle Marksmanship Ribbon
Coast Guard Pistol Marksmanship Ribbon

# Current U.S. Air Force Ribbons & Devices

**Correct Order of Ribbon Wear**

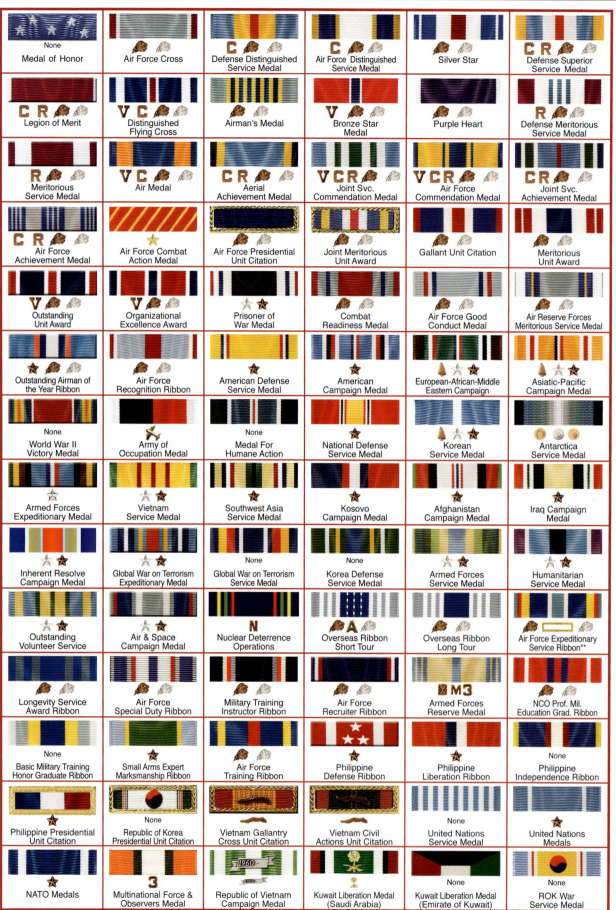

Note: Per Air Force regulations, no row may contain more than four (4) ribbons. The above display is arranged solely to conserve space on the page.
** Frame around ribbon denotes deployed in combat zone.

# Air Force Order of Precedence *(Other Services in Italics)*

Medal of Honor (Air Force, Army, Navy)
Air Force Cross
Distinguished Service Cross
*Navy Cross*
*Coast Guard Cross*
Defense Distinguished Service Medal
Air Force Distinguished Service Medal
Army Distinguished Service Medal
*Navy Distinguished Service Medal*
*Homeland Security Dist. Service Medal*
*Transportation Distinguished Service Medal*
*Coast Guard Distinguished Service Medal*
Silver Star
Defense Superior Service Medal
Legion of Merit
Distinguished Flying Cross
Airman's Medal
Soldier's Medal
*Navy & Marine Corps Medal*
*Coast Guard Medal*
Bronze Star Medal
Purple Heart
Defense Meritorious Service Medal
Meritorious Service Medal
Air Medal
Aerial Achievement Medal
Joint Service Commendation Medal
Air Force Commendation Medal
Army Commendation Medal
*Navy & Marine Corps Commendat'n Medal*
*Coast Guard Commendation Medal*
*Transportation 9-11 Medal*
Joint Service Achievement Medal
Air Force Achievement Medal
*Army Achievement Medal*
*Navy & Marine Corps Achievement Medal*
*Coast Guard Achievement Medal*
*Coast Guard Commandant's Letter of Commendation Ribbon*
*Combat Action Ribbon (Navy, Marine Corps)*
Air Force Combat Action Medal
*Combat Action Ribbon (Coast Guard)*
Air Force Presidential Unit Citation
*Coast Guard Presidential Unit Citation*
Army Presidential Unit Citation
*Navy Presidential Unit Citation*

Joint Meritorious Unit Award
*Army Valorous Unit Award*
Air Force Gallant Unit Citation
*D.O.T. Secretary's Outstanding Unit Award*
*Coast Guard Unit Commendation*
*Navy Unit Commendation*
*Coast Guard Meritorious Unit Commendation*
*Coast Guard Meritorious Team Commendation*
*Army Meritorious Unit Commendation*
*Navy Meritorious Unit Commendation*
Air Force Meritorious Unit Award
Air Force Outstanding Unit Award
Air Force Organizatonal Excellence Award
*Army Superior Unit Award*
*Navy "E" Ribbon*
*Coast Guard "E" Ribbon*
*Coast Guard Bicentennial Unit Commendation*
    Gold Lifesaving Medal

Silver Lifesaving Medal
Prisoner of War Medal
Air Force Combat Readiness Medal
Air Force Good Conduct Medal
Army Good Conduct Medal
*Reserve Special Commendation Ribbon*
*Navy Good Conduct Medal*
*Marine Corps Good Conduct Medal*
*Coast Guard Good Conduct Medal*
Air Reserve Forces Meritorious Service Medal
*Army Reserve Components Achievement Medal*
*Naval Reserve Meritorious Service Medal*
*Selected Marine Corps Reserve Medal*
*Coast Guard Reserve Good Conduct Medal*
*Coast Guard Enlisted Person of the Year Ribbon*
*Navy Fleet Marine Force Ribbon*
Outstanding Airman of the Year Ribbon
Air Force Recognition Ribbon

*Navy Expeditionary Medal*
*Marine Corps Expeditionary Medal*
China Service Medal
American Defense Service Medal
Women's Army Corps Service Medal
American Campaign Medal
Asiatic-Pacific Campaign Medal
European-African-Middle Eastern Campaign Medal
World War II Victory Medal
Army of Occupation Medal
*Navy Occupation Service Medal*
Medal for Humane Action
National Defense Service Medal
Korean Service Medal
Antarctica Service Medal
*Coast Guard Arctic Service Medal*
Armed Forces Expeditionary Medal
Vietnam Service Medal
Southwest Asia Service Medal
Kosovo Campaign Medal
Afghanistan Campaign Medal
Iraq Campaign Medal
Inherent Resolve Campaign Medal
Global War on Terrorism Expeditionary Medal
 Global War on Terrorism Service Medal
 Korea Defense Service Medal
 Armed Forces Service Medal
 Humanitarian Service Medal
Outstanding Volunteer Service Medal
Air Force Air & Space Campaign Medal
Air Force Nuclear Deterrence Operation Medal
Air Force Overseas Ribbon (Short Tour)
Air Force Overseas Ribbon (Long Tour)
Air Force Expeditionary Service Ribbon
*Army Overseas Service Ribbon*
*Army Reserve Components Overseas Training Ribbon*
*Navy Sea Service Deployment Ribbon*
*Navy Arctic Service Ribbon*
*Naval Reserve Sea Service Ribbon*
*Navy & Marine Corps Overseas Service Ribbon*

*Navy Recruiting Service Ribbon*
*Navy Recruit Training Service Ribbon*
*Navy Ceremonial Guard Ribbon*
*Navy Recruit Honor Graduate Ribbon*
*Marine Corps Recruiting Ribbon*
*Marine Corps Drill Instructor Ribbon*
*Marine Security Guard Ribbon*
*Marine Combat Instructor Ribbon*
*Transportation 9-11 Ribbon*
*Coast Guard Special Operations Service Medal*
*Coast Guard Sea Service Ribbon*
*Coast Guard Restricted Duty Ribbon*
Air Force Longevity Service Award Ribbon
Air Force Special Duty Ribbon
Air Force Military Training Instructor Ribbon
Air Force Recruiter Ribbon
*Army Sea Duty Ribbon*
Armed Forces Reserve Medal
*Naval Reserve Medal*
*Marine Corps Reserve Ribbon*
Air Force N.C.O. Professional Military Education Graduate Ribbon
*Army N.C.O. Professional Development Ribbon*
Air Force Basic Military Training Honor Graduate Ribbon
*Coast Guard Basic Training Honor Graduate Ribbon*
*Coast Guard Recruiting Service Ribbon*
Air Force Small Arms Expert Marksmanship Ribbon

**No Specific Restrictions in Air Force Uniform or Award Regulations.**

# Coast Guard Order of Precedence *(Other Services in Italics)*

Medal of Honor (Navy, Army, Air Force)
Coast Guard Cross; Navy Cross
*Distinguished Service Cross*
*Air Force Cross*
Homeland Security Dist. Service Medal
Transportation Dist. Service Medal
Defense Distinguished Service Medal
Coast Guard Distinguished Service Medal
*Navy Distinguished Service Medal*
*Army Distinguished Service Medal*
*Air Force Distinguished Service Medal*
Silver Star
D.O.T. Secretary's Award for Outstanding Achievement
Defense Superior Service Medal
Transportation Guardian Medal
Legion of Merit
Distinguished Flying Cross
Coast Guard Medal
*Navy & Marine Corps Medal*
*Soldier's Medal*
*Airman's Medal*
Gold Lifesaving Medal
Bronze Star Medal
Purple Heart
Defense Meritorious Service Medal
Meritorious Service Medal
Air Medal
Silver Lifesaving Medal
D.O.T. Secretary's Award for Meritorious Achievement
*Aerial Achievement Medal*
Joint Service Commendation Medal
Coast Guard Commendation Medal
*Navy & Marine Corps Commendat'n Medal*
*Army Commendation Medal*
*Air Force Commendation Medal*
D.O.T. Secretary's Award for Superior Achievement
Joint Service Achievement Medal
Transportation 9-11 Medal
Coast Guard Achievement Medal
*Navy & Marine Corps Achievement Medal*
*Army Achievement Medal*
*Air Force Achievement Medal*
Coast Guard Commandant's Letter of Commendation Ribbon
Combat Action Ribbon (Coast Guard)
Combat Action Ribbon (Navy, Marine Corps)
*Air Force Combat Action Medal*

Coast Guard Presidential Unit Citation
Navy Presidential Unit Citation
*Army Presidential Unit Citation*
*Air Force Presidential Unit Citation*
*Air Force Gallant Unit Citation*
Joint Meritorious Unit Award
D.O.T. Secretary's Outstand'g Unit Award
Coast Guard Unit Commendation
*Navy Unit Commendation*
*Army Valorous Unit Award*
*Air Force Meritorious Unit Award*

*Air Force Outstanding Unit Award*
*Air Force Organizational Excellence Award*
Coast Guard Meritorious Unit Commendation
Coast Guard Meritorious Team Commendation
*Navy Meritorious Unit Commendation*
*Army Meritorious Unit Commendation*
*Army Superior Unit Award*
Coast Guard "E" Ribbon
*Navy "E" Ribbon*
Coast Guard Bicentennial Unit Commendation

Prisoner of War Medal
Coast Guard Good Conduct Medal
*Reserve Special Commendation Ribbon*
*Navy Good Conduct Medal*
*Marine Corps Good Conduct Medal*
*Army Good Conduct Medal*
*Air Force Good Conduct Medal*
Coast Guard Reserve Good Cond. Medal
*Naval Reserve Meritorious Service Medal*
*Selected Marine Corps Reserve Medal*
Coast Guard Enlisted Person of the Year Ribbon
*Navy Fleet Marine Force Ribbon*
Navy Expeditionary Medal
*Marine Corps Expeditionary Medal*
China Service Medal
American Defense Service Medal
*Women's Army Corps Service Medal*
American Campaign Medal
European-African-Middle Eastern Campaign Medal
Asiatic-Pacific Campaign Medal
World War II Victory Medal
U.S. Antarctic Expedition Medal
Navy Occupation Service Medal
*Army of Occupation Medal*
Medal for Humane Action
National Defense Service Medal
Korean Service Medal
Antarctica Service Medal
Coast Guard Arctic Service Medal
Armed Forces Expeditionary Medal
Vietnam Service Medal
Southwest Asia Service Medal
Kosovo Campaign Medal
Afghanistan Campaign Medal
Iraq Campaign Medal
Inherent Resolve Campaign Medal
Global War on Terrorism Expeditionary Medal
Global War on Terrorism Service Medal
Korea Defense Service Medal
Armed Forces Service Medal
Humanitarian Service Medal
Outstanding Volunteer Service Medal
Transportation 9-11 Ribbon
USCG Special Operations Service Ribbon
Coast Guard Sea Service Ribbon
Coast Guard Restricted Duty Ribbon
Coast Guard Overseas Service Ribbon
*Navy Sea Service Deployment Ribbon*

*Army Reserve Components Overseas Training Ribbon*
*Navy & Marine Corps Overseas Service Ribbon*
*Army Overseas Service Ribbon*
*Navy Recruiting Service Ribbon*
*Navy Recruit Training Service Ribbon*
*Navy Ceremonial Guard Ribbon*
*Navy Recruit Honor Graduate Ribbon*
*Marine Corps Recruiting Ribbon*
*Marine Corps Drill Instructor Ribbon*
*Marine Security Guard Ribbon*
*Marine Combat Instructor Ribbon*
*Air Force Air & Space Campaign Medal*
*Air Force Nuclear Deterrence Operation Medal*
*Air Force Overseas Ribbon (Short Tour)*
*Air Force Overseas Ribbon (Long Tour)*
*Air Force Expeditionary Service Ribbon*
*Navy Arctic Service Ribbon*
*Naval Reserve Sea Service Ribbon*
Coast Guard Basic Training Honor Graduat Ribbon
*Air Force Basic Military Training Honor Graduate Ribbon*
Coast Guard Recruiting Service Ribbon
*Army Sea Duty Ribbon*
Armed Forces Reserve Medal
*Naval Reserve Medal*
*Marine Corps Reserve Ribbon*
*Army Reserve Components Achievement Medal*
*Air Reserve Forces Meritorious Service Medal*
*Air Force Military Training Instructor Ribbon*
*Air Force Recruiter Ribbon*

Philippine Presidential Unit Citation
Korean Presidential Unit Citation
Vietnam Presidential Unit Citation
Vietnam Gallantry Cross Unit Citation
Vietnam Civil Actions Unit Citation

Philippine Defense Ribbon
Philippine Liberation Ribbon
Philippine Independence Ribbon
United Nations Korean Service Medal
United Nations Medal

Foreign Decorations

NATO Medal for Bosnia
NATO Medal for Kosovo
NATO Article 5 & Non-Article 5 Medals
Multinational Force & Observers Medal
Inter-American Defense Board Medal
Republic of Vietnam Campaign Medal
Kuwait Liberation Medal (Saudi Arabia)
Kuwait Liberation Medal (Kuwait)
Korean War Service Medal
Coast Guard Rifle Marksmanship Ribbon
Coast Guard Pistol Marksmanship Ribbon

## The following awards may not be worn on the Coast Guard Uniform

Air Force Training Ribbon
Army Service Ribbon
Army N.C.O. Professional Development Ribbon

Air Force N.C.O. Professional Military Education Graduate Ribbon
Outstanding Airman of the Year Ribbon
Air Force Recognition Ribbon
Air Force Combat Readiness Medal

Air Force Longevity Service Award Ribbon
Air Force Small Arms Expert Marksmanship Ribbon
Navy Rifle Marksmanship Ribbon
Navy Pistol Marksmanship Ribbon

Medals of America 113

# Right Breast Displays on Full Dress Uniforms

The three Naval Services prescribe the wear of "ribbon only" awards on the right breast of the full dress uniform when large medals are worn. The Navy and Coast Guard align their ribbons inboard to outboard while the Marines align theirs outboard to inboard.

## U.S. Navy

| Navy Presidential Unit Citation | Combat Action Ribbon | |
|---|---|---|
| Navy Meritorious Unit Commendation | Navy Unit Commendation | Joint Meritorious Unit Award |
| Fleet Marine Force Ribbon | Reserve Special Commendation Ribbon | Navy "E" Ribbon |
| Navy Reserve Sea Service Service Ribbon | Arctic Service Ribbon | Sea Service Deployment Ribbon |
| Navy Recruit Training Service Ribbon | Navy Recruiting Service Ribbon | Navy & Marine Corps Overseas Service Ribbon |
| Philippine Presidential Unit Citation | Navy Recruit Honor Graduate Ribbon | Navy Ceremonial Guard Ribbon |
| Vietnam Gallantry Cross Unit Citation | Vietnam Presidential Unit Citation | Korean Presidential Unit Ribbon |
| Philippine Liberation Ribbon | Philippine Defense Ribbon | Vietnam Civil Actions Unit Citation |
| Pistol Marksmanship Ribbon | Rifle Marksmanship Ribbon | Philippine Independence Ribbon |

## U.S. Marine Corps

| | Combat Action Ribbon | |
|---|---|---|
| Navy Presidential Unit Citation | Joint Meritorious Unit Award | Navy Unit Commendation |
| Navy Meritorious Unit Commendation | Navy "E" Ribbon | Sea Service Deployment Ribbon |
| Arctic Service Ribbon | Navy & Marine Corps Overseas Service Ribbon | Marine Corps Recruiting Ribbon |
| Marine Corps Drill Instructor Ribbon | Marine Security Guard Ribbon | Marine Combat Instructor Ribbon |
| Marine Corps Reserve Ribbon | Philippine Presidential Unit Citation | Korean Presidential Unit Citation |
| Vietnam Presidential Unit Citation | Vietnam Gallantry Cross Unit Citation | Vietnam Civil Actions Unit Citation |
| Philippine Defense Ribbon | Philippine Liberation Ribbon | Philippine Independence Ribbon |

## U.S. Coast Guard

USCG ribbon only awards are worn inboard to outboard.

| Coast Guard Combat Action Ribbon | Commandant's Letter of Commendation Ribbon | |
|---|---|---|
| Joint Meritorious Unit Award | Navy Presidential Unit Citation | Coast Guard Presidential Unit Citation |
| Coast Guard Meritorious Unit Commendation | Coast Guard Unit Commendation | D.O.T. Outstanding Unit Award |
| Coast Guard Bicentennial Unit Commendation | Coast Guard "E" Ribbon | Coast Guard Meritorious Team Commendation |
| Special Operations Service Ribbon | Transportation 9-11 Ribbon | Enlisted Person of the Year Ribbon |
| Coast Guard Overseas Service Ribbon | Restricted Duty Ribbon | Coast Guard Sea Service Ribbon |
| Philippine Presidential Unit Citation | Coast Guard Recruiting Service Ribbon | Basic Training Honor Graduate Ribbon |
| Vietnam Gallantry Cross Unit Citation | Vietnam Presidential Unit Citation | Korean Presidential Unit Citation |
| Philippine Liberation Ribbon | Philippine Defense Ribbon | Vietnam Civil Actions Unit Citation |
| Coast Guard Pistol Marksmanship Ribbon | Coast Guard Rifle Marksmanship Ribbon | Philippine Independence Ribbon |

# United Nations Ribbons for Wear on the U.S. Military Uniform

Originally, U.S. military personnel serving with United Nations Missions were permitted to wear only two UN medals, the United Nations Korean Service Medal and the United Nations Medal. However, changes in DOD policy brought the total to 28. However, only one ribbon may be worn on the US military uniform and awards for any subsequent missions are denoted by the three-sixteenth inch bronze stars.

**AUTHORIZED 30 SEPTEMBER 2011**

- UNTSO — Middle East
- UNMOGIP — India, Pakistan
- UNOGIL — Lebanon
- UNSF/UNTEA — West New Guinea
- UNIKOM — Iraq, Kuwait
- MINURSO — Western Sahara
- UNAMIC — Cambodia
- UNPROFOR — Former Yugoslavia
- UNTAC — Cambodia
- UNOSOM II — Somalia
- UNMIH — Haiti
- UNSSM — Special Service Medal
- ONUMOZ — Mozambique
- UNOMIG — Georgia
- UNPREDEP — Macedonia
- UNTAES — E. Slavonia, Baranja
- UNSMIH — Haiti
- MINUGUA — Guatemala
- UNMIK — Kosovo
- UNTAET — East Timor
- MONUC — Congo
- UNMEE — Ethiopia, Eritrea
- UNMISET — East Timor
- UNMIL — Liberia
- MINUSTAH — Haiti
- UNAMID — Darfur
- MINURCAT — Cent. Afr. Rep, Chad
- MONUSCO — Congo
- UNAMI — UN Assistance Mission in Iraq

# United States Merchant Marine Ribbons and Attachments

= Silver Service Star Indicates crew member forced to abandon ship.

= Bronze Service Star Denotes second and subsequent awards of a service award or participation in a campaign or operation.

= Silver Seahorse Worn in Gallant Ship Citation Bar upon initial issue but has no significance.

| | | | |
|---|---|---|---|
| Distinguished Service Medal — None | Meritorious Service Medal — None | | Mariner's Medal — None |
| Outstanding Achievement Medal — None | Gallant Ship Citation Bar — Silver | Merchant Marine Combat Bar — Silver | Prisoner of War Medal — Bronze |
| Merchant Marine Defense Medal — None | Atlantic War Zone Medal — None | Pacific War Zone Medal — None | Mediterranean-Middle East War Zone Medal — None |
| World War II Victory Medal — None | Korean Service Medal — None | Vietnam Service Medal — None | Merchant Marine Expeditionary Medal — Bronze |
| Philippine Defense Ribbon — Bronze | Philippine Liberation Ribbon — Bronze | 40th Anniversary of World War II (USSR) — None | 50th Anniversary of World War II (Russia) — None |

# Armed Forces Ribbon Devices (Listed Alphabetically)

### 1. Airplane, C-54, Gold

**Services:** All
**Worn on:** World War II Occupation Medals
**Denotes:** Service during Berlin Airlift (1948-49)

### 2. Arrowhead, Bronze

**Services:** Army, Air Force
**Worn on:** Campaign awards since World War II
**Denotes:** Combat assault or invasion

### 3. Bar, Date, Silver

**Services:** All
**Worn on:** Republic of Vietnam Campaign Medal
**Denotes:** Worn upon initial issue; has no significance

### 4a. Bar, Knotted, Bronze

**Services:** Army
**Worn on:** Army Good Conduct Medal
**Denotes:** Additional periods of service (awards 2 through 5)

### 4b. Bar, Knotted, Silver

**Services:** Army
**Worn on:** Army Good Conduct Medal
**Denotes:** Additional periods of service (awards 6 through 10)

### 4c. Bar, Knotted, Gold

**Services:** Army
**Worn on:** Army Good Conduct Medal
**Denotes:** Additional periods of service (awards 11 through 15)

### 5a. Disk, Bronze

**Services:** All
**Worn on:** Antarctica Service Medal
**Denotes:** Wintered over on the Antarctic continent

### 5b. Disk, Gold

**Services:** All
**Worn on:** Antarctica Service Medal
**Denotes:** Wintered over twice on the Antarctic continent

### 5c. Disk, Silver

**Services:** All
**Worn on:** Antarctica Service Medal
**Denotes:** Wintered over three times on the Antarctic continent

### 6. Frame, Gold

**Services:** Air Force
**Worn on:** Expeditionary Service Ribbon
**Denotes:** Satisfactory participation in combat operations

### 7. Globe, Gold

**Services:** Navy
**Worn on:** Navy Presidential Unit Citation
**Denotes:** Service with USS Triton during 1st submerged cruise around the world

### 8a. Hourglass, Bronze

**Services:** All
**Worn on:** Armed Forces Reserve Medal
**Denotes:** 10 Years of service in the Reserve Forces

### 8b. Hourglass, Silver

**Services:** All
**Worn on:** Armed Forces Reserve Medal
**Denotes:** 20 Years of service in the Reserve Forces

### 8c. Hourglass, Gold

**Services:** All
**Worn on:** Armed Forces Reserve Medal
**Denotes:** 30 Years of service in the Reserve Forces

### 9. Hurricane Device, Gold

**Services:** Coast Guard
**Worn on:** USCG Presidential Unit Citation
**Denotes:** Service during the aftermath of Hurricane Katrina

### 10. Letter "A", Block, Bronze

**Services:** Navy, Marine Corps, Coast Guard
**Worn on:** American Defense Service Medal
**Denotes:** Atlantic Fleet service prior to World War II

### 11. Letter "A", Serif, Bronze

**Services:** Air Force
**Worn on:** Overseas Service Ribbon (Short Tour)
**Denotes:** Service at bases above the Arctic Circle

### 12. Letter "E", Serif, Bronze

**Services:** Navy, Coast Guard
**Worn on:** Marksmanship Ribbons
**Denotes:** First "Expert" qualification **(Obsolete)**

### 13. Letter "E", Serif, Silver

**Services:** Navy, Coast Guard
**Worn on:** Marksmanship Ribbons
**Denotes:** "Expert" weapons qualification

### 14. Letter "E", Block, Silver

**Services:** Navy, Marine Corps.
**Worn on:** Navy "E" Ribbon
**Denotes:** Initial and subsequent awards (3 maximum)

### 15. Letter "E", Wreathed, Silver

**Services:** Navy, Marine Corps.
**Worn on:** Navy "E" Ribbon
**Denotes:** Fourth (Final) award

### 16. Letter "M", Block, Bronze

**Services:** All
**Worn on:** Armed Forces Reserve Medal
**Denotes:** Mobilization for active military service

### 17. Letter "N", Block, Gold

**Services:** Navy
**Worn on:** Navy Presidential Unit Citation
**Denotes:** Service aboard USS Nautilus during 1st cruise under the Arctic ice cap

### 18. Letter "O", Block, Silver

**Services:** Coast Guard
**Worn on:** Meritorious Service Medal and USCG decorations
**Denotes:** Distinguished operational service by individual

### 19. Letter "O", Block, Silver

**Services:** Coast Guard
**Worn on:** Coast Guard Unit Awards
**Denotes:** Distinguished operational service by cited unit

### 20. Letter "S", Block, Bronze

**Services:** Navy
**Worn on:** Navy Marksmanship ribbons
**Denotes:** Sharpshooter qualification

### 21. Letter "S", Block, Silver

**Services:** Coast Guard
**Worn on:** Coast Guard Marksmanship ribbons
**Denotes:** Sharpshooter qualification

### 22. Letter "V", Serif, Bronze

**Services:** All (Except Marine Corps)
**Worn on:** Personal decorations
**Denotes:** Valorous actions in combat

### 23. Letter "V", Serif, Bronze

**Services:** Air Force
**Worn on:** Outstanding Unit Award and Organizational Excellence Award
**Denotes:** Valorous actions by unit in combat

### 24. Letter "V", Serif, Bronze

**Services:** All
**Worn on:** Joint Service Commendation Medal
**Denotes:** Valorous actions in combat

# Armed Forces Ribbon Devices *(Listed Alphabetically)*

**25. Letter "V", Serif, Gold**

Services: Marine Corps
Worn on: Personal Decorations
Denotes: Valorous actions in combat

**26. Letter "W", Block, Silver**

Services: Navy, Marine Corps.
Worn on: Expeditionary Medals
Denotes: Participation in the defense of Wake Island (Dec, 1941)

**27. Maltese Cross, Bronze**

Services: Navy
Worn on: World War I Victory Medal
Denotes: Service by Navy personnel with the AEF

**28. Marine Device, Bronze**

Services: Navy
Worn on: Campaign medals since World War II
Denotes: Service by Naval combat personnel with Marine Corps units

**29a. Medal, Miniature, Gold**

Services: Foreign military personnel
Worn on: Legion of Merit
Denotes: Level of award ("Chief Commander")

**29b. Medal, Miniature, Silver**

Services: Foreign military personnel
Worn on: Legion of Merit
Denotes: Level of award ("Commander")

**29c. Medal, Miniature, Gold**

Services: Foreign military personnel
Worn on: Legion of Merit
Denotes: Level of award ("Officer")

**30. Numeral, Block, Bronze**

Services: Navy, Marine Corps.
Worn on: Air Medal
Denotes: Total number of Strike/Flight awards

**31. Numeral, Block, Bronze**

Services: Army
Worn on: Air Medal
Denotes: Total number of awards

**32. Numeral, Block, Bronze**

Services: All (Except Coast Guard)
Worn on: Humanitarian Service Medal
Denotes: Number of additional awards **(Obsolete)**

**33. Numeral, Block, Bronze**

Services: All
Worn on: Armed Forces Reserve Medal
Denotes: Number of times mobilized for active duty

**34. Numeral, Block, Bronze**

Services: Navy
Worn on: Navy Recruiting Service Ribbon
Denotes: Total number of "Gold Wreath" awards

**35. Numeral, Block, Bronze**

Services: Army
Worn on: Overseas Service and Reserve Components Overseas Training Ribbons
Denotes: Total number of awards

**36. Numeral, Block, Bronze**

Services: All
Worn on: Multinational Force & Observers Medal
Denotes: Total number of awards

**37a. Numeral "2", Block, Bronze**

Services: Army
Worn on: NCO Professional Development Ribbon
Denotes: Level of professional training achieved ("Basic")

**37b. Numeral "3", Block, Bronze**

Services: Army
Worn on: NCO Professional Development Ribbon
Denotes: Level of professional training achieved ("Advanced")

**37c. Numeral "4", Block, Bronze**

Services: Army
Worn on: NCO Professional Development Ribbon
Denotes: Level of professional training achieved ("Senior")

**37d. Numeral "5", Block, Bronze**

Services: Army
Worn on: NCO Professional Development Ribbon
Denotes: Completion of Sergeants-Major Academy **(Obsolete)**

**38. Numeral, Block, Gold**

Services: Navy, Marine Corps
Worn on: Air Medal
Denotes: Total number of individual awards

**39. Numeral, Scroll, Bronze**

Services: Marine Corps
Worn on: Marine Corps Good Conduct and Expeditionary Medals
Denotes: Number of awards **(Obsolete)**

**40. Numeral, Scroll, Bronze**

Services: Navy
Worn on: World War II Campaign Medals
Denotes: Number of battle clasps earned **(Obsolete)**

**41. Oak Leaf Cluster, Bronze**
Services: Army, Air Force
Worn on: Personal Decorations
Denotes: One (1) additional award

**42. Oak Leaf Cluster, Bronze**

Services: Army, Air Force
Worn on: Unit Awards
Denotes: One (1) additional award

**43. Oak Leaf Cluster, Bronze**

Services: Air Force
Worn on: Service and Reserve Awards
Denotes: One (1) additional award

**44. Oak Leaf Cluster, Bronze**

Services: Army
Worn on: Reserve Components Achievement Medal
Denotes: One (1) additional award

**45. Oak Leaf Cluster, Bronze**

Services: All
Worn on: Joint Service Decorations and Joint Meritorious Unit Award
Denotes: One (1) additional award

**46. Oak Leaf Cluster, Bronze**

Services: Air Force
Worn on: Recognition Awards
Denotes: One (1) additional award

**47. Oak Leaf Cluster, Bronze**

Services: Army
Worn on: National Defense Service Medal
Denotes: One (1) additional award **(Obsolete)**

**48. Oak Leaf Cluster, Silver**

Services: Army, Air Force
Worn on: Personal Decorations
Denotes: Five (5) additional awards

**49. Oak Leaf Cluster, Silver**

Services: Army, Air Force
Worn on: Unit Awards
Denotes: Five (5) additional awards

# Armed Forces Ribbon Devices *(Listed Alphabetically)*

**50. Oak Leaf Cluster, Silver**

**Services:** Air Force
**Worn on:** Service and Reserve Awards
**Denotes:** Five (5) additional awards

**51. Oak Leaf Cluster, Silver**

**Services:** All
**Worn on:** Joint Service decorations and Joint Meritorious Unit Award
**Denotes:** Five (5) additional awards

**52. Oak Leaf Cluster, Silver**

**Services:** Air Force
**Worn on:** Recognition Awards
**Denotes:** Five (5) additional awards

**53. Palm, Bronze**

**Services:** All (Except Army)
**Worn on:** Vietnam Gallantry Cross Unit Citation
**Denotes:** No significance, worn upon initial issue

**54. Palm, Bronze**
**Services:** All
**Worn on:** Vietnam Civil Actions Unit Citation
**Denotes:** No significance, worn upon initial issue

**55. Palm, Bronze**

**Services:** Army
**Worn on:** Vietnam Gallantry Cross Unit Citation
**Denotes:** Level of Award ("Cited before the Army")

**56. Palm & Swords Device, Gold**

**Services:** All
**Worn on:** Kuwait Liberation Medal (Saudi Arabia)
**Denotes:** No significance, worn upon initial issue

**57. Pistol, M1911A1, Bronze**

**Services:** Coast Guard
**Worn on:** Pistol Marksmanship Ribbon
**Denotes:** Recipient of Pistol Shot Excellence in Competition Badge (Bronze)

**58. Pistol, M1911A1, Silver**

**Services:** Coast Guard
**Worn on:** Pistol Marksmanship Ribbon
**Denotes:** Recipient of Pistol Shot Excellence in Competition Badge (Silver)

**59. Rifle, M-14, Bronze**

**Services:** Coast Guard
**Worn on:** Rifle Marksmanship Ribbon
**Denotes:** Recipient of Rifleman Excellence in Competition Badge (Bronze)

**60. Rifle, M-14, Silver**

**Services:** Coast Guard
**Worn on:** Rifle Marksmanship Ribbon
**Denotes:** Recipient of Rifleman Excellence in Competition Badge (Silver)

**61. Seahorse, Silver**

**Services:** Merchant Marine
**Worn on:** Gallant Ship Citation Bar
**Denotes:** No significance, worn upon initial issue

**62. Star 3/16" dia., Blue**

**Services:** Navy, Marine Corps
**Worn on:** Navy Presidential Unit Citation
**Denotes:** Initial and subsequent awards **(Obsolete)**

**63. Star 3/16" dia., Bronze**

**Services:** All
**Worn on:** Campaign awards since World War II
**Denotes:** Battle participation (one star per major engagement)

**64. Star 3/16" dia., Bronze**

**Services:** All
**Worn on:** Expeditionary Medals
**Denotes:** Additional service (one star per designated expedition)

**65. Star 3/16" dia., Bronze**

**Services:** All
**Worn on:** Prisoner of War and Humanitarian Service Medals
**Denotes:** One (1) additional award

**66. Star 3/16" dia., Bronze**

**Services:** Navy, Marine Corps.
**Worn on:** Unit Awards
**Denotes:** One (1) star per each additional award

**67. Star 3/16" dia., Bronze**

**Services:** All
**Worn on:** Service Awards
**Denotes:** One (1) star per each additional award

**68. Star 3/16" dia., Bronze**

**Services:** Navy
**Worn on:** Letter of Commendation Ribbon with Pendant
**Denotes:** One additional award **(Obsolete)**

**69. Star 3/16" dia., Bronze**

**Services:** Navy and Marine Corps.
**Worn on:** Air Medal
**Denotes:** First individual award **(Obsolete)**

**70. Star 3/16" dia., Bronze**

**Services:** Air Force
**Worn on:** Outstanding Airman of the Year Award
**Denotes:** "One of 12" competition finalist

**71. Star 3/16" dia., Bronze**

**Services:** Air Force
**Worn on:** Small Arms Expert Marksmanship Ribbon
**Denotes:** Additional weapon qualification

**72. Star 3/16" dia., Bronze**

**Services:** All
**Worn on:** World War I Victory Medal
**Denotes:** One (1) star for each campaign clasp earned

**73. Star 3/16" dia., Bronze**

**Services:** Navy, Marine Corps, Coast Guard
**Worn on:** China Service Medal (1937-39)
**Denotes:** Additional award for service during (1945-57)

**74. Star 3/16" dia., Bronze**

**Services:** Coast Guard
**Worn on:** Combat Action Ribbon
**Denotes:** One (1) additional award

**75. Star 3/16" dia., Bronze**

**Services:** All
**Worn on:** American Defense Service Medal
**Denotes:** Overseas service prior to World War II

**76. Star 3/16" dia., Bronze**

**Services:** All
**Worn on:** National Defense Service Medal
**Denotes:** Additional awards (one star per designated period)

**77. Star 3/16" dia., Bronze**

**Services:** Coast Guard
**Worn on:** Joint Meritorious Unit Award
**Denotes:** One (1) additional award

**78. Star 3/16" dia., Bronze**

**Services:** Coast Guard
**Worn on:** Antarctica Service Medal
**Denotes:** One (1) additional award

**79. Star 3/16" dia., Bronze**

**Services:** All
**Worn on:** Philippine Defense and Liberation Ribbons
**Denotes:** Additional battle honors

**80. Star 3/16" dia., Bronze**

Services: All (Except Army)
Worn on: Philippine Presidential Unit Citation
Denotes: Additional award

**81. Star 3/16" dia., Bronze**
Services: All
Worn on: United Nations and NATO mission medals
Denotes: One (1) star for each additional mission

**82. Star 3/16" dia., Silver**
Services: All
Worn on: Campaign awards since World War II
Denotes: Battle participation in five (5) major engagements

**83. Star 3/16" dia., Silver**
Services: All
Worn on: Expeditionary Medals
Denotes: Five (5) additional expeditions

**84. Star 3/16" dia., Silver**
Services: All
Worn on: Prisoner of War and Humanitarian Service Medals
Denotes: Five (5) additional awards

**85. Star 3/16" dia., Silver**

Services: Navy, Marine Corps
Worn on: Unit awards
Denotes: Five (5) additional awards

**86. Star 3/16" dia., Silver**

Services: All
Worn on: Service Awards
Denotes: Five (5) additional Awards

**87. Star 3/16" dia., Silver**
Services: Navy
Worn on: World War I Victory Medal
Denotes: Receipt of Letter of Commendation

**88. Star 3/16" dia., Silver**

Services: Army
Worn on: Campaign medals up to World War I
Denotes: Citation for Gallantry

**89. Star 3/16" dia., Silver**
Services: Coast Guard
Worn on: Joint Meritorious Unit Award
Denotes: Five (5) additional awards

**90. Star 3/16" dia., Silver**

Services: Merchant Marine
Worn on: Combat Bar
Denotes: Crew member forced to abandon ship (one star per sinking)

**91. Star 5/16" dia., Bronze**

Services: Navy, Marine Corps.
Worn on: Navy, USMC Expeditionary Medals
Denotes: One (1) additional award (**Obsolete**)

**92. Star 5/16" dia., Bronze**

Services: Navy, Marine Corps.
Worn on: Haitian Campaign Medal (1915)
Denotes: Subsequent award of the "1919-1920" Clasp

**93. Star 5/16" dia., Gold**

Services: Navy, Marine Corps, Coast Guard
Worn on: Personal Decorations
Denotes: One (1) additional award

**94. Star 5/16" dia., Gold**

Services: Coast Guard
Worn on: Unit awards
Denotes: One (1) additional award

**95. Star 5/16" dia., Gold**

Services: Air Force
Worn on: Combat Action Medal
Denotes: One (1) additional award

**96. Star 5/16" dia., Gold**

Services: Navy, Marine Corps
Worn on: Combat Action Ribbon
Denotes: One (1) additional award

**97. Star 5/16" dia., Gold**

Services: Coast Guard
Worn on: Joint Service Awards
Denotes: One (1) additional award (**Obsolete**)

**98. Star 5/16" dia., Gold**

Services: Coast Guard
Worn on: Lifesaving Medals
Denotes: One (1) additional award

**99. Star 5/16" dia., Gold**

Services: All
Worn on: Inter-American Defense Board Medal
Denotes: One (1) additional award

**100. Star 5/16" dia., Gold**

Services: Army
Worn on: Army Sea Duty Ribbon
Denotes: 10th (final) award

**101. Star 5/16" dia., Silver**

Services: Navy, Marine Corps, Coast Guard
Worn on: Personal Decorations
Denotes: Five (5) additional awards

**102. Star 5/16" dia., Silver**

Services: Coast Guard
Worn on: Unit Awards
Denotes: Five (5) additional awards

**103. Star 5/16" dia., Silver**

Services: Coast Guard
Worn on: Joint Service Awards
Denotes: Five (5) additional awards (**Obsolete**)

**104. Star 5/16" dia., Silver**

Services: Navy
Worn on: World War II Campaign Medals
Denotes: Five (5) major campaigns (**Obsolete**)

**105. Star 3/8" dia., Bronze**

Services: Army
Worn on: Vietnam Gallantry Cross Unit Citation
Denotes: Level of award ("Cited before the Regiment")

**106. Star 3/8" dia., Silver**

Services: Army
Worn on: Vietnam Gallantry Cross Unit Citation
Denotes: Level of award ("Cited before the Division")

**107. Star 3/8" dia., Gold**

Services: Army
Worn on: Vietnam Gallantry Cross Unit Citation
Denotes: Level of award ("Cited before the Corps")

**108. Target, Pistol, Gold**

Services: Coast Guard
Worn on: Pistol Marksmanship Ribbon
Denotes: Recipient of Distinguished Pistol Shot Badge

**109. Target, Rifle, Gold**

Services: Coast Guard
Worn on: Rifle Marksmanship Ribbon
Denotes: Recipient of Distinguished Marksman Badge

**110 Letter "C", Serif, Bronze**

Services: New for all
Worn on: Personal decorations
Denotes: award was earned in a combat setting

**111. Letter "R", Serif, Bronze**

Services: New for All
Worn on: Personal decorations
Denotes: Recognize remote combat action.

# Placement of the Letter "V" on the Ribbon and Medal

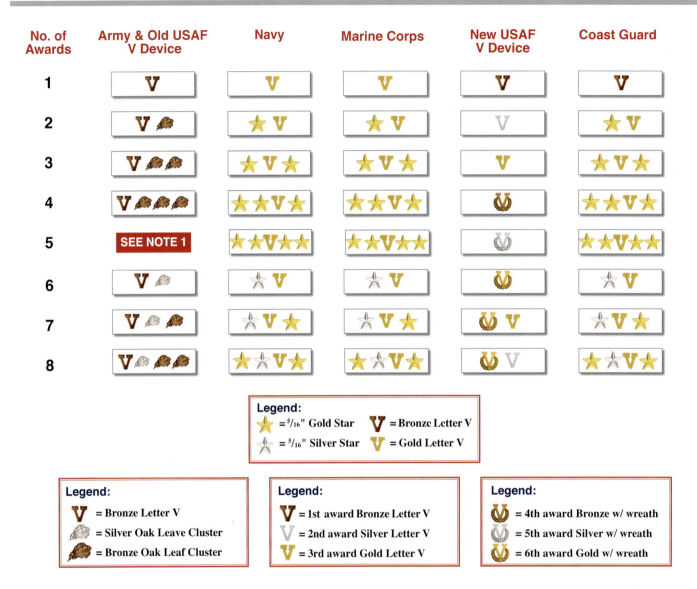

# Placement of Devices on the Armed Forces Reserve Medal

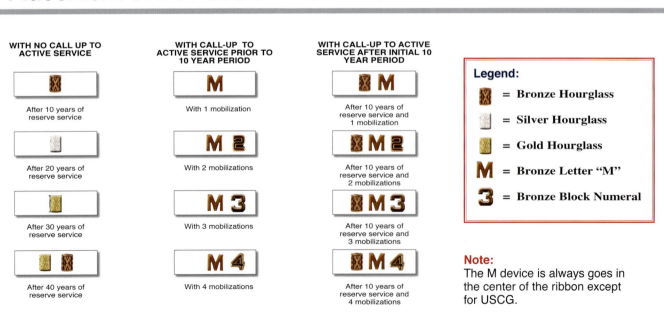

# Placement of Silver & Gold Stars and Bronze & Silver Oak Leaf Devices on Ribbons

# Placement of Oak Leaf Cluster Devices on the Ribbon

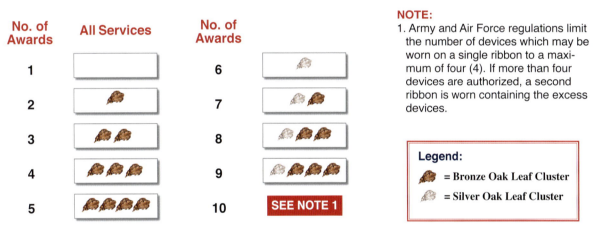

# Device Usage on the Navy Air Medal

## Navy and Marine Corps (Individual Awards)

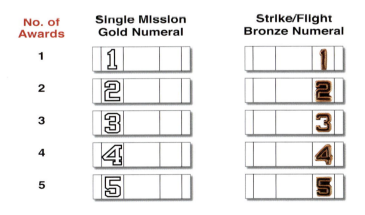

Since April 5, 1974, the Combat "V" may be authorized for awards for heroism or meritorious action in conflict with an armed enemy.

**Ribbon devices (1989–2006)**

Between November 22, 1989, and September 27, 2006, 3/16 inch bronze stars, 5/16 inch gold stars, and 5/16 inch silver stars denoted the number of "Individual" Air Medals. A bronze star denoted a first award. Gold stars were used for the second through the fifth awards with Silver stars used for five gold stars. For "Individual" Air Medals, the Combat "V" could be authorized.

Bronze Strike/Flight numerals denoted the number of Strike/Flight awards authorized for operations in hostile or disputed territory and count the total number of Strikes (operations that faced enemy opposition) and Flights (operations that did not encounter enemy opposition) added together.

**Air Medal Device Arrangements.** As of September 27, 2006, gold Numeral devices are used to denote the number of "Individual" Air Medals.

Bronze Strike/Flight numerals denote the total number of Strike/Flight awards. Strikes are combat sorties that encounter enemy opposition. Flights are combat sorties that do not encounter enemy opposition.

# Placement Campaign Stars on the Ribbon

| No. of Campaigns | All Service | No. of Campaigns | Army & Air Force | Navy | Marine Corps | Coast Guard |
|---|---|---|---|---|---|---|
| 1 | ★ | 5 | ✰ | ✰ | ✰ | ✰ |
| 2 | ★★ | 6 | ✰★ | ✰★ | ✰★ | ✰★ |
| 3 | ★★★ | 7 | ✰★★ | ★✰★ | ★✰★ | ★✰★ |
| 4 | ★★★★ | 8 | ✰★★★ | ★★✰★ | ★✰★★ | ★★✰★ |
| 5 | ✰ | 9 | SEE NOTE 1 | ★★✰★★ | ★★✰★★ | ★★✰★★ |

**NOTE:**
1. Army and Air Force regulations limit the number of devices which may be worn on a single ribbon to a maximum of four. If more than four devices are authorized, a second ribbon is worn containing the excess devices.
2. Campaign stars are often referred to as "Battle Stars".

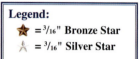

Legend:
★ = 3/16" Bronze Star
✰ = 3/16" Silver Star

# C Combat & R Remote Device Placement on the Ribbon

| No. of Awards | Army C Device | Navy | Marine Corps | New USAF C Device | Coast Guard |
|---|---|---|---|---|---|
| 1 | C | C | C | C | C |
| 2 | C🍂 | ★C | ★C | C | ★C |
| 3 | C🍂🍂 | ★C★ | ★C★ | C | ★C★ |
| 4 | C🍂🍂🍂 | ★★C★ | ★★C★ | Ⓒ | ★★C★ |
| 5 | SEE NOTE 1 | ★★C★★ | ★★C★★ | Ⓒ | ★★C★★ |

| No. of Awards | Army R Device | Navy | Marine Corps | Coast Guard |
|---|---|---|---|---|
| 1 | R | R | R | R |
| 2 | R🍂 | ★R | ★R | ★R |
| 3 | R🍂🍂 | ★R★ | ★R★ | ★R★ |
| 4 | R🍂🍂🍂 | ★★R★ | ★★R★ | ★★R★ |
| 5 | SEE NOTE 1 | ★★R★★ | ★★R★★ | ★★R★★ |

When both C and R device are awarded the C goes before the R and the V before both.

CR    VCR    CR🍂    ★CR

# Placement of the USAF V, C and R Devices

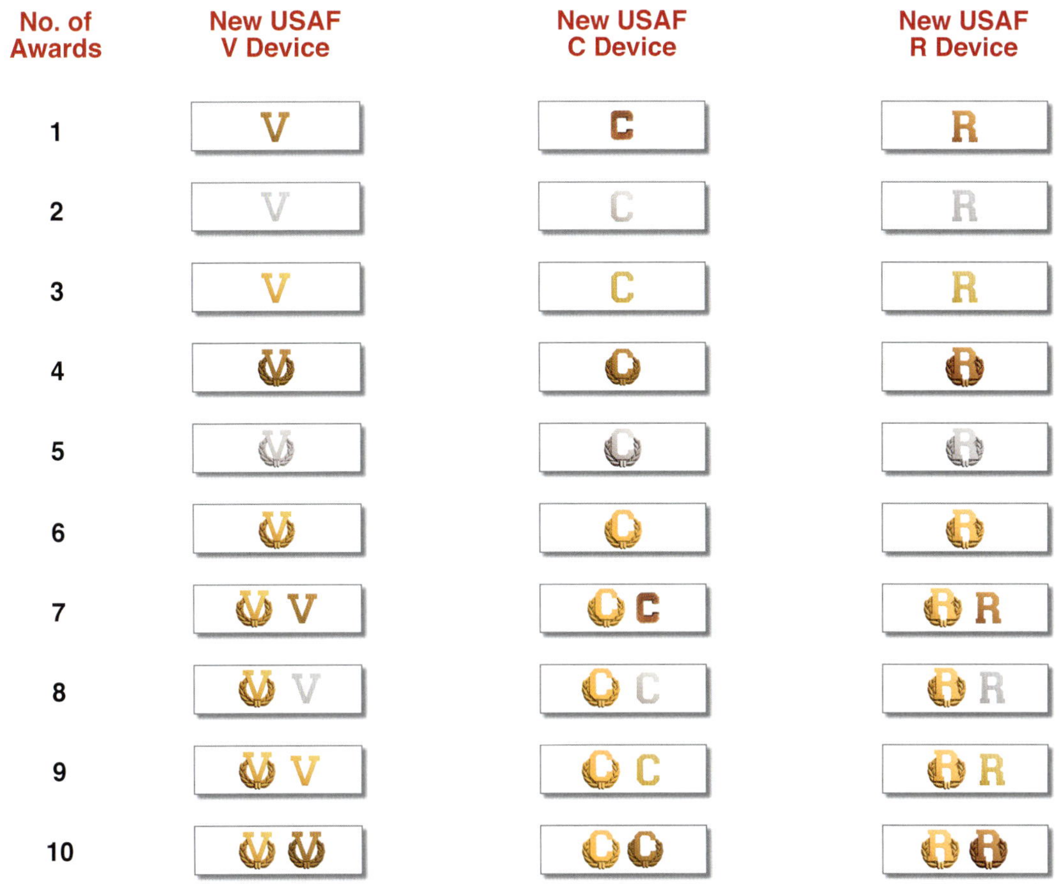

Air Force

| No. of Awards | New USAF V Device | New USAF C Device | New USAF R Device |
|---|---|---|---|
| 1 | V | C | R |
| 2 | V (silver) | C (silver) | R (silver) |
| 3 | V (gold) | C (gold) | R (gold) |
| 4 | Bronze V w/ wreath | Bronze C w/ wreath | Bronze R w/ wreath |
| 5 | Silver V w/ wreath | Silver C w/ wreath | Silver R w/ wreath |
| 6 | Gold V w/ wreath | Gold C w/ wreath | Gold R w/ wreath |
| 7 | Bronze wreath V + V | Bronze wreath C + C | Bronze wreath R + R |
| 8 | Bronze wreath V + Silver V | Bronze wreath C + Silver C | Bronze wreath R + Silver R |
| 9 | Bronze wreath V + Gold V | Bronze wreath C + Gold C | Bronze wreath R + Gold R |
| 10 | Two bronze wreath V | Two bronze wreath C | Two bronze wreath R |

**Legend:**
- V 1st award Bronze Letter V
- V 2nd award Silver Letter V
- V 3rd award Gold Letter V

**Legend:**
- 4th award Bronze w/ wreath
- 5th award Silver w/ wreath
- 6th award Gold w/ wreath

**Legend:**
- C 1st award Bronze Letter C
- C 2nd award Silver Letter C
- C 3rd award Gold Letter C

**Legend:**
- 4th award Bronze C w/ wreath
- 5th award Silver C w/ wreath
- 6th award Gold C w/ wreath

**Legend:**
- R 1st award Bronze Letter R
- R 2nd award Silver Letter R
- R 3rd award Gold Letter R

**Legend:**
- 4th award Bronze R w/ wreath
- 5th award Silver R w/ wreath
- 6th award Gold R w/ wreath

# The Early United States Military Medals

The first military medals of the United States clearly showed the country's elected leadership's identification with the private soldier, volunteers, militia and a basic avoidance of awards for the professional officer corps. The first six awards on this page were originally only for private Soldiers, Sailors and Marines. The Marine Corps Brevet Medal came into being reflecting the frustration of Marine Corps officers who were not eligible for the Medal of Honor until 1915. Only when Theodore Roosevelt, a former volunteer officer became President did the Congress begin to truly recognize both volunteers and professional military service.

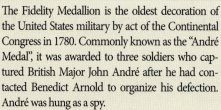

The Fidelity Medallion is the oldest decoration of the United States military by act of the Continental Congress in 1780. Commonly known as the "André Medal", it was awarded to three soldiers who captured British Major John André after he had contacted Benedict Arnold to organize his defection. André was hung as a spy.

The face of the medallion contains the inscription "FIDELITY" and the reverse "AMOR PATRIÆ VINCIT", which means: "The love of country conquers."

The Fidelity Medallion, was never again awarded and became regarded as a commemorative decoration. The Badge of Military Merit is generally considered the first U.S. military decoration although, created two years later in 1782.

The Badge of Military Merit was announced in General Washington's General Orders to the Continental Army on 7 August 1782. Designed by Washington in the form of a purple heart, it was intended as a military order for soldiers who exhibited: "not only instances of unusual gallantry in battle, but also extraordinary fidelity and essential service in any way." General Washington created three badges, two Honorary Badges of Distinction and a Badge of Military Merit on 7 August 1782. These are the first awards presented to the private soldier as opposed to the European practice of honoring high-ranking officers for victory, rather than private soldiers. However General Washington said, "the road to glory in a patriot army and a free country is open to all".

The Army Certificate of Merit was issued in medal form between the years of 1905 to 1918, Replacing the much older Certificate of Merit issued in 1847 for valor in action during the Mexican-American War. Originally only authorized for Privates in 1854 it was approved for Sergeants but never authorized for officers.

In 1892, the criteria was changed to include distinguished service in action. Although awarded for non-combat heroism, it was generally awarded for gallantry against the enemy.

It could only be awarded once and became obsolete July 9, 1918 with the establishment of the Distinguished Service Cross and Distinguished Service Medal.

The Army Medal of Honor was signed into law on July 12, 1862. To be awarded: "to such non-commissioned officers and privates as shall most distinguish themselves by their gallantry in action, and other soldier-like qualities, during the present insurrection." The original design of the Army Medal of Honor shows the goddess Minerva fending off a symbol of discord. The thirty-four stars surrounding the figures represent the number of states in the Union. Later in the war it was approved for award to Army Officers.

The Navy Medal of Valor was signed into law by President Lincoln on December 21, 1861. Soon renamed the Medal of Honor, it was "to be bestowed upon such Petty Officers, Seamen, Landsmen and Marines as shall most distinguish themselves by their gallantry and other seaman like qualities during the present war." It was not approved for Officers until 1915.

The Secretary of the Navy authorized a Good Conduct Badge on April 26, 1869 to help re-enlistments. The badge, a Maltese cross, had the words "FIDELITY - ZEAL - OBEDIENCE" in a circle with "U.S.N." in the center of the disc. The reverse was for the engraved recipients name. A one-half inch wide red, white and blue ribbon was supplied without a suspension pin. Initially, the badge was awarded to "... any man holding a Continuous Service Certificate who: "has distinguished himself for obedience, sobriety, and cleanliness, and is proficient in seamanship and gunnery..." Sailors were presented a separate badge for each discharge and promoted to Petty Officer upon receipt of their third award. It was replaced in 1884 by the now-familiar Navy Good Conduct Medal.

The Marine Corps Brevet Medal was authorized in 1921 for Marine officers who had received brevet commissions between April 15, 1861 and March 3, 1915. As the Medal of Honor was not available to Marine officers until 1915, the brevet promotion was the only means to reward these individuals for outstanding service or gallantry in action. Although originally intended for all Marine officers who qualified, it was ultimately limited to 20 surviving active duty and retired officers. Since the last action for which brevet promotions had been bestowed was the Boxer Rebellion (1900-01), the Brevet Medal became obsolete on the day it was issued. After many years of indecision, the Brevet Medal was elevated to its final precedence immediately after the Medal of Honor in 1937 and declared obsolete in 1940.

*With malice toward none with charity for all.*

### Civil War Campaign Medal (Army)
**Service:** Army **Instituted:** 1905
**Dates:** 1861-1866
**Criteria:** Active Federal service between April 1861 and April 1865 or service in Texas between April 1861 and August 1866.
**Devices:** ★ (88)

### Civil War Service Medal (Navy)
**Service:** Navy, Marine Corps.
**Instituted:** 1908 **Dates:** 1861-1865
**Criteria:** Active service in the Union Navy or Marine Corps afloat or ashore between April 1861 and April 1865.

The Civil War Campaign Medal is chronologically the first campaign service medal and was authorized in 1905 on the fortieth anniversary of the Civil War. The blue and gray ribbon reflects the uniform colors of both U.S. and Confederate soldiers. The Army Civil War Campaign Medal required that a soldier had to serve between 1861 and 1866 when President Johnson signed a Proclamation officially ending the war. The Navy and Marine Civil War Medal was established June 27, 1908.

The front of the Army Civil War Campaign Medal displayed a bust of Abraham Lincoln while the Navy and Marine Corps versions depicted the USS Monitor and CSS Virginia's battle in Hampton Roads. The reverse of the medal displays "The Civil War 1861-1865" encircled by a wreath.

The medal was first established as a badge due to costs. In 1956, some 90 years after the Civil War, Congress provided the government provide the medal to all Civil War qualified veterans (whether they were Union or Confederate).

In the center the bronze medal is the head of Lincoln encircled by inscription, WITH MALICE TOWARD NONE WITH CHARITY FOR ALL.

The back of the medal is inscribed THE CIVIL WAR over a bar, under which appear the dates 1861-1865; surrounded by a wreath composed of a branch of oak on the left and a branch of laurel on the right, joined at the base by a bow. The oak representing the strength of the United States and the laurel representing its victory.

The Navy and Marine Corps versions have different backs as shown above. The medal was designed by Francis D. Millet, a noted sculptor who perished on the RMS Titanic in 1912. The Civil War Campaign Medal was the first campaign medal authorized for Marine Corps veterans and only about 200 medals were minted and numbered on the rims for Marine Corps Civil War veterans. Less than two dozen original issued numbered medals are known to exist making them the rarest of all Marine Corps Campaign Medals.

Confederate soldiers, sailors, and marines who fought in the Civil War, were made U.S. Veterans by an act of Congress in 1957. U.S. Public Law 85-425 May 23, 1958 (H.R. 358) (Attached & Link Below)

This made the Confederate Army, Navy, and Marine Veterans equal to U.S. Veterans. Additionally, under U.S. Public Law 810 (Link Below), approved by the 17th Congress on 26 Feb 1929, The War Department was directed to erect headstones and recognize Confederate grave sites as U.S. War grave sites.

US. Public Law 85-425 May 23, 1958 (H.R. 358)

"(e) For the purpose of this section, and section 433, the term 'veteran' includes a person who served in the military or naval forces of the Confederate States of America during the Civil War, and the term 'active, military or naval service' includes active service in such forces. The Act of Congress can be founded at:

http://uscode.house.gov/statutes/pl/85/425.pdf
http://uscode.house.gov/statutes/pl/85/810.pdf

### Indian Campaign Medal (Army)

**Service:** Army
**Instituted:** 1905
**Dates:** 1865-1891
**Criteria:** Service during the above years in campaigns in the Western United States against hostile indian tribes.
**Devices:** ★ (88)

### Spanish Campaign Medal (Army)

**Service:** Army
**Instituted:** 1905  **Dates:** 1898
**Criteria:** Services ashore or en route to any of the following areas:
*Cuba:* May-July 1898
*Puerto Rico:* July-Aug 1898
*Philippine Islands:* June-Aug 1898
**Devices:** ★ (88)

### Spanish Campaign Medal (Navy)

**Service:** Navy, Marine Corps
**Instituted:** 1908  **Dates:** 1898
**Criteria:** Service by all Navy & Marine Corps personnel in the naval activities of the Spanish-American War.

### West Indies Campaign Medal (Navy)

**Service:** Navy, Marine Corps.
**Instituted:** 1908 **Dates:** 1898
**Criteria:** Originally awarded to Naval veterans of the West Indies Campaign. Later replaced by the Spanish Campaign Medal.
**Notes:** First ribbon version.

### Manila Bay ("Dewey") Medal (Navy)

**Service:** Navy
**Instituted:** 1898
**Dates:** 1898
**Criteria:** Awarded to all officers and men under Commodore George Dewey's command during the defeat of the Spanish Navy at Manila Bay.

### West Indies Naval Campaign ("Sampson") Medal (Navy)

**Service:** Navy, Marine Corps.
**Instituted:** 1901
**Dates:** 1868
**Criteria:** Participation in the naval engagements in the West Indies and on the shores of Cuba.

### Specially Meritorious Medal (Navy)

**Service:** Navy, Marine Corps.
**Instituted:** 1901
**Dates:** 1898
**Criteria:** Performance of specially meritorious service other than battle during the Spanish-American War.

### Spanish War Service Medal (Army)

**Service:** Army
**Instituted:** 1918
**Dates:** 1898
**Criteria:** Awarded to all regular or volunteer army personnel who served during the above period but did not qualify for the Spanish Campaign Medal.

### Army of Cuban Occupation Medal (Army)
**Service:** Army
**Instituted:** 1915
**Dates:** 1898-1902
**Criteria:** Service by Army personnel who participated in the occupation of Cuba during the above dates at the end of the War with Spain.

### Army of Occupation of Puerto Rico Medal (Army)
**Service:** Army
**Instituted:** 1919
**Dates:** 1898
**Criteria:** Service during the occupation of Puerto Rico between 14 August and 10 December, 1898

### Philippine Campaign Medal (Army)
**Service:** Army
**Instituted:** 1905
**Dates:** 1899-1913
**Criteria:** Awarded to Army personnel who served in campaigns ashore during the above dates to quell the Philippine Insurrection.
**Devices:** ★ (88)

### Philippine Campaign Medal (Navy)
**Service:** Navy, Marine Corps.
**Instituted:** 1908  **Dates:** 1899-1906
**Criteria:** Awarded to Navy & Marine Corps personnel who served on ships in Philippine waters and four shore stations.

### Philippine Congressional Medal (Army)
**Service:** Army
**Instituted:** 1906
**Dates:** 1899-1902
**Criteria:** Awarded to Army personnel who volunteered to serve beyond their discharge date and were ashore in the Philippine Islands during above dates.

### China Campaign Medal (Army)
**Service:** Army
**Instituted:** 1905  **Dates:** 1900-1905
**Criteria:** Service ashore with the Peking Relief Expedition during the Boxer Rebellion between 20 June 1900 and 27 May 1901.
**Devices:** ★ (88)

### China Relief Expedition Medal (Navy)
**Service:** Navy, Marine Corps.
**Instituted:** 1908  **Dates:** 1900-1901
**Criteria:** Service ashore in China or as crew members on specific vessels during the period of the Boxer Rebellion.

### Army of Cuban Pacification Medal (Army)
**Service:** Army
**Instituted:** 1909  **Dates:** 1906-1909
**Criteria:** Awarded to all Army personnel who served in Cuba between October 1906 and April 1909 to assist the new government during the insurrection.

### Cuban Pacification Medal (Navy)
**Service:** Navy & Marine Corps.
**Instituted:** 1909   **Dates:** 1898-1902
**Criteria:** Service by personnel who served on land and aboard ship in Cuban waters during the specified time period.

### Nicaraguan Campaign (Navy)
**Service:** Navy & Marine Corps.
**Instituted:** 1913  **Dates:** 1912
**Criteria:** Awarded to personnel who served ashore and specific ships in Nicaraguan waters between Sept 1906 and April 1909.

### Mexican Service Medal (Army)
**Service:** Army
**Instituted:** 1917
**Dates:** 1914-1919
**Criteria:** Awarded to Army personnel who participated in engagements or expeditions in Mexico during 10 specific time periods from April 1914 to June, 1919.
**Devices:** ★ (88)

### Mexican Service Medal (Navy)
**Service:** Navy, Marine Corps.
**Instituted:** 1918   **Dates:** 1914-1917
**Criteria:** Awarded to Navy & Marine Corps personnel who served ashore or on ships in Mexican waters during the above period.

### Haitian Campaign Medal (Navy)
**Service:** Navy & Marine Corps.
**Instituted:** 1917   **Dates:** 1915
**Criteria:** Awarded to personnel who served ashore in Haiti or on ships in Haitian waters during the period of July 9 to Dec. 1915.
**Devices:** ★ (92)

### Dominican Campaign (Navy)
**Service:** Navy & Marine Corps.
**Instituted:** 1921   **Dates:** 1916
**Criteria:** Service ashore in Santo Domingo or on specific ships operating in Dominican waters between May and Dec., 1916.

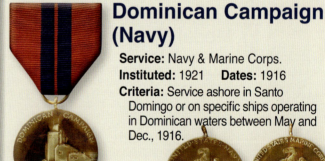

### Mexican Border Service Medal (Army)
**Service:** Army
**Instituted:** 1918
**Dates:** 1916-1917
**Criteria:** Awarded to Army and National Guard troops who served on the Mexican border between January 1916 and April 1917.

Note: Device numerals refer to expanded information on pages 116-119

# World War I Victory Medal

Regulation Ribbon Bar

WW I Style Ribbon with Silver Star

Bronze

Medal Reverse

| Service | All Services |
| --- | --- |
| Instituted | 1919 |
| Criteria | Awarded to all military personnel who served in the Continental United States or overseas between April, 1917 and April, 1920. |
| Devices | Bronze Star, Silver Star |

Battle Clasp

Service Clasp

*Unlike the army, the navy only allowed one clasp of any type to be worn on the ribbon. Members of the marine or medical corps who served in France but were not eligible for a battle clasp would receive a bronze Maltese across on their ribbons.*

*Known until 1947 simply as the "Victory Medal", the World War I Victory Medal was awarded to any member of the U.S. military who had served in the armed forces between the following dates in the following locations: 6 April 1917 to 11 November 1918 for any military service. 12 November 1918 to 5 August 1919 for service in European Russia and 23 November 1918 to 1 April 1920 for service with the American Expeditionary Force Siberia.*

The 14 Allied Nations decided on a single ribbon, but pendant design was left up to each Nation. Mr. James E. Fraser was the designer of the U.S. Victory Medal. The bronze medal front shows a Winged Victory holding a shield and sword. The back of the medal reads "The Great War For Civilization" curved along the top of the medal. On the bottom of the back of the medal are six stars, three on either side of the center column of seven Roman staffs wrapped in a cord. The top of the staff has a round ball on top and is winged on the side. The staff overlays a shield saying "U" on the left side of the staff and "S" on the right side. Left of the staff are listed World War I Allied countries: France, Italy, Serbia, Japan, Montenegro, Russia, and Greece. On the right side of the staff are: Great Britain, Belgium, Brazil, Portugal, Rumania (now spelled Romania), and China.

A 3/16 inch Silver Citation Star was authorized to be worn on the ribbon of the Victory Medal by any member of the U.S. Army who had been cited for gallantry in action between 1917 and 1920. In 1932, the Silver Citation Star was redesigned as the Silver Star and, upon application, any holder of the Silver Citation Star could have it converted to a Silver Star decoration. Only one bronze star was authorized for wear on the ribbon regardless of the number of campaign bars earned. The Navy Commendation Star to the World War I Victory Medal was authorized to any person who had been commended by the Secretary of the Navy for performance of duty during the First World War. A 3/16 inch silver star was worn on the World War I Victory Medal, identical in appearance to the Army's Citation Star. Unlike the Army's version, however, the Navy Commendation Star could not be upgraded to the Silver Star medal. Marines and Navy Medical Corps personnel attached to the Army in France earned, and were authorized to wear any Army clasps authorized by their parent command.

For sea-related war duty, the Navy issued operational clasps, which were worn on the World War I Victory Medal and inscribed with the name of the duty type which had been performed:

1. **Armed Guard**: Merchant personnel (freighters, tankers, and troop ship), 2. **Asiatic**: Service on any vessel that visited a Siberian port, 3. **Asiatic**; Port visit Atlantic Fleet: Service in the Atlantic Fleet; 4. **Aviation**: Service involving flying over the Atlantic Ocean, 5. **Destroyer**: Service on destroyers on the Atlantic Ocean, 6. **Escort**: Personnel regularly attached to escort vessels on the North Atlantic, 7. **Grand Fleet**: Personnel assigned to any ship of the "United States Grand Fleet", 8. **Mine Laying**: Service in mine laying sea duty, 9. **Mine Sweeping**: Service in mine sweeping sea duty, 10. **Mobile Base**: Service on tenders and repair vessels, 11. **Naval Battery**: Service as a member of a naval battery detachment, 12. **Overseas**: Service on shore in allied or enemy countries of Europe, 13. **Patrol**: War patrol service on the Atlantic Ocean, 14. **Salvage**: Salvage duty performed on the seas, 15. **Submarine**: Submarine duty performed on the Atlantic Ocean, 16. **Submarine Chaser**, 17. **Anti-submarine**: duty performed on the Atlantic Ocean, 18. **Transport**: Personnel regularly attached to a transport or cargo vessel, 19. **White Sea**: Service on any vessel which visited a Russian port or war patrols in the White Sea.

### Texas Cavalry Congressional Medal (Army)

**Service:** Army  **Instituted:** 1924
**Dates:** 1917-1918
**Criteria:** Awarded to two Texas Cavalry Brigades used to relieve Regular Army units then serving on the Texas-Mexican Border.

### Army of Occupation of Germany Medal (Army)

**Service:** Army  **Instituted:** 1942
**Dates:** 1918-1923
**Criteria:** Awarded to Army personnel who served in the occupation of Germany or Austria-Hungary between November, 1918 and July, 1923. Navy personnel on shore duty were also eligible.

### NC-4 Medal (Navy)

**Service:** Navy, Coast Guard
**Instituted:** 1929
**Dates:** 1919
**Criteria:** Awarded to personnel who participated in the first Trans-Atlantic flight by Curtiss Army seaplanes from May 8 to May 31, 1919.

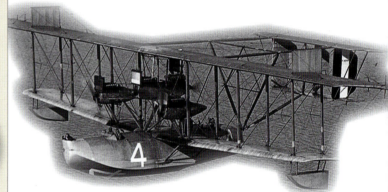

### 2nd Haitian Campaign Medal (Navy)

**Service:** Navy, Marine Corps
**Instituted:** 1921   **Dates:** 1919-1920
**Criteria:** Awarded to personnel who reinforced the Marine garrison in Haiti to assist in the restoration of order to the country.

### 2nd Nicaraguan Campaign Medal (Navy)

**Service:** Navy and Marine Corps.
**Instituted:** 1929   **Dates:** 1926-1933
**Criteria:** Awarded to personnel who served ashore in Nicaragua between Aug 1926 and Jan 1933 to put an end to local violence.

### Yangtze Service Medal (Navy)

**Service:** Navy & Marine Corps.
**Instituted:** 1930   **Dates:** 1926-1932
**Criteria:** Service in the Yangtze River Valley or in surrounding Chinese waters between Sept, 1926 and Dec 1932.

# Introduction to United States Military Medals and Ribbons from World War II to Present

The decorations and awards, which represent the rich United States military heritage of all the Armed Forces from 1939 onward, are presented in the order of precedence for the Army as it is the Senior Service. Each service has a different order of precedence which is shown on the services ribbon charts to include commonly awarded foreign medals. Most of the medals pertain to all branches of the service but many are branch specific and are identified so.

Medals of America 131

# THE PYRAMID OF HONOR

The awards system of the United States has evolved into a structured program often referred to as the "Pyramid of Honor." It is an awards program designed to reward services ranging from heroism of individuals and units on the battlefield to superior meritorious performance of noncombat duties.

The Armed Services for the most part embraced Napoleon's concept of liberally awarding medals and ribbons to enhance morale and esprit de corps. This expanded and specifically tailored awards program is generally very popular in all-volunteer armed forces and has played a significant part in improving morale, job performance, recruitment and reenlistment among all military personnel.

The decorations and awards, which represent the rich United States military heritage of all the Armed Forces from 1939 onward, are presented in the chart to the right; displaying the United States Armed Forces' "Pyramid of Honor" and includes commonly awarded foreign medals. Most of the medals pertain to all branches of the service but many are branch specific.

Decorations, medals, ribbons and unit awards as well as commonly awarded foreign medals are shown in the senior service (U.S. Army) order of precedence for wear. These awards paint a wonderful portrait of the Armed Forces dedication to the ideals of freedom, honor and sacrifice required of each member to support those ideals.

# United States and Foreign Awards

## United States and Foreign Awards

Army
Medal of Honor

Air Force
Medal of Honor

Navy, Marine Corps and
Coast Guard Medal of Honor

Sgt. Dakota Meyer received the Medal of Honor for bravery in Afghanistan.

# Introduction to U.S. Military Medals

Beginning with the Army, Navy, Marine Corps and Coast Guard and Air Force Medals of Honor, the decorations, medals and ribbon and unit awards of the U.S. Armed Forces are presented in Army order of precedence from World War II to present. Consult the various services' ribbon charts for their order of wear precedence.

## THE MEDAL OF HONOR

In a country whose government is based upon a totally democratic society, it is fitting that the first medal to reward heroic acts on the field of battle should be for private soldiers, marines, and seamen (although later extended to officers).

The Congressional Medal of Honor (referred to universally as the Medal of Honor in all statutes, awards manuals and uniform regulations) was born in conflict and steeped in controversy during its early years, finally emerging, along with Great Britain's Victoria Cross, as one of the World's premier awards for bravery.

The Medal of Honor comes in three forms (Army, Navy and Air Force); all three medals represent our county's highest reward for bravery. Today there is only one set of directives governing the award of this, the highest of all U.S. decorations.

The medal was created during the Civil War as a reward for "gallantry in action and other soldier-like qualities." However, the reference to "other qualities" led to many awards for actions which would seem less than heroic, including the bestowal of 864 awards upon the entire membership of the 27th Maine Volunteer Infantry for merely reenlisting.

The inconsistencies in this and other dubious cases were apparently resolved in the early 20th Century when 910 names were removed from the lists (including the 864 awarded to the 27th Maine). At the same time, the statutes which intrepidity govern the award of the medal were revised to reflect the present-day criteria of "gallantry and at the risk of one's own life above and beyond the call of duty."

# Medal of Honor

The **Medal of Honor** is the highest military award for bravery that can be given to an individual in the United States of America. Conceived in the early 1860's and first presented in 1863, the medal has a colorful and inspiring history which has culminated in the standards applied today for awarding this respected honor.

To judge whether a man is entitled to the Medal of Honor, all of the Armed Services apply regulations which permit no margin of doubt or error: (1.) The deed of the person must be proved by incontestable evidence of at least two eyewitnesses (2.) It must be so outstanding that it clearly distinguishes gallantry beyond the call of duty from lesser forms of bravery and (3.) It must involve the risk of life. However, until passage of Public Law 88-77, the Navy awarded Medals of Honor for bravery in saving lives, and deeds of valor performed in submarine rescues, boiler explosions, turret fires and other types of disasters unique to the naval profession.

A recommendation for the Army or Air Force Medal must be made within 2 years from the date of the deed upon which it depends. Award of the medal must be made within 3 years after the date of the deed. The recommendation for a Navy Medal of Honor must be made within 3 years and awarded within 5 years.

The Medal of Honor was the result of group thought and action and evolved in response to a need of the times. In the winter of 1861-62, following the beginning of hostilities in the Civil War, there was much thought in Washington concerning the necessity for recognizing the deeds of the American soldiers, sailors and marines who were distinguishing themselves in the fighting. The United States, which had given little thought to its Armed Forces during times of peace, now found them to be the focal point of attention. The serviceman was not just fighting, but was fighting gallantly, sometimes displaying a sheer heroism which a grateful Nation now sought to reward in a meaningful and dignified manner.

It was in this spirit that a bill was introduced in the Senate to create a Navy Medal of Honor. It was passed and approved by President Abraham Lincoln on December 21, 1861. It established the Medal of Honor for enlisted men of the Navy and Marine Corps - The first decoration formally authorized by the American Government to be worn as a badge of honor. Action on the Army medal was started two months later, when, on February 17, 1862, a Senate resolution was introduced providing for presentation of "medals of honor" to enlisted men of the Army and Voluntary Forces who "shall most distinguish themselves by their gallantry in action and other soldier like qualities." President Lincoln's approval made the resolution law on July 12, 1862. The law was extended later to include Army officers as well as enlisted men and made retroactive to the beginning of the Civil War. Awards to Navy and Marine Corps officers were not authorized until 1915.

There were some sincere men who believed that the idea of a Medal of Honor would not prove popular with Americans. But after the Civil War and in succeeding years, the medal turned out to be too popular and the honors conferred upon its recipients had the effect of inspiring the human emotion of envy. A flood of imitators, including a number by prestigious veteran and patriotic organizations, sprang up following the Civil War and had the effect of causing Congress, eventually, to take steps to protect the dignity of the original medal. This took the form of major changes to the medal and ribbon and over the years, resulted, depending on the source, in seventeen Medal of Honor variations (six Army, ten Navy and one Air Force). Illustrations of the most notable variants are presented on the following page.

On April 27, 1916, Congress approved an act which created a "Medal of Honor Roll" upon which the names of honorably discharged recipients who had earned the Medal of Honor in combat were to be recorded. The purpose of the act was to provide a special pension of $10 per month for life and to give medal recipients the same recognition shown to holders of similar British and French decoration for valor. Unfortunately, the act had some unforeseen consequences since not all of the awards seemed to be for combat actions. Given these doubts, the Secretary of War appointed a board of five retired general officers for the purpose of "investigating and reporting upon past awards of the medal of honor by the War Department with a view to ascertaining what medals of honor, if any, had been awarded or issued for any cause other than distinguished conduct involving actual conflict with an enemy."

By October 16, 1916, the Board had met, gathered all records on the 2,625 Medals of Honor which had been awarded up to that time, prepared statistics, organized evidence and began its deliberations. On February 15, 1917, all of the pertinent documentation had been examined and considered by the Board and 910 names were stricken from the list.

Of these 910 names, 864 were involved in one group, the 27th Maine Volunteer Infantry. The regiment's enlistment was to have expired in June of 1863 but, to keep the regiment on active duty during a critical period (the Battle of Gettysburg), President Lincoln authorized Medals of Honor for any members who volunteered for another tour of duty. It was felt that the 309 men who volunteered for extended duty in the face of possible death, were certainly demonstrating "soldier like" qualities and as such were entitled to the Medal under the original law. But their act in no way measured up to the 1916 standards and a clerical error compounded the abuse. Not only did the 309 volunteers receive the medal, but the balance of the regiment, which had gone home in spite of the President's offer, also received the award.

In that case, as well as in the remaining 46 scattered instances, the Board felt that the medal had not been properly awarded for distinguished services by the definition of the act of June 3, 1916. Among the 46 others who lost their medals were William F. ("Buffalo Bill") Cody, Dr. Mary Walker, the only female medal recipient and the 29 members of the special Honor Guard that had accompanied the body of Abraham Lincoln from Washington, DC to its final resting place in Springfield, Illinois. There have been no instances of cancellation of Medal of Honor awards within the Naval services due to failure to meet the 1916 award criteria.

# Medal of Honor

In the United States the Government is based on a totally democratic society, therefore, it is fitting that the first medal to reward valor on the battlefield was for private soldiers and seamen (although extended in later years to officers).

The Congressional Medal of Honor (referred to universally as the Medal of Honor in all official documents) was born in conflict, steeped in controversy during its early years and finally emerged, along with Britain's Victoria Cross, as one of the world's premier awards for bravery.

The medal is actually a statistical oddity, proving the unlikely equation that "Three equals One". Although there are three separate medals representing America's highest reward for bravery (illustrated above), there is now only a single set of directives governing the award of this, the most coveted of all U.S. decorations.

Many Americans today are confused by the term: "Congressional Medal of Honor" when, in fact, the proper term is "Medal of Honor". Part of this confusion stems from a law that was passed on July 1918 authorizing the President to present the medal" … in the name of Congress". The fact that all Medals of Honor recipients belong to the Congressional Medal of Honor Society, an official organization chartered by Congress, does not help the situation. However, suffice it to state that the medal is referred to universally as the "Medal of Honor" in all statues, awards manuals, uniform regulations and official documents.

# Army Medals of Honor

Ribbon

Rosette

The Army Medal of Honor was first awarded in 1862 but, owing to extensive copying by veterans groups, was redesigned in 1904 and patented by the War Department to ensure the design exclusivity.

The present medal, a five pointed golden star, lays over a green enamelled laurel wreath. The center of the star depicts Minerva, Goddess of righteous war and wisdom, encircled by the words: "United States of America". The back of the medal is inscribed, "The Congress to", with a place for the recipient's name. The medal hangs from a bar inscribed: "Valor", which is held by an American Eagle with laurel leaves (denoting peace) in its right talon and arrows (war) in its left. The eagle is fastened by a hook to a light blue silk pad on which are embroidered 13 stars.

Army Medal of Honor
(1862-1896)

Army Medal of Honor
(1896-1904)

Army Medal of Honor
(1904-1944)

**Establishing Authority:** The Army Medal of Honor was established by Joint Resolution of Congress, July 12, 1862 *(as amended)*

**Effective Date:** April 15, 1861

**Criteria:** Awarded for conspicuous gallantry and intrepidity at the risk of one's own life, above and beyond the call of duty. This gallantry must be performed either while engaged in action against an enemy of the United States, while engaged in military operations involving conflict with an opposing foreign force or while serving with friendly foreign forces engaged in an armed conflict against an opposing armed force in which the United States is not a belligerent party. Recommendation must be submitted within three years of the act and the medal must be awarded within five years of the act.

The current Army Medal of Honor was designed by the firm of Arthus Bertrand, Beranger & Magdelaine of Paris, France and is based on the original design of the Medal of Honor created in 1862 by William Wilson & Son Company of Philadelphia, Pennsylvania.

The Medal of Honor is a five-pointed gold-finished star (point down) with each point ending in a trefoil. Every point of the star has a green enamel oak leaf in its center and a green enamel laurel wreath surrounds the center of the star, passing just below the trefoils. In the center of the star is a profile of the Goddess Minerva encircled by the inscription, "UNITED STATES OF AMERICA", with a small shield at the bottom. The star is suspended by links from a bar inscribed, "VALOR", topped by a spread winged eagle grasping laurel leaves in its right talon and arrows in the left. The star represents each State in the United States. The oak leaf represents strength and the laurel leaf represents achievement. The head of Minerva represents wisdom with the shield from the Great Seal of the United States representing lawful authority. The laurel leaves clasped in the right claw of the Federal eagle offer peace while the arrows represent military might if the country's offer of peace is rejected. The back of the bar holding the star is engraved, "THE CONGRESS TO." The rest of the medal is smooth to permit engraving the recipient's name. The ribbon is a light blue moiré patterned silk neck band one and three sixteenths inches wide and twenty four inches long, with a square pad in the center of the same ribbon. Thirteen white stars are woven into the pad.

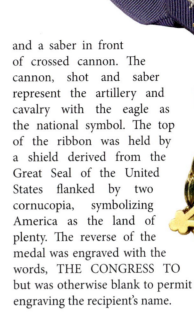

and a saber in front of crossed cannon. The cannon, shot and saber represent the artillery and cavalry with the eagle as the national symbol. The top of the ribbon was held by a shield derived from the Great Seal of the United States flanked by two cornucopia, symbolizing America as the land of plenty. The reverse of the medal was engraved with the words, THE CONGRESS TO but was otherwise blank to permit engraving the recipient's name.

### Army Medal of Honor (July 12, 1862 to May 1, 1896)

The first Army Medal of Honor had the same five-pointed star and flag ribbon as the Navy. The only differences were in the means of suspension. While the Navy medal was suspended by a fouled anchor, the Army's was suspended from an American eagle with outstretched wings with a stack of eight cannon balls

### Army Medal of Honor (May 2, 1896 to April 23, 1904)

In the years following the Civil War, many veteran's organizations and other patriotic societies adopted membership badges and insignia which were thinly-disguised replicas of the Medal of Honor. To protect the sanctity of the Medal of Honor, Congress authorized a new ribbon for the Army Medal of Honor in 1896 to clearly distinguish it from veterans association's badges. The basic colors of the original ribbon were not changed, but simply altered.

### Army Medal of Honor (April 23, 1904 to 1944)

Unfortunately, the Army Medal of Honor continued to be widely copied and its design criticized. On April 23, 1904 a new design was approved and was granted Patent Number 197,369. In addition to the new planchet, the redesigned award was suspended from the now familiar light blue moire ribbon symbolic of the loyalty and vigilance, containing 13 embroidered white stars representing the 13 original states. This new version of the Medal of Honor is the design that is still used to the present day. The only change that has taken place since its adoption in 1904 is the suspension which was modified in 1942 from a pin on breast ribbon to a neck ribbon.

# Navy, Marine Corps and Coast Guard Medals of Honor

For conspicuous gallantry and intrepidity at the risk of one's own life, above and beyond the call of duty, in action involving actual conflict with an opposing armed force.

Ribbon   Rosette

### Navy Medal of Honor

The 1861 Navy Medal of Honor was redesigned by Tiffany & Co. in 1917 but returned to the basic 1861 design in 1942 and a neck ribbon was added. The design is a five point bronze star with a central circular plaque depicting Minerva repulsing Discord.

Navy Medal of Honor (1861)

Navy Medal of Honor (1913-1917)

Navy Medal of Honor (1917-1942)

Marine Corps Brevet Medal (1921) was for distinguished conduct and service and was only awarded 20 times. It Is the rarest of decorations and out of date when approved and is not a current award.

**Establishing Authority:** The Navy Medal of Honor arose from a Public Resolution signed into law by President Lincoln on December 21, 1861 authorizing the preparation of "200 medals of honor" to promote the efficiency of the Navy. It was followed by a Joint Resolution of Congress on July 12, 1862 (as amended) which actually approved the design and further defined the eligibility and required deeds of potential recipients.

**Criteria:** For conspicuous gallantry and intrepidity at the risk of one's own life, above and beyond the call of duty, in action involving actual conflict with an opposing armed force. The Navy Medal of Honor is a five pointed star with a standing figure of the Goddess Minerva surrounded by a circle of stars representing the number of States in the Union at the outbreak of the Civil War. Minerva, the Roman Goddess of Strength and Wisdom, holds a shield taken from the Great Seal of the United States, and in her left hand she holds a fasces, representing the lawful authority of the state with which she is warding off a crouching figure representing Discord. The medal is suspended from an anchor and the reverse is plain for engraving the recipient's name. The ribbon is light blue and has a light blue eight-sided central pad with thirteen white stars.

### Navy Medal of Honor
*(December 21, 1861 to August 11, 1913)*

Since its inception, the Navy Medal of Honor has been revised three times. The original version was quite similar to its Army counterpart with a planchet virtually identical to that used on the present Navy Medal of Honor. The same suspension ribbon ("Flag design") as the Army, a solid dark blue field on its top half and thirteen alternating vertical stripes of red and white on the bottom was also fitted. The major differences lay in the hangers used for ribbon suspension. Where the Army used an eagle as its hanger (the transition between the ribbon and the medal), the Navy employed a gold rectangular frame on which was superimposed a gold star, both pieces supporting a gold anchor.

### Navy Medal of Honor

*(August 12, 1913 to April 5, 1917)*

The first modification to the Medal of Honor by the Navy was authorized on August 12, 1913 as part of a general update to their uniform regulations. In a change which was mostly cosmetic, the original ribbon was discarded in favor of the same light blue ribbon with white stars that was used on the Army medal since 1904. Along with a few minor changes to the planchet, the regulations now stated that the medal was to be worn from a cravat-style neck ribbon.

### Navy Medal of Honor
*(April 6, 1917 to August 6, 1942)*

In 1919, a new Medal of Honor version, retroactive to the start of World War I, came into use and remained until 1942 when the current Navy Medal of Honor was reinstituted. This version was often referred to as the "Tiffany Cross," since the firm of Tiffany & Co. were the designers of the new award. The medal was a gold cross patee on a wreath of oak and laurel leaves. In the center of the cross was an octagon with the inscription, "UNITED STATES NAVY 1917-1918". Inside the octagon was an eagle design of the United States Seal and an anchor appeared on each arm of the cross. The reverse of the medal had the raised inscription, "AWARDED TO" and space for the recipient's name. The medal was suspended from a light blue ribbon with thirteen white stars. The ribbon was suspended from a rectangular gold pin bar inscribed with the word, "VALOUR".

### Navy Medal of Honor
*(August 7, 1942 to Present)*

In August 1942, Congress readopted the original, Civil War-style five-pointed star, adding a neckband of light blue and eight-sided pad charged with 13 white stars. Although some minor modifications have been made to the neck ribbon/pad in the interim, the award as adopted in 1942 is basically identical to the Medal of Honor design used by the Navy and Marine Corps today.

### The Marine Corps Brevet Medal *(Obsolete)*

On June 7, 1921, the Secretary of the Navy approved Marine Commandant John A. Lejeune's request for a medal for award to the holder of a brevet promotion. Marine Corps Order #26 was issued on June 27, 1921, authorizing the medal. The decoration was justified on the grounds that, until 1915, Marine Corps officers were not eligible for the Medal of Honor.

Award of the medal was awarded to twenty Marine officers. The Marine Corps Brevet Medal was considered to be the equivalent of the Navy Cross, although in precedence it ranks just behind the Medal of Honor. In 1940 the Marine Corps declared the Brevet Medal obsolete; the medal was never issued again. (See page 140 for picture).

# Air Force Medals of Honor

The Army Medal of Honor was awarded to members of the Army Air Force and United States Air Force until May 1954.

Rosette

Ribbon

Air Force Medal of Honor (1917-1965)

**Army Medal of Honor**

The Army Medal of Honor was first awarded in 1862 but, owing to extensive copying by veterans groups, was redesigned in 1904 and patented by the War Department to ensure the design exclusivity.

The Army medal is a five pointed golden star, lays over a green enamelled laurel wreath. The center of the star depicts Minerva, Goddess of righteous war and wisdom, encircled by the words: "United States of America".

Captain Eddie Rickenbacker did not start flying combat missions until 7 months before the war ended, Rickenbacker shot down a total of 26 German aircraft. That was the highest total of any American pilot in the war, making him officially the American "ace of aces."
He was awarded the Medal of Honor for his actions in World War I. He was known to Americans simply as "Captain Eddie."

Military Medals of America

Congress authorized the Air Force Medal of Honor in 1960, 13 years after the establishment of the Air Force as an independent Service (prior to 1960, airmen received the Army medal). The medal design is fashioned after the Army version and is a five pointed star with a green enameled laurel wreath. The center depicts the head of the Statue of Liberty surrounded by 34 stars. The star hangs from a representation of the Air Force coat of arms and is suspended from a bar inscribed "VALOR".

**Establishing Authority:** The Air Force design of the Medal of Honor was established by Congress on July 6, 1960 and presented to all Air Force recipients of the MOH on or after November 1, 1965. Air Force decorations are generally considered as deriving from their earlier comparable Army awards; that is, they are not legally "new" decorations but rather the Air Force design versions of previously established Army decorations. The Air Force is authorized to issue its own version of the Army Medal of Honor by Section 8741 of Title 10 of the U.S. Code.

**Criteria** for awarding the Air Force Medal of Honor is the same as for the Army and Navy, to wit: "conspicuous gallantry and intrepidity at the risk of one's own life above and beyond the call of duty." Each recommendation for the Medal of Honor must incontestably prove that the self sacrifice or personal bravery involved conspicuous risk of life.

The Air Force Medal of Honor became effective on November 1, 1965 and was designed by Lewis J. King, Jr. of the Army's Institute of Heraldry. The first recipient of the Air Force Medal of Honor was Major Bernard E. Fisher on January 19, 1967 for his heroic actions in rescuing a fellow pilot who had crash landed on a landing strip in the A Shau Valley on March 10, 1966. Airman First Class John L. Levitow was the first USAF enlisted person to receive the Medal. He was awarded the MOH for saving his AC-47 gunship and crew in Vietnam (See page 85). Five airmen received the Medal of Honor during the Vietnam War.

The medal is officially described as follows: within a wreath of laurel in green enamel, a gold-finished five-pointed star, one point down, tipped with trefoils and each point containing a crown of laurel and oak on a green enamel background. Centered upon the star is an annulet of thirty-four stars which surround the profile of the head from the Statue of Liberty. The star is suspended by a connecting bar and pinned hinge from a trophy consisting of a bar inscribed with the word, "VALOR", above an adaptation of a thunderbolt. The bar is suspended from a pale blue moire silk neck band behind an elongated square pad in the center, with the corners turned back and charged with thirteen white stars in the form of a triple chevron. The star is a replica of the design originally adopted by the Navy and the Army. The profile taken from the Statue of Liberty represents those ideals for which the United States is known throughout the world. The thunderbolt is taken from the Air Force coat of arms and distinguishes the medal as an Air Force decoration. The medal is two inches in overall height and two and one-sixteenth inches in overall width, making it larger than either the Army or Navy Medals of Honor. The reverse is plain, providing space for the name of the recipient.

Reverse

### Medal of Honor (Air Force)

For conspicuous gallantry and intrepidity at the risk of one's own life, above and beyond the call of duty, in action involving actual conflict with an opposing armed force.

# Distinguished Service Cross, First Version 1918

The first 100 Distinguished Service Crosses were manufactured in the Philadelphia Mint and numbered on the right side of the lower arm. The arms of the cross were embossed with oak leaves with an American Eagle in the center of a diamond shape with stars on the corner of the diamond. Below the eagle was a scroll reading" E Pluribus Unum". The reverse of the medal had the words "For Valor" surrounded by a laurel wreath.

The overall medal was influenced by the art deco design of the period and was soon replaced by a second design with decorative, fluted edges and a small ornamental scroll topped by a ball at the end of each arm. The diamond and stars design was replaced by a wreath behind an enlarged eagle. Several variations of the first type DSC were made in France and are generally thinner and slightly smaller in size. None of the French made DSCs were numbered.

**Service:** Army
**Instituted:** 1918
**Criteria:** Extraordinary heroism in action against an enemy of the U.S. while engaged in military operations involving conflict with an opposing foreign force or while serving with friendly foreign forces.
**Devices:**
(41)
(48)

# Distinguished Service Cross

Authorized by Congress on July 9, 1918. Awarded for extraordinary heroism against an armed enemy but of a level not justifying the award of the Medal of Honor. It may be awarded to both civilians and military serving in any capacity with the Army who distinguish themselves by heroic actions in combat. The act or acts of heroism must be so notable and have involved risk of life so extraordinary as to set the individual apart from his comrades. The medal had been initially proposed for award to qualifying members of the American Expeditionary Forces in Europe during World War I but was authorized permanently by Congress in the Appropriations Act of 1918. The Cross was designed by 1st Lt. Andre Smith and Captain Aymar Embury with the final design sculpted by John R. Sinnock at the Philadelphia Mint.

While DSCs were originally numbered, the practice was discontinued during World War II. In 1934 the DSC was authorized to be presented to holders of the Certificate of Merit which had been discontinued in 1918 when the Distinguished Service Medal was established. The medal is a cross with an eagle with spread wings centered on the cross behind which is a circular wreath of laurel leaves. The cross has decorative fluted edges with a small ornamental scroll topped by a ball at the end of each arm. The laurel wreath is tied at its base by a scroll which upon which are written the words, "FOR VALOR." The eagle represents the United

**Service:** Army
**Instituted:** 1918
**Criteria:** Extraordinary heroism in action against an enemy of the U.S. while engaged in military operations involving conflict with an opposing foreign force or while serving with friendly foreign forces.
**Devices:**
(41)
(48)

States and the laurel leaves surrounding the eagle representing victory and achievement. The reverse of the cross features the same decorations at the edges that appear on the front. The eagle's wings, back and tips also show. Centered on the reverse of the cross is a laurel wreath. In the center of the wreath is a decorative rectangular plaque for engraving the soldier's name. The ribbon has a one inch wide center of national blue edged in white and red. The national colors taken from the flag stand for sacrifice (red), purity (white) and high purpose (blue).

The numbers in parentheses next to the Devices refer to the tables in "Attachments and Devices" on page 116-119.

## Navy Cross

For extraordinary heroism in connection with military operations against an opposing armed force. The Navy Cross is worn after the Medal of Honor and before all other decorations.

The Navy Cross was established by an Act of Congress and approved on February 4, 1919. Initially the Navy Cross was awarded for extraordinary heroism or distinguished service in either combat or peacetime. The criteria was upgraded in August 1942 to limit the award to those individuals demonstrating extraordinary heroism in connection with military operations against an armed enemy.

The Navy Cross medal is a cross pattée with the ends of the cross rounded. It has four laurel leaves with berries in each re-entrant angle, which symbolizes victory. In the center of the cross is a sailing ship on waves. The ship is a caravel, symbolic of ships of the fourteenth century. On the reverse are crossed anchors with cables attached with the letters USN amid the anchors. The ribbon is navy blue with a white center stripe. Additional awards of the Navy Cross are denoted by gold stars five-sixteenths of an inch in diameter.

**Service:** Navy/Marine Corps/Coast Guard
**Instituted:** 1919
**Criteria:** Extraordinary heroism in action against an enemy of the U.S. while engaged in military operations involving conflict with an opposing foreign force or while serving with friendly foreign forces.
**Devices:**
★ (93)
☆ (101)

## Air Force Cross

Authorized on November 1, 1965 for extraordinary heroism while engaged in a military action against an enemy of the United States; previous to the effective date of July 6, 1960, deserving Air Force personnel received the Army Distinguished Service Cross (DSC). It is awarded for heroic actions not justifying the Medal of Honor and is presented in the name of the President.

The first award of the Air Force Cross was made posthumously to Major Rudolf Anderson, Jr. who was shot down and killed over Cuba during the Cuban missile crisis while flying a U-2 aircraft. The first living enlisted man to receive the award was Sgt. Duane D. Hackney who received it for rescuing a downed Air Force pilot in Vietnam. As of this writing, the two latest awards of the Air Force Cross were the result of actions occurring during Operation Enduring Freedom in Afghanistan, coincidentally on the same date, March 4, 2002. The first was to Technical Sergeant John Chapman of the 24th Special Tactics Squadron. After his helicopter, containing a U.S. Navy sea-air-land team was shot down, TSgt Chapman established communications with a gunship, directed fire to protect the team, controlled a rescue helicopter to effect the extraction and provided fire which covered the rescue until he succumbed to his wounds. The second award was made to Senior Airman Jason D. Cunningham of the USAF Quick Reaction Force for extraordinary heroism while acting as a primary Combat Search & Rescue medic. After the crash of his helicopter, Airman Cunningham, in spite of effective enemy fire and

**Service:** Air Force
**Instituted:** 1960
**Criteria:** Extraordinary heroism in action against an enemy of the U.S. while engaged in military operations involving conflict with an opposing foreign force or while serving with friendly foreign forces.
**Devices:**
(41)
(48)

risk to his own life, gave ten gravely wounded soldiers life-saving medical treatment until he was, himself, mortally wounded. The design of the Air Force Cross medal and ribbon are based on the design of the Army Distinguished Service Cross. The medal is a bronze cross containing a gold-plated American bald eagle with wings against a cloud formation encircled by a green laurel wreath. The awardees name may be engraved on the reverse. The blue in the center of the ribbon is a lighter shade than that of the DSC. Additional awards are denoted by bronze and silver oak leaf clusters.

## Coast Guard Cross

For extraordinary heroism in action against an enemy of the U.S. while engaged in military operations against an opposing armed force. The Coast Guard Cross is worn after the Medal of Honor and before all other decorations.

The Coast Guard Cross was established by Act of Congress (Public Law 111-281) approved on October 2010 which authorized 14 USC 491A). The Coast Guard Cross was designed by the Coast Guard in conjunction with the Institute of Heraldry. The medal is a cross in gold metal and colored epoxy and is two and one quarter inches in height and one and three quarters inches in width. The four arms of the cross are pointed and faceted with ship's anchors between each arm. Centered on the obverse is a wreath of twenty-six laurel leaves, thirteen to either side of a depiction of the coat of arms of the United States of America, all of appropriate epoxy colors. The suspension ring is part of the medal and is a looped rope with crossed oars.

The reverse is the same as the obverse except that it does not display the wreath and shield ; in their place is a central circle with the words FOR arched at the top and VALOR arched below.

The ribbon is one and three-eighths inches wide and is dark blue with a central stripe of ultramarine blue-flame

**Service:** Coast Guard
**Instituted:** 15 October 2010
**Criteria:** Extraordinary heroism in action against an enemy of the U.S. while engaged in military operations involving conflict with an opposing foreign force or while serving with friendly foreign forces.
**Devices:**
(93)
(101)

red-ultramarine blue all of the central stripes being separated by thin white stripes.

Additional awards of the Coast Guard Cross are denoted by gold and silver stars, each five-sixteenths of an inch in diameter.

## Defense Distinguished Service Medal

Authorized on July 9, 1970 and awarded to military officers for exceptionally meritorious service while assigned to a Department of Defense joint activity. The Secretary of Defense is the awarding authority for the medaland it is usually only awarded to very senior officers. Examples of assignments that may allow qualification for this medal are: Chairman, Joint Chiefs of Staff; Chiefs and Vice Chiefs of the Military Services, including the Commandant and Assistant Commandant of the Marine Corps and Commanders and Vice Commanders of Unified and Specified Commands. It may also be awarded to other senior officers who serve in positions of great responsibility or to an officer whose direct and individual contributions to national security or defense are also recognized as being so exceptional in scope and value as to be equivalent to contributions normally associated with positions encompassing broader responsibilities. Subsequent awards are denoted by bronze and silver oak leaf clusters.

The medal depicts an American bald eagle with wings spread and the United States shield on its breast; the eagle is superimposed on a medium blue pentagon (which represents the five services) and is surrounded by a gold circle that has thirteen stars in the upper half and a laurel and olive wreath in the lower half. On the reverse of the medal is the inscription, "FOR DISTINGUISHED SERVICE...FROM THE SECRETARY OF DEFENSE

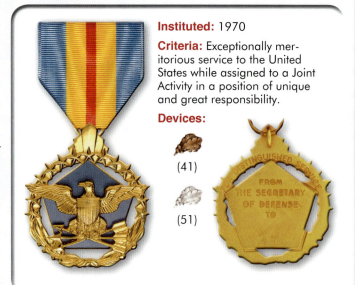

**Instituted:** 1970
**Criteria:** Exceptionally meritorious service to the United States while assigned to a Joint Activity in a position of unique and great responsibility.
**Devices:**
(41)
(51)

TO" Space is provided below the TO for engraving of the recipient's name. The ribbon has a central stripe of red flanked by stripes of gold and blue. The red represents zeal and courageous action, the gold denotes excellence and the medium blue represents the Department of Defense.

The Defense Distinguished Service Medal was designed by Mildred Orloff and sculpted by Lewis J. King, Jr., both of the Institute of Heraldry.

The numbers in parentheses next to the Devices refer to the tables in "Attachments and Devices" on page 116-119.

# Distinguished Service Medal *(Army)*

Authorized by Congress on July 9, 1918 for exceptionally meritorious service to the United States while serving in a duty of great responsibility with the U.S. Army. It was originally intended for qualifying actions during wartime only but was later authorized during both wartime or peacetime. As this country's highest award for meritorious service or achievement, it has been awarded to both military and civilians, foreign and domestic. The first American to receive this medal on October 12, 1918 was General John J. Pershing, Commanding General of the American Expeditionary Forces during World War I. Individuals who had received the Certificate of Merit before its disestablishment in 1918 were authorized to receive the DSM. The Army DSM is seldom awarded to civilians and personnel below the rank of Brigadier General.

The medal is a circular design containing the U.S. Coat of Arms encircled by a blue ring with the inscription, "FOR DISTINGUISHED SERVICE MCMXVII". Subsequent awards are denoted by the attachment of a bronze oak leaf cluster to the medal and ribbon. In the center of the reverse of the medal, amidst several flags and weapons, is a blank scroll for engraving the awardees name.

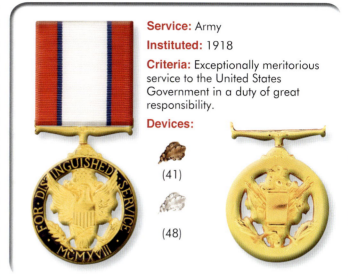

**Service:** Army
**Instituted:** 1918
**Criteria:** Exceptionally meritorious service to the United States Government in a duty of great responsibility.
**Devices:**
(41)
(48)

The ribbon has a central wide white stripe edged with blue and an outer red band representing the colors of the U.S. flag. The Army Distinguished Service Medal was designed by Captain Aymar E. Embury III and sculpted by Private Gaetano Cecere.

# Distinguished Service Medal *(Navy)*

For exceptionally meritorious service to the U.S. Government in a duty of great responsibility. The Navy Distinguished Service Medal is worn after the Defense Distinguished Service Medal and before the Silver Star.

The Navy Distinguished Service Medal was established by an Act of Congress and approved on February 4, 1919 and, like the Navy Cross, was made retroactive to April 6, 1917. During this period there was confusion about what criteria constituted the award of the Navy Distinguished Service Medal and what criteria constituted the award of the Navy Cross. At the outbreak of World War II, laws governing the award of naval decorations were changed with Public Law 702, which placed the Navy Cross above the Navy Distinguished Service Medal and clearly limited the Navy Distinguished Service Medal for exceptionally meritorious service and not for acts of heroism. The first Navy Distinguished Service Medal was awarded, posthumously, to Brigadier General Charles M. Doyen, USMC.

The Navy Distinguished Service Medal is a gold medallion with an American bald eagle with displayed wings in the center. The eagle is surrounded by a blue enameled ring which contains the words, "UNITED STATES OF AMERICA" with "NAVY" at the bottom. Outside the blue ring is a gold border of waves. The medal is suspended from its ribbon by a five pointed white enameled star with an anchor in the center. Behind the star are gold rays emanating from the re-entrant angles of

**Service:** Navy/Marine Corps
**Instituted:** 1919
**Criteria:** Exceptionally meritorious service to the United States Government in a duty of great responsibility.
**Devices:**
(93)
(101)

the star. The reverse of the medal contains a trident surrounded by a wreath of laurel. The wreath is surrounded by a blue enamel ring with the inscription, "FOR DISTINGUISHED SERVICE". The blue enamel ring is surrounded by a gold border of waves the same as on the front of the medal. The ribbon is navy blue with a gold stripe in the center. Additional awards of the Navy Distinguished Service Medal are denoted by gold stars five sixteenths of an inch in diameter.

**Medals of America** 147

# Distinguished Service Medal (Air Force)

The Air Force Distinguished Service Medal was authorized by Congress on July 6, 1960; it evolved from the Army Distinguished Service Medal authorized in 1918. The medal is awarded for exceptionally meritorious service to the U.S. in a duty of great responsibility; the term "great responsibility" denotes the success of a major operation or program attributed to the proper exercise of authority and judgement. This is the highest peacetime Air Force decoration awarded. It is presented to all recipients who are awarded this decoration on or after November 1, 1965; AAF and USAF personnel who were awarded this decoration prior to this date received the Army version. The Air Force Distinguished Service Medal is rarely awarded to officers below the rank of Brigadier General. The medal should be referred to as "Distinguished Service Medal - Air Force design." Major General Osmond J. Ritland, Air Force Systems Command, was the first recipient of the Air Force Distinguished Service Medal on November 30, 1965 for his efforts as Deputy Commander for Manned Space Flight. Subsequent awards are denoted by bronze and silver oak leaf clusters. The medal is a blue stone centered within 13 gold rays, each separated by 13 white stars. The recipient's name may be engraved on the reverse of the medal.

**Service:** Air Force
**Instituted:** 1960
**Criteria:** Exceptionally meritorious service to the United States Government in a duty of great responsibility.
**Devices:** (47) (48)

**Notes:** Original design was modified and used as the Airman's Medal.

# Department of Homeland Security Distinguished Service Medal (Coast Guard)

This decoration was originally established as the Transportation Distinguished Service Medal via Executive Order 12824 signed by President George H. W. Bush on December 7, 1992 under his authority as Commander in Chief of the U.S. Armed Forces. On February 28, 2003, President George W. Bush signed Executive Order 13286 establishing the Department of Homeland Security Distinguished Service Medal by striking "Transportation" from the original medal authorization and inserting "Homeland Security" in its place. The action rendered the Transportation Distinguished Service Medal obsolete. The effective date of the new medal is March 1, 2002, the date when the Coast Guard was transferred from the Department of Transportation (D.O.T.) to the Department of Homeland Security (D.H.S.). The first recipient of the new medal was the Commandant of the Coast Guard, Admiral Thad W. Allen, in 2006 for his extraordinary efforts during and after Hurricane Katrina.

The design of the medal is based on the Transportation Distinguished Service Medal created by Nadine Russell of the Institute of Heraldry with the central disk that originally contained D.O.T. logo replaced by the D.H.S. shield. In the center of a silver medallion one half inch in diameter, the D.H.S. logo is placed over crossed anchors on a circular field scored with raised rays. This field is in turn surrounded by a raised laurel wreath in green enamel, finished in gold. The laurel leaves form a continuous circle and the leaves point counter-clockwise. The suspender which connects the medal to its ribbon is integral to the medal and consists of a miniature Coast Guard officer's cap device in gold. The encircling wreath of laurel symbolizes honor and achievement.

In the upper-central portion of the reverse, there is a raised plaque for engraving the recipient's name. Above the plaque in two lines are the raised words, "AWARDED TO"; and below the plaque in four lines, the words "FOR EXTRAORDINARY MERITORIOUS SERVICE." The plaque and inscription are contained within an incomplete circle (open at the bottom) consisting of the raised words, " UNITED STATES DEPARTMENT OF HOMELAND SECURITY."

**Service:** Coast Guard
**Instituted:** 2006
**Criteria:** Exceptionally meritorious service in a duty of great responsibility while assigned to the Department of Homeland Security or other activities under the responsibility of the Secretary of Homeland Security.
**Devices:** None

# Transportation Distinguished Service Medal *(Department of Transportation)*

The Transportation Distinguished Service Medal was established by Executive Order 12824 signed by President George Bush on December 7, 1992. It may be awarded to any member of the Coast Guard who has provided exceptionally meritorious service in a duty of great responsibility while assigned to the Department of Transportation, or in other activities under the responsibility of the Secretary of Transportation, either national or international as may be assigned by the Secretary. The Transportation Distinguished Service Medal is worn only by Coast Guard officers. It is worn after the Defense Distinguished Service Medal and before the Coast Guard DSM.

The Transportation Distinguished Service Medal was designed by Nadine Russell of the Institute of Heraldry. In the center of the obverse is a silver medallion containing a narrow-bordered blue triskelion adapted from the Department of Transportation Seal. It is contained within a raised border of continuous cable in gold, superimposed over crossed anchors on a circular field. This field is in turn surrounded by a raised laurel wreath in green enamel, finished in gold.

The suspender which connects the medal to its ribbon is integral to the medal and consists of a miniature Coast Guard officer's cap device in gold. In the upper-central portion of the reverse there is a raised plaque for engraving the recipient's name. Above the plaque in two lines are the raised words, "AWARDED TO" and below the plaque in four lines, the words "FOR EXTRAORDINARY MERITORIOUS SERVICE". The plaque and inscription

**Service:** Coast Guard
**Instituted:** 1992
**Criteria:** Exceptionally meritorious service in a duty of great responsibility while assigned to the Department of Transportation or other activities under the responsibility of the Secretary of Transportation.
**Devices:** (93)
**Notes:** Since the transfer of the Coast Guard to The Department of Homeland Security, this medal will no longer be awarded to USCG personnel.

are contained within an incomplete circle (open at the bottom) consisting of the raised words, "UNITED STATES DEPARTMENT OF TRANSPORTATION".

The ribbon to the Transportation Distinguished Service Medal is predominantly Old Glory Blue edged in white with two stripes of paprika near each edge, the colors traditionally associated with other Department of Transportation awards. Additional awards are denoted by gold stars. However, since the entire Coast Guard organization was transferred to the U.S. Department of Homeland Security after the 9-11 attacks, this medal will no longer be awarded to Coast Guard personnel.

# Distinguished Service Medal *(Coast Guard)*

The Coast Guard Distinguished Service Medal was officially established by an Act of Congress on August 4, 1949 but its design was not approved until February 1, 1961. It is awarded to any person who, while serving in any capacity with the Coast Guard, distinguishes himself or herself by exceptionally meritorious service to the United States in a duty of great responsibility. To justify an award of the Distinguished Service Medal, exceptional performance of duty, clearly above that normally expected, which has contributed materially to the success of a major command or project, is required. In general, the Coast Guard Distinguished Service Medal is awarded only to those officers in principal commands whose service is such as to justify the award.

The Coast Guard Distinguished Service Medal was designed and sculpted by Thomas Hudson Jones of the Institute of Heraldry. It is a gold disc which, on its obverse, shows a representation of the U.S. Revenue Cutter Massachusetts under full sail on a moderate sea. In a circle surrounding the ship are the words, "U.S. COAST GUARD" in the upper portion, and "DISTINGUISHED SERVICE" in the lower. On the reverse is the Coast Guard Seal above a blank streamer (used for engraving the recipient's name) which follows the contour of the lower half of the medal. In terms of its symbolism, the Massachusetts was the first U.S. Revenue Cutter. Built in 1791, it was the forerunner of a long

**Service:** Coast Guard
**Instituted:** 1961
**Criteria:** Exceptionally meritorious service to the United States Government in a duty of great responsibility.
**Devices:** (93) (101)
**Notes:** Originally authorized in 1949 but the design was not approved until 1961.

line of similar vessels which rendered distinguished service to U.S. Maritime history and was considered a fitting symbol to use on the Coast Guard Distinguished Service Medal. The ribbon consists of a central stripe of light blue, bordered on each side by a pinstripe of white. The ribbon is edged in purple. Additional awards are denoted by gold stars.

## Silver Star

Awarded for gallantry in action against an enemy of the United States or while engaged in military operations involving conflict against an opposing armed force in which the United States is not a belligerent party. The level of gallantry required, while of a high degree, is less than that required for the Medal of Honor, Distinguished Service Cross or Navy Cross. The Silver Star is derived from the Army's "Citation Star", a 3/16" dia. silver star device which was worn on the ribbon bar and suspension ribbon of the "appropriate Army campaign medal" by any soldier cited in orders for gallantry in action. Although most applicable to the World War I Victory Medal, it was retroactive to all Army campaign medals dating back to the Civil War.

The actual Silver Star Medal was instituted in 1932 with the first award presented to General Douglas MacArthur, the Army's then-Chief-of-Staff. The Silver Star was designed by Rudolf Freund of the firm of Bailey, Banks and Biddle. On August 7, 1942, the award was extended to Navy personnel and, later that year, authorized for civilians serving with the armed forces who met the stated criteria specified in the initial regulation.

The medal is a five-pointed star finished in gilt-bronze. In the center of the star is a three-sixteenths inch silver five-pointed star within a wreath of laurel, representing the silver [citation] star prescribed by the original legislation. The rays of both stars align. The top of the medal has a rectangular-shaped loop for the suspension ribbon. The laurel wreath signifies achievement and the larger gilt-bronze star represents military service. The reverse contains the inscription, "FOR GALLANTRY IN ACTION" with a space to engrave the name of the recipient.

The ribbon, based on the colors of the National flag, has a center stripe of red flanked by a stripes of white which are flanked by blue bands with borders of white edged in blue. Additional awards are denoted by a bronze or silver oak leaf clusters or gold and silver stars depending on the recipient's Branch of Service.

**Instituted:** 1932

**Criteria:** Gallantry in action against an armed enemy of the United States or while serving with friendly foreign forces.

**Devices:**
- (41)
- (48)
- (93)
- (101)

**Notes:** Derived from the 3/16" silver "Citation Star" previously worn on Army campaign medals.

## Defense Superior Service Medal

Authorized on February 6, 1976 by an executive order signed by President Gerald R. Ford. Awarded by the Secretary of Defense to any member of the armed forces for superior meritorious service after February 6, 1976 in a position of significant responsibility while assigned to a DOD joint activity, including the Office of the Secretary of Defense, the Joint Chiefs of Staff, and specified and unified commands. The medal was created to provide recognition to those assigned to joint duty on a level equivalent to that recognition provided by the Legion of Merit. Prior to establishment of the Defense Superior Service Medal, the Office of the Secretary of Defense had to provide recognition through equivalent awards that were approved through individual service channels. Although it was established as equivalent to the Legion of Merit, its precedence is before the Legion of Merit when both are worn. Oak leaf clusters denote additional awards.

The medal depicts a silver American bald eagle with wings spread and the United States shield on its breast; the eagle is superimposed on a medium blue pentagon (which represents the five services) and is surrounded by a silver circle that has thirteen stars in the upper half and a laurel and olive wreath in the lower half. On the reverse of the medal is the inscription, "FOR SUPERIOR SERVICE FROM THE SECRETARY OF DEFENSE TO…." Space is provided below the TO for engraving of the recipient's name. The ribbon consists of a central stripe of red, flanked on either side by stripes of white, blue and gold.

**Service:** All Services (by Secretary of Defense)

**Instituted:** 1976

**Criteria:** Superior meritorious service to the United States while assigned to a Joint Activity in a position of significant responsibility

**Devices:**
- (45)
- (51)

# Legion of Merit

Authorized by Congress on July 20, 1942 for award to members of the Armed Forces of the United States for exceptionally meritorious conduct in the performance of outstanding service. Superior performance of normal duties will not alone justify award of this decoration. It is not awarded for heroism but rather service and achievement while performing duties in a key position of responsibility. It may be presented to foreign personnel but is not authorized for presentation to civilian personnel. There are four degrees of this decoration that are awarded to foreign personnel only (Chief Commander, Commander, Officer and Legionnaire). The first two degrees are comparable in rank to the Distinguished Service Medal and are usually awarded to heads of state and to commanders of armed forces, respectively. The last two degrees are comparable in rank to the award of the Legion of Merit to U.S. service members. The Legion of Merit was designed by Colonel Robert Townsend Heard and sculpted by Katharine W. Lane of Boston.

**Service:** All Services
**Instituted:** 1942
**Criteria:** Exceptionally meritorious conduct in the performance of outstanding services to the United States.
**Devices:**
V (22, 25)
(41)
(48)
★ (93)
★ (101)

The name and design of the Legion of Merit was strongly influenced by the French Legion of Honor. The medal is a white enameled five-armed cross with ten points, each tipped with a gold ball and bordered in red enamel. In the center of the cross, thirteen stars on a blue field are surrounded by a circle of heraldic clouds. A green enameled laurel wreath circles behind the arms of the cross. Between the wreath and the center of the medal, in between the arms of the cross are two crossed arrows pointing outward. The blue circle with thirteen stars surrounded by clouds is taken from the Great Seal of the United States and is symbolic of a "new constellation," as the signers of the Declaration of Independence called our new republic. The laurel wreath represents achievement, while the arrows represent protection of the nation. The reverse of the cross is a gold colored copy of the front with blank space to be used for engraving The raised inscription, "ANNUIT COEPTIS MDCCLXXXII" with a bullet separating each word encircles the area to be engraved. The words, "UNITED STATES OF AMERICA" and "ANNUIT COEPTIS" (He [God] Has Favored Our Undertaking) come from the Great Seal of the United States and the date, "MDCCLXXXII" (1782) refers to the year General Washington established the Badge of Military Merit. The ribbon is a purple-red called American Beauty Red which is edged in white. The color is a variation of the original color of the Badge of Military Merit.

# Legion of Merit for Foreign Military Personnel

Chief Commander Legion of Merit — Commander Legion of Merit — Officer Legion of Merit — Legionnaire Legion of Merit

The degrees of Chief Commander, Commander, Officer and Legionnaire are awarded only to members of armed forces of foreign nations under the criteria outlined in U.S. Army Regulation 672-7 based on the relative rank or position of the recipient as follows: Chief Commander - Chief of State or Head of Government. Commander - Equivalent of a U.S. military Chief of Staff or higher position but not to Chief of State. Officer - General or Flag Officer below the equivalent of a U.S. military Chief of Staff; Colonel or equivalent rank for service in assignments equivalent to those normally held by a General or Flag Officer in U.S. military service; or Military Attaches. Legionnaire - All recipients not included above.

# Distinguished Flying Cross

**Service:** All Services
**Instituted:** 1926
**Criteria:** Heroism or extraordinary achievement while participating in aerial flight.
**Devices:**
- V (22, 25)
- (oak leaf) (41)
- (silver oak leaf) (48)
- (gold star) (93)
- (silver star) (101)

Authorized on July 2, 1926 and implemented by an executive order signed by President Calvin Coolidge on January 28, 1927. It is awarded to United States military personnel for heroism or extraordinary achievement that is clearly distinctive involving operations during aerial flight that are not routine. It is the first decoration authorized in identical design and ribbon to all branches of the U.S. Armed Forces. Captain Charles A. Lindbergh was the first recipient of the Distinguished Flying Cross for his solo flight across the Atlantic. The Wright Brothers were awarded the DFC by an Act of Congress for their first manned flight at Kitty Hawk, North Carolina in 1903. Amelia Earhart became the only female civilian to be awarded the DFC when it was presented to her by the United States Army Air Corps for her aerial exploits. Such awards to civilians were prohibited on March 1, 1927 by Executive Order 4601.

While the Distinguished Flying Cross was never intended to be an automatic award, the Army Air Force did use it in that capacity many times during World War II by awarding DFCs for specific number of sorties and flying hours in a combat theater.

The front of the medal is a four-bladed propeller contained within a bronze cross suspended from a straight bar attached to the medal drape. The reverse is blank and provides space for the recipient's name and date of the award. The ribbon is blue with a narrow stripe of red bordered by white in the center. The ribbon edges are outlined with bands of white inside blue. Additional awards are denoted by bronze and silver oak leaf clusters or gold and silver stars depending on the recipient's Service Branch.

---

*The President of the United States takes pleasure in presenting the*

**Distinguished Flying Cross**

to

**Lieutenant, Junior Grade, George Herbert Walker Bush
United States Naval Reserve**

*for service as set forth in the following*

**Citation:** "For heroism and extraordinary achievement in aerial flight as Pilot of a Torpedo Plane in Torpedo Squadron FIFTY ONE, attached to the U.S.S. San Jacinto, in action against enemy Japanese forces in the vicinity of the Bonin Islands, on September 2, 1944. Leading one section of a four-plane division in a strike against a radio station, Lieutenant, Junior Grade, Bush pressed home an attack in the face of intense antiaircraft fire. Although his plane was hit and set afire at the beginning of his dive, he continued his plunge toward the target and succeeded in scoring damaging bomb hits before bailing out of the craft. His courage and devotion to duty were in keeping with the highest traditions of the United States Naval Reserve."

---

**Did You Know?** Lieut. Bush was the youngest pilot in the Navy when he qualified in 1942. After his rescue by a submarine Lieut. Bush returned to the USS San Jacinto and participated in operations in the Philippines until his squadron was replaced and sent home to the United States. Through 1944, he flew 58 combat missions for which he received the Distinguished Flying Cross, three Air Medals, and the Presidential Unit Citation awarded to the USS San Jacinto. Lieut. Bush was then reassigned to Norfolk Navy Base and put in a training wing for new torpedo pilots. His final assignment was as a naval aviator in a new torpedo squadron, VT-153, based at Naval Air Station Grosse Ile, Michigan. Bush was honorably discharged from the U.S. Navy in September 1945, one month after the unconditional surrender of Japan. George Herbert Walker Bush (born June 12, 1924) served as the 41st President of the United States from 1989 to 1993.

## Soldier's Medal

Authorized by Congress on July 2, 1926 to any member of the Army, National Guard or Reserves for heroism not involving actual conflict with an armed enemy.

The bronze octagonal medal has, as its central feature, a North American bald eagle with raised wings representing the United States. The eagle grasps an ancient Roman fasces symbolizing the State's lawful authority and conveys the concept that the award is to a soldier from the Government. There are seven stars on the eagle's left side and six stars and a spray of leaves to its right. The octagonal shape distinguishes the Soldier's Medal from other decorations. The stars represent the thirteen original colonies that formed the United States. The laurel spray balances the groups of stars and represents achievement. The reverse has a U.S. shield with sprays of laurel and oak leaves representing achievement and strength in front of a scroll. The words, "SOLDIER'S MEDAL" and "FOR VALOR" are inscribed on the reverse.

The ribbon contains thirteen alternating stripes of white (seven) and red (six) in the center, bordered by blue and are taken from the United States flag. The thirteen red and white stripes are arranged in the same manner as the thirteen vertical stripes in the U.S. Coat of Arms shield and also represent the thirteen original colonies.

**Service:** Army
**Instituted:** 1926
**Criteria:** Heroism not involving actual conflict with an armed enemy of the United States.
**Devices:**
(41)

Gaetano Cecere designed and sculpted the Soldier's Medal (the art deco influence of the 1920's can certainly be seen in this medal more than in any other Army award.) The Soldier's Medal is one of four decorations for which an enlisted soldier may increase his retirement by ten percent. The increase is not automatic, however; recipients of the Soldier's Medal must petition the Army Decorations Board for the bonus. Additional awards are denoted by oak leaf clusters.

## Navy and Marine Corps Medal

For heroism that involves the voluntary risk of life under conditions other than those of conflict with an opposing armed force. The Navy and Marine Corps Medal is worn after the Distinguished Flying Cross and before the Bronze Star Medal.

The Navy and Marine Corps Medal was established by an Act of Congress and approved on August 7, 1942. The medal was established to recognize non-combat heroism. For acts of lifesaving, or attempted lifesaving, it is required that the action be performed at the risk of one's own life. The Navy and Marine Corps Medal is prized above many combat decorations by those who have received it.

The Navy and Marine Corps Medal was designed by Lt. Commander McClelland Barclay, USNR. The medal is a bronze octagon with an eagle perched upon a fouled anchor. Beneath the anchor is a globe and below that is the inscription, "HEROISM" in raised letters. The reverse of the medal is blank to allow for engraving the recipient's name. The ribbon consists of three equal stripes

**Service:** Navy/Marine Corps
**Instituted:** 1942
**Criteria:** Heroism not involving actual conflict with an armed enemy of the United States.
**Devices:**
(93)

of navy blue, gold and scarlet - the blue-gold representing the Navy and the scarlet-gold being the Marine Corps' official colors. Additional awards are denoted by five-sixteenth inch gold stars.

**Did You Know?** The Navy and Marine Corps Medal may be awarded to service members of the Navy or Marine Corps who distinguish themselves by heroism not involving actual conflict with an enemy. Usually, it is awarded for actions involving the risk of one's own life. Before World War II, the Silver or Gold Lifesaving Medal was awarded for sea rescues involving risk of life. The Navy and Marine Corps Medal replaced the Lifesaving medals since military decorations are considered more prestigious than the Lifesaving Medal. The Navy and Marine Corps Medal was first bestowed during the Second World War. Its most famous recipient was President John F. Kennedy who was awarded the Navy and Marine Corps Medal for service as Commanding Officer of Motor Torpedo Boat PT-109.

## Airman's Medal

Authorized on August 10, 1956 and instituted on July 6, 1960, the authorizing directive was an amendment to the same order which created the Soldier's Medal (prior to that time, USAF personnel qualifying for such an award were awarded the Soldier's Medal). The medal's name is also fashioned as a carryover from the Soldier's Medal but does not make the casual observer aware of the medal's significance and the acts required to earn the decoration. The Airman's Medal is awarded for actions involving voluntary risk of life under conditions other than combat. A successful voluntary heroic act or the saving of a life is not essential to the award of this decoration. The first Airman's Medal was awarded to Captain John Burger on July 21, 1960 at McDill Air Force Base, Florida for saving a fellow airman's life by removing a live power line that laid across his body after having been severely shocked. Another example of the heroism required for the award was the bravery exhibited by Senior Airman Joe Sampson of Charleston Air Force Base, South Carolina when he saved an Army jumpmaster's life at the risk of his own aboard a C-141 aircraft carrying Army paratroopers. When the jumpmaster's reserve parachute inadvertently deployed and threatened to pull him out of the aircraft, Sr. Airman Sampson, without hesitation, grabbed the jumpmaster and his chute and pulled him back into the

**Service:** Air Force
**Instituted:** 1960
**Criteria:** Heroism involving voluntary risk of life under conditions other than those of actual conflict with an armed enemy.
**Devices:**
(41)

aircraft despite the tremendous forces of the airstream. The American bald eagle is depicted on the face of the medal along with the Greek god Hermes, herald and messenger of other gods. Around the edge of the medal is the curved inscription, "AIRMAN'S" on the left and "MEDAL" on the right. The reverse contains space for engraving just below the inscription, "FOR VALOR." Additional awards of the Airman's Medal are denoted by oakleaf clusters.

## Coast Guard Medal

The Coast Guard's search and rescue mission makes it inevitable that personnel of that service will occasionally be faced with extremely hazardous situations. After World War II, to provide a parallel Coast Guard decoration to the Navy and Marine Corps Medal, the Coast Guard sought legislation for an appropriate counterpart decoration. Authority for the new decoration, known as the Coast Guard Medal, was accordingly granted by an Act of Congress on August 4, 1949 but it was not designed and struck until 1958. The Coast Guard Medal is awarded to any person who, while serving in any capacity with the Coast Guard, distinguishes himself by heroism not involving actual combat with an enemy. To justify the Coast Guard Medal, the individual must have performed a voluntary act of heroism in the face of great danger which also extended beyond that normally been expected of the individual. For lifesaving, the individual must have displayed heroism at the risk of his life. It was first awarded in June of 1958. The first recipients were Engineman Third Class Earl A. Leyda and Boatswain's Mate Third Class Raymond A. Johnson, both of whom received the medal for their attempted rescue of workers trapped 5,800 feet below Lake Ontario after a tunnel explosion at Oswego, New York. The Coast Guard Medal was designed and sculpted by Thomas Hudson Jones of the Army's Institute of Heraldry and is a bronze octagon. On its

**Service:** Coast Guard
**Instituted:** 1958 (Authorized in 1949 but not designed and issued until 1958)
**Criteria:** Heroism not involving actual conflict with an armed enemy of the United States.
**Devices:**
(93)

**Notes:** Ribbon design used briefly in 1999.

obverse it bears the Coast Guard Seal enclosed within a circle of continuous cable. The reverse is plain except for the inscription, "FOR HEROISM" in raised letters. The ribbon is medium blue in the center and at the edges, with two sets of alternating white and red stripes (four white and three red). An additional award is denoted by a five-sixteenth inch diameter gold star.

# Gold Lifesaving Medal

The Lifesaving Medals has had three designs in their history. The original design in 1874 was "non-portable" and could not be worn by the recipient, but rather displayed much like a trophy.

**Service:** All Services and Civilians

**Instituted:** 1874 (modified 1882 and 1946)

**Criteria:** Heroic conduct at the risk of one's own life during the rescue or attempted rescue of a victim of drowning or shipwreck.

**Devices:**

(98)

Notes: Normally a "Non-Military Decoration" but considered a personal decoration by the Coast Guard. Originally a "table" (non-wearable) medal, then worn with a 2" wide ribbon.

The Gold Lifesaving Medal may be awarded to any person who rescues or endeavors to rescue another person from drowning, shipwreck or other peril of the water. The rescue or attempted rescue must take place in waters within the United States or, if the rescue or attempted rescue takes place outside of such waters, one of the parties must be a citizen of the United States or from a vessel or aircraft owned or operated by citizens of the United States. To qualify for the Gold Lifesaving Medal, the rescue or attempted rescue must be made at the risk of one's own life and must evince extreme and heroic daring. The medal was designed by Anthony C. Paquet, Chief Engraver of the Philadelphia Mint. The original Gold Lifesaving Medal was not intended to be worn; it was a so-called "table" medal, one and three-fourths inches in circumference showing three men in a boat in a heavy sea attempting to help a fourth figure, a mariner in distress. The whole is surrounded by the words, "LIFESAVING MEDAL OF THE FIRST CLASS" in the upper half and, "UNITED STATES OF AMERICA" in the lower half. The reverse contains an American eagle with spread wings perched atop a monument. To its left is the figure of a woman holding an oak wreath in her left hand. Under the monument, in two lines, are the words, "ACT OF CONGRESS JUNE 20th 1874." The whole is surrounded by the words, "IN TESTIMONY OF HEROIC DEEDS IN SAVING LIFE FROM THE PERILS OF THE SEA". On June 18, 1878, some minor changes were made when the words, "LIFESAVING MEDAL OF THE FIRST CLASS" were removed from the upper half of the obverse and replaced with "UNITED STATES OF AMERICA", taken from the lower half, which was in turn replaced by "ACT OF CONGRESS JUNE 20, 1874", which was removed from the reverse of the medal. The Gold Lifesaving Medal was again modified in May 4, 1882, when it was fitted with a red, 2 inch wide ribbon and a suspension device, a gold eagle's head and outstretched wings. On March 13, 1946, several changes were made to the Lifesaving Medals. The ribbons were changed to avoid confusion with the ribbons of other medals and the size of the medals was reduced to standardize their appearance when worn on the uniform with other medals and ribbons. The only other change to the medal is an inscription change on the lower obverse to "ACT OF CONGRESS AUGUST 4, 1949". The ribbon was changed to one and three-eighths inches in width and consists of a center stripe of gold bordered on either side by a stripe of white and edged with a stripe of red.

The 1882 the design was changed so that the medal was suspended from a two inch wide ribbon. The ribbon was red for the Gold Lifesaving Medal and light blue for the Silver Lifesaving medal.

# Bronze Star Medal

Authorized on February 4, 1944, retroactive to December 7, 1941. It is awarded to individuals who, while serving in the United States Armed Forces in a combat theater, distinguish themselves by heroism, outstanding achievement or by meritorious service not involving aerial flight.

The Bronze Star was originally conceived by the U.S. Navy as a junior decoration comparable to the Air Medal for heroic or meritorious actions by ground and surface personnel. The level of required service would not be sufficient to warrant the Silver Star if awarded for heroism or the Legion of Merit if awarded for meritorious achievement. In a strange twist of fate, the Bronze Star Medal did not reach fruition until championed by General George C. Marshall, the Army Chief of Staff during World War II. Marshall was seeking a decoration that would reward front line troops, particularly infantrymen, whose ranks suffered the heaviest casualties and were forced to endure the greatest danger and hardships during the conflict. Once established, the Bronze Star Medal virtually became the sole province of the Army in terms of the number of medals awarded.

Although Marshall wanted the Bronze Star Medal to be awarded with the same freedom as the Air Medal, it never came close to the vast numbers of Air Medals distributed during the war. The only exception was the award of the Bronze Star Medal to every soldier of the 101st Airborne Division who had fought in the Normandy invasion, Operation Market Garden in Holland, the Battle of the Bulge or were wounded.

After the war, when the ratio of Air Medals to airmen was compared to the numbers of Bronze Star Medals awarded to combat soldiers, it became clear that a huge disparity existed and many troops who deserved the award for their service had not received it. Therefore, in September 1947, the Bronze Star Medal was authorized for all personnel who had received either the Combat Infantryman's Badge (CIB) or the Combat Medical Badge (CMB) between December 7, 1941 to September 2, 1945. In addition, personnel who had participated in the defense of the Philippine Islands between December 7, 1941 and May 10, 1942 were awarded the Bronze Star Medal if their service was on the island of Luzon, the Bataan Peninsula or the harbor defenses on Corregidor Island and they had been awarded the Philippine Presidential Unit Citation. The Bronze Star Medal also replaced some awards of the Purple Heart from early in World War II when that medal was awarded for meritorious or essential service rather than for wounds.

Recipients of the Bronze Star Medal are entitled to wear a "V" device on the ribbon bar and suspension ribbon if the Medal is awarded for heroism in combat. The "V" device was approved in 1945 to clearly distinguish between awards of the medal for heroism in combat or for meritorious service. Additional awards are

**Service:** All Services
**Instituted:** 1944
**Criteria:** Heroic or meritorious achievement or service not involving participation in aerial flight.
**Devices:**
- V (22, 25)
- (41)
- (48)
- ★ (93)
- ☆ (101)

denoted by bronze and silver oak leaf clusters or gold and silver stars, depending on the recipient's Service Branch.

The Bronze Star Medal is a five-pointed bronze star with a smaller star in the center (similar in design to the Silver Star Medal); the reverse contains the inscription, "HEROIC OR MERITORIOUS ACHIEVEMENT" in a circular pattern. The ribbon is red with a white-edged blue band in the center and white edge stripes. The Bronze Star Medal was designed by Rudolf Freund of Bailey, Banks and Biddle.

**Notes:** Awarded to World War II holders of Army Combat Infantryman Badge or Combat Medical Badge.

The numbers in parentheses next to the Devices refer to the tables in "Attachments and Devices" on page 116-119.

# Purple Heart

The Purple Heart is America's oldest military decoration. It was originally established on August 7, 1782 by General George Washington who designed the original award called the "Badge of Military Merit." The Badge of Military Merit was awarded for singularly meritorious action to a deserving hero of the Revolutionary War. There were only three recipients of the award, all of whom were noncommissioned officers of the Continental Army. The Badge of Military Merit was intended by Washington to be a permanent decoration but was never used again after the three initial presentations until it was reestablished as the Purple Heart Medal on February 22, 1932 (the 200th anniversary of Washington's birth) by the Army War Department.

During the First World War, War Department General Order No.134 of October 12, 1917 authorized a red ribbon with a narrow white center stripe to be worn on the right breast for wounds received in action. However, the order was rescinded 32 days later and the ribbon never became a reality. Instead the Army authorized wound chevrons which were worn on the lower right sleeve of the tunic.

On July 21, 1932, General Douglas MacArthur, who was a key figure in its revival, received the first Purple Heart after it was reestablished. President Franklin D. Roosevelt signed an executive order on December 3, 1942 that expanded the award to members of the Navy, Marine Corps and Coast Guard as well. Although the Purple Heart was awarded for meritorious service between 1932 and 1943, the primary purpose of the award has always been to recognize those who received wounds while in the service of the United States military.

Later Presidential Executive Orders extended eligibility for the Purple Heart to military and civilian personnel who received wounds from a terrorist attack or while performing peace keeping duties. Currently, it is awarded for wounds received while serving in any capacity with one of the U.S. Armed Forces after April 5, 1917; it may be awarded to civilians as well as military personnel. The wounds may have been received while in combat against an enemy, while a member of a peacekeeping force, while a Prisoner of War, as a result of a terrorist attack or as a result of a friendly fire incident in hostile territory. The 1996 Defense Authorization Act extended eligibility for the Purple Heart to prisoners of war before April 25, 1962; previous legislation had only authorized the medal to POWs after April 25, 1962. Wounds that qualify must have required treatment by a medical officer and must be a matter of official record.

The Purple Heart was originally last in precedence of all other personal decorations but was elevated in 1985 by an act of Congress to a position just behind the Bronze Star.

**Service:** All Services (originally Army only)

**Instituted:** 1932

**Criteria:** Awarded to any member of the U.S. Armed Forces killed or wounded in an armed conflict.

**Devices:** (41) (48) (93) (101)

**Notes:** Wound Ribbon appeared circa 1917-18 but was never officially authorized. (Army used wound chevrons during World War I).

The medal is a heart-shaped, gold-rimmed medallion with a profile of George Washington on a purple enameled base. Above Washington's profile is the shield from his family's coat of arms. "FOR MILITARY MERIT" is inscribed on the reverse. The ribbon is a dark purple with narrow white edges. The original Badge of Military Merit was a satin purple heart edged in white. The format may have been used since the strongest wood available for gun carriages and weapons during the Revolution was called "Purpleheart", a very strong smooth grain wood from Latin America that was stronger than the famous English oak. Here was an American wood that was stronger, more resistant to rot and termites than any other known wood. Perhaps General Washington chose the American Purpleheart wood as a symbol of strength and resistance over the British hearts of English Oak (a popular English military song of the time).

Additional awards of the Purple Heart are denoted by bronze and silver oak leaf clusters or gold and silver stars, depending on the recipient's Service Branch.

**Notes:** Early Purple Heart Medals were numbered on the edge but this ended in World War II.

Medals of America 157

## Defense Meritorious Service Medal

Authorized on November 3, 1977. The Defense Meritorious Service Medal is awarded to any active member of the U.S. Armed Forces who distinguishes him/herself by noncombat meritorious achievement or service while serving in a Joint Activity after November 3, 1977. Examples of Joint assignments that may allow qualification for this medal are: Office of the Secretary of Defense, Office of the Joint Chiefs of Staff, Unified or Specified Commands, Joint billets in NATO or NORAD, Defense Agencies, National Defense University, National War College, Industrial College of the Armed Forces, Armed Forces Staff College and the Joint Strategic Target Planning Staff.

The bronze medal has an eagle with spread wings in the center superimposed on a pentagon in the center of a laurel wreath. The reverse is inscribed with the words, "DEFENSE MERITORIOUS SERVICE" and "UNITED STATES OF AMERICA". The ribbon has a wide white center stripe with three light blue stripes in the middle. The white stripe is flanked by ruby red and white. The ruby red and white are copied from the ribbon of the Meritorious Service Medal with the blue stripes representing the Department of Defense. Subsequent awards are denoted by bronze and silver oak leaf clusters. The Defense Meritorious Service Medal was designed by Lewis J. King, Jr. of the Institute of Heraldry.

**Service:** All Services (by Secretary of Defense)
**Instituted:** 1977
Criteria: Noncombat meritorious achievement or service while assigned to Joint Activity.
**Devices:**
(45)
(51)
R (111)

## Meritorious Service Medal

Authorized on January 16, 1969 and awarded to members of the Armed Forces for noncombat meritorious achievement or meritorious service after that date. The Meritorious Service Medal evolved from an initial recommendation in 1918 by General John J. Pershing, the Commander of the American Expeditionary Forces during World War I. He suggested that an award for meritorious service be created to provide special recognition to deserving individuals by the U.S. government. Although the request by General Pershing was disapproved, it was revisited several more times during World War II and afterwards. During the Vietnam War the proposal to create the medal received significant attention and was eventually approved when President Lyndon B. Johnson signed the executive order on January 16, 1969. The Meritorious Service Medal cannot be awarded for service in a combat theater. It has often been the decoration of choice for both end of tour and retirement recognition for field grade officers and senior enlisted personnel.

The MSM is a bronze medal with six rays rising from the top of a five-pointed star with beveled edges with two smaller stars outlined within. On the lower part of the medal in front of the star there is an eagle with its wings spread. It is standing on two curving laurel branches tied between the eagle's talons. The eagle, symbol of the nation, holds laurel branches representing achievement. The star represents military service with the rays symbolizing individual efforts to achieve excellence. The reverse of the medal has the inscription, "UNITED STATES OF AMERICA" at the top and "MERITORIOUS SERVICE" at the bottom; the space inside the circle formed by the text is to be used for engraving the recipient's name. The ribbon is ruby red with two white stripes and is a variation of the Legion of Merit ribbon. Jay Morris and Lewis J. King of the Institute of Heraldry designed and sculpted the Meritorious Service Medal. Additional awards are indicated by bronze and silver oak leaf clusters or gold and silver stars depending on the recipient's Service Branch.

**Service:** All Services
**Instituted:** 1969
**Criteria:** Outstanding noncombat meritorious achievement or service to the United States.
**Devices:**
(18)
(41)
(48)
(93)
(101)
R (111)

The numbers in parentheses next to the Devices refer to the tables in "Attachments and Devices" on page 116-119.

# Air Medal

**Service:** All Services
**Instituted:** 1942
**Criteria:** Heroic actions or meritorious service while participating in aerial flight.
**Devices:**
- V (22, 25)
- 3 (30, 31)
- (41)
- (48)
- (38)
- ★ (69)
- ★ (93)
- ★ (101)

Authorized on May 11, 1942, the Air Medal is awarded for single acts of achievement after September 8, 1939 to any member of the U.S. Armed Forces who distinguishes him/herself by heroism, outstanding achievement or by meritorious service while participating in aerial flight. During World War II, the Air Medal was to be awarded for a lesser degree of heroism or achievement than required for the Distinguished Flying Cross. However, many Army Air Force units began to award the Air Medal on a quota basis, e.g., 20 missions equaled one Air Medal or an Air Medal for every enemy aircraft shot down. Some commands carried this to extremes by awarding a DFC for every five Air Medals. By the end of the war, over a million Air Medals were awarded (many of which were, of course, oak leaf clusters). While this might appear extreme, the generous award of the Air Medal provided combat aircrews a visible sign that their devotion and determination were appreciated by the country. The Air Medal helped keep morale up in a force that suffered the highest casualty rate of the war after the Infantry.

Although the Naval Services were authorized to award the Air Medal during World War II, the numbers never approached those received by the Army Air Force amidst the European bombing campaigns. Subsequent to World War II, however, with the increased role of the Navy in joint operations, the use of the Air Medal was subtly redefined. The Air Medal was still awarded for single acts of outstanding achievement which involve superior airmanship but of a lesser degree than would justify an award of a Distinguished Flying Cross. However, during the Korean, Vietnam and Gulf conflicts, awards for meritorious service were made for sustained distinction in the performance of duties involving regular and frequent participation in aerial flight operations. These operations include "strikes" (sorties which deliver ordnance against the enemy; those which land or evacuate personnel in an assault; or, those which involve search and rescue operations which encounter enemy opposition), "flights" (sorties which involve the same kinds of operations as strikes but which do not encounter enemy opposition) or "direct combat support" (sorties which include such activities as reconnaissance, combat air patrol, electronic countermeasures support, psychological warfare, coastal surveillance, etc.). In addition, the Air Medal was awarded for noncombat aerial achievement, such as, to air weather crews who gather major storm data by flying into hurricanes. The Air Force ceased all noncombat awards of the Air Medal with the institution of the Aerial Achievement Medal in 1988 but without a comparable peacetime medal, the other Services still award the Air Medal under circumstances not involving actual combat.

The Air Medal was designed and sculpted by Walker Hancock and is a bronze sixteen point compass rose suspended by a fleur-de-lis. In the center there is an diving eagle carrying a lighting bolt in each talon. The compass rose represents the global capacity of American air power. The lightning bolts show the United States' ability to wage war from the air and the Fleur-de-lis, the French symbol of nobility, represents the high ideals of American airmen. The reverse of the compass rose is plain with an area for engraving the recipient's name. The ribbon is ultramarine blue with two golden orange stripes representing the original colors of the Army Air Force.

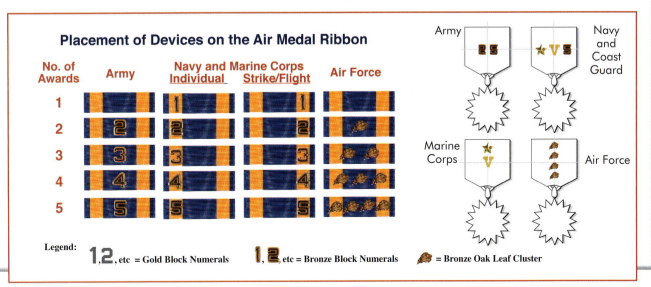

# Silver Lifesaving Medal

The Silver Lifesaving Medal is awarded under the same conditions as the Gold Lifesaving Medal, except that the act need not involve the degree of heroism and risk called for in the case of the Gold Medal. The Silver Lifesaving Medal, like the Gold Lifesaving Medal, was designed by Anthony C. Paquet and was also originally a table medal. It was one and three-fourths inches in diameter and showed a man struggling in a heavy sea; hovering above him is the figure of a woman who is offering him one end of a long scarf. The whole is encircled by the words, "LIFESAVING MEDAL OF THE SECOND CLASS" in the upper half, and "UNITED STATES OF AMERICA" in the lower half. The reverse contains a large wreath of laurel knotted at the bottom with a flowing ribbon. Within the wreath at the top are the words, "ACT OF CONGRESS JUNE 20th 1874". The whole is encircled by the words, "IN TESTIMONY OF HEROIC DEEDS IN SAVING LIFE FROM THE PERILS OF THE SEA". There is a small decorative scroll at the bottom of the medal.

The Act of Congress on June 18, 1878, which modified the Gold Lifesaving Medal also modified the Silver Lifesaving Medal. The obverse was altered to replace the words, "LIFESAVING MEDAL OF THE SECOND CLASS" with "UNITED STATES OF AMERICA", taken from the lower half. The latter was replaced with "ACT OF CONGRESS JUNE 20th 1874", which was removed from the reverse of the medal. In 1882 the Silver Lifesaving Medal was again modified, this time to add a silver suspension bar (of the same design as that of the Gold Lifesaving Medal) and to add a light blue two-inch wide ribbon. The final modification of the Silver Lifesaving Medal occurred in 1949 at the same time and under the same circumstances that the Gold Lifesaving Medal was changed. The current Silver Lifesaving Medal was reduced in size to one and seven-sixteenths of an inch in diameter, the date on the obverse was changed to "AUGUST 4, 1949" and the ribbon reduced in width to one and three-eighths inches. The ribbon is composed of a center stripe of silver gray, bordered by a stripe of white and edged with a stripe of blue. Additional awards of a Gold or Silver Lifesaving Medal are denoted by ornate bars which are inscribed with the recipient's name. A gold star denotes an additional award on the ribbon bar.

**Service:** All Services and Civilians
**Instituted:** 1874 (modified 1882 and 1946)
**Criteria:** Heroic conduct during rescue or attempted rescue of a victim of drowning or shipwreck.
**Devices:** ★ (98)
**Notes:** Normally a "Non-Military Decoration" but considered a personal decoration by the Coast Guard. Originally a "table" (non-wearable) medal, then worn with a 2" wide ribbon.

# Aerial Achievement Medal

The Aerial Achievement Medal was established on February 3, 1988 and has been in effect since January 1, 1990. It is awarded to U.S. Air Force personnel for sustained meritorious achievement while participating in aerial flight. It is not awarded for single event flights. In contrast to the normal procedure for award of all other military decorations, the individual performance which may qualify for the Aerial Achievement Medal can vary based on the requirements and criteria established by each Major Air Force Command. This is due to the many variations posed by each Command's location, mission, environment, available aircraft types, local political conditions and the general world situation.

The American bald eagle is depicted on the front of the Aerial Achievement Medal just below 13 stars symbolic of the original colonies and in front of two intercepting arcs symbolic of flight paths. The eagle is clutching six lightning bolts which represent the U.S. Air Force. The reverse contains the words "FOR MILITARY MERIT" surrounding a space for engraving the awardees name. Additional awards of the Aerial Achievement Medal are denoted by bronze and silver oak leaf clusters.

**Service:** Air Force
**Instituted:** 1988
**Criteria:** Sustained meritorious achievement while participating in aerial flight.
**Devices:**
C (110)
R (111)
🥉 (41)
🥈 (48)

**Notes:** Considered on a par with the Air Medal but more likely to be awarded for peacetime actions.

## Joint Service Commendation Medal

Authorized on June 25, 1963, this was the first medal specifically authorized for members of a Joint Service organization. Awarded to members of the Armed Forces for meritorious achievement or service while serving in a Joint Activity after January 1, 1963. The "V" device is authorized if the award is made for direct participation in combat operations.

The medal consists of four conjoined green enameled hexagons edged in gold which represent the unity of the Armed Forces. The top hexagon has thirteen gold five-pointed stars (representing the thirteen original states) and the lower hexagon has a gold stylized heraldic device (for land, air and sea). An eagle with spread wings and a shield on its breast is in the center of the hexagons. The eagle is grasping three arrows in its talons. The hexagons are encircled by a laurel wreath bound with gold bands (representing achievement). On the reverse there is a plaque for engraving the recipient's name. Above the plaque are the raised words, "FOR MILITARY" and below, "MERIT" with a laurel spray below. The words and laurel spray are derived from the Army and Navy Commendation Medals. The ribbon is a center stripe of green flanked by white, green, white and light blue stripes.

**Service:** All Services (by Secretary of Defense)
**Instituted:** 1963
**Criteria:** Meritorious service or achievement while assigned to a Joint Activity.
**Devices:**
V (24,25)
C (110)
R (111)
(45)
(48)

The green and white are from the Army and Navy Commendation ribbons and the light blue represents the Department of Defense.

The Joint Service Commendation Medal was designed by the Institute of Heraldry's Stafford F. Potter. Oak leaf clusters denote additional awards.

## Army Commendation Medal

Authorized on December 18, 1945 as a commendation ribbon and awarded to members of the Army for heroism, meritorious achievement or meritorious service after December 6, 1941. It was meant for award where the Bronze Star Medal was not appropriate, i.e., outside of operational areas.

The Army Commendation Medal, commonly called the ARCOM, is unique as it is the first and only Army award that started as a ribbon-only award and then became a medal. After World War II, it became the only award created for the express purpose of peacetime and wartime meritorious service as well as the only award designed expressly for presentation to junior officers and enlisted personnel. In short, the ARCOM became the peacetime version of the Bronze Star Medal to recognize outstanding performance and boost morale. Subsequent to World War II, retroactive awards of the Commendation Ribbon were authorized for any individual who had received a Letter of Commendation from a Major General or higher before January 1, 1946.

In 1947, the rules were changed allowing the ARCOM to be awarded in connection with military operations for which the level of service did not meet the requirements for the Bronze Star or Air Medal. In 1949 the change from a ribbon-only award to a pendant was approved. Anyone who received the ribbon could apply for the new medal. The Army redesignated the Commendation Ribbon With Metal Pendant as the Army Commendation Medal in 1960. In 1962, it was authorized for award to a member of the Armed Forces of a friendly nation for the same level of achievement or service which was mutually beneficial to that nation and the United States. The next big change occurred on February 29, 1964 with the approval of the "V"

**Service:** Army
**Instituted:** 1945 (retroactive to 1941)
Criteria: Heroism, meritorious achievement or meritorious service.
**Devices:**
V (22)
C (110)
R (111)
(41)
(48)

device to denote combat heroism of a degree less than that required for the Bronze Star Medal. Additionally, the ARCOM continued to be awarded for acts of courage not qualifying for the Soldier's Medal.

The medal, a bronze hexagon, depicts the American bald eagle with spread wings on the face. The eagle has the U.S. shield on its breast and is grasping three crossed arrows in its talons. On the reverse of the medal are inscriptions "FOR MILITARY" and "MERIT" with a plaque for engraving the recipient's name between the two inscriptions. A spray of laurel, representing achievement is at the bottom. The ribbon is a field of myrtle green with five white stripes in the center and white edges. The Army Commendation Medal was designed and sculpted by Thomas Hudson Jones of the Institute of Heraldry.

## Navy and Marine Corps Commendation Medal

For heroic and meritorious achievement or service. The Navy and Marine Corps Commendation Medal is worn after the Joint Service Commendation Medal and before the Joint Service Achievement Medal.

The Navy and Marine Corps Commendation Medal was originally established as a ribbon-only award on January 11, 1944. The current medal was authorized by the Secretary of the Navy on March 22, 1950. The medal is awarded for both heroism and meritorious achievement. To be awarded for heroism, the act must be worthy of recognition, but to a lesser degree than required for the Bronze Star Medal in combat or the Navy and Marine Corps Medal in a noncombat situation. To be awarded for meritorious achievement, the act must be outstanding and worthy of special recognition, but to a lesser degree than required for the Bronze Star Medal in combat or the Meritorious Service Medal or Air Medal when in a noncombat situation.

The Navy and Marine Corps Commendation Medal was designed by the Institute of Heraldry. The medal is a bronze hexagon with the eagle from the Seal of the Department of Defense in the center. The reverse of the medal has a plaque for inscribing the recipient's name and the raised words, "FOR MILITARY" (above the plaque) and "MERIT" (below the plaque). The ribbon is dark green with a narrow stripe of white near each edge. Additional awards of the Navy and Marine Corps Commendation Medal are denoted by five-sixteenth inch gold stars. A Combat Distinguishing Device (Bronze letter "V") may be authorized.

**Service:** Navy/Marine Corps
**Instituted:** 1944 (retroactive to 1941)
**Criteria:** Heroic or meritorious achievement or service.
**Devices:**
V (22, 25)
C (110)
R (111)
★ (93)
☆ (101)

**Notes:** Originally a ribbon only award then designated "Navy Commendation Ribbon with Metal Pendant". Redesignated: "Navy Commendation Medal" in 1960. Change to present name was made in 1994.

## Air Force Commendation Medal

Authorized on March 28, 1958; Awarded to personnel below the rank of Brigadier General for outstanding achievement, meritorious service or acts of courage that do not meet the requirements for award of the Airman's Medal or the Bronze Star Medal. Previous to its establishment, the Army Commendation Medal was awarded to Air Force personnel who met the criteria for the award. The medal has often been used for end of tour recognition, especially to junior officers and noncommissioned officers. In 1996, the Secretary of the Air Force authorized the award of a bronze letter "V" with this medal, retroactive to January 11, 1996, if the award's recipient distinguishes him/herself while under attack or during a hazardous situation resulting from hostilities. The "V" may be awarded for actions taken during single acts of terrorism and isolated combat incidents. The first instances of the "V" device being awarded with this medal occurred during the terrorist bombing in Saudi Arabia in 1996. The front of the medal contains an American eagle with outstretched wings in front of a cloud formation and perched above the Air Force Coat of Arms.

The reverse contains the words, "FOR MILITARY MERIT" above a blank area which may be used to engrave the recipient's name. The ribbon stripe pattern was designed using the official Air Force colors. The center stripe and other blue stripes are ultramarine blue. They are flanked by stripes of golden yellow.

**Service:** Air Force
**Instituted:** 1958
**Criteria:** Outstanding achievement or meritorious service rendered on behalf of the United States Air Force.
**Devices:**
V (22)
C (110)
R (111)
(41)
(48)

The numbers in parentheses next to the Devices refer to the tables in "Attachments and Devices" on page 116-119.

# Coast Guard Commendation Medal

Following the lead of the other Services, the Coast Guard Commendation Ribbon with Metal Pendant was established on August 26, 1947. This award was to be granted to members of the Armed Forces of the United States serving in any capacity with the Coast Guard, for meritorious service resulting in unusual and outstanding achievement rendered while the Coast Guard is serving under Treasury Department jurisdiction. On October 2, 1959, it was redesignated as the Coast Guard Commendation Medal by order of the Commandant of the Coast Guard. To merit this decoration, the outstanding achievement or meritorious service must have been accomplished in a manner above that normally expected and be sufficient to distinguish the individual from those of comparable grade or ratings performing similar acts or services. The heroism, outstanding achievement or meritorious service must be worthy of special recognition, but not of a level which would justify a higher award (e.g.: Bronze Star Medal, etc.) yet more than that required for award of the Coast Guard Achievement Medal. The Coast Guard Commendation Medal has gone through two designs both executed by the Army's Institute of Heraldry. The first was designed and sculpted by Frank Gasparro. The second version was designed by Jay Morris and sculpted by Lewis J. King, Jr. The first design was employed while the Coast Guard was under the jurisdiction of the Treasury Department and the second was adopted when it was placed under the Department of Transportation. The first design was a bronze hexagon, point up. In the center of the obverse is the former Coast Guard Seal which embodied elements of the Treasury Department Seal, the whole being encircled by a continuous cable. There is a blank plaque in the center of the reverse, which is encircled by a laurel wreath. Above the plaque, in two lines, are the words, "FOR OUTSTANDING" and below it, the word, "SERVICE". The plaque, words and wreath are encircled by a continuous cable. The second design, which was approved by the Commandant on June 11, 1968, is very similar to the first and also employs a bronze hexagon, point up. In the center of the obverse is the current Coast Guard Seal. The continuous cable used in the first design is deleted from the second. The reverse contains an annulet consisting of the word, "AWARDED" at the top and, separated by stylized laurel leaves, the words, "OUTSTANDING SERVICE" in the bottom. In the center are the words, "TO" and "FOR", separated by space for engraving the recipient's name.

**Service:** Coast Guard
**Instituted:** 1947
**Criteria:** 1. Heroic or meritorious achievement or service. 2. Meritorious service resulting in unusual or outstanding achievement.
**Devices:**
◻ (18)
V (22)
C (110)
R (111)
★ (93)
☆ (101)

**Notes:** Originally "Commendation Ribbon with Metal Pendant".

# Joint Service Achievement Medal

The Joint Service Achievement Medal was established in 1983 specifically to complete the Department of Defense awards hierarchy and thereby provide a system of decorations for meritorious achievement comparable to those of the separate services. In so doing, the integrity of the more senior Joint Service medals was protected and the opportunity to earn recognition while assigned to a Joint Activity was provided.

It is awarded for meritorious service or achievement while serving in a Joint Activity after August 3, 1983 to military personnel below the rank of colonel. Oak leaf clusters denote additional awards. The medal features an American eagle with the United States coat of arms on its breast holding three arrows in the center of the bronze medal which consists of a star of twelve points chosen to make it distinctive. The eagle was taken from the Seal designed for the National Military Establishment in 1947 by the President and the arrows were adapted from the seal of the Department of Defense. This is the same design seen on the Army and Navy Commendation Medals.

The reverse of the medal contains the inscriptions, "JOINT SERVICE" and "ACHIEVEMENT AWARD" in a circle. There is space in the center for inscribing the recipient's name. The ribbon consists of a center stripe of red flanked on either side by stripes of light blue, white, green, white and blue.

The Joint Service Achievement Medal was designed by Jay Morris and sculpted by Donald Borja, both of the Institute of Heraldry.

**Service:** All Services (by Secretary of Defense)
**Instituted:** 1983
**Criteria:** Meritorious service or achievement while serving with a Joint Activity.
**Devices:**
C (110)
R (111)
(45)
(51)

## Army Achievement Medal

Key elements of the Department of the Army Seal are centered in a bronze octagon one and a half inches in diameter. The medal shape was chosen to distinguish it from other Army decorations. The Army Seal represents the authority under which the award is given.

On the reverse are three lines in the upper half reading, "FOR MILITARY ACHIEVEMENT". At the bottom of the medal there is a double spray of laurel which represents achievement. The ribbon has a central stripe of blue with a white center stripe. The blue is bordered by white, green, white and is edged in green.

The Army Achievement Medal is awarded for significant achievement deserving recognition but not considered adequate to qualify for an award of the Army Commendation Medal. Award authority rests with commanders in the grade of Lieut. Colonel and above. The Army Achievement Medal is limited to noncombat achievement and that members of other branches of the Armed Forces may be eligible for it under certain circumstances.

**Service:** Army
**Instituted:** 1981
**Criteria:** Meritorious service or achievement while serving in a non-combat area.
**Devices:**
C (110)
R (111)
(41)
(48)

At the same time the Secretary of the Army approved the Army Achievement medal he also approved the Overseas Service Ribbon, the NCO Academy Ribbon (renamed the NCO Professional Development Ribbon) and the Army Service Ribbon. Additional awards of the Army Achievement Medal are denoted by oak leaf clusters. The Army Achievement Medal was designed by Jay Morris and sculpted by Donald Borja of the Institute of Heraldry.

## Navy and Marine Corps Achievement Medal

For junior officers and enlisted personnel whose professional and/or leadership achievements on or after May 1, 1961 are clearly of a superlative nature. The Navy and Marine Corps Achievement Medal is worn after the Joint Service Achievement Medal and before the Combat Action Ribbon.

The Navy and Marine Corps Achievement Medal was originally established as a ribbon-only award on May 1, 1961. The current medal was authorized by the Secretary of the Navy on July 17, 1967. The medal is awarded for both professional and leadership achievement. To be awarded for professional achievement, the act must clearly exceed that which is normally required or expected and must be an important contribution to benefit the United States Naval Service. To be recognized for leadership achievement, the act must be noteworthy and contribute to the individual's unit mission.

The Navy and Marine Corps Achievement Medal was designed by the Institute of Heraldry. The medal is a bronze square (having clipped corners) with a fouled anchor in the center. There is a star in each of the four corners. The reverse of the medal is blank to allow for engraving the recipient's name. The ribbon is myrtle green with stripes of orange near each edge. Additional awards

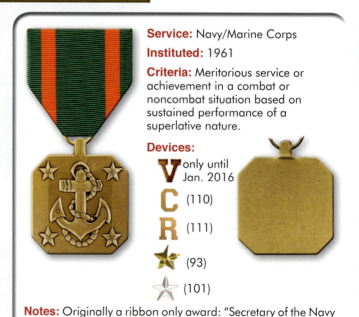

**Service:** Navy/Marine Corps
**Instituted:** 1961
**Criteria:** Meritorious service or achievement in a combat or noncombat situation based on sustained performance of a superlative nature.
**Devices:**
V only until Jan. 2016
C (110)
R (111)
★ (93)
★ (101)

**Notes:** Originally a ribbon only award: "Secretary of the Navy Commendation for Achievement Award with Ribbon".

of the Navy and Marine Corps Achievement Medal are denoted by five-sixteenth inch gold stars. A Combat Distinguishing Device (Combat "V") may be authorized before Jan. 2016.

The numbers in parentheses next to the Devices refer to the tables in "Attachments and Devices" on page 116-119.

## Air Force Achievement Medal

The Air Force Achievement Medal was established by the Secretary of the Air Force on October 12, 1980 and may be awarded to U.S. military personnel below the rank of colonel for meritorious service or outstanding achievement. This medal is the first decoration established for Air Force personnel under Air Force authority. The primary use of the medal has been to recognize specific individual achievements or accomplishments rather than continuing periods of service such as might be associated with a change in permanent assignment, although it has been used for end of tour recognition for some junior ranking personnel. A bronze letter "V" was authorized retroactive to January 11, 1996 for those receiving the award for actions during combat conditions, hostile acts or single acts of terrorism. The first instances of the "V" device being awarded with the medal were to airmen who received the medal for actions during the 1996 terrorist bombing of an Air Force dormitory in Saudi Arabia. The front of the medal has eleven cog-like shapes on the outer border; within the medal are a set of wings with four thunderbolts crossing through them. The

**Service:** Air Force
**Instituted:** 1980
**Criteria:** Outstanding achievement or meritorious service not warranting award of the Air Force Commendation Medal.
**Devices:**
V only until Jan. 2016
C (110)
R (111)
(41)
(48)

reverse of the medal bears the circular inscription, "AIR FORCE MERITORIOUS ACHIEVEMENT" around its outer edge.

## Transportation 9-11 Medal

The Transportation 9-11 Medal is awarded to employees of the Department of Transportation and private citizens for meritorious service resulting from unusual and outstanding achievement in response to the attacks on September 11, 2001. The award may be made posthumously and the decoration, certification and citation presented to the next of kin with appropriate ceremony. Specifically this award is authorized for the following personnel:

a. Employees of the Department of Transportation who were on scene at the World Trade Center Complex in New York, the crash site in Pennsylvania or at the Pentagon on September 11, 2001 and performed a role in the initial rescue and recovery operations.
b. All personnel directly involved in the evacuation of lower Manhattan to include DOT employees, masters and crews of commercial vessels and masters and crews of recreational boats that actually transported evacuees during the evacuation on September 11, 2001. The level of effort must clearly set the member above that described in the 9-11 Ribbon.
c. Personnel that demonstrated extraordinary participation or leadership while patrolling harbors, securing critical infrastructure facilities, escorting high interest vessels and conducting boarding of vessels entering U.S. waters during the period of September 11, 2001 to September 11, 2002. The level of effort must clearly set the member above that described in the 9-11 Ribbon.
d. Employees of the DOT who demonstrated extraordinary dedication or leadership between September 11, 2001 and September 11, 2002. Participation must have

**Service:** Coast Guard
**Instituted:** 2002
**Dates:** 2001- 2002
**Criteria:** Meritorious service and outstanding achievement in response to the attacks on September 11, 2001.
**Devices:** None

been at an exceptional level to warrant consideration for the awarding of the 9-11 Medal. The level of effort must clearly set the member well above that described in the 9-11 Ribbon.

The front of the medal is dominated by a lighted candle from which 11 beams of light emanate with nine stars located between the beams. Below the candle are two olive branches representing peace and the Latin inscription, "NE OBLIVISCARIS" (Never Forget). Around the periphery of the medal are the inscriptions, "DEPARTMENT OF TRANSPORTATION" at the top and "UNITED STATES OF AMERICA" at the bottom. The medal's reverse contains the inscription, "FOR SERVICE AND SACRIFICE TO THE UNITED STATES OF AMERICA DURING AND AFTER THE TRAGIC EVENTS OF SEPTEMBER 11, 2001."

## Coast Guard Achievement Medal

Following the lead of the "Secretary of the Navy Commendation for Achievement with Ribbon" in 1961, (subsequently designated the Navy Achievement Medal), the Secretary of the Treasury established a similar ribbon for Coast Guard personnel on January 29, 1964. The ribbon was formally redesignated as the Coast Guard Achievement Medal on June 11, 1968.

The Coast Guard Achievement Medal may be awarded to all members of the Coast Guard, including reserves, as well as to members of other branches of the Armed Forces when serving with Coast Guard units. It is given for professional or leadership achievement in either peacetime or combat situations. It may be awarded based on sustained performance or for specific achievement of a superlative nature, but not of a level which would justify award of a Commendation Medal.

The Coast Guard Achievement Medal was designed by Irving Lyons and sculpted by Lewis J. King, Jr., both of the Institute of Heraldry. It is a bronze disc in the center of which is the Coast Guard Seal surrounded by a laurel wreath, which is in turn surrounded by a border of cable. The reverse bears the inscription (in raised letters), "AWARDED TO" in the upper portion and "FOR ACHIEVEMENT" in the lower. The ribbon is the same as

**Service:** Coast Guard
**Instituted:** 1968
**Criteria:** Professional and/or leadership achievement in a combat or noncombat situation.
**Devices:**
V only until Jan. 2016 (110)
C (111)
R
◻ (18)
★ (93)
☆ (101)

**Notes:** Originally a ribbon-only award. until 1968.

that of the Navy Achievement Medal except that it has a narrow stripe of white in the center of the ribbon.

Symbolically, the laurel wreath represents achievement and the continuous cable stands for fidelity of the seaman in support of the Coast Guard, which is represented by the Coast Guard Seal.

## Coast Guard Commandant's Letter of Commendation Ribbon

With the establishment of the Coast Guard Commandant's Letter of Commendation Ribbon in 1979, the Coast Guard formalized one of its oldest awards. Like the Navy's Letter of Commendation, the award had previously existed only as a paper certificate and an entry into the Coast Guardsman's service record before its appearance as a tangible, wearable part of the uniform. It is awarded to any member of the Armed Forces of the United States who, while serving in any capacity with the Coast Guard, is awarded a Letter of Commendation by the Coast Guard Commandant. The service for which the ribbon is awarded

**Service:** Coast Guard Instituted: 1979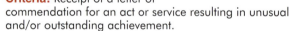
**Criteria:** Receipt of a letter of commendation for an act or service resulting in unusual and/or outstanding achievement.
**Devices:** ◻ (18)  ★ (99)  ☆ (101)

must be of a degree less than that required for award of the Coast Guard Achievement Medal.

## Navy Combat Action Ribbon

For active participation in ground or surface combat subsequent to December 6, 1941, while in the grade of Colonel or below. The Combat Action Ribbon is worn after the Navy and Marine Corps Achievement Medal and before the Navy Presidential Unit Citation in a ribbon display. It is worn as the senior ribbon on the right breast when full sized medals are worn on the left breast.

The Combat Action Ribbon was authorized by the Secretary of the Navy on February 17, 1969 and recently made retroactive to December 6, 1941. The principal requirement is that the individual was engaged in combat during specifically listed military operations at which time he/she was under enemy fire and that his/her performance was satisfactory.

**Service:** Navy/Marine Corps Instituted: 1979 (Retroactive to 6th Dec. 1941)
**Criteria:** Active participation in ground or surface combat during specifically listed military operations.
**Devices:** ★ (96)  ☆ (101)

The Combat Action Ribbon is a ribbon only award. The ribbon is gold with thin center stripes of red, white and blue and border stripes of dark blue on the left and red on the right. Additional awards are authorized for each separate conflict/war and are represented by five-sixteenth inch gold stars.

## Air Force Combat Action Medal

On January 2007, the SECAF approved establishment of the Air Force Combat Action Medal (AFCAM) to recognize any military member of the Air Force (airman through colonel) who actively participated in combat (ground or air). The principal eligibility criterion is that the individual must have been under direct and hostile fire while operating in enemy domain (outside the wire) or physically engaging hostile forces with direct and lethal fire.

Combat conditions defined: for the purposes of this award, combat conditions are met when: 1) individuals deliberately go outside the wire to conduct official duties—either ground or air; and 2) they come under enemy attack by lethal weapons while performing those duties; and 3) are at risk of grave danger. Or 1) individuals defending the base (on the wire); and 2) come under fire and engage the enemy with direct and lethal fire; and 3) are at risk of grave danger, also meet the intent of combat conditions for this award. Additionally, personnel in ground operations who actively engage the enemy with direct and lethal fire may qualify even if no direct fire is taken—as long as there was risk of grave danger and other criteria are met. Central to the integrity of this combat recognition is the adherence to those combat conditions prerequisites.

The symbolism to the medal is as follows: The eagle represents strength and vigilance and embodies the American spirit of freedom. The star and eagle, as

**Service:** Air Force
**Instituted:** 2006
**Criteria:** Awarded to Airmen who have directly participated in active combat, either in the air or on the ground, as part of their official duties.
**Devices:** (95)

well as the ribbon colors are adapted from the art insignia on the aircraft of Billy Mitchell and give this medal the heritage and honor of that history. Billy Mitchell was an airpower advocate who planned and led the first coordinated air ground offensive in history during World War I. The eagle is facing toward the arrows represent lethal capability while the olive branch emphasizes looking forward to peace. The laurel wreath is symbolic of respect and high achievement.

## Coast Guard Combat Action Ribbon

For active participation in ground or maritime combat subsequent to July 16, 2008 by Coast Guard members while in the grade of Captain (O-6) or below. The Combat Action Ribbon is worn after the Commandant's Letter of Commendation Ribbon and before the Coast Guard Presidential Unit Citation. The Combat Action Ribbon is an individual service award, the principal eligibility criterion is satisfactory performance under enemy fire while actively participating in a ground or maritime engagement. Neither service in a combat area, being awarded the Purple Heart nor a combat award or badge from another Service automatically makes a Service member eligible for the Combat Action Ribbon.

Coast Guard members who experience direct expo-

**Service:** Coast Guard
**Instituted:** 2008 Criteria: Awarded to members of the Coast Guard who have actively participated in ground or maritime combat.
**Devices:**  (74)  (86)

sure to the detonation of an improvised explosive device (IED) and/or who serve in clandestine or special operations may be eligible for this award. Additional awards of the Coast Guard Combat Action Ribbon are denoted by three-sixteenth inch bronze and silver stars. Only one award per operation is authorized.

## Army Presidential Unit Citation

The Army Presidential Unit Citation (PUC) was established on February 26, 1942 as the "Distinguished Unit Badge" or the "Distinguished Unit Citation" and redesignated as the Presidential Unit Citation in 1966. It is awarded to Army units that display the same degree of heroism in combat as would warrant the Distinguished Service Cross for an individual. Like all Army unit awards, the PUC is worn above the pocket on the right breast of the uniform. The gold-colored frame around the ribbon is worn with the open end of the "V" of the laurel leaf pattern pointing upward. The badge may only be worn permanently by those individuals who were assigned to the unit for the period for which it was cited. Current members of the unit who were not assigned to

**Service:** Army
**Instituted:** 1942
**Criteria:** Awarded to U.S. Army units for extraordinary heroism in action against an armed enemy.
**Devices:**  (42)  (49)

the unit for the award period are entitled to wear the ribbon but only for the duration of their assignment with the cited unit. Such personnel must remove it from their uniform upon reassignment. Additional awards of the Army Presidential Unit Citation are denoted by bronze oak leaf clusters.

## Navy Presidential Unit Citation

 (62)

The Navy Presidential Unit Citation is awarded in the name of the President for service in a unit with outstanding performance in action. The Navy Presidential Unit Citation was established on February 6, 1942 and amended on June 28, 1943. The citation is conferred on units for displaying extraordinary heroism subsequent to October 16, 1941, the degree of heroism required is the same as that which is required for the award of the Navy Cross to an individual. Unlike the Army, only individuals actually assigned to the unit when the award was granted may wear the ribbon on their uniform. The ribbon consists of three equal horizontal stripes of navy blue (top), gold (middle) and red (bottom)

**Service:** Navy/Marine Corps/ Coast Guard
**Instituted:** 1942 **Criteria:** Awarded to Navy/ Marine Corps units for extraordinary heroism in action against an armed enemy.
**Devices:**  (7) N (17) ★ (66) ☆ (85)

and is worn after the Combat Action Ribbon and before the Joint Meritorious Unit Award. Additional awards of the Navy Presidential Unit Citation are denoted by three-sixteenth inch bronze stars.

## Air Force Presidential Unit Citation

The Air Force Presidential Unit Citation owes its heritage to the original Army award which was created in February 26, 1942 and modified by Executive Order on December 2, 1943. The order created the Distinguished Unit Citation which was redesignated as the Presidential Unit Citation on January 10, 1957. It is conferred upon units of the Army and Air Force of the United States for extraordinary heroism in action against an armed enemy on or after December 7, 1941. The unit must display such gallantry, determination and esprit de corps as to set it apart from and above other units participating in the same campaign. The degree of heroism required is the same that which would warrant award of the Distinguished Service Cross or Air Force Cross

**Service:** Air Force
**Instituted:** 1957
**Criteria:** Awarded to Air Force units for extraordinary heroism in action against an armed enemy.
**Devices:**  (42)  (49)

to an individual. Unlike the Army, the Air Force PUC may only be worn by individuals who are assigned or permanently attached to and also present for duty with a unit in the action for which the Presidential Unit Citation is awarded. Subsequent awards of the Presidential Unit Citation are denoted by bronze oak-leaf clusters.

## Coast Guard Presidential Unit Citation

Following a tradition set by the Coast Guard twice before in their history (with the Bicentennial Unit Commendation and the D.O.T. Secretary's Outstanding Unit Award), the Coast Guard issued their version of the Presidential Unit Citation to all active duty, reserve, auxiliary and civilian members of the Service on duty during a specific time period. At a change of command ceremony at Fort McNair in Washington, DC, President George W. Bush announced the establishment of the award under Executive Order 13286. This initial award was for meritorious achievement and outstanding performance in action from August 29 to September 13, 2005 in preparation for, response to, and recovery from, the devastation wrought by Hurricane Katrina. In coordination with the

**Service:** Coast Guard
**Instituted:** 2006
**Criteria:** Awarded for meritorious achievement and outstanding performance in conjunction with efforts during Hurricane Katrina.
**Devices:**  (9)

Department of Homeland Security and the Institute of Heraldry, the ribbon is worn with a specially-designed device in the form of the familiar hurricane symbol used on road signs and shelters in areas prone to these disastrous storms. Curiously, the device is worn by all Coast Guard personnel no matter where they were serving at the time of the storm.

## Joint Meritorious Unit Award

The Joint Meritorious Unit Award was authorized by the Secretary of Defense on June 10, 1981 (retroactive to January 23, 1979) and was originally called the Department of Defense Meritorious Unit Award. It is awarded in the name of the Secretary of Defense for meritorious service, superior to that which would normally be expected during combat, a declared national emergency or under extraordinary circumstances that involve national interest. The service performed by the unit would be similar to that performed by an individual awarded

**Service:** All Services
**Instituted:** 1981
**Criteria:** Awarded to Joint Service units for meritorious achievement or service in combat or extreme circumstances.
**Devices:**  (42) (49)

the Defense Superior Service Medal. The ribbon is similar to the Defense Superior Service Medal ribbon with a gold metal frame with laurel leaves. The Army award is larger.

## Army Valorous Unit Award

The Army Valorous Unit Award was approved and established by the Army Chief of Staff on January 12, 1966. It is awarded to units of the Armed Forces of the United States for extraordinary heroism in action against an armed enemy of the United States while engaged in conflict with an opposing foreign force on or after August 3, 1963. The Valorous Unit Award requires a lesser degree of gallantry than that required for the Presidential Unit Citation. Nevertheless, the unit must have performed with marked distinction under difficult and hazardous conditions so as to set it apart from the other units participating in the same conflict. The degree of heroism required is the same as that which would warrant award of the Silver Star to an individual.

**Service:** Army
**Instituted:** 1963
**Criteria:** Awarded to U.S. Army units for outstanding heroism in armed combat against an opposing armed force.
**Devices:**  (42)  (49)

This award will normally be earned by units that have participated in single or successive actions covering relatively brief time spans but only on rare occasions will a unit larger than a battalion qualify for this award. Additional awards are denoted by bronze oak leaf clusters

## Air Force Gallant Unit Citation

The Gallant Unit Citation (GUC) was established in 2004 by the Secretary of the Air Force and is awarded to active duty, Reserve and Guard units for extraordinary heroism in action against an armed enemy of the United States while engaged in military operations involving conflict with an opposing foreign force on or after September 11, 2001. The unit must have performed with marked distinction under difficult and hazardous conditions in accomplishing its mission so as to set it apart from and above other units participating in the same conflict. The degree of heroism is the same as that

**Service:** Air Force
**Instituted:** 2004
**Criteria:** Awarded to U.S. Air Force units for extraordinary heroism against an armed enemy of the United States.
**Devices:**  (42) (49)

which would warrant award of the Silver Star to an individual. Bronze and silver oak leaf clusters are worn to denote additional awards.

## Navy Unit Commendation

The Navy Unit Commendation was established by the Secretary of the Navy on December 18, 1944. The Commendation is awarded by the Secretary of the Navy with the approval of the President to units which, subsequent to December 6, 1941, distinguish themselves by outstanding heroism in action against an enemy, but to a lesser degree than required for the Presidential Unit Citation. The Commendation may also be awarded for extremely meritorious service not involving combat, but in support of military operations, which is outstanding when compared to other units performing similar service. The ribbon is dark green with narrow border

**Service:** Navy/Marine Corps
**Instituted:** 1944
**Criteria:** Awarded to Navy & Marine Corps units for outstanding heroism in action or extremely meritorious service.
**Devices:**  (66) (85)

stripes of red, gold and blue and is worn after the Joint Meritorious Unit Award and before the Navy Meritorious Unit Commendation. Additional awards are denoted by three-sixteenth inch bronze stars.

## Army Meritorious Unit Commendation

The Army Meritorious Unit Commendation is awarded to units for exceptionally meritorious conduct in performance of outstanding services for at least six continuous months during the period of military operations against an armed enemy occurring on or after January 1, 1944. Service in a combat zone is not required but must be directly related to the combat effort. Units based within the continental U.S. or outside the area of operation are excluded from this award. The unit must display such outstanding devotion and superior performance of exceptionally difficult tasks as to set it apart and above other units with similar missions. The award is usually given to units larger than battalions. The degree of achievement required is the same as that which would warrant award

**Service:** Army and Army Air Force
**Instituted:** 1944
**Criteria:** Awarded to U.S. Army units for exceptionally meritorious conduct in the performance of outstanding service.
**Devices:**  (42)  (49)

of the Legion of Merit to an individual. It was originally authorized as a wreath emblem that was worn on the lower right sleeve of the Army uniform but was redeveloped in its present form in 1961. As with other unit citations, it has a gold frame surrounding the ribbon; the open end of the "V" shaped design on the frame points upward and is worn with other unit citations on the right side of the uniform. Additional awards are denoted by bronze and silver oak leaf clusters.

## Navy Meritorious Unit Commendation

The Navy Meritorious Unit Commendation was established by the Secretary of the Navy on July 17, 1967 and is awarded by the Secretary of the Navy to units which distinguish themselves by either valorous or meritorious achievement considered outstanding, but to a lesser degree than required for the Navy Unit Commendation. The Commendation may be awarded for services in combat or noncombat situations. The ribbon is dark green with a narrow red center stripe flanked on either side by stripes of gold, navy blue and gold. The Meritorious Unit Commendation is worn after the Navy Unit Commendation and before the Navy "E" ribbon. Additional awards are denoted by three-sixteenth inch bronze and silver stars.

**Service:** Navy/Marine Corps
**Instituted:** 1967
**Criteria:** Awarded to Navy/Marine Corps units for valorous actions or meritorious achievement (combat or noncombat).
**Devices:**  (66)   (85)

## Air Force Meritorious Unit Award

The Meritorious Unit Award was established in 2004 by the Secretary of the Air Force to reward Active duty, Reserve and Guard units for exceptionally meritorious conduct in the performance of outstanding services for at least 90 continuous days during a period of military operations against an armed enemy on or after September 11, 2001. The unit must display such outstanding devotion and superior performance of exceptionally difficult tasks so as to set it above and apart from other units with similar missions. The degree of achievement required is the same as that which would warrant award of the Legion of Merit to an individual. Bronze and silver oak leaf clusters are worn to denote additional awards.

**Service:** Air Force
**Instituted:** 2004
**Criteria:** Awarded to Air Force units for exceptionally meritorious conduct in the performance of outstanding service.
**Devices:**  (42)  (49)

## Air Force Outstanding Unit Award

The Outstanding Unit Award was established on January 6, 1954 and is awarded by the Secretary of the Air Force to units for exceptionally meritorious service or outstanding achievement that clearly sets the unit above and apart from similar units. A unit must clearly perform at a high level for a sustained period of time to receive such recognition as afforded by this award. The exceptionally meritorious service must have been performed for a period of not more than two years and not less than one year. A bronze letter "V" is worn on the ribbon when awarded for combat or direct combat support actions. Bronze and silver oak leaf clusters are worn to denote additional awards.

**Service:** Air Force
**Instituted:** 1954
**Criteria:** Awarded to U.S. Air Force units for exceptionally meritorious achievement or meritorious service.
**Devices:**  (No longer awarded)    (42)  (49)

## Air Force Organizational Excellence Award

The Air Force Organizational Excellence Award was established on August 26, 1969 to recognize unique, unnumbered organizations/units that have performed exceptionally meritorious service for a nominated time period of not less than two years. It is awarded to recognize the achievements and accomplishments of Air Force organizations or activities that do not meet the eligibility requirements of the Air Force Outstanding Unit Awards such as Headquarters organizations and Air Force Academy units. The letter "V" is authorized if awarded for combat or direct combat support actions. Additional awards are signified by bronze and silver oak leaf clusters.

**Service:** Air Force
**Instituted:** 1969
**Criteria:** Same as Outstanding Unit Award but awarded to unique unnumbered organizations performing staff functions.
**Devices:**  (No longer awarded)    (42)  (49)

The numbers in parentheses next to the Devices refer to the tables in "Attachments and Devices" on page 116-119.

## Army Superior Unit Award

The Army Superior Unit Award was approved in April, 1985 (modified in July, 1986) and is awarded for outstanding meritorious performance of a unit during peacetime in a difficult and challenging mission under extraordinary circumstances. The unit must display such outstanding devotion and superior performance of exceptionally difficult tasks to set it apart from and above other units with similar missions. For the purpose of this award, peacetime is defined as any period during which wartime or combat awards are not authorized in the geographical area in which the mission was executed. The award may be given for operations of a humanitarian nature. The award is designed for battalion-size and smaller or comparable units, but, under most circumstances, headquarters type units would not be eligible.

**Service:** Army
**Instituted:** 1985
**Criteria:** Awarded to U.S. Army units for meritorious performance in difficult and challenging peacetime missions.
**Devices:**  (42)  (49)

Awards to units larger than battalion size would be infrequent. As with other Army unit citations, it has a gold frame surrounding the ribbon; the open end of the "V" shaped design on the frame points upward and is worn with other unit citations on the right side of the uniform. Additional awards are denoted by bronze and silver oak leaf clusters.

## Department of Transportation Outstanding Unit Award

The Department of Transportation Outstanding Unit Award was authorized by the Secretary of Transportation effective Nov. 3, 1994 as an award to Coast Guard units for valorous or extremely meritorious service on behalf of the Transportation Dept. It has been awarded only twice, the first being to all Coast Guard active duty personnel, civilian employees, Reservists, Auxiliarists, cadets, U.S. Public Health Service personnel and Dept. of Defense personnel serving with the Coast Guard for any length of honorable service between Oct. 1, 1993 and Sept. 30, 1994. It was again awarded to Coast Guard personnel who served with the Guarding Liberty Task Force (New York City) between Sept. 11, 2001 and

**Service:** Coast Guard
**Instituted:** 1995
**Criteria:** Awarded to U.S. Coast Guard units for valorous or extremely meritorious service on behalf of the Transportation Dept.
**Devices:** (19) (94) (102)

Oct. 22, 2001. The second award is denoted by a gold star. However, since the entire Coast Guard organization was transferred to the U.S. Department of Homeland Security after the 9-11 attacks, this award will not longer be presented to Coast Guard personnel.

## Coast Guard Unit Commendation

The Coast Guard Unit Commendation was authorized by the Coast Guard Commandant effective January 1, 1963 for award to any unit which has distinguished itself by valorous or extremely meritorious service not involving combat but in support of Coast Guard operations, which renders the unit outstanding compared to other units performing similar service. This award may also be conferred upon a unit of another branch of the Armed Forces of the United States. To justify this award, the unit must have performed service as a unit of a character comparable to that which would merit the award of the Coast Guard Commendation Medal or higher

**Service:** Coast Guard
**Instituted:** 1963
**Criteria:** Awarded to U.S. Coast Guard units for valorous or extremely meritorious service not involving combat.
**Devices:** (19) (94) (102)

award to an individual. The silver letter "O" (Operational Distinguishing Device) may be authorized. Additional awards are denoted by 5/16 inch dia. gold and silver stars.

## Coast Guard Meritorious Unit Commendation

The Coast Guard Meritorious Unit Commendation was authorized by the Coast Guard Commandant effective November 13, 1973 and is awarded to any unit of the Coast Guard which distinguishes itself by either valorous or meritorious achievement or service in support of Coast Guard operations not involving combat which renders the unit outstanding compared to other units performing similar service but not sufficient to justify the award of the Coast Guard Unit Commendation. The service performed as a unit must be of a character comparable to that which would merit the award of the Coast Guard Achievement Medal to an individual.

**Service:** Coast Guard
**Instituted:** 1973
**Criteria:** Awarded to U.S. Coast Guard units for valorous or meritorious achievement (combat or noncombat).
**Devices:** (19) (94) (102)

This award may also be conferred by the Commandant upon a unit of other branches of the Armed Forces of the United States. The silver letter "O" (Operational Distinguishing Device) may be authorized. Additional awards are denoted by gold and silver stars.

## Coast Guard Meritorious Team Commendation

The Coast Guard Meritorious Team Commendation was authorized on December 22, 1993 by the Coast Guard Commandant to recognize outstanding performance by small groups, e.g., teams, detachments or sub-units, which do not constitute a Coast Guard Unit. To justify the award, the individual members of these groups must perform service which makes a significant contribution to the group's outstanding accomplishment of a study, process, mission, etc. The service performed as a group or team must be of a character comparable to that which would merit the award of the Commandant's Letter of Commendation to an individual. The silver letter "O" (Operational Distinguishing Device) may be authorized. Additional awards are denoted by gold and silver stars.

**Service:** Coast Guard
**Instituted:** 1993
**Criteria:** Awarded to smaller U.S. Coast Guard units for valorous or meritorious achievement (combat or noncombat).
**Devices:** ▭ (19)  ★ (94)  ☆ (102)

## Navy "E" Ribbon

The Navy "E" Ribbon was established in June 1976 to recognize individuals who, subsequent to July 1, 1974, are permanently assigned to ships or squadrons that win battle efficiency competitions. It may be worn by all personnel who served as permanent members of the ship's company or squadrons winning the Battle Efficiency Award. The Navy "E" Ribbon is worn after the Meritorious Unit Commendation and before the Prisoner of War Medal. The ribbon is navy blue with borders of white and gold and is issued with a silver "E" device in the center denoting the first award. Subsequent awards are signified by additional "E" devices with the fourth (and final) award indicated by a silver "E" surrounded by a silver wreath.

**Service:** Navy/Marine Corps
**Instituted:** 1976
**Criteria:** Awarded to ships or squadrons which have won battle efficiency competitions.
**Devices:** Ⓔ (14)  E (15)

## Coast Guard "E" Ribbon

The Coast Guard "E" Ribbon was authorized by the Coast Guard Commandant on September 25, 1990. It is awarded by area commanders to provide visible recognition for personnel of cutters earning the overall operational readiness "E" award during Refresher Training. All personnel serving aboard their unit for more than 50 percent of the period during which it undergoes Refresher Training are eligible for the "E" Ribbon. Additional awards are denoted by 5/16 inch diameter gold and silver stars.

**Service:** Coast Guard
**Instituted:** 1990
**Criteria:** Awarded to U.S. Coast Guard ships and cutters which earn the overall operational readiness efficiency award.
**Devices:** ★ (94)  ☆ (102)

## Coast Guard Bicentennial Unit Commendation

The Coast Guard Bicentennial Unit Commendation was authorized by the Coast Guard Commandant effective January 2, 1990. It was awarded to all Coast Guard members, including selected Reservists, civilians and Auxiliarists, serving satisfactorily during any period from June 4, 1989 to August 4, 1990. Personnel of other Services who were assigned to and served with the Coast Guard during this period were also eligible for this award. Since this was a "one-time only" award, no devices were authorized.

**Service:** Coast Guard
**Instituted:** 1990
**Criteria:** Awarded to all Coast Guard personnel serving satisfactorily at any time between June 4, 1989 and June 4, 1990.
**Devices:** None

The numbers in parentheses next to the Devices refer to the tables in "Attachments and Devices" on page 116-119.

## Prisoner of War Medal

The Prisoner of War Medal is awarded to any person who was taken prisoner of war and held captive after April 5, 1917. It was authorized by Public Law Number 99-145 in 1985 and may be awarded to any person who was taken prisoner or held captive while engaged in an action against an enemy of the United States, while engaged in military operations involving conflict with an opposing armed force or while serving with friendly forces engaged in armed conflict against an opposing armed force in which the United States is not a belligerent party. The recipient's conduct while a prisoner must have been honorable.

The Prisoner of War Medal is worn after all unit awards (after personal decorations in the case of the Army) and before the various Armed Service Good Conduct Medals (before the Combat Readiness Medal in the case of the Air Force).

The Prisoner of War Medal was designed by the Institute of Heraldry. The medal is a circular bronze disc with an American eagle centered and completely surrounded by a ring of barbed wire and bayonet points. The reverse of the medal has a raised inscription, "AWARDED TO" with a space for the recipient's name and, "FOR HONORABLE SERVICE WHILE A PRISONER OF WAR" set in three lines. Below this is the shield of the United States and the words, "UNITED STATES OF AMERICA." The ribbon is black with thin border stripes of white, blue, white and red. Additional awards are denoted by three-sixteenth inch bronze stars.

**Service:** All Services
**Instituted:** 1985
**Criteria:** Awarded to any member of the U.S. Armed Forces taken prisoner during any armed conflict dating from World War I.
**Devices:** ★ (65)

## Combat Readiness Medal

Authorized on March 9, 1964. Awarded for periods of qualifying service in a combat or mission ready status for direct weapon system employment. Direct weapon system employment is defined as: (1) An aircrew whose wartime mission places them into enemy territory or in the threat envelope of ground enemy defenses, (2) A missile operation which could employ weapons to destroy enemy targets and (3) Individuals who directly control in-flight manned aircraft whose wartime mission is to seek and destroy enemy targets. An individual must be a member of a unit subject to combat readiness reporting under Joint Chiefs of Staff requirements, must have completed all prerequisite training and be certified as combat or mission ready in performing the unit's mission and must be subject to a continuous individual positional evaluation program. In previous regulations, eligibility was extended to Air Force members on special duty with another U.S. military service provided they were certified as combat ready in that service and the combat ready status closely correlated to that of the Air Force. Originally an individual was required to be combat ready for three years to earn this award. Currently, individuals must have 24 months of sustained combat ready status to receive the award. Eligibility for the award is certified by the individual's unit commander and is filed in the unit's personnel records group. An oak leaf cluster attachment is awarded for each additional 24 months of combat ready status provided there is no break greater than 120 days. The front of the medal has a border of concentric rays encircling a ring of stylized cloud forms with two intersecting triangles on a compass rose that has small triangles at the points. The reverse of the medal contains the inscription, "FOR COMBAT READINESS-AIR FORCE."

**Service:** Air Force
**Instituted:** 1964
**Criteria:** Awarded for specific periods of qualifying service in a combat or mission-ready status.
**Devices:** (43) (50)

# Army Good Conduct Medal

**Service:** Army (also Air Force until 1963)
**Instituted:** 1941
**Criteria:** Exemplary conduct, efficiency and fidelity during three years of active enlisted service with the U.S. Army (1 year during wartime).
**Devices:**
(4)

Authorized on June 28, 1941 for exemplary conduct, efficiency and fidelity and awarded to Army personnel who, on or after August 27, 1940, had honorably completed three years of active Federal military service. The medal could also be awarded for one year of service after December 7, 1941 while the U.S. was at war. The award was not automatic and required certification by a commanding officer (usually a battalion commander or higher).

The Army Good Conduct Medal was designed by Joseph Kiselewski with an eagle perched on a roman sword atop a closed book. Around the outside are the words, "EFFICIENCY, HONOR, FIDELITY." The reverse of the medal has a five pointed star just above center with a blank scroll for engraving the soldier's name. Above the star are the words, "FOR GOOD" and below the scroll is the word, "CONDUCT." A wreath of half laurel leaves, denoting accomplishment and half oak leaves, denoting bravery surrounds the reverse design.

The ribbon was designed by Arthur E. DuBois, the legendary Director of the Army Institute of Heraldry, and is scarlet with three narrow white stripes on each side. The ribbon is divided by the white stripes so as to form thirteen stripes representing the thirteen original colonies of the United States. During the Revolutionary War, the color scarlet symbolized the mother country and the white stripe symbolized the virgin land separated by force from the mother country.

Unlike other additional award devices, e.g., oak leaf clusters, bronze, silver, or gold clasps with knots (or loops) are used to indicate the **total** number of awards of the Army Good Conduct Medal. For instance, two awards of the medal are indicated by two bronze knots, three by three, etc. Six total awards are indicated by one silver knot, seven by two silver knots, etc. Eleven total awards are indicated by one gold knot, twelve by two gold knots, etc. While all regulations since World War II only authorize a clasp to be worn after the second award or higher; it is not unusual to see veterans with a clasp having a single bronze knot on their Army Good Conduct Medal or ribbon; this may have indicated either a single or second award and seems to have been an accepted practice.

Although the Good Conduct Medal was officially instituted by executive order in 1941, it really goes back to the American Revolution. When General George Washington established the Badge of Military Merit in 1782 he also created an award called the Honorary Badge of Distinction. This was the first good conduct award since it was to be conferred on veteran noncommissioned officers and soldiers of the Army who served more than three years with bravery, fidelity and good conduct. General Washington directed that the good conduct badge be made of cloth and each soldier who received it sew a narrow piece of white cloth on the left arm of his uniform jacket. Soldiers with more than six years service were to be distinguished by two pieces of cloth set parallel to each other. General Washington went on to express that this good conduct badge was a high honor and those who received it should be treated with particular confidence and consideration. However, just as the Badge of Military Merit disappeared after the Revolution so did the Honorary Badge of Distinction.

When President Roosevelt signed executive order 9323 on March 31, 1943 he officially changed the policy that the Army Good Conduct Medal could be awarded after one year. It should be understood, however, that additional awards of the Good Conduct Medal cannot be given for each additional year of service in World War II but required completion of a subsequent additional three-year period.

During the Korean War, President Eisenhower approved a first award only which could be presented for service after June 27, 1950 with less than three years but more than one year service.

The Air Force ceased using the Army Good Conduct Medal June, 1 1963. Qualifying airmen were then awarded the Air Force Good Conduct Medal which differed from the Army Good Conduct Medal only in design of the ribbon. The medal remained the same. Personnel who earned the Army Good Conduct medal before earning the Air Force Good Conduct Medal can wear both with the Air Force Good Conduct Medal coming first.

There is often some discussion if the Army Good Conduct Medal is a decoration or service medal. Historically going back to World War II, the Good Conduct Medal was considered a decoration and was one of a few medals to be manufactured throughout the war when service medal production was restricted due to the need to divert metal to the arms industry. Today however, it is considered a service award.

There was no certificate to denote the award of the Army Good Conduct Medal until 1981 when the Army began issuing an 8" x 10" paper certificate. The army regulations covering the issue of the paper certificate prohibited the issue of the certificate of those awarded the Good Conduct Medal prior to January 1 1981.

The Army has changed policy on official engraving of a Good Conduct Medal several times during its history. Currently the Army authorizes engraving at the government's expense by the U.S. Army Support Activity in Philadelphia PA.

The Good Conduct Medal is especially interesting in that it is the last United States Army award established prior to World War II. It was also the last medal that the War Department attempted to issue with a serial number (a practice dropped in WW II). It is the only United States Army medal awarded which specifically excludes officers from eligibility and is only authorized for enlisted personnel.

The numbers in parentheses next to the Devices refer to the tables in "Attachments and Devices" on page 116-119.

# Reserve Special Commendation Ribbon (Obsolete)

The Reserve Special Commendation Ribbon was established by the Secretary of the Navy on April 16, 1946. The ribbon was awarded to those officers of the Naval Reserve or Organized Marine Corps Reserve who had commanded at the battalion, squadron or separate division level in a meritorious manner for a period of four years between January 1, 1930 and December 7, 1941 and had a total service in the Reserve of at least ten years. The period of command need not have been continuous, but the officer must have been regularly assigned to command such units for a total of four years within a ten year period of time. Owing to the date of promulgation of the award, it was obsolete the day it was instituted and, as a result, no device was ever authorized.

**Service:** Navy/Marine Corps
**Instituted:** 1946
**Criteria:** Awarded to Reserve Officers with 4 years of successful command and a total Reserve service of 10 years.
**Devices:** None

# Navy Good Conduct Medal

The Navy Good Conduct Medal was authorized on November 21, 1884. The medal is awarded to enlisted personnel of the United States Navy and Naval Reserve (active duty) for creditable, above average professional performance, military behavior, leadership, military appearance and adaptability based on good conduct and faithful service for three-year periods of continuous active service.

Those receiving the award must have had no convictions by court martial and no nonjudicial punishment during the three year period (there was a time from November 1963 to January 1996 when the period was four years). For the first award the medal may be awarded to the next-of-kin in those cases where the individual is missing in action or dies of wounds received in combat. Naval personnel may also receive the medal if separated from the service as a result of wounds incurred in combat.

The Navy Good Conduct Medal is a circular bronze disc with a raised anchor and anchor chain circling a depiction of the **U.S.S. Constitution** and the words, "CONSTITUTION and UNITED STATES NAVY." The reverse side of the medal has the raised inscription, "FIDELITY - ZEAL - OBEDIENCE" around the border with space provided in the center to stamp the recipient's name. The medal is suspended from a plain bronze suspender and is worn after the Prisoner of War Medal and before the Naval Reserve Meritorious Service Medal. The ribbon of the Navy Good Conduct Medal is maroon. Additional awards are denoted by three-sixteenth inch diameter bronze and silver stars.

The forerunner of the Navy Good Conduct Medal was the Navy Good Conduct Badge which was established in 1868 by the Secretary of the Navy, making it our country's second oldest award. The badge, in use from 1868 to 1884, was awarded to men holding a Continuous Service Certificate received upon the successful completion of a term of enlistment. In those early days, any seaman who qualified for three awards was promoted to petty officer.

The Good Conduct Badge was a Maltese cross with a circular medallion in the center. The medallion was bordered with a border inscribed around the edge with the words, "FIDELITY - ZEAL - OBEDIENCE and U.S.A." in the center. The cross was suspended from a 1/2 inch wide red, white and blue ribbon.

In 1880, the Navy redesigned the Good Conduct Badge. The new medallion was proposed by Commodore Winfield Scott Schley from the design used on the letterhead of the Navy Department's Bureau of Equipment and Recruiting. This new medallion was suspended from a 1-5/8 inch wide red ribbon with thin border stripes of white and blue.

In 1884, the medal was redesigned and in 1896, the award period was changed to three years of continuous active service. This new medal maintained the 1880 design but was suspended from a maroon ribbon by a straight bar clasp. Subsequent awards were recognized by the addition of clasps placed on the suspension ribbon between the top of the ribbon and the medallion. These clasps were bordered with rope and were engraved with the recipient's ship or duty station. During World War I, medals were impressed with rim numbers but many were issued without engraving. In the 1930's, the ship or duty station name on the clasps was replaced by the recipient's enlistment discharge date. In 1942, all engraved clasps were replaced with generic clasps having, "SECOND AWARD", "THIRD AWARD", etc. in raised letters. Finally, subsequent to World War II, the Navy discontinued the clasps, began stamping the recipient's information on the medal's reverse and authorized the use of three-sixteenth bronze stars to denote additional awards.

**Service:** Navy (see page 44 for WW II version of medal.)
**Instituted:** 1888
**Criteria:** Outstanding performance and conduct during 3 years of continuous active enlisted service in the U.S. Navy.
**Devices:**
★ (66)
☆ (85)

## Marine Corps Good Conduct Medal

The Marine Corps Good Conduct Medal is awarded for outstanding performance, based on good conduct and faithful service for three- year periods of continuous active enlisted service. This medal is worn after the Prisoner of War Medal and before the Selected Marine Corps Reserve Medal.

The Marine Corps Good Conduct Medal was established by the Secretary of the Navy on July 20, 1896. The medal is awarded to an enlisted Marine for obedience, sobriety, military proficiency, neatness and intelligence during three years of continuous active service. The Marine receiving the award must have had no convictions by court martial and no more than one nonjudicial punishment during the three-year period. For the first award, the medal may be awarded to the next-of-kin in those cases where the individual is missing in action or dies of wounds received in combat. A Marine may also receive the medal if separated from the service as a result of wounds incurred in combat.

The Marine Corps Good Conduct Medal was designed by Major General Charles Heywood, the ninth Commandant of the Marine Corps. The medal is a circular bronze disc with an anchor and anchor chain circling an enlisted Marine in the uniform of the late nineteenth century. The Marine is holding the lanyard of a naval rifle (gun) and below this is a scroll with the motto of the Corps, "SEMPER FIDELIS." In the space between the Marine and the anchor chain is the raised inscription, "UNITED STATES MARINE CORPS." The reverse side of the medal has the raised inscription, "FIDELITY - ZEAL - OBEDIENCE" centered in between two concentric raised circles and with room in the center to inscribe the recipient's name.

The medal has undergone several design mod-

**Service:** Marine Corps (see page 44 for WW II version of medal.)
**Instituted:** 1896
**Criteria:** Outstanding performance and conduct during 3 years of continuous active enlisted service in the U.S. Marine Corps.
**Devices:**
★ (66)
☆ (85)

ification since its inception. The original medal incorporated an upper bronze suspension bar bearing the raised inscription, "U.S. MARINE CORPS." Number clasps, placed on the suspension ribbon between the upper suspension bar and the medallion were used on the original medal to indicate additional awards. Prior to World War I, medals were engraved with the recipient's name, service number and date span. During World War I, medals were impressed with rim numbers and many were issued without engraving. Following World War II, the Marine Corps changed from engraving to stamping the recipient's information on the medal's reverse. The practice of using a suspension bar and clasps was also eliminated during this period.

The ribbon of the Marine Corps Good Conduct Medal is dark red with a dark blue stripe in the center. Additional awards are denoted by three-sixteenth bronze stars.

## Air Force Good Conduct Medal

Authorized on June 1, 1963. Awarded to Air Force personnel in an enlisted status upon recommendation of the unit commander for exemplary conduct while in active military service on or after June 1, 1963 after three years of continuous service (1 year in wartime - this was rarely done). The U. S. Air Force used the Army Good Conduct Medal to recognize deserving service by enlisted personnel from 1947 to 1963 when the Air Force Good Conduct Medal was created. As with the Army Good Conduct Medal, the award was never automatic and required commander certification prior to being awarded. Commanders usually receive notification from their personnel center that an individual is eligible for this award. The commander then reviews the individual's record and affixes his/her signature to the personnel document verifying that the person is eligible and deserving of the award. The absence of an award of the Air Force Good Conduct medal to an individual having a qualifying period of enlistment would be noteworthy to supervisory personnel. The front of the medal bears the inscription, "EFFICIENCY, HONOR, FIDELITY," surrounding the American eagle which stands

**Service:** Air Force
**Instituted:** 1963
**Criteria:** Exemplary conduct, efficiency and fidelity during three years of active enlisted service with the U.S. Air Force.
**Devices:**
🜸 (43)
🜸 (50)

**Notes:** Air Force used Army Good Conduct Medal until 1963.

on a closed book and sword. On the reverse is a five-pointed star above a blank scroll; the words, "FOR GOOD" are above the star and below the scroll is the word, "CONDUCT." Bronze and silver oak leaf attachments denote additional awards of the medal.

# Coast Guard Good Conduct Medal

The Coast Guard Good Conduct Medal was first authorized on December 12, 1923 to recognize superior performance of duty by enlisted Coast Guardsmen during a four year period of service. The time requirement was changed in 1934 to conform to the three year requirement then in effect for the Navy and Marine Corps Good Conduct Medals. Originally, the Coast Guard Good Conduct Medal was attached to a 1-1/2 inch wide ribbon suspended from a rectangular top bar having the inscription, "U.S. COAST GUARD." The metal pendant was 1-7/16 inches in diameter with the likeness of a cutter in the center surrounded by the Coast Guard's motto, "SEMPER PARATUS" (Always Prepared). The pendant is suspended from a straight crossbar looped through the bottom of the suspension ribbon. Subsequent awards were indicated by the addition of bronze Good Conduct Bars. These bars were attached to the suspension ribbon with the recipient's ship or duty station engraved on the front and the date of award on the reverse. Both the suspension top bar and the Good Conduct Bars were discontinued following the Korean War.

The current Coast Guard Good Conduct Medal is suspended from a 1-3/8 inch wide ribbon and the planchet has been reduced to 1-1/4 inches. The new planchet also replaces the small ship in the center with the seal of the U.S. Coast Guard. The reverses of both versions are quite similar with a blank center disk surrounded by an outer ring upon which are inscribed the words, "FIDELITY ZEAL OBEDIENCE."

The current medal also does not use the "square" suspension and bottom crossbar but is attached directly to the ribbon by means of a suspension ring. The ribbon is maroon with a central stripe of white. Additional awards are denoted by bronze and silver stars.

**Service:** Coast Guard
**Instituted:** 1921
**Criteria:** Outstanding proficiency, leadership and conduct during 3 continuous years of active enlisted Coast Guard service.
**Devices:** ★ (67)  ☆ (86)
**Notes:** Earlier ribbon was 1½" wide.

# Army Reserve Components Achievement Medal

Authorized by the Secretary of the Army on March 3, 1971 and amended by Dept. of the Army General Order 4, 1974, this medal is awarded to any person in the rank of Colonel or below for exemplary behavior, efficiency and fidelity while serving as a member of the Army National Guard (ARNG), a United States Army Reserve troop program unit (TPU) or as an individual augmentee.

The medal is 1-1/4 inches in diameter. In the center is a flaming torch symbolizing the vigilance of the Guard and the Reserve and their readiness to come to the Nation's aid. Two crossed swords in front of and behind the torch represent the history of the Guard and Reserve forged in combat. Left and right of the torch are five pointed stars and the entire design is surrounded by a laurel wreath symbolizing accomplishment. Around these symbols is a twelve pointed star superimposed over a smaller twelve-pointed star indicating the Guard and Reserve's ability to travel where needed in the United States or the world. In between the points of the larger star are laurel leaves and a berry representing achievement.

On the reverse side of the medal in the upper center is a miniature breast plate taken from the Army seal. Above this, the outside edge of the medal is inscribed either, "UNITED STATES ARMY RESERVE" or "ARMY NATIONAL GUARD." Along the bottom edge of the medal are the words, "FOR ACHIEVEMENT."

The ribbon has a wide center stripe of red flanked by narrow stripes of white and blue, reflecting our national colors and patriotism. The outside gold stripes are symbolic of merit. Additional awards are denoted by bronze and silver oak leaf clusters.

**Service:** Army
**Instituted:** 1971
**Criteria:** Exemplary conduct, efficiency and fidelity during 3 years of service with the U.S. Army Reserve or National Guard.
**Devices:** 🍂 (44)  🍃 (48)

## Naval Reserve Meritorious Service Medal

For Naval Reservists who fulfill, with distinction, obligations above a level that is normally expected. The Naval Reserve Meritorious Service Medal is worn after the Navy Good Conduct Medal and before the Fleet Marine Force Ribbon.

The Naval Reserve Meritorious Service Medal was authorized on September 12, 1959 originally as a ribbon-only award. The medal was authorized on June 22, 1962 with eligibility backdated to July 1, 1958. The award is made on a selected basis to U.S. Navy Reservists who fulfill, with distinction, the obligations of an inactive Reservists at a higher level than normally expected. The obligations pertain to attendance and performance.

**Service:** Navy
**Instituted:** 1964
**Criteria:** Outstanding performance and conduct during 3 years of enlisted service in the Naval Reserve.
**Devices:**
★ (67)
☆ (86)

**Notes:** Originally a ribbon-only award.

The Naval Reserve Meritorious Service Medal is a circular bronze disc showing an fouled anchor covered with a scroll with the raised words, "MERITORIOUS SERVICE." The words, "UNITED STATES NAVAL RESERVE" encircle the anchor. The reverse of the medal is blank. The ribbon is red with a blue center stripe and thin border stripes of gold and blue. Additional awards are denoted by three-sixteenth bronze stars.

## Selected Marine Corps Reserve Medal

Awarded for four consecutive years service in the Selected Marine Corps Reserve. The Selected Marine Corps Reserve Medal is worn after the Marine Corps Good Conduct Medal and before the Marine Corps Expeditionary Medal.

The Selected Marine Corps Reserve Medal was established by the Secretary of the Navy on February 19, 1939 as the Fleet Marine Corps Reserve Medal. Later the name was changed to the Organized Marine Corps Reserve Medal and finally to its current designation in the late 1980's. The medal is awarded to members of the Marine Corps Reserve who, subsequent to July 1, 1925, and prior to April 24, 1961, attended 80 percent of all scheduled drills during a four year period. Since April 24, 1961, the attendance criteria was raised to 90 percent.

The Selected Marine Corps Reserve Medal was designed by the United States Mint. The medal is a circular bronze disc with two walking figures. The figure in the foreground is wearing a pre-World War II uniform and the other is wearing civilian clothes. Above the figures is the raised circular inscription, "MARINE CORPS RESERVE" and below the figures is the inscription, "FOR SERVICE." The reverse of the medal is identical to the that of the Marine Corps Good Conduct Medal with the raised inscription, "FIDELITY - ZEAL - OBEDIENCE"

**Service:** Marine Corps
**Instituted:** 1939
**Criteria:** Outstanding performance and conduct during 4 years of enlisted service in the Selected Marine Corps Reserve.
**Devices:**
★ (67)
☆ (86)

**Notes:** Formerly: "Organized Marine Corps Reserve Medal".

centered in between two concentric raised circles and with room in the center to inscribe the recipient's name. The ribbon is gold and has a red center stripe with narrow border stripes of blue, white and red. Additional awards are denoted by three-sixteenth bronze stars.

## Air Reserve Forces Meritorious Service Medal

**Service:** Air Force
**Instituted:** 1964
**Criteria:** Exemplary behavior, efficiency and fidelity during three years of active enlisted service with the Air Force Reserve.
**Devices:** (43) (50)

Authorized on April 1, 1964 as a ribbon-only award, the medal was created in 1973. Awarded on specific recommendation of the unit commander to enlisted members of the Air Reserve Forces for exemplary behavior, efficiency and fidelity for a period of four continuous years service prior to July 1, 1972 and for three years on/after July 1, 1972. Creditable service ends when the Reservist is called to active duty or is appointed a commissioned officer. The front of the medal has the American eagle perched atop a small circle containing a five-pointed star. A banner sits above the eagle and contains the words, "MERITORIOUS SERVICE." On the outer edge of the medal are the words, "AIR RESERVE FORCES." On the reverse is a cloud design with thunderbolts and wings with the word, "TO" inscribed below it with space to engrave the recipient's name. Along the circular outer edge, the words, "EXEMPLARY BEHAVIOR" are in raised letters on the upper half of the ring and "EFFICIENCY-FIDELITY" appear on the lower half.

The ribbon has a wide, light blue center with stripes of, reading outward from the center on each side, dark blue, yellow, dark blue, white and light blue selvedges. Additional awards are denoted by bronze and silver oak leaf clusters.

## Coast Guard Reserve Good Conduct Medal

**Service:** Coast Guard
**Instituted:** 1963
**Criteria:** Outstanding proficiency, leadership and conduct during 3 years of enlisted service in the Coast Guard Reserve.
**Devices:** (67) (86)

**Notes:** Originally a ribbon-only award - "Coast Guard Reserve Meritorious Service Ribbon".

On February 1, 1963, the Commandant of the Coast Guard established a ribbon-only award known as the Coast Guard Reserve Meritorious Service Ribbon to recognize enlisted members of the active reserve in much the same manner as the Coast Guard Good Conduct Medal recognizes active duty enlisted personnel. It rewards outstanding proficiency, leadership and conduct during three years of enlisted service in the Coast Guard Reserve. It was renamed and reauthorized in its present form as the Coast Guard Reserve Good Conduct Medal on Sept. 3, 1981. The medal is a circular bronze planchet containing the Coast Guard seal in the center. Surrounding the seal at the edge of the medal is the circular inscription "UNITED STATES COAST GUARD RESERVE." The reverse contains the raised inscription, "GOOD CONDUCT" with no other adornment.

The ribbon of the Coast Guard Reserve Good Conduct Medal is identical to that of the Naval Reserve Meritorious Service Medal with the addition of a thin white stripe in the center. Additional awards of the Coast Guard Reserve Good Conduct Medal are denoted by three-sixteenth inch diameter bronze and silver stars.

## Coast Guard Enlisted Person of the Year Ribbon

The Coast Guard Enlisted Person of the Year (EPOY) Program is designed to recognize exemplary Coast Guard personnel from the active and reserve enlisted work forces. Such personnel must be in pay grades E-2 through E-6, may have no nonjudicial punishments nor civil convictions and must have a mark of "Satisfactory" during the 36 months prior to the nomination. He or she must have demonstrated exceptional performance in the areas of leadership, Coast Guard rating skills, personal and work ethics and Coast Guard knowledge and must be a role model for all other personnel to strive to emulate. Each recipient of the award shall be advanced to the next higher pay grade, shall be recommended for the Coast Guard Commendation Medal and will have their name inscribed on the perpetual plaque displayed in Coast Guard Headquarters.

**Service:** Coast Guard
**Instituted:** 2003
**Criteria:** Awarded to exemplary men and women in the enlisted force who demonstrate sustained exceptional standards of proficiency, conduct and impeccable military appearance and bearing.
**Devices:** None

## Navy Fleet Marine Force Ribbon (Obsolete)

Traditionally, the U.S. Marine Corps has relied upon the Navy to provide trained personnel in specific areas not covered by the USMC's table of organization, e.g., Chaplains, Medical Personnel, etc. The Navy Fleet Marine Force Ribbon was authorized by the Secretary of the Navy on September 1, 1984 to recognize the service of these Navy officers and enlisted personnel who serve with the Fleet Marine Force. Qualification for the Navy Fleet Marine Force Ribbon signifies acquisition of specific professional skills, knowledge and military experience that result in qualifications above those normally required of Navy personnel serving with the Fleet Marine Force (FMF). A recipient may qualify only once for the Fleet Marine Force Ribbon, therefore, there are no additional award devices.

**Service:** Navy
**Instituted:** 1984
**Criteria:** Active participation by professionally skilled Navy personnel with the Fleet Marine Force.
**Devices:** None

> **Did You Know?** Effective October 1, 2006, the Fleet Marine Force Ribbon became obsolete as a result of the creation of the Fleet Marine Force Qualified Officer Insignia and Fleet Marine Force Enlisted Warfare Specialist Insignia programs. The Enlisted Fleet Marine Force Warfare Specialist designation is most commonly awarded to the Hospital Corpsman (HM) and Religious Programs Specialist (RP) ratings, although it is also awarded to other sailors who support Marine Corps Commands. The FMF Qualified Officer Insignia is most commonly earned by staff officers in the Medical Fields and Chaplains, although it is also awarded to other officer communities, such as Civil Engineer Corps and line officers.

## Outstanding Airman of the Year Ribbon

Authorized on February 21, 1968. Awarded to those 12 airmen chosen from nominees throughout the Air Force, field operation agencies, the Air Force Reserve and Air National Guard in the 12 Outstanding Airmen of the Year Program. The award of the ribbon is retroactive to include those selected for this program as of June 1970. The 12 current designees wear a bronze service star and multiple winners wear oak leaf clusters to denote additional awards.

**Service:** Air Force
**Instituted:** 1968 Criteria: Awarded to airmen for selection to the "12 Outstanding Airmen of the Year" Competition Program.
**Devices:**  (46)  (52)  (70)

The numbers in parentheses next to the Devices refer to the tables in "Attachments and Devices" on page 116-119.

## Air Force Recognition Ribbon

Authorized on October 12, 1980 and effective January 1, 1981. Awarded to individual recipients of Air Force level special trophies and awards, as listed in appropriate Air Force regulations, except the 12 Outstanding Airmen of the Year nominees. It is not awarded to individuals of a unit which receives a special award. The ribbon is not awarded retroactively. The ribbon design is patterned after the Air Force Cross ribbon with a red stripe in the center. Bronze and silver oak leaf clusters are used to denote additional awards.

**Service:** Air Force
**Instituted:** 1980
**Criteria:** Awarded to individual recipients of Air Force-level special trophies and awards.
**Devices:**  (46)  (52)

## Navy Expeditionary Medal

The Navy Expeditionary Medal was authorized on August 5, 1936. The medal is awarded to members of the Navy who have engaged in operations against armed opposition in foreign territory or have served in situations warranting special recognition where no other campaign medal was awarded. Many operations have qualified for the award, beginning (retroactively) with operations by Navy and Marine Corps personnel in Honolulu, Hawaii in 1874 and culminating in the operations involving the attack on the *USS Cole* between 2000 and 2002.

The Navy Expeditionary Medal is a circular bronze disc depicting a sailor beaching a boat containing an officer and Marines with a flag of the United States and the word, "EXPEDITIONS." The reverse of the medal shows an American eagle perched atop an anchor and laurel branches. On either side of the eagle are the words, "FOR SERVICE." Above, in a semicircle is a raised inscription, "UNITED STATES NAVY." The ribbon contains the official colors of the Navy with a wide blue center stripe flanked by gold with narrow blue edges. Additional awards are denoted by three-sixteenth inch diameter bronze stars. For those who served in the defense of Wake Island in December, 1941, a one-quarter inch silver "W" is worn on the ribbon bar and a bronze clasp bearing the inscription, "WAKE ISLAND" is affixed to the suspension ribbon of the medal. This represents the last time in the 20th century that a named bar has been issued by any Service to commemorate a specific battle or engagement. The Navy Expeditionary Medal is worn after the Navy Fleet Marine Force Ribbon and before all other service and campaign awards.

**Service:** Navy
**Instituted:** 1936
**Dates:** 1936 to Present
**Criteria:** Landings on foreign territory and operations against armed opposition for which no specific campaign medal has been authorized.
**Devices:**
W (26)
★ (64)
☆ (83)
**Bars:** "Wake Island"

★ Cuban Military Operation, Jan. 3, 1961 - Oct. 23, 1962
★ Thailand Military Operation, May 16, 1962 - Aug. 10, 1962
★ Iranian, Yemen & Indian Ocean Operation, Dec. 8, 1978 - Jun. 6, 1979, Nov. 21, 1979 - Oct. 20, 1981
★ Lebanon, Aug. 20, 1982 - May 31, 1983
★ Libyan Expedition, Jan. 20, 1986 - Jun. 27, 1986
★ Persian Gulf, Feb. 1, 1987 - Jul. 23, 1987
★ Panama, Apr. 1, 1988 - Dec. 19, 1989.
  *(Pre and post invasion)* Feb. 1, 1990 - Jun. 13, 1990
★ Operation Sharp Edge - Liberia, Aug. 5, 1990 - Feb. 21, 1991
★ Operation Distant Runner - Rwanda, Apr. 7-18, 1994
  *(11th Marine Exped. Unit USS Peleliu)*
★ Operation Safe Departure - Eritrea, Jun. 6-25, 1998
★ Operation Determined Response - USS Cole, Oct. 12, 2000-Dec. 15, 2002

# Marine Corps Expeditionary Medal

For opposed landing on a foreign territory or operations deserving special recognition. The Marine Corps Expeditionary Medal is worn after the Selected Marine Corps Reserve Medal and before the China Service Medal.

The Marine Corps Expeditionary Ribbon was authorized by Marine Corps General Order on May 8, 1919. The medal pendant was added on July 28, 1921 by Executive Order 3524. The medal is awarded to members of the Marine Corps who have engaged in operations against armed opposition in foreign territory, or have served in situations warranting special recognition where no other campaign medal was awarded. To date, more than sixty operations have qualified for the award, the first (retroactively) being operations by Navy and Marine Corps personnel in Honolulu, Hawaii in 1874 and the latest being operations involving the attack on the *USS Cole* between 2000 and 2002. The Navy had actually planned to discontinue the medal after World War II (it was awarded only three times in twenty years) in favor of the Navy Expeditionary Medal but the concept was never implemented.

The Marine Corps Expeditionary Medal was designed by Walter Hancock. The medal is a circular bronze disc showing a Marine charging from the sea (depicted by wave scrolls at his feet). The Marine is in a uniform of the post World War I period with a full pack and fixed bayonet. Above, in a semicircle, is a raised inscription, "EXPEDITIONS." The reverse of the medal shows an American eagle perched on an anchor and laurel branches. On either side of the eagle are the words, "FOR SERVICE." Above, in a semicircle is a raised inscription, "UNITED STATES MARINE CORPS." The ribbon is cardinal red and gold, the official colors of the Corps. The ribbon has a wide red center stripe flanked by gold (sometimes mistaken for khaki) with narrow red edges. Additional awards are denoted by three-sixteenth inch diameter bronze stars. For those who served in the defense of Wake Island in December, 1941, a one-quarter inch silver "W" is worn on the ribbon bar and a bronze clasp bearing the inscription, "WAKE ISLAND" is affixed to the suspension ribbon of the medal.

**Service:** Marine Corps
**Instituted:** 1919
**Dates:** 1919 to Present
**Criteria:** Landings on foreign territory and operations against armed opposition for which no specific campaign medal has been authorized.
**Devices:** W (26), ★ (64), ☆ (83)
**Bars:** "Wake Island"
**Notes:** Originally a "ribbon-only" award.

# China Service Medal

For service in China during the periods just prior to and just following World War II, the China Service Medal is worn after the Navy or Marine Corps Expeditionary Medal and before the American Defense Service Medal.

The China Service Medal was authorized by the Department of the Navy on August, 23 1940 for members of the Navy and Marine Corps who served in China or were attached to ships in the area during the period July 7, 1937 to September 7, 1939. The second period was for those who were present for duty during operations in China, Taiwan and the Formosa Straits during the period September 2, 1947 to April 1, 1957.

The China Service Medal was designed by George Snowden. The medal is a circular bronze disc showing a Chinese junk under full sail with the raised inscribed words, "CHINA" above and "SERVICE" below. The reverse of the medal shows an American eagle perched on an anchor and laurel branches. On either side of the eagle are the words, "FOR SERVICE." Above, in a semicircle is a raised inscription, "UNITED STATES NAVY" or "UNITED STATES MARINE CORPS" depending on the recipient's branch of service. The ribbon is yellow with a narrow red stripe near each edge. If an individual served during both periods, a bronze three-sixteenth inch star is worn.

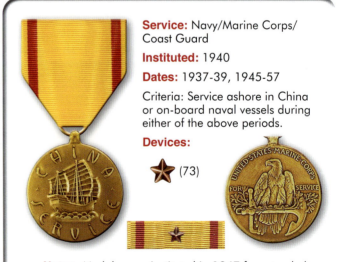

**Service:** Navy/Marine Corps/Coast Guard
**Instituted:** 1940
**Dates:** 1937-39, 1945-57
**Criteria:** Service ashore in China or on-board naval vessels during either of the above periods.
**Devices:** ★ (73)
**Notes:** Medal was reinstituted in 1947 for extended service during dates shown above.

# American Defense Service Medal

Authorized on June 28, 1941 for military service during the limited emergency proclaimed by President Roosevelt on Sept. 8, 1939 or during the unlimited emergency proclaimed on May 27, 1941 until December 7, 1941 if under orders to active duty for 12 months or longer. In addition to the bars depicted to the right, a bronze star is worn on the service ribbon to denote receipt of any of the bars. The Navy also authorized the wear of a bronze letter "A" if the recipient served with the Atlantic Fleet during the period of the national emergency. The bronze star was not worn if the letter "A" was awarded.

On the front of the medal is the Grecian figure, Columbia, representing America or Liberty, holding a shield and sword while standing on an oak branch, symbolic of strength. The oak leaves represent the strength of the Army, Navy, Marine Corps and Coast Guard. The inscription, "AMERICAN DEFENSE," is around the outside upper edge. The reverse of the medal carries the inscription, "FOR SERVICE DURING THE LIMITED EMERGENCY PROCLAIMED BY THE PRESIDENT ON SEPTEMBER 8, 1939 OR DURING THE UNLIMITED EMERGENCY PROCLAIMED BY THE PRESIDENT ON MAY 27, 1941."

The golden yellow color of the ribbon symbolizes the golden opportunity of United States youth to serve the nation, represented by the blue, white and red stripes on both sides of the ribbon.

**Service:** All Services
**Instituted:** 1941
**Dates:** 1939-41
**Criteria:** Army: 12 months of active duty service during the above period; Naval Services: Any active duty service.
**Devices:** ★ (75)  A (10)

Navy — FLEET
Navy — BASE
Army — FOREIGN SERVICE
Coast Guard — SEA

**Bars:** "Foreign Service", "Base", "Fleet", "Sea"

# Women's Army Corps Service Medal

Authorized on July 29, 1943 for service in both the Women's Army Auxiliary Corps (WAAC) between July 10, 1942 and August 31, 1943 and the Women's Army Corps (WAC) between September 1, 1943 and September 2, 1945. After 1945, members of the WAC received the same medals as other members of the Army. No attachments are authorized for the medal.

The front of the medal contains the head of Pallas Athena, goddess of victory and wisdom, superimposed on a sword crossed with oak leaves and a palm branch. The sword represents military might; the oak leaves represent strength and the palm branch represents peace. The reverse contains thirteen stars, an eagle and a scroll along with the words, "FOR SERVICE IN THE WOMEN'S ARMY AUXILIARY CORPS," and the dates "1942-1943." The dates on the medal, 1942-1943, remained the same

**Service:** Army
**Instituted:** 1943
**Dates:** 1942-45
**Criteria:** Service with both the Women's Army Auxiliary Corps and Women's Army Corps during the above period.
**Devices:** None

**Note:** Only U.S. award authorized for women only.

even after the WAAC became the WAC. The ribbon is moss green with old gold edges, the branch colors of the Women's Army Corps. Green indicates merit and gold refers to achievement.

Fewer than 100,000 women in World War II qualified for the Women's Army Corps Service Medal; over 40,000 WAC members were assigned to the U.S. Army Air Force by 1945. This is the only U.S. service medal specifically created and authorized for women in the military.

## American Campaign Medal

For service during World War II within the American Theater of Operations. The American Campaign Medal was established by Executive Order on November 6, 1942 and amended on March 15, 1946, which established a closing date. The medal is awarded to any member of the Armed Forces who served in the American Theater of Operations during the period from December 7, 1941 to March 2, 1946 or was awarded a combat decoration while in combat against the enemy. The service must have been an aggregate of one year within the continental United States, or thirty consecutive days outside the continental United States, or sixty nonconsecutive days outside the continental United States, but within the American Theater of Operations. Maps of the three theaters of operations during World War II were drawn on November 6, 1942 to include the American Theater, European- African - Middle Eastern Theater and Asiatic-Pacific Theater.

The American Campaign Medal was designed by the Army's Institute of Heraldry. The medal is a circular bronze disc showing a Navy cruiser, a B-24 bomber and a sinking enemy submarine above three waves. Shown in the background are some buildings representing the United States. Above is the raised inscription, "AMERICAN CAMPAIGN." The reverse of the medal shows an American eagle standing on a rock. On the left of the eagle are the raised inscribed dates, "1941-1945"

**Service:** All Services
**Instituted:** 1942
**Dates:** 1941-46
**Criteria:** Service outside the U.S. in the American theater for 30 days, or within the continental U.S. for one year.
**Devices:** ★ (63)

and on the right, "UNITED STATES OF AMERICA." The ribbon is azure blue with three narrow stripes of red, white and blue (United States) in the center and four stripes of white, red (Japan), black and white (Germany) near the edges. Three-sixteenth inch bronze stars indicated participation in specialized antisubmarine, escort or special operations. The American Campaign Medal is worn after the Women's Army Corps Service Medal by Army & Air Force personnel and after the American Defense Service Medal by the Naval Services.

## Asiatic-Pacific Campaign Medal

Authorized on November 6, 1942 and amended on March 15, 1946. Awarded to members of the U.S. Armed Forces for at least 30 consecutive (60 nonconsecutive) days service (less if in combat) within the Asiatic-Pacific Theater between December 7, 1941 and March 2, 1946.

The front of the medal shows a palm tree amidst troops with an aircraft overhead and an aircraft carrier, battleship and submarine in the background. The reverse has the American eagle, symbolizing power, on a rock, symbolizing stability, with the inscription, "UNITED STATES OF AMERICA" on the eagle's back. The orange yellow of the ribbon represents Asia while the white and red stripes toward each edge represent Japan. The center blue, white and red thin stripes are taken from the American Defense Service Medal, referring to America's continued defense preparedness after Pearl Harbor. A bronze star denoted participation in a campaign. A silver star attachment is used to represent five bronze stars. An arrowhead attachment is authorized by the Army and Air Force for participation in a combat parachute jump, combat glider landing

**Service:** All Services
**Instituted:** 1942
**Dates:** 1941-46
**Criteria:** Service in the Asiatic-Pacific theater for 30 days or receipt of any combat decoration.
**Devices:**
▲ (2)
★ (63)
☆ (82)
⚓ (28)

or amphibious assault landing (only one arrowhead may be worn on the medal/ribbon despite the number of qualification events). The ribbon is worn with the center blue stripe on the wearer's right.

### Designated Army & AAF campaigns for the Asiatic-Pacific Campaign Medal are:

- ★ Burma, 1941-1942
- ★ Philippine Islands, 1941-1942
- ★ Central Pacific, 1941-1943
- ★ East Indies, 1942
- ★ Aleutian Islands, 1942-1943
- ★ Guadalcanal, 1942-1943
- ★ Papua, 1942-1943
- ★ Air Offensive, Japan, 1942-1945
- ★ China Defensive, 1942-1945
- ★ India-Burma, 1942-1945
- ★ Bismark Archipelago, 1943-1944
- ★ New Guinea, 1943-1944
- ★ Northern Solomons, 1943-1944
- ★ Eastern Mandates (Air), 1943-1944
- ★ Eastern Mandates (Ground), 1944
- ★ Leyte, 1944-1945
- ★ Luzon, 1944-1945
- ★ Western Pacific, 1944-1945
- ★ Central Burma, 1945
- ★ China Offensive, 1945
- ★ Ryukyus, 1945
- ★ Southern Philippines, 1945
- ★ Air Combat, 1941-1945
- ★ Antisubmarine, 1941-1945
- ★ Ground Combat, 1941-1945

# Asiatic-Pacific Campaign Medal

**Designated Navy and Marine Corps campaigns for the Asiatic-Pacific Campaign Medal are:**

★ Pearl Harbor-Midway, 1941
★ Wake Island, 1941
★ Philippine Islands Operation, 1941-1942
★ Netherlands East Indies, 1942
★ Pacific Raids, 1942
★ Coral Sea, 1942
★ Midway, 1942
★ Guadalcanal, Tulagi Landings, 1942
★ Capture and defense of Guadalcanal, 1942-1943
★ Makin Raid, 1942
★ Eastern Solomons (Stewart Island), 1942
★ Buin-Faisi-Tonolai Raid, 1942
★ Cape Esperance (Second Savo), 1942
★ Santa Cruz Islands, 1942
★ Guadalcanal (Third Savo), 1942
★ Tassafaronga (Fourth Savo), 1942
★ Eastern New Guinea, 1942-1944
★ Rennel Island Operation, 1943
★ Solomon Islands Consolidation, 1943-1945
★ Aleutians Operations, 1943
★ New Georgia Group Operation, 1943
★ Bismarck Archipelago, 1943-1944
★ Pacific Raids, 1943
★ Treasury-Bougainville Operation, 1943
★ Gilbert Island Operation, 1943
★ Marshall Islands Operation, 1943-1944
★ Asiatic-Pacific Raids, 1944
★ Western New Guinea, 1944-1945
★ Marianas Operation, 1944
★ Western Caroline Islands, 1944
★ Leyte Operation, 1944
★ Luzon Operation, 1944-1945
★ Iwo Jima Operation, 1945
★ Okinawa Gunto Operation, 1945
★ Third Fleet Operations against Japan, 1945
★ Kurile Islands Operation, 1944-1945
★ Borneo Operation, 1945
★ Tinian Capture and Occupation, 1944
★ Consolidation of Southern Philippines, 1945
★ Hollandia Operation, 1944
★ Manila Bay-Bicol Operation, 1945
★ Escort, Antisubmarine, etc, 1942-1945
★ Minesweeping Operations, 1945-1946
★ Submarine War Patrols, 1941-1945

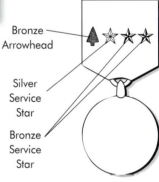

**Army**

Bronze Arrowhead
Silver Service Star
Bronze Service Star

**Navy**

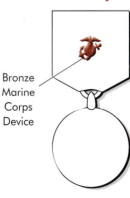

Bronze Marine Corps Device

Follows same rules as Letter "V"

# European-African-Middle Eastern Campaign Medal

Authorized on November 6, 1942, as amended on March 15, 1946. Awarded to members of the U.S. Armed Forces for at least 30 days of consecutive (60 days non-consecutive) service within the European Theater of Operations between December 7, 1941 and November 8, 1945 (lesser periods qualify if individual was in actual combat against the enemy during this period).

The front of the bronze medal shows a Landing Ship, Tank (LST) unloading troops while under fire with an airplane overhead. The reverse has the American eagle, symbol of power, standing on a rock, symbol of stability, with the inscription, "UNITED STATES OF AMERICA" and dates, "1941-1945."

Three-sixteenth inch diameter bronze and silver stars denoted participation in the specific campaigns described below. A bronze arrowhead indicated participation in a combat parachute jump, combat glider landing or amphibious assault landing. The ribbon's central blue, white and red stripes represent the United States. The wide green stripes represent the green fields of Europe, the brown edges represent the African desert sands, the thin green, white, and red stripes represent Italy and the thin black and white stripes represent Germany.

**Service:** All Services
**Instituted:** 1942
**Dates:** 1941-45
Criteria: Service in the European-African-Middle Eastern theater for 30 days or receipt of any combat decoration.

**Devices:**
- (2) bronze arrowhead
- (63) bronze star
- (82) silver star
- (28) Marine Corps device

**Designated Army (& AAF) campaigns for the European-African-Middle Eastern Campaign Medal are as follows:**

- Algeria-French Morocco, 1942
- Egypt-Libya, 1942-1943
- Tunisia, 1942-1943
- Air Offensive, Europe, 1942-1944
- Sicily, 1943
- Naples-Foggia, 1943-1944
- Anzio, 1944
- Rome-Arno, 1944
- Normandy, 1944
- Northern France, 1944
- Southern France, 1944
- North Apennines, 1944-1945
- Rhineland, 1944-1945
- Ardennes-Alsace, 1944-1945
- Central Europe, 1945
- Po Valley, 1945
- Air Combat, 1941-1945
- Antisubmarine, 1941-1945
- Ground Combat, 1941-1945

**Designated Navy and Marine Corps campaigns for the European-African-Middle Eastern Campaign Medal are as follows:**

- Reinforcement of Malta, 1942
- North African Occupation, 1942-1943
- Sicilian Occupation, 1943
- Salerno Landings, 1943
- West Coast of Italy Operations, 1944
- Invasion of Normandy, 1944
- Northeast Greenland Operation, 1944
- Invasion of Southern France, 1944
- Escort, antisubmarine, armed guard special operations, 1941-1944

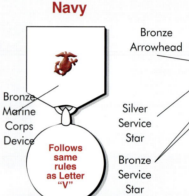

Navy — Bronze Marine Corps Device — Follows same rules as Letter "V"

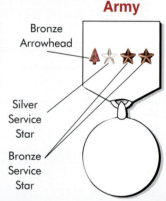

Army — Bronze Arrowhead, Silver Service Star, Bronze Service Star

US Army Photo

## World War II Victory Medal

Authorized by an Act of Congress on July 6, 1945 and awarded to all members of the Armed Forces who served at least one day of honorable, active federal service between December 7, 1941 and December 31, 1946, inclusive.

The front of the medal depicts the Liberty figure resting her right foot on a war god's helmet with the hilt of a broken sword in her right hand and the broken blade in her left hand. The reverse contains the words, "FREEDOM FROM FEAR AND WANT, FREEDOM OF SPEECH AND RELIGION, and UNITED STATES OF AMERICA 1941-1945." The red center stripe of the ribbon is symbolic of Mars, the God of War, representing both courage and fortitude. The twin rainbow stripes, suggested by the World War I Victory Medal, allude to the peace following a storm. A narrow white stripe separates the center red stripe from each rainbow pattern on both sides of the ribbon. The World War

**Service:** All Services
**Instituted:** 1945
**Dates:** 1941-46
**Criteria:** Awarded for service in the U.S. Armed Forces during the above period.
**Devices:** None

II Victory Medal provides deserving recognition to all of America's veterans who served during World War II.

No attachments are authorized although some veterans received the medal with an affixed bronze star which, according to rumors at the time, was to distinguish those who served in combat from those who did not. However, no official documentation has ever been found to support this supposition. Although eligible for its award, many World War II veterans never actually received the medal since many were discharged prior to the medal's being struck in late 1946.

## U.S. Antarctic Expedition Medal

The U.S. Antarctic Expedition Medal was created by an Act of Congress on September 24, 1945 and was awarded in gold, silver and bronze to the participants. 160 medals were authorized, with 60 minted in gold and 50 each in silver and bronze. Rear Admiral Richard E. Byrd, who headed the endeavor, received one of the medals in gold. Unlike previous expeditions headed by Admiral Byrd, this effort was not named for him as it was an official undertaking of the United States Government rather than a privately funded enterprise.

The 1939-1941 expedition was envisioned as the first of a long series of efforts to explore the South Pole but the advent of World War II forced all such plans to be shelved indefinitely.

The medal was designed by John R. Sinnock. The lower half of the obverse shows a partial map with the engraved names, "SOUTH PACIFIC OCEAN, LITTLE AMERICA, SOUTH POLE, ANTARCTICA, AND PALMERLAND." Above this is a three-part scroll inscribed, "SCIENCE, PIONEERING, EXPLORATION." Around the edge is the inscription, "THE UNITED STATES ANTARCTIC EXPEDITION 1939 1941." On the reverse, the inscription, "BY ACT OF CONGRESS OF THE UNITED STATES OF AMERICA TO" is set in four lines over a blank space for the

**Service:** Navy/Coast Guard
**Instituted:** 1945
Dates: 1939-41
**Criteria:** Awarded in gold, silver and bronze to members of the U.S. Antarctic Expedition of 1939-41.
**Devices:** None

recipient's name. Below is the inscription, "IN RECOGNITION OF INVALUABLE SERVICE TO THIS NATION BY COURAGEOUS PIONEERING IN POLAR EXPLORATION WHICH RESULTED IN IMPORTANT GEOGRAPHICAL AND SCIENTIFIC DISCOVERIES," in seven lines.

The ribbon has three equal stripes - ice blue, white, ice blue - and the white center stripe has two narrow dark red stripes near each edge.

The numbers in parentheses next to the Devices refer to the tables in "Attachments and Devices" on page 116-119.

# Army of Occupation Medal

Authorized on June 7, 1946 and awarded to both Army and Army Air Force personnel for at least 30 consecutive days of service in formerly held enemy territories, including Germany (1945-1955), Berlin (1945-1990), Austria (1945-1955), Italy (1945-1947), Japan (1945-1952) and Korea (1945-1949).

The front of the medal depicts the Remagen Bridge on the Rhine River with the inscription, "ARMY OF OCCUPATION" at the top. The reverse depicts Mount Fujiyama in Japan with two Japanese junks in front of the mountain. Although not specifically authorized by regulations, many veterans received Occupation Medals with reversed medallions, apparently to indicate the theater of occupation service, i.e., if occupation service was in Japan, the reverse side showing Mount Fujiyama became the front of the medal. The white and black colors of the ribbon represent Germany and the white and red colors represent Japan.

A gold-colored C-54 airplane device is authorized to denote participation in the Berlin airlift. Medal clasps inscribed: Germany and Japan are authorized for the suspension ribbon of the medal for occupation service in those respective territories. An individual who performed occupational service in both areas is authorized to wear both clasps with the upper clasp representing the area where occupation was first performed. However, regardless of the clasp configuration, no attachment is authorized for the ribbon bar.

★ Italy, May 9, 1945 - Sept. 15, 1947
★ Germany (except West Berlin), May 9, 1945 - May 5, 1955
★ Austria, May 9, 1945 - Jul. 27, 1945 - Oct. 2, 1990
★ Germany (West Berlin), May 9, 1945 - Oct. 2, 1990
★ Korea, Sept. 3, 1945 - Jun. 29, 1949
★ Japan, Sept. 3, 1945 - Apr. 27, 1952

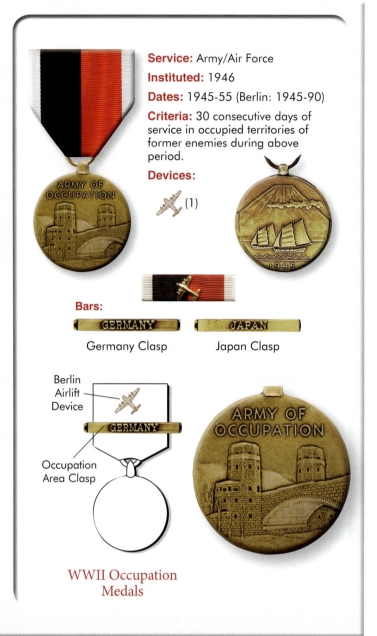

**Service:** Army/Air Force
**Instituted:** 1946
**Dates:** 1945-55 (Berlin: 1945-90)
**Criteria:** 30 consecutive days of service in occupied territories of former enemies during above period.
**Devices:** (1)
**Bars:** Germany Clasp, Japan Clasp

WWII Occupation Medals

# Navy Occupation Service Medal

For thirty consecutive days of service in occupied zones following World War II. The Navy Occupation Service Medal is worn after the World War II Victory Medal and before the Medal for Humane Action.

The Navy Occupation Service Medal was authorized on January 22, 1947 and Navy Department GO on January 28, 1948. The medal was awarded for occupation duty in Japan and Korea from September 2, 1945 to April 27, 1952. The medal was also awarded for occupation service in Germany, Italy, Trieste and Austria.

The Navy Occupation Service Medal was designed by the Army's Institute of Heraldry. The medal is a circular bronze disc showing Neptune, god of the sea, riding a sea serpent with the head and front legs of a horse. Neptune is holding a trident in his right hand and is pointing to an image of land, at the left of the medal, with his left hand. The lower front of the medal depicts the ocean with the words, "OCCUPATION SERVICE" in two lines. The reverse of the medal shows an American eagle perched on an anchor and laurel branches. On either side of the eagle are the words, "FOR SERVICE." Above, in a semicircle is a raised inscription, "UNITED STATES NAVY" or "UNITED STATES MARINE CORPS." The ribbon has two wide stripes of red and black in the center with border stripes of white. Clasps, similar to those used on the World War I Victory Medal, are used to denote service in EUROPE and ASIA, which are authorized for wear with the medal. There are no devices to represent these clasps authorized for wear on the ribbon bar. However, Navy and Marine personnel who served 90 consecutive days in support of the Berlin Airlift (1948-1949) are authorized to wear the Berlin Airlift device, a three-eighths inch gold C-54 airplane, on the ribbon bar and suspension ribbon.

**Service:** Navy/Marine Corps/Coast Guard
**Instituted:** 1947
**Dates:** 1945-55 (Berlin: 1945-90)
**Criteria:** 30 consecutive days of service in occupied territories of former enemies during above period.
**Devices:** (1)
**Bars:** Europe Clasp, Asia Clasp

★ Italy, May 8, 1945 - Dec. 15, 1947
★ Trieste, May 8, 1945 - Oct. 26, 1954
★ Germany (except West Berlin), May 8, 1945 - May 5, 1955
★ Austria, May 8, 1945 - Oct. 25, 1955
★ Asiatic Pacific, Sep. 2, 1945 - Apr. 27, 1952

## Medal for Humane Action

Authorized for members of the U.S. Armed Forces on July 20, 1949 for at least 120 days of service while participating in or providing direct support for the Berlin Airlift during the period June 26, 1948 and September 30, 1949. The prescribed boundaries for qualifying service include the area between the north latitudes of the 54th and the 48th parallels and between the 14th east longitude and the 5th west longitude meridians. Posthumous award may be made to any person who lost his/her life while, or as a direct result of, participating in the Berlin Airlift, without regard to the length of such service.

The front of the medal depicts the C-54 aircraft, which was the primary aircraft used during the airlift, above the coat of arms of Berlin which lies in the center of a wreath of wheat. The reverse has the American eagle with shield and arrows and bears the inscriptions, "FOR HUMANE ACTION and TO SUPPLY NECESSITIES OF LIFE TO THE PEOPLE OF BERLIN GERMANY."

On the ribbon, the black and white colors of Prussia refer to Berlin, capital of Prussia and Germany. Blue alludes to the sky and red represents the fortitude and zeal of the personnel who participated in the airlift.

**Service:** All Services
**Instituted:** 1949
**Dates:** 1948-49
**Criteria:** 120 consecutive days of service participating in the Berlin Airlift or in support thereof. Was also awarded posthumously.
**Devices:** None
**Notes:** This medal was only awarded for Berlin Airlift service and is not to be confused with the Humanitarian Service Medal (established in 1977).

No attachments are authorized. However, instances have been noted where the gold C-54 airplane device was incorrectly placed on this award rather than its proper usage, the Occupation Medal.

## National Defense Service Medal

Initially authorized by executive order on April 22, 1953. It is awarded to members of the U.S. Armed Forces for any honorable active federal service during the Korean War (June 27, 1950 - July 27, 1954), Vietnam War (January 1, 1961- August 14, 1974), Desert Shield/Desert Storm (August 2, 1990 - November 30, 1995) and/or Operations Iraqi Freedom and Enduring Freedom (Afghanistan) (September 11, 2001 to a date TBD). President Bush issued an Executive Order 12776 on October 8, 1991 authorizing award of the medal to all members of the Reserve forces whether or not on active duty during the designated period of the Gulf War. The latest award of the medal was promulgated in a memo, dated April 2, 2002, from the Office of the Deputy Secretary of Defense, Mr. Paul Wolfowitz who authorized the award to all U.S. Service Members on duty on or after September 11, 2001 to a date TBD. Today, there are probably more people authorized this medal than any other award in U.S. history. Circumstances not qualifying as active duty for the purpose of this medal include: (1) Members of the Guard and Reserve on short tours of active duty to fulfill training obligations; (2) Service members on active duty to serve on boards, courts, commissions, and like organizations; (3) Service members on active duty for the sole purpose of undergoing a physical examination; and (4) Service members on active duty for purposes other than extended active duty. Reserve personnel who have received the Armed Forces Expeditionary Medal or the Vietnam Service Medal are eligible for this medal. The National Defense Service Medal is also authorized to those individuals serving as cadets or midshipmen at the Air Force, Army or Naval Academies. The front of the medal shows the American bald eagle with inverted wings standing on a sword and palm branch and contains the

**Service:** All Services
**Instituted:** 1953
**Dates:** 1950-54, 1961-74, 1990-95, 2001 - TBD
**Criteria:** Any honorable active duty service during any of the above periods.
**Devices:**
★ (76)
🍂 (47)

**Notes:** Reinstituted in 1966, 1991 and 2001 for Vietnam, Southwest Asia (Gulf War) and Iraq/Afghanistan actions respectively.

words, "NATIONAL DEFENSE"; the reverse has the United States shield amidst an oak leaf and laurel spray. Symbolically, the eagle is the national emblem of the United States, the sword represents the Armed Forces and the palm is symbolic of victory. The reverse contains the shield from the great seal of the United States flanked by a wreath of laurel and oak representing achievement and strength. The ribbon has a broad center stripe of yellow representing high ideals. The red, white and blue stripes represent the national flag. Red for hardiness and valor, white for purity of purpose and blue for perseverance and justice. No more than one medal is awarded to a single individual but a three-sixteenth inch diameter. bronze star denotes an additional award of the medal.

# Korean Service Medal

Authorized by executive order on November 8, 1950 and awarded for service between June 27, 1950 and July 27, 1954 in the Korean theater of operations. Members of the U.S. Armed Forces must have participated in combat or served with a combat or service unit in the Korean Theater for 30 consecutive or 60 nonconsecutive days during the designated period. Personnel who served with a unit or headquarters stationed outside the theater but in direct support of Korean military operations are also entitled to this medal. The combat zone designated for qualification for the medal encompassed both North and South Korea, Korean waters and the airspace over these areas. The first campaign began when North Korea first invaded South Korea and the last campaign ended when the Korean Armistice cease-fire became effective. The period of Korean service was extended by one year from the cease fire by the Secretary of Defense; individuals could qualify for the medal during this period if stationed in Korea but would not receive any campaign credit. An award of this medal qualifies personnel for award of the United Nations (Korean) Service Medal and the Republic of Korea War Service Medal (approved 1999).

A Korean gateway is depicted on the front of the medal along with the inscription, "KOREAN SERVICE" and on the reverse are the "Taeguk" symbol from the Korean flag that represents unity and the inscription,

**Service:** All Services
**Instituted:** 1950
**Dates:** 1950-54
**Criteria:** Participation in military operations within the Korean area during the above period.
**Devices:**
▲ (2)
★ (63)
☆ (82)
🦅 (28)

"UNITED STATES OF AMERICA." A spray of oak and laurel line the bottom edge. The suspension ribbon and ribbon bar are both blue and white representing the United Nations. Bronze and silver stars are affixed to the suspension drape and ribbon bar to indicate participation in any of the 10 designated campaigns in the Korean War (see below). Army and Air Force personnel who participated in an amphibious assault landing are entitled to wear the arrowhead attachment.

### Campaigns designated by the Army and Air Force for the Korea Service Medal are:

- ★ UN Defensive, 27 June - 15 Sept, 1950
- ★ UN Offensive, 16 Sept - 2 Nov, 1950
- ★ CCF Intervention, 3 Nov, 1950 - 24 Jan, 1951
- ★ 1st UN Counteroffensive, 25 Jan - 21 Apr, 1951
- ★ CCF Spring Offensive, 22 Apr - 8 July, 1951
- ★ UN Summer-Fall Offensive, 9 July - 27 Nov, 1951
- ★ Second Korean Winter, 28 Nov, 1951 - 30 Apr, 1952
- ★ Korea, Summer-Fall, 1 May - 30 Nov, 1953
- ★ Third Korean Winter, 1 Dec, 1952 - 30 Apr, 1953
- ★ Korea, Summer, 1 May - 27 July, 1953

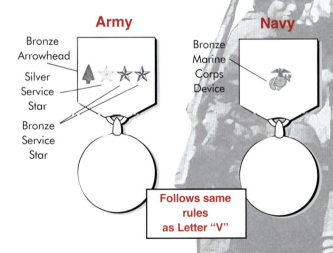

**Army**
- Bronze Arrowhead
- Silver Service Star
- Bronze Service Star

**Navy**
- Bronze Marine Corps Device

Follows same rules as Letter "V"

The ten Navy & Marine Corps campaign designations for the Korean Service Medal are:

- ★ North Korean aggression, 27 June - 2 Nov 1950
- ★ Communist China aggression, 3 Nov 1950 - 24 Jan 1951
- ★ Inchon Landing, 13 September - 17 Sept 1950
- ★ 1st United Nations counteroffensive, 25 Jan - 21 Apr 1951
- ★ Communist China spring offensive, 22 Apr - 8 July 1951
- ★ United Nations summer-fall offensive, 9 July - 27 Nov 1951
- ★ 2nd Korean winter, 28 November 1951 - 30 Apr 1952
- ★ Korean defensive, summer-fall 1952, 1 May - 30 Nov 1952
- ★ 3rd Korean winter, 1 December 1952 - 30 Apr 1953
- ★ Korean summer 1953, 1 May - 27 July 1953

The numbers in parentheses next to the Devices refer to the tables in "Attachments and Devices" on page 116-119.

# Antarctica Service Medal

Authorized on July 7, 1960 and awarded to any member of the Armed Forces who, from January 2, 1946, as a member of a U.S. Antarctic expedition, participates in, or performs services in direct support of scientific or exploratory operations on the Antarctic Continent. Qualifying service includes personnel who participate in flights or naval operations supporting operations in Antarctica. The medal may also be awarded to any U.S. citizen who participates in Antarctic expeditions under the same conditions as Service personnel.

The front of the medal depicts a figure appropriately clothed in cold weather gear with his hood thrown back, arms extended and legs spread, symbolizing stability, determination, courage and devotion. The reverse depicts a map of the Antarctic continent in polar projection across which are three centered lines containing the inscription, "COURAGE SACRIFICE DEVOTION."

A clasp containing the raised inscription, "WINTERED OVER" is worn on the medal and a disc of the same metal, containing the outline of the Antarctic Continent is worn on the ribbon bar if the individual remains on the continent during the winter months. For the first stay, the disc and bar are made of bronze, for the second stay, they are gold-colored and for the third and all subsequent winter tours, the devices are silver. The Coast Guard alone specifies the small three-sixteenths inch diameter bronze star as an additional award device.

**Service:** All Services
**Instituted:** 1960
**Dates:** 1946 to Present
**Criteria:** 30 calendar days of service on the Antarctic Continent.
**Devices:** (5a) (5b) (5c) (78)
**Bars:** "Wintered Over" in bronze, gold, silver.

# Arctic Service Medal

The Coast Guard Arctic Service Medal was authorized by the Coast Guard Commandant on May 20, 1976 and made retroactive to Jan 1, 1946. It is awarded for 21 days consecutive service aboard a Coast Guard vessel in Polar waters north of the Arctic Circle from May 1 through October 31 or 21 days consecutive service north of latitude 60 degrees N from November 1 through April 30. Personnel who serve at any of the following Coast Guard Stations for the required 21 days also qualify for the medal:

★ Loran Station, Cape Atholl, Greenland
★ Loran Station, Cape Christian, Baffin Island, Canada
★ Loran Station, Port Clarence, Alaska
★ Radio Station, Barrow, Alaska
★ Loran Station, Bo, Norway
★ Loran Station, Jan Mayen Island, Norway

**Service:** Coast Guard
**Instituted:** 1976
**Dates:** 1946 to Present
**Criteria:** Awarded for 21 days of service on vessels operating in polar waters north of the Arctic Circle.
**Devices:** (67) (86)

The front of the medal depicts a polar bear on the Arctic tundra beneath a stylized Polar star. Above this, on the medal's edge is the curved inscription, "ARCTIC SERVICE." The reverse contains the Coast Guard Shield in the center of an otherwise unadorned planchet. Although no devices were initially authorized, the regulations now specify three-sixteenths inch diameter bronze and silver stars to denote additional awards for all deployments subsequent to January 1, 1989.

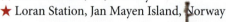

# Armed Forces Expeditionary Medal

**Service:** All Services
**Instituted:** 1961
**Dates:** 1958 to Present
**Criteria:** Participation in military operations not covered by specific war medal.
**Devices:**
▲ (2)
★ (64) (bronze)
☆ (83) (silver)
🦅 (28)

**Notes:** Authorized for service in Vietnam until establishment of Vietnam Service Medal.

President John F. Kennedy characterized the post World War II period as: "a twilight that is neither peace nor war." During the period commonly referred to as the Cold War, the Armed Services agreed to one medal to recognize major actions not otherwise covered by a specific campaign medal.

The Armed Forces Expeditionary Medal was authorized on December 4, 1961 to any member of the United States Armed Forces for U.S. military operations, U.S. operations in direct support of the United Nations and U.S. operations of assistance to friendly foreign nations after July 1, 1958. Operations that qualify for this medal are authorized in specific orders. Participating personnel must have served at least 30 consecutive (60 nonconsecutive) days in the qualifying operation or less if the operation was less than 30 days in length. The medal may also be authorized for individuals who do not meet the basic criteria but who do merit special recognition for their service in the designated operation.

The first qualifying operation was Operation Blue Bat, a peacekeeping mission in Lebanon from July 1 to November 1, 1958. This medal was initially awarded for Vietnam service between July 1, 1958 and July 3, 1965; an individual awarded the medal for this period of Vietnam service may elect to keep the award or request the Vietnam Service Medal in its place. However, both awards may not be retained for the same period of Vietnam service. Many personnel received this medal for continuing service in Cambodia after the Vietnam cease-fire. The medal was also authorized for those serving in the Persian Gulf area who previously would have qualified for the Southwest Asia Service Medal and the National Defense Service Medal whose qualification periods for that area terminated on November 30, 1995. Individuals who qualify for both the Southwest Asia Service Medal and the Armed Forces Expeditionary Medal must elect to receive the Expeditionary medal.

The front of the medal depicts an American eagle with wings raised, perched on a sword. Behind this is a compass rose with rays coming from the angles of the compass points. The words "ARMED FORCES EXPEDITIONARY SERVICE" encircle the design. The reverse of the medal depicts the Presidential shield with branches of laurel below and the inscription, "UNITED STATES OF AMERICA." The American national colors are located at the center position or honor point of the ribbon. The light blue sections on either side suggest water and overseas service, while various colors representing areas of the world where American troops may be called upon to serve run outward to the edge.

Army — Bronze Arrowhead, Silver Service Star, Bronze Service Star

Navy — Bronze Marine Corps Device

### The qualifying campaigns:

★ Lebanon, Jul. 1, 1958 - Nov. 1, 1958
★ Taiwan Straits, Aug. 23, 1958 - Jan. 1, 1959
★ Quemoy & Matsu Islands, Aug. 23, 1958 - Jun. 1, 1963
★ Vietnam, Jul. 1, 1958 - Jul. 3, 1965
★ Congo, Jul. 14, 1960 - Sep. 1, 1962
★ Laos, Apr. 19, 1961 - Oct. 7, 1962
★ Berlin, Aug. 14, 1961 - Jun. 1, 1963
★ Cuba, Oct. 24, 1962 - Jun. 1, 1963
★ Congo, Nov. 23-27, 1964
★ Dominican Republic, Apr. 23, 1965 - Sep. 21, 1966
★ Korea, Oct. 1, 1966 - Jun. 30, 1974
★ Cambodia, Mar. 29, 1973 - Aug. 15, 1973
★ Thailand, Mar. 29, 1973 - Aug. 15, 1973 (Only those in direct support of Cambodia)
★ Operation Eagle Pull - Cambodia, Apr. 11-13, 1975 (Includes evacuation)
★ Operation Frequent Wind - Vietnam, Apr. 29-30, 1975
★ Mayaquez Operation, May 15, 1975
★ El Salvador, Jan. 1, 1981 - Feb. 1, 1992
★ Lebanon, Jun. 1, 1983 - Dec. 1, 1987
★ Operation Urgent Fury - Grenada, Oct. 23, 1983 - Nov. 21, 1983
★ Eldorado Canyon - Libya, Apr. 12-17, 1986
★ Operation Earnest Will - Persian Gulf, Jul. 24, 1987 - Aug. 1, 1990 (Only those participating in, or in direct support)
★ Operation Just Cause - Panama, Dec. 20, 1989 - Jan. 31, 1990 (USS Vreeland & other SVS-designated aircrew mbrs. outside the Conus in direct support)
★ United Shield - Somalia, Dec. 5, 1992 - Mar. 31, 1995
★ Operation Restore Hope - Somalia, Dec. 5, 1992 - Mar. 31, 1995
★ Operation Uphold Democracy - Haiti, Sept. 1994 - Mar. 31, 1995
★ Operation Joint Endeavor - Bosnia, Croatia, the Adriatic Sea & Airspace, Nov. 20, 1995 - Dec. 19, 1996
★ Operation Vigilant Sentinel - Iraq, Saudi Arabia, Kuwait, & Persian Gulf Dec. 1, 1995 - Sep. 1, 1997
★ Operation Southern Watch - Iraq, Saudi Arabia, Kuwait, Persian Gulf, Bahrain, Qatar, UAE, Oman, Gulf of Oman W of 62° E Long., Yemen, Egypt, & Jordan
★ Operation Maritime Intercept - Iraq, Saudi Arabia, Kuwait, Red Sea, Persian Gulf, Gulf of Oman W of 62° E Long., Bahrain, Qatar, UAE, Oman, Yemen, Egypt & Jordan Dec. 1, 1995 - Open
★ Operation Joint Guard - Bosnia, Herzegovina, Croatia, Adriatic Sea & Airspace, Dec. 20, 1996 - Jun. 20, 2008
★ Operation Northern Watch - Iraq, Saudi Arabia, Kuwait, Persian Gulf of W of 56° E Long., and Incirlik AB, Turkey (Only pers. TDY to ONW), Jan. 1, 1997 - 18 March 2003
★ Operation Joint Forge - Bosnia-Herzegovina, Croatia, Adriatic Sea & Airspace, Jun. 21, 1998 - Open
★ Operation Desert Thunder - Iraq, Saudi Arabia, Kuwait, Bahrain, Qatar, UAE, Omar, Yemen, Egypt, Jordan, Persian Gulf, Gulf of Oman, Red Sea support, Nov. 11, 1998 - Dec. 22, 1998
★ Operation Desert Fox - Iraq, Saudi Arabia, Kuwait, Bahrain, Qatar, UAE, Oman, Yemen, Egypt, Jordan, Persian Gulf, Gulf of Oman, USN Red Sea support, 16 Dec. -22 Dec. 1998
★ Operation Desert Spring, Haiti, Southwest Asia, 31 Dec.1998-18 Mar. 2003
★ Operation Secure Tomorrow, 29 Feb. 2004- 15 Jun. 2004

# Vietnam Service Medal

**Service:** All Services
**Instituted:** 1965
**Dates:** 1965-73
**Criteria:** Service in Vietnam, Laos, Cambodia or Thailand during the above period.
**Devices:**
- (2) Bronze Arrowhead
- (63) Bronze Star
- (82) Silver Star
- (28) Marine Corps Device

Authorized by executive order on July 8, 1965 for U.S. military personnel serving in the Vietnam Theater of Operations after July 3, 1965 through March 28, 1973. Personnel must have served in Vietnam on temporary duty for at least 30 consecutive/60 nonconsecutive days or have served in combat with a unit directly supporting a military operation in Southeast Asia. Military personnel serving in Laos, Cambodia or Thailand in direct support of operations in Vietnam are also eligible for this award. The Armed Forces Expeditionary Medal was awarded for earlier service in Vietnam from July 1, 1958 to July 3, 1965, inclusive; personnel receiving that award may be awarded the Vietnam Service Medal but are not authorized both awards for Vietnam service. The front of the medal depicts an oriental dragon behind a grove of bamboo trees; below the base of the trees is the inscription, "REPUBLIC OF VIETNAM SERVICE." The reverse of the medal depicts a crossbow with a torch through the center and contains the inscription, "UNITED STATES OF AMERICA" along the bottom edge. The colors of the suspension drape and ribbon suggest the flag of the Republic of Vietnam (the red stripes represent the three ancient Vietnamese empires of Tonkin, Annam, and Cochin China) and the green represents the Vietnamese jungle. Bronze and silver stars are authorized to signify participation in any of the 17 designated campaigns during the inclusive period.

### Army

Bronze Arrowhead, Silver Service Star, Bronze Service Star

### Navy
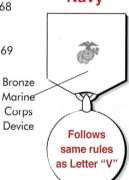
Bronze Marine Corps Device
Follows same rules as Letter "V"

**Designated campaigns for the Vietnam Service Medal are as follows:**

**Army and Naval Services:**
- ★ Vietnam (VN) Advisory, 1962 - 1965
- ★ VN Defense, 1965 - 1965
- ★ VN Counteroffensive Campaign, 1965 - 1966
- ★ VN Counteroffensive Campaign Phase II, 1966 -1967
- ★ VN Counteroffensive Campaign Phase III, 1967 - 1968
- ★ TET Counteroffensive, 1968
- ★ VN Counteroffensive Campaign Phase IV, 1968
- ★ VN Counteroffensive Campaign Phase V, 1968
- ★ VN Counteroffensive Campaign Phase VI, 1968 - 1969
- ★ TET69 Counteroffensive, 1969
- ★ VN Summer - Fall 1969, 1969
- ★ Vietnam Winter - Spring 1970, 1969 - 1970
- ★ Sanctuary Counteroffensive, 1970
- ★ VN Counteroffensive Campaign Phase VII, 1970 - 1971
- ★ Consolidation I, 1971
- ★ Consolidation II, 1971 - 1972
- ★ Vietnam Cease-Fire Campaign, 1972 - 1973

**Air Force:**
- ★ Vietnam (VN) Advisory, 1961 - 1965
- ★ VN Defense, 1965 - 1966
- ★ VN Air Campaign, 1966
- ★ VN Air Offensive Phase I, 1966 - 1967
- ★ VN Air Offensive Phase II, 1967 - 1968
- ★ VN Air/Ground Campaign, 1968
- ★ VN Air Offensive Phase III, 1968
- ★ VN Air Offensive Phase IV, 1968 - 1969
- ★ TET 69/Counteroffensive, 1969
- ★ VN Summer-Fall, 69, 1969
- ★ VN Winter-Spring, 1969 - 1970
- ★ Sanctuary Counteroffensive, 1970
- ★ Southwest Monsoon, 1970
- ★ Commando Hunt V, 1970 - 1971
- ★ Commando Hunt VI, 1971
- ★ Commando Hunt VII, 1971 - 1972
- ★ Vietnam Cease-Fire, 1972 - 1973

# Southwest Asia Service Medal

Awarded to members of the United States Armed Forces who participated in, or directly supported, military operations in Southwest Asia or in surrounding areas between August 2, 1990 and November 30, 1995 (Operations Desert Shield, Desert Storm and follow-up). The medal was established by an executive order signed by President George Bush on March 15, 1991.

The front of the medal depicts the tools of modern desert warfare, i.e., aircraft, helicopter, tank, armored personnel carrier, tent and troops, battleship, in both desert and sea settings along with the inscription, "SOUTHWEST ASIA SERVICE" in the center. The reverse of the medal contains a sword entwined with a palm leaf representing military preparedness and the maintenance of peace and the inscription "UNITED STATES OF AMERICA" around the periphery. The ribbon is predominately tan, symbolizing the sands of the desert and contains thin stripes of the U.S. national colors towards each edge. The green and black center stripes and the black edges, along with the red and white, suggest the flag colors of most Arab nations in the region of Southwest Asia.

**Service:** All Services
**Instituted:** 1991
**Dates:** 1991 to 1995
**Criteria:** Active participation in, or support of, Operations Desert Shield and/or Desert Storm.
**Devices:**
★ (63)
⚓ (28)
**Notes:** Terminal date of service was 30 Nov 1995.

**Approved campaigns for the Southwest Asia Service Medal, each being represented by a bronze star:**

★ Operation Desert Shield, August 2, 1990 - January 16, 1991
★ Operation Desert Storm, January 17, 1991 - April 11, 1991
★ Southwest Asia Cease-fire Campaign, April 12, 1991- November 30, 1995
★ Operation Provide Comfort, June 1, 1992 - November 30, 1995

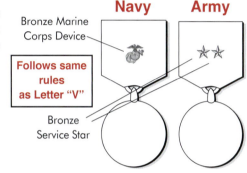

# Kosovo Campaign Medal

For participation in, or in direct support of Kosovo operations. The Kosovo Campaign Medal is worn after the Southwest Asia Service Medal and before the Afghanistan Campaign Medal. The Kosovo Campaign Medal was established by executive order on May 15, 2000. The medal is awarded to all members of the Armed Forces who participated in or provided direct support to Kosovo operations within established areas of eligibility (AOE) from March 24, 1999 to December 31, 2013. The service member must have been a member of a unit participating in, or engaged in support of one or more of the following operations for 30 consecutive days or 60 nonconsecutive days.

- ★ Allied Force: 24 March - 10 June 1999
- ★ Task Force Hawk: 5 April - 24 June 1999
- ★ Joint Guardian: 11 June 1999- TBD
- ★ Task Force Saber: 31 March - 8 July 1999
- ★ Allied Harbour: 4 April - 1 Sept 1999
- ★ Task Force Falcon: 11 June - TBD
- ★ Sustain Hope/Shining Hope: 4 April - 10 July 1999
- ★ Task Force Hunter: 1 April - 1 Nov 1999
- ★ Noble Anvil: 24 March - 20 July 1999

The Kosovo Campaign Medal was designed by the Institute of Heraldry. The medal is a circular bronze disk depicting rocky terrain, a fertile valley and sunrise behind a mountain pass in Kosovo. Above the scene, on two lines, are the words, "KOSOVO CAMPAIGN." At the lower edge is a stylized wreath of grain reflecting the ag-

**Service:** All Services
**Instituted:** 2000
**Dates:** 1999-2013
**Criteria:** Service in Kosovo, Former Yugoslavia during the above period.
**Devices:**
★ (63)
🦅 (28)

ricultural nature of the area. The reverse shows an outline of the province of Kosovo with the curved inscription, "IN DEFENSE OF HUMANITY" across the top. To date, there are two bronze service stars authorized for the Kosovo Campaign Medal as follows:
(1) Kosovo Air Campaign - 24 March 1999 to 10 June 1999
(2) Kosovo Defense Campaign - 11 June 1999 to a date TBD

In addition, Naval personnel who were attached to Marine Corps units are entitled to wear a miniature bronze Marine device on the suspension ribbon and ribbon bar.

# Afghanistan Campaign Medal

Presidential Executive Order 13363 established the Afghanistan Campaign Medal.

Service members authorized the Afghanistan Campaign Medal must have served in direct support of Operation Enduring Freedom on or after Oct. 24, 2001, to a future date to be determined by the Secretary of Defense or the cessation of the operation. The area of eligibility encompasses all land areas of the country of Afghanistan and all air spaces above the land.

Service members must have been assigned, attached or mobilized to units operating in these areas of eligibility for 30 consecutive days or for 60 non-consecutive days or meet one of the following criteria:

a. Be engaged in combat during an armed engagement, regardless of the time in the area of eligibility; or
b. While participating in an operation or on official duties, is wounded or injured and requires medical evacuation from the area of eligibility; or
c. While participating as a regularly assigned air crewmember flying sorties into, out of, within or over the area of eligibility in direct support of the military operations; each day of operations counts as one day of eligibility.

**Service:** All Services
**Instituted:** 2004
**Dates:** 2001-TBD
**Criteria:** Active participation in Operation Enduring Freedom, the liberation of Afghanistan.
**Devices:**
▲ (2)
★ (63)
☆ (82)
🦅 (28)

Service members qualified for the Global War on Terrorism Expeditionary Medal by reasons of service between Oct. 24, 2001, and April 30, 2005, in an area for which the Afghanistan Campaign Medal was subsequently authorized and between March 19, 2003, and Feb. 28, 2005, in an area for which the Iraq Campaign Medal was subsequently authorized, shall remain qualified for the medal.

Upon application, any such service member may be awarded the Afghanistan Campaign Medal in lieu of the Global War on Terrorism Expeditionary Medal for such service. No service member shall be entitled to both medals for the same act, achievement or period of service.

The awarding authority for the Afghanistan campaign medals shall be prescribed by the member's respective military service regulations. The medal may be awarded posthumously.

Only one award of the Afghanistan Campaign Medal may be authorized for any individual. A bronze service star is worn on the suspension and campaign ribbon for one or more days of participation in each designated campaign phase. The Afghanistan Campaign Medal shall be positioned below the Kosovo Campaign Medal and above the Iraq Campaign Medal.

On the front of the medal, above a range of mountains is a map of Afghanistan in the center with the inscription, "AFGHANISTAN CAMPAIGN" around the top. On the reverse side on top is a radiating demi-sun superimposed by an eagle's head. Inscribed across the bottom half of the reverse side are the three lines, "FOR SERVICE IN AFGHANISTAN" all enclosed by a laurel wreath symbolizing victory.

*The designated Afghanistan Campaign Medal campaigns are:*

★ Liberation of Afghanistan: 11 September 2001 - 30 November 2001
★ Consolidation I: 1 December 2001 - 30 September 2006
★ Consolidation II: 1 October 2006 - 30 November 2009
★ Consolidation III: 1 December, 2009–30 June 2011
★ Transition I: 1 July 2011–date to be determined.

The numbers in parentheses next to the Devices refer to the tables in "Attachments and Devices" on page 116-119.

# Iraq Campaign Medal

**Service:** All Services
**Instituted:** 2004
**Dates:** 2003-31 December 2011
**Criteria:** Active participation in Operation Iraqi Freedom.
**Devices:**
(2)
(63)
(82)
(28)

Presidential Executive Order 13363 established the Iraq Campaign Medal.

Those authorized the Iraq Campaign Medal must have served in direct support of Operation Iraqi Freedom on or after March 19, 2003, to a future date to be determined by the Secretary of Defense or the cessation of the operation. The area of eligibility encompasses all land area of the country of Iraq and the contiguous water area out to 12 nautical miles and all air spaces above the land area of Iraq and above the contiguous water area out to 12 nautical miles.

Service members must have been assigned, attached or mobilized to units operating in these areas of eligibility for 30 consecutive days or for 60 non-consecutive days or meet one of the following criteria:

a. Be engaged in combat during an armed engagement, regardless of the time in the area of eligibility; or

b. While participating in an operation or on official duties, is wounded or injured and requires medical evacuation from the area of eligibility; or

c. While participating as a regularly assigned air crewmember flying sorties into, out of, within or over the area of eligibility in direct support of the military operations; each day of operations counts as one day of eligibility.

Service members qualified for the Global War on Terrorism Expeditionary Medal by reasons of service between Oct. 24, 2001, and April 30, 2005, in an area for which the Iraq Campaign Medal was subsequently authorized, shall remain qualified for the medal.

Upon application, any such service member may be awarded the Iraq Campaign Medal in lieu of the Global War on Terror Expeditionary Medal for such service. No service member shall be entitled to both medals for the same act, achievement or period of service.

The awarding authority for the Iraq campaign medals shall be prescribed by the member's respective military service regulations. Medals may be awarded posthumously.

Only one award of the Iraq Campaign Medal may be authorized for any individual. Individuals may receive both the medals if they meet the requirement of both awards; however, the qualifying period of service used to establish eligibility for one award cannot be used to justify eligibility for the other.

The Iraq Campaign Medal shall be positioned below the Afghanistan Campaign Medal and above the Global War on Terrorism Expeditionary Medal.

The medal's obverse features a relief map of Iraq displaying two irregular lines representing the Tigris and Euphrates Rivers surmounting a palm wreath. Above is the inscription, "IRAQ CAMPAIGN". The Statue of Freedom is shown on the reverse surmounting a sunburst, encircle by two scimitars, points down, crossed at the tips of the blades, all above the inscription, "FOR SERVICE IN IRAQ".

A bronze star is worn on the suspension and campaign ribbon for one or more days of participation in each designated campaign phases. A silver campaign service star device is used for participation in five campaigns.

**The designated Iraq campaigns are:**

★ Liberation of Iraq: 19 March 2003 - 1 May 2003
★ Transition of Iraq: 2 May 2003 - 28 June 2004
★ Iraqi Governance: 29 June 2004 - 15 December 2005
★ National Resolution: 16 December 2005 - Date to be determined
★ Iraqi Surge: 10 January 2007–31 December 2008
★ Iraqi Sovereignty: 1 January 2009–31 August 2010
★ New Dawn: 1 September 2010–31 December 2011

# Inherent Resolve Campaign Medal

The Inherent Resolve Campaign Medal was established 30 March, 2016. It provides special recognition for members of the Armed Forces serving, or having served, 30 consecutive days or 60 nonconsecutive days in Iraq, Syria, or contiguous waters or airspace on or after 15 June, 2014 to a future date to be determined by the Secretary of Defense. Personnel are also authorized the medal regardless of the time criteria if they were engaged in combat during an armed engagement or while participating in an operation or official duties and were killed or wounded. Aircrew members accrue one day of eligibility for each day they fly into, out of, with in, or over the area of engagement.

Previously the Global War on Terror Expeditionary Medal was authorized for service in Iraq and Syria for operation INHERENT RESOLVE, however, that award is now terminated. Service members who were awarded a GWOT–EM for their Inherent Resolve Campaign Medal qualifying service in Iraq or Syria during the period of 15 June, 2014 to 30 March, 2016 remain qualified for the GWOT–EM. However, service members, may apply to be awarded the IRCM in lieu of the GWOT–EM. Service members can not be awarded both medals for the same qualifying periods.

The Inherent Resolve Campaign Medal is worn after the Iraq Campaign Medal and before the GWOT–EM. The medal is only presented upon initial award and a separate bronze campaign star is worn on the suspension and campaign ribbon to recognize each designated campaign phase in which a member participated for one or more days.

The scorpion, symbolic for treachery and destruction, is found on most major land masses. The dagger alludes to swiftness and determination. The eagle represents the United States and is symbolic of might and victory. The decorated star panels are common in the Arabian and Moorish styles of ornamentation.

The ribbon is blue, teal, sand and orange. This color combination is inspired by the colors of the Middle East landscape and the Ishtar Gate, the eighth gate leading to the historic inner city of Babylon.

**Service:** All Services
**Instituted:** 30 March 2016
**Dates:** 15 June, 2014 to TBD
**Criteria:** Active service indirect support of Operation Inherent Resolve.
**Devices:**
★ (63)
☆ (82)
🦅 (28)

**Designated Inherent Resolve campaigns are:**

Abeyance: 15 June 2014 - 24 November 2015
Intensification: 25 November 2015 - TBD

# Global War on Terrorism Expeditionary Medal

For deployed service abroad in support of Global War on Terrorism operations on, or after September 11, 2001. The Global War on Terrorism Expeditionary Medal is worn after the Iraq Campaign Medal and before the Global War on Terrorism Service Medal.

The Global War on Terrorism Expeditionary Medal was authorized by executive order. The medal is awarded to any member of the Armed Forces who is deployed in an approved operation, such as ENDURING FREEDOM. The Chairman of the Joint Chiefs of Staff shall designate the specific area of deployed eligibly per qualifying operation. To be eligible personnel must have participated in the operation by authority of written order. Qualification includes at least 30 consecutive days or 60 nonconsecutive days, or be engaged in actual combat (hostile weapons fire is exchanged), or duty that is equally as hazardous as combat duty, or wounded or injured requiring evacuation from the operation, or while participating as a regularly assigned air crewmember flying sorties into, out of, within or over the are of eligibility in direct support of the military operations.

**Service:** All Services
**Instituted:** 2003
**Dates:** 2002-TBD
**Criteria:** For the deployment abroad for 30 days in support of the Global War on Terrorism operations on or after 11 Sept. 2001.
**Devices:** None

Earlier design with the word "Medal"

New design without word "Medal"

Personnel may receive both the Global War on Terrorism Expeditionary Medal and the Global War on Terrorism Service Medal if they meet the requirements of both awards; however, service eligibility for one cannot be used to justify service eligibility for the other.

The Global War on Terrorism Expeditionary Medal was designed by the Institute of Heraldry. The medal is a circular bronze disc which displays a shield adapted from the Great Seal of the United States surmounting two sword hilts enclosed within a wreath of laurel; overall an eagle, wings displayed, grasping a serpent in its claws. The reverse of the medal displays the eagle, a serpent and swords from the front of the medal within the encircling inscription, "WAR ON TERRORISM EXPEDITIONARY." The ribbon is scarlet, white and blue representing the United States; light blue refers to worldwide cooperation against terrorism; gold denotes excellence. Effective 2005, the GWOTEM is no longer authorized to be awarded for service in Afghanistan and/or Iraq.

**To date, the Areas of Eligibility associated with the operations ENDURING FREEDOM, IRAQI FREEDOM and NOMAD SHADOW are:**

- ★ Afghanistan
- ★ Bahrain
- ★ Bulgaria (Bourgas)
- ★ Crete
- ★ Cyprus
- ★ Diego Garcia
- ★ Djibouti
- ★ Egypt
- ★ Eritrea
- ★ Ethiopia
- ★ Iran
- ★ Iraq
- ★ Israel
- ★ Jordan
- ★ Kazakhstan
- ★ Kenya
- ★ Kuwait
- ★ Kyrgyzstan
- ★ Lebanon
- ★ Oman
- ★ Pakistan
- ★ Philippines
- ★ Qatar
- ★ Romania (Constanta)
- ★ Saudi Arabia
- ★ Somalia
- ★ Syria
- ★ Tajikistan
- ★ Turkey (east of 35 degrees east lat.)
- ★ Turkmenistan
- ★ United Arab Emirates
- ★ Uzbekistan
- ★ Yemen
- ★ That portion of the Arabian Sea north of 10 degrees north latitude and west of 68 degrees longitude
- ★ Bab el Mandeb
- ★ Gulf of Aden
- ★ Gulf of Aqaba
- ★ Gulf of Oman
- ★ Gulf of Suez
- ★ That portion of the Mediterranean Sea east of 28 degrees east longitude
- ★ Persian Gulf
- ★ Red Sea
- ★ Strait of Hormuz
- ★ Suez Canal

# Global War on Terrorism Service Medal

Awarded to members of the United States Armed Forces who participated in, or served in support of operations relating to the Global War on Terrorism between September 11, 2001 and a date to be determined at a later date. The medal was established by an executive order signed by President George W. Bush on October 28, 2003. Initial award of the Global War on Terrorism Service Medal was limited to Airport Security Operations from September 27, 2001 until May 31, 2002 and to Service members who supported Operations ENDURING FREEDOM, NOBLE EAGLE and IRAQI FREEDOM.

Qualifying Service members must be assigned, attached or mobilized to a unit participating in or service in direct support of designated for 30 consecutive days or 60 nonconsecutive days. It is to be noted that eligibility for the Global War on Terrorism Service Medal is defined as support for the War on Terrorism in a non-deployed status, whether stationed at home or overseas. By contrast, service in an operationally deployed status abroad within a designated area of eligibility merits primary eligibility for the Global War on Terrorism Expeditionary Medal.

**Service:** All Services
**Instituted:** 2001
**Dates:** 2002-TBD
**Criteria:** For service for 30 days in support of the Global War on Terrorism operations in the U.S. or overseas on or after 11 Sept. 2001.
**Devices:** None

New design without word "Medal"

Earlier design with the word "Medal"

Personnel may receive both the Global War on Terrorism Service and Expeditionary Medals if they meet the requirements of both awards. However, the qualifying period for one cannot be used to justify eligibility for the other. Establishing the award of the GWOTSM for general support of the war on terror makes the medal similar to the award of the National Defense Service Medal. The major difference between the National Defense Service Medal and GWOTSM is that the NDSM is authorized when an individual joins the Armed Forces and the GWOTSM is only authorized after 30 days of active service or 60 days non consecutive service for reserve forces.

Although qualifying circumstances would be extremely rare, Battle Stars may be applicable for personnel who were engaged in actual combat against the enemy under circumstances involving grave danger of death or serious bodily injury from enemy action.

The Global War on Terrorism Service Medal was designed by the Institute of Heraldry. The medal is a circular bronze disc which displays an eagle, wings displayed, with a stylized shield of thirteen vertical bars on its breast and holding in dexter claw an olive branch and in sinister claw three arrows, all in front of a terrestrial globe with the inscription above, "WAR ON TERRORISM SERVICE." The reverse of the medal displays a laurel wreath on a plain field. The ribbon is scarlet, white and blue representing the United States; gold denoting excellence.

## Korea Defense Service Medal

For the defense of the Republic of Korea. The Korea Defense Service Medal is worn after the Global War on Terrorism Service Medal and before the Armed Forces Service Medal.

The Korea Defense Service Medal was provided for in the Fiscal Year 2003 National Defense Authorization Act. The medal is awarded to members of the Armed Forces who served in the Republic of Korea or waters adjacent thereto for a qualifying period of time between July 28, 1954 and a date to be determined.

The Korea Defense Service Medal was designed by the Institute of Heraldry. The medal is a circular bronze disc bearing a Korean circle dragon within an encircling scroll inscribed, "KOREA DEFENSE SERVICE" with, in base, two sprigs, laurel to dexter side, bamboo to sinister. Symbolism: The four-clawed dragon is a traditional symbol of Korea and represents intelligence and strength of purpose. The sprig of laurel denotes honorable endeavor and victory, the bamboo refers to the land of Korea. The medal's reverse displays a representation of the land mass of Korea surmounted by two swords points up saltirewise within a circlet with five points.

Symbolism: The swords placed saltirewise over a map of Korea signify defense of freedom in that country and the readiness to engage in combat to that end. The circlet enclosing the device recalls the forms of five-petal symbols common in Korean armory.

**Service:** All Services
**Instituted:** 2003
**Dates:** 1954-TBD
**Criteria:** For service in the Republic of Korea, or the waters adjacent thereto, for a qualifying period of time between 28 July, 1954 and a date to be determined.
**Devices:** None

New design without word "Medal"

Earlier design with the word "Medal"

The ribbon is dark green representing the land of Korea, blue indicates overseas service and commitment to achieving peace. Gold denotes excellence, white symbolizes idealism and integrity. Light blue with a thin white stripe in the center and narrow white stripes at the edges.

## Armed Forces Service Medal

Authorized on January 11, 1996 for U.S. military personnel who, on or after June 1, 1992, participate in a U.S. military operation deemed to be a significant activity in which no foreign armed opposition or imminent hostile action is encountered and for which no previous U.S. service medal is authorized. The medal can be awarded to service members in direct support of the United Nations or North Atlantic Treaty Organization and for assistance operations to friendly nations. The initial awards of this medal were for operations that have occurred in the Balkans since 1992. Qualifications include at least one day of participation in the designated area. Direct support of the operation and aircraft flights within the area also qualify for award of this medal as long as at least one day is served within the designated area. Recent operations that qualify for the medal are Provide Promise, Joint Endeavor, Able Sentry, Deny Flight, Maritime Monitor and Sharp Guard.

The front of the medal contains the torch of liberty within its center and contains the inscription "ARMED FORCES SERVICE" around its periphery. The reverse of the medal depicts the American eagle with the U.S. shield in its chest and spread wings clutching three arrows in its talons encircled by a laurel wreath and the inscription, "IN PURSUIT OF DEMOCRACY." Bronze and silver service stars are worn to denote additional awards.

**Service:** All Services
**Instituted:** 1996
**Dates:** 1995 to Present
**Criteria:** Participation in military operations not covered by specific war medal or the Armed Forces Expeditionary Medal.
**Devices:** ★ (67)  ☆ (86)

New design without word "Medal"

Earlier design with the word "Medal"

# Humanitarian Service Medal

Authorized on January 19, 1977 and awarded to Armed Forces personnel (including Reserve components) who, subsequent to April 1, 1975, distinguish themselves by meritorious direct participation in a DOD-approved significant military act or operation of a humanitarian nature. According to regulations, the participation must be "hands-on" at the site of the operation; personnel assigned to staff functions geographically separated from the operation are not eligible for this medal. Service members must be assigned and/or attached to participating units for specific operations by official orders. Members who were present for duty at specific qualifying locations for the medal but who did not make a direct contribution to the action or operation are specifically excluded from eligibility. It should be noted that some of the earliest recipients of the Humanitarian Service Medal, e.g., for the evacuations of Laos, Cambodia and Vietnam, would more likely be awarded the Armed Forces Service Medal in today's environment.

The medal was designed by the Institute of Heraldry. The front of the medal depicts a human right hand with open palm within a raised circle. At the top of the medal's reverse is the raised inscription, "FOR HUMANITARIAN SERVICE" set in three lines. In the center is an oak branch with three acorns and leaves and, below this, is the raised circular inscription, "UNITED STATES ARMED FORCES" around the lower edge of the medal. The ribbon is medium blue with a wide center stripe of navy blue. It is edged by a wide stripe of purple which is separated from the light blue field by a narrow white stripe. Bronze and silver stars are authorized for additional awards.

**Service:** All Services
**Instituted:** 1977
**Dates:** 1975 to Present
**Criteria:** Direct participation in specific operations of a humanitarian nature.
**Devices:**
2 (32)
★ (67)
☆ (86)

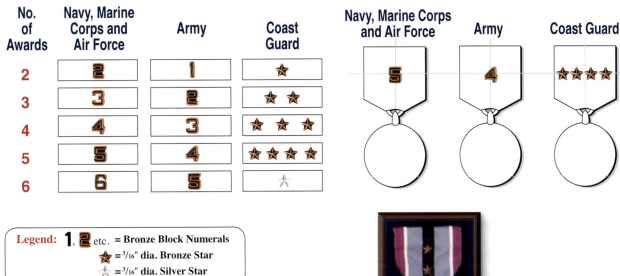

## Former Placement of Devices on the Humanitarian Service Medal

| No. of Awards | Navy, Marine Corps and Air Force | Army | Coast Guard | Navy, Marine Corps and Air Force | Army | Coast Guard |
|---|---|---|---|---|---|---|
| 2 | 2 | 1 | ★ | | | |
| 3 | 3 | 2 | ★ ★ | | | |
| 4 | 4 | 3 | ★ ★ ★ | | | |
| 5 | 5 | 4 | ★ ★ ★ ★ | 5 | 4 | ★ ★ ★ ★ |
| 6 | 6 | 5 | ☆ | | | |

**Legend:** 1, 2 etc. = Bronze Block Numerals
★ = 3/16" dia. Bronze Star
☆ = 3/16" dia. Silver Star

**NOTE:**
1. When medals overlap, Navy regulations require the wear of all attachments: ...to the wearer's left on suspension ribbons". In practice, the devices are still mounted horizontally and centered on the exposed portion of the suspension ribbon. Marine Corps regulations make no such provision so the devices remain as shown, centered on the suspension ribbon regardless of the degree of overlap.

**Note:** All branches now use stars. USAF example shown.

The numbers in parentheses next to the Devices refer to the tables in "Attachments and Devices" on page 116-119.

## Outstanding Volunteer Service Medal

The Outstanding Volunteer Service Medal was authorized in 1993 to members of the U.S. Armed Forces and reserve components and is awarded for outstanding and sustained voluntary service to the civilian community after December 31, 1992. It may be awarded to active duty and reserve members who perform outstanding volunteer service over time as opposed to a single event. The service performed must have been to the civilian community and must be strictly voluntary and not duty-related. The volunteerism must be of a sustained and direct nature and must be significant and produce tangible results while reflecting favorably on the Armed Forces and the Department of Defense. There are no specific time requirements as to how many hours must be spent on the volunteer activity, but the activity should consist of significant action and involvement rather than, for example, simply attending meetings as a member of a community service group. An individual would normally be considered for only one award during an assignment. Group level commanders, including commanders of provisional and composite groups, have approval authority for the medal.

The front of the bronze medal has a five-pointed star with a circular ring over each point; the star, a symbol

**Service:** All Services
**Instituted:** 1993
**Dates:** 1993 to Present
**Criteria:** Awarded for outstanding and sustained voluntary service to the civilian community.
**Devices:** ★ (67)  ☆ (86)

of the military and representing outstanding service, is encircled by a laurel wreath which represents honor and achievement. The reverse has an oak leaf branch, symbolic of strength and potential, with three oak leaves and two acorns along with the inscriptions, "OUTSTANDING VOLUNTEER SERVICE," and "UNITED STATES ARMED FORCES." Bronze and silver stars are authorized to denote additional awards.

## Navy Sea Service Deployment Ribbon

The Navy Sea Service Deployment Ribbon was approved by the Secretary of the Navy in 1981 and made retroactive to August 15, 1974. The ribbon was created to recognize the unique and demanding nature of sea service and the arduous duty attendant with such service deployments. The award is made to Navy and Marine Corps personnel for twelve months of accumulated sea duty or duty with the Fleet Marine Force, which includes at least one, ninety day deployment.

The ribbon consists of a wide center stripe of light blue, bordered on either side by a narrow stripe of medium blue and equal stripes of gold, red and navy blue.

**Service:** Navy/Marine Corps
**Instituted:** 1981
**Criteria:** 12 months active duty on deployed vessels operating away from their home port for extended periods.
**Devices:** ★ (67)  ☆ (86)

Additional awards are denoted by three-sixteenth inch bronze stars. The Navy Sea Service Deployment Ribbon is worn after the Outstanding Volunteer Service Medal and before the Navy Arctic Service Ribbon.

## Navy Arctic Service Ribbon

The Navy Arctic Service Ribbon was established by the Secretary of the Navy on May 8, 1986 and authorized for wear on June 3, 1987. The ribbon is awarded to members of the Naval Service who participate in operations in support of the Arctic Warfare Program. To be eligible, the individual must have served 28 days north of, or within 50 miles of the Marginal Ice Zone (MIZ). The MIZ is defined as an area consisting of more than 10% ice concentration. The ribbon is medium blue with a narrow center stripe of navy blue flanked on either side by three thin stripes of gradually lighter shades of blue, a narrow stripe of white, followed

**Service:** Navy/Marine Corps
**Instituted:** 1987
**Criteria:** 28 days of service on naval vessels operating above the Arctic Circle.
**Devices:** None.

again by two thin stripes of gradually darker shades of blue. There are no provisions for additional awards. The Navy Arctic Service Ribbon is worn after the Navy Sea Service Deployment Ribbon and before the Naval Reserve Sea Service Ribbon.

## Naval Reserve Sea Service Ribbon

The Naval Reserve Sea Service Ribbon was authorized by the Secretary of the Navy on May 28, 1986. It is awarded to officer and enlisted personnel of the U.S. Navy and Naval Reserve who perform active duty or Selected Reserve service, or any combination of active or Selected Reserve service after August 15, 1974 aboard a Naval Reserve ship or its Reserve unit or an embarked active or Reserve staff, for a cumulative total of 24 months. Qualifying ship duty includes duty in a self-propelled Naval Reserve ship, boat or craft operated under the operational control of fleet or type commanders. Selected Reserve duty with staffs which regularly embark in such Naval Reserve ships, craft, or boats, is also qualifying provided at least 50 percent of the drills performed for each creditable period have been underway drills. A 3/16 inch bronze star denotes a subsequent award.

**Service:** Navy
**Instituted:** 1987
**Criteria:** 24 months of cumulative service embarked on Naval Reserve vessels or an embarked Reserve unit.
**Devices:** (67) (86)

## Navy and Marine Corps Overseas Service Ribbon

The Navy and Marine Corps Overseas Service Ribbon was approved by the Secretary of the Navy on June 3, 1987 and made retroactive to August 15, 1974. The award is made to active duty members of the Naval Service who serve 12 months consecutive or accumulated active duty at an overseas duty station; or 30 consecutive days or 45 cumulative days of active duty for training or temporary active duty.

The ribbon was originally intended to recognize individuals who serve overseas, but are not members of ships, squadrons or detachments of the Fleet Marine Force and do not qualify for the Navy Sea Service Deployment Ribbon. However, as of Dec 1, 1999, members of the U.S. Navy may receive the award for active duty at an overseas sea or shore based duty station. Note that the original award requirement (shore-based duty only) remains in place for U.S. Marine Corps personnel.

The Navy and Marine Corps Overseas Service Ribbon is worn after the Navy Arctic Service Ribbon and before the Navy Recruiting Service Ribbon (USN) or Marine Corps Recruiting Ribbon (USMC). Additional awards are denoted by three-sixteenth inch bronze stars.

**Service:** Navy/Marine Corps
**Instituted:** 1987
**Criteria:** 12 months consecutive or accumulated duty at an overseas duty station. (Navy: sea or shore base; Marine Corps: shore base only)
**Devices:** (67) (86)

## Navy Recruiting Service Ribbon

The Navy Recruiting Service Ribbon was established in 1986 (retroactive to August 15, 1974) and is awarded for successful completion of three consecutive years of recruiting duty. The ribbon is gold with navy blue stripes near the borders and at the center. The blue center stripe has a thin red stripe and is bordered by stripes of light green on either side. A bronze numeral is worn to denote the total number of Gold Wreath awards for superior productivity. Additional individual awards are denoted by three-sixteenth inch bronze and silver service stars.

**Service:** Navy
**Instituted:** 1989
**Criteria:** Successful completion of 3 consecutive years of recruiting duty.
**Devices:** (67) (86) (34)

## Navy Recruit Training Service Ribbon

The Navy Recruit Training Service Ribbon was established in 1998 (retroactive to 1995) and is awarded for successful service as a Navy Recruit Division Commander (RDC) and training at least nine divisions over a minimum tour of three years. The ribbon has a broad scarlet center with equal-sized blue stripes on either side and gold edges. The Navy Recruit Training Service Ribbon is worn after the Navy Recruiting Service Ribbon and before the Ceremonial Guard Ribbon. Additional awards are denoted by three-sixteenth inch bronze and silver stars.

**Service:** Navy
**Instituted:** 1998 - retroactive to 1995
**Criteria:** Successful service as Recruit Division Commander (RDC) and training at least nine Divisions over a minimum tour of three years.
**Devices:** (67) (86)

## Navy Ceremonial Guard Ribbon

The Navy Ceremonial Guard Ribbon was established in 2003 and is awarded to Naval personnel who successfully complete a tour of duty as members of Ceremonial Guard units. The ribbon has equal stripes of dark blue, golden yellow and white (from outboard to inboard) with a narrow silver-gray center stripe. The Navy Ceremonial Guard Ribbon is worn after the Navy Recruit Training Service Ribbon and before the Armed Forces Reserve Medal. Additional awards are denoted by three-sixteenth inch bronze and silver stars.

**Service:** Navy
**Instituted:** 2003
**Criteria:** Awarded to recognize personnel who complete a satisfactory tour of duty in Navy Ceremonial Guard units.
**Devices:**  (67)  ☆ (86)

## Navy Recruit Honor Graduate Ribbon

The Navy Honor Graduate Ribbon is awarded to recruits for superb performance during basic military training, in academics, physical fitness, recruit leadership and commitment to the Navy core values of honor, courage and commitment. No more than three percent of each training group are designated as honor graduates.

**Service:** Navy
**Instituted:** 2015
**Criteria:** Awarded to recruits for superb performance during basic military training.
**Devices:** None

## Marine Corps Recruiting Ribbon

The Marine Corps Recruiting Ribbon was established in 1995 and made retroactive to 1973. The ribbon is awarded to Marines who successfully complete three consecutive years of recruiting duty.

The ribbon is dark blue with a wide red center stripe. The Marine Corps Recruiting Ribbon is worn after the Navy and Marine Corps Overseas Service Ribbon and before the Marine Corps Drill Instructor Ribbon. Additional awards are denoted by three-sixteenth inch bronze and silver stars.

**Service:** Marine Corps
**Instituted:** 1995 - retroactive to 1973
**Criteria:** Successful completion of 3 consecutive years of recruiting duty.
**Devices:** ★ (67)  ☆ (86)

## Marine Corps Drill Instructor Ribbon

The Marine Corps Drill Instructor Ribbon was established in 1997 (retroactive to October 6, 1952) and is awarded to Marines who serve successfully in a drill instructor assignment. An assignment is defined as a tour of a minimum of 20 months for those who received their 8511 MOS before December 1996 or 30 months thereafter.

The Marine Corps Drill Instructor Ribbon is worn after the Marine Corps Recruiting Ribbon and before the Marine Security Guard Ribbon.

**Service:** Marine Corps
**Instituted:** 1997- retroactive to 1952
**Criteria:** Successful completion of a tour of duty as a drill instructor (staff billets require completion of 18 months to be eligible).
**Devices:** ★ (67)  ☆ (86)

## Marine Security Guard Ribbon

The Marine Security Guard Ribbon was established in 1997 and made retroactive to January 28, 1949. The ribbon is awarded to Marines assigned to Marine Security Guard duty (MOS 8151), who have successfully completed 24 months service at a foreign service establishment. Marines who served successful tours at a lettered company headquarters within MSGBn are also eligible to receive the ribbon upon completion of 24 months service. The ribbon is medium blue with a narrow red center stripe bordered by bands of white.

**Service:** Marine Corps
**Instituted:** 1997- retroactive to 1949
**Criteria:** Successful completion of 24 months of cumulative security guard duty service at a foreign service establishment.
**Devices:** ★ (67)   (86)

## Marine Combat Instructor Ribbon

The Marine Corps Combat Instructor Ribbon was established by the Secretary of the Navy in August 2014. The ribbon recognizes the successful completion of a tour as a combat instructor, or in a high-profile leadership position, at the School of Infantry East or West. The ribbon is chamois in color with edges of olive green. In the center is a stripe of black. Subsequent awards of the ribbon are denoted by bronze service stars, with a silver 3/16 inch star worn to denote a sixth award. To be eligible Marines must complete a three-year tour, in a qualifying billet. Those include the 0913 Marine Combat Instructor billet or when it was designated 8513. Additionally, Marines who serve in a billet with the advanced Infantry Training Battalion are eligible.

**Service:** Marine Corps
**Instituted:** 2014- retroactive to 2002
**Criteria:** Successful completion of a tour as a combat instructor, or in a high-profile leadership position, at the School of Infantry East or West.
**]Devices:** ★ (67)  ☆ (86)

## Air Force Air and Space Campaign Medal

The Air Force Air & Space Campaign Medal (ASCM) was authorized on April 24, 2002 to recognize personnel not eligible for other DOD campaign medals but provide direct support of combat operations at home stations or from outside the geographical area of combat.

To qualify, Air Force personnel must be assigned or attached to a unit engaged in the operation and have provided 30 consecutive or 60 nonconsecutive days of direct support. No individual may be eligible for both the ASCM and a DOD campaign/service medal awarded during a single tour in the same operation. Additional awards are denoted by bronze and silver service stars on the ribbon. Operations related to the Global War on Terrorism (to include Iraqi Freedom and Enduring Freedom) are not eligible for the ASCM.

The Air and Space Campaign Medal is a bronze circle with a eagle clutching a shield on a backdrop of a stylized earth

**Service:** Air Force
**Instituted:** 2002
**Dates:** 1999 to Present
**Criteria:** Awarded for providing direct support of combat operations at home station or from outside the area of combat.
**Devices:**
★ (67)
☆ (86)

## Air Force Nuclear Deterrence Operations Medal

Authorized May 27, 2014, for award to individuals for their direct support of nuclear deterrence operations.

The medal is worn with an "N" device for those who serve in for 179 nonconsecutive days in direct support of intercontinental ballistic missile operations or are in direct support of nuclear laden aircraft. Only one "N" device is worn, regardless of the number of qualifying assignments. An oak leaf cluster is worn for additional awards. Eligibility is retroactive to Dec. 27, 1991. Retired or separated Airmen can request the award from the Air Force Personnel Center.

The medal is gold in color to represent the nuclear deterrence mission. The ribbon is blue representing "nuclear dominance of the sky with the red stripe representing "power and passion" in providing nuclear deterrence, the green stripe represents Earth and global capability, and gold is for participating Airmen, "the wealth of our nuclear enterprise"

**Service:** Air Force
**Instituted:** 2014
**Dates:** 1991 to Present
**Criteria:** Awarded for providing direct support of Nuclear Deterrence Operations.
**Devices:** N Device, Bronze Oak Leaf Cluster

(43)

Medals of America 207

## Air Force Overseas Ribbon *(Short Tour)*

The Air Force Overseas Ribbon (Short Tour) was created on October 12, 1980 and is awarded to Air Force personnel for less than two years of duty or as directed by Air Force policies. The Short Tour Ribbon is awarded for a permanent duty assignment of at least 181 consecutive days or, if stationed overseas, 300 days within an 18 month time span.

Additional awards are denoted by bronze and silver oak leaf clusters. The "A" device is authorized on the Short Tour Ribbon to any service member who performs a tour of duty at an Arctic-based Air Force facility.

**Service:** Air Force
**Instituted:** 1980
**Criteria:** Successful completion of an overseas tour designated as "short term" by appropriate authority.
**Devices:** (43) (50) **A** (11)

Presently, Thule Air Force Base in Greenland is the only facility within the Arctic Circle boundary.

## Air Force Overseas Ribbon *(Long Tour)*

The Air Force Overseas Ribbon (Long Tour) was created on October 12, 1980 by order of General Lew Allen, Air Force Chief of Staff and is awarded to Air Force personnel for completing a standard overseas service assignment greater than two years in length. Long tour credit is awarded for completion of a prescribed overseas long tour (two years) by Air Force Instructions, or to any member assigned to a United States or overseas location who is subsequently sent under temporary duty orders (to include combat tours) for 365 or more days within a

**Service:** Air Force
**Instituted:** 1980
**Criteria:** Successful completion of an overseas tour designated as "long term" by appropriate authority.
**Devices:** (43) (50)

3-year time frame. Additional awards are denoted by bronze and silver oak leaf clusters.

## Air Force Expeditionary Service Ribbon

The Air Force Expeditionary Service Ribbon was approved in October, 2003 to recognize service members who support air expeditionary force deployments subsequent to Oct. 1, 1999. For the award, "deployed status" is defined as either deployment on contingency, exercise, deployment orders or in direct support, in theater or out, of expeditionary operations. To qualify, members must have deployed for 45 consecutive or 90 nonconsecutive days with no time limit.

In Apr. 2004, the addition of a gold border to the Air Force Expeditionary Service Ribbon was approved to signify satisfactory participation in combat operations.

**Service:** Air Force
**Instituted:** 2004
**Criteria:** Awarded to recognize personnel who complete a contingency tour of duty in support of air expeditionary deployments.
**Devices:**  (6)

The gold border is the same device as is used on the Air Force Presidential Unit Citation as well as many other U.S. unit awards.

## Air Force Longevity Service Award Ribbon

Awarded to USAF personnel for 4 years honorable active federal military service with any branch of the U.S. Armed Forces or reserve components. An additional four years' of creditable service is denoted by a bronze oak leaf cluster. As an example, an individual who retires after 20 years service would wear 4 bronze oak leaf clusters on the ribbon. Individuals who served both in the Army Air Force and continued their service into the U.S. Air Force until 1957 or later would be authorized to wear the Longevity Service Award with appropriate oak leaf clus-

**Service:** Air Force
**Instituted:** 1957
**Criteria:** Successful completion of an aggregate total of four years of honorable active service.
**Devices:**  (43)  (50)

ters to properly represent their total service during both periods.

*The numbers in parentheses next to the Devices refer to the tables in "Attachments and Devices" on page 116-119.*

## Air Force Special Duty Ribbon

The Air Force Special Duty Ribbon recognized Airman who successfully complete a developmental special duty assignment. It replaces the Air Force Military Training Instructor Ribbon and the Air Force Recruiter Ribbon. Instructors and Recruiters are now eligible for the Air Force Special Duty award. The award is to recognize successful completion of a difficult and or highly responsible duty. Additional awards are noted by oak leaf clusters.

**Service:** Air Force
**Instituted:** 2014
**Criteria:** Satisfactory completion of a special duty assignment.
**Devices:**  (43) (50)

## Air Force Military Training Instructor Ribbon (Obsolete)

The Secretary of the Air Force established the Air Force Military Training Instructor Ribbon on December 7, 1998 to acknowledge past, present and future Military Training Instructors (MTI's) who display commitment and dedication to the training of Air Force personnel. This ribbon is intended for MTI's at Air Force Basic Military Training (BMT) and Officer Training School (OTS) (instructors at Technical Training Schools do not qualify). The basic award is presented to Air Force active duty, Reserve and National Guard personnel upon graduation from Military Training Instructor School. Wear of the ribbon becomes permanent after successful completion of at least 12 months tour of duty as an MTI. Each additional three years of MTI duty following the basic tour entitles the member to an oak leaf cluster.

**Service:** Air Force
**Instituted:** 1998
**Criteria:** Graduation from Military Training Instructor (MTI) School. Permanently worn after completion of a 12 month tour of duty as an MTI.
**Devices:** (43) (50)

The ribbon is retroactive for any individual who has successfully completed 12 months duty as an MTI and is currently on active duty or a member of a reserve component as of the establishment date (Dec 7, 1998). The ribbon is worn between the Air Force Longevity Service Award Ribbon and the Air Force Recruiter Ribbon.

## Air Force Recruiter Ribbon (Obsolete)

The Secretary of the Air Force established the Air Force Recruiter Ribbon on June 21, 2000 to recognize officers and enlisted personnel who perform the challenging duties involved in Air Force recruiting. To qualify for the award, individuals must perform recruiting duty for a minimum period of three years. The award is retroactive to earlier recruiting assignments but only for persons who were on active duty status on the date of establishment, (June 21, 2000).

Each additional three years of recruiting duty following the basic tour entitles the member to wear a bronze oak leaf

**Service:** Air Force
**Instituted:** 2000
**Criteria:** Satisfactory performance as an Air Force Recruiter for a period of 3 years.
**Devices:** (43) (50)

cluster on the ribbon. The ribbon is worn between the Air Force Military Training Instructor Ribbon and the Armed Forces Reserve Medal.

## Transportation 9-11 Ribbon

Awarded to an individual serving in any capacity within the DOT, Merchant Marine or other civilians, for an act or service that contributed to recovery from the attacks of September 11 2001, force protection following the attacks or efforts that directly contributed to the increased infrastructure security effort between September 11, 2001 and September 11, 2002. The award may be made posthumously.

**Service:** Coast Guard
**Instituted:** 2002
**Criteria:** Acts or services that contributed to recovery from the attacks of September 11, 2001 or force protection following the attacks.
**Devices:** None

## Coast Guard Special Operations Service Ribbon

The Coast Guard Special Operations Service Ribbon was authorized on July 1, 1987 and is awarded to any member of the U.S. Armed Forces serving with the Coast Guard who, after July 1, 1987, participates in a major Coast Guard operation of a special nature not involving combat and not recognized by another award. Personnel must be attached to a unit for at least 21 days during the the special operation or serve for the full period when an operation is less than 21 days. The Ribbon may also be authorized for multi-unit or multi-service operations involving national security/law enforcement, Coast Guard involvement with foreign governments in all areas at sea and Coast Guard operations of assistance to friendly and/or developing nations. Additional awards of the Special Operations Service Ribbon are denoted by three-sixteenth inch diameter bronze and silver stars.

**Service:** Coast Guard
**Instituted:** 1987
**Criteria:** Participation in a Coast Guard special noncombat operation not recognized by another service award.
**Devices:** ★(67) ★(86)

## Coast Guard Sea Service Ribbon

The Coast Guard Sea Service Ribbon was established by the Coast Guard Commandant on March 3, 1984. It is awarded to active duty members of the Coast Guard and Coast Guard Reserve, inactive duty members of the Coast Guard Reserve or non-Coast Guard personnel who, under temporary or permanent assignment, satisfactorily complete a minimum of 12 months of cumulative sea duty. Sea duty is defined as duty performed aboard any Coast Guard cutter 65 feet or more in length in an active status). A three-sixteenth inch bronze service star is authorized for each additional three years of sea duty.

**Service:** Coast Guard
**Instituted:** 1984
**Criteria:** Satisfactory completion of a minimum of 12 months of cumulative sea duty.
**Devices:** ★(67) ★(86)

## Coast Guard Restricted Duty Ribbon

The Coast Guard Restricted Duty Ribbon was established on March 3, 1984. It is awarded to all Coast Guard personnel who have completed a permanent change of station (PCS) tour of duty at a remote shore station (such as LORAN stations, light stations, etc.) where no accompanying dependents are permitted. A three-sixteenth inch bronze star is authorized for each subsequent PCS tour of duty at a restricted shore unit.

**Service:** Coast Guard
**Instituted:** 1984
**Criteria:** Successful completion of a tour of duty at remote shore stations (LORAN stations, light ships, etc.) without family.
**Devices:** ★(67) ★(86)

## Coast Guard Overseas Service Ribbon

The Coast Guard Overseas Service Ribbon was approved on October 28, 2009. It is awarded to active duty members on a permanent assignment and who successfully complete a tour of duty of at least 12 months at an overseas shore-based duty station or on-board a cutter permanently assigned to an overseas area. It is also awarded to reservists who are permanently assigned and have satisfactorily completed a minimum of 36 cumulative days of service at an overseas duty station during each 12-month period of the total tour of duty. Personnel who receive the Coast Guard's Restricted Duty Ribbon are not eligible to receive the Overseas Service Ribbon for the same period. The ribbon may be awarded retroactively to qualifying individuals for initial award only. Subsequent awards are indicated by bronze or silver service stars.

**Service:** Coast Guard
**Instituted:** 2009
**Criteria:** Successful completion of a tour of duty of at least 12 months at an overseas shore-based duty station or on-board a cutter permanently assigned to an overseas area.
**Devices:** ★(67) ★(86)

The numbers in parentheses next to the Devices refer to the tables in "Attachments and Devices" on page 116-119.

## Coast Guard Basic Training Honor Graduate Ribbon

The Coast Guard Basic Training Honor Graduate Ribbon was established by the Commandant of the Coast Guard on March 3, 1984. Effective April 1, 1984, it is awarded to Coast Guard personnel comprising the top 3 percent of each Coast Guard recruit training graduating class. Individuals who graduated from Coast Guard recruit training prior to April 1, 1984 and meet the above criteria and believe themselves eligible for this award may submit a request, with supporting documentation to the Coast Guard Commandant.

Prior service personnel who graduated from other than Coast Guard recruit training are not eligible for the award. Since this is a "one-time only" award, no devices are authorized.

**Service:** Coast Guard
**Instituted:** 1984
**Criteria:** Successful attainment of the top 3 percent of the class during Coast Guard recruit training.
**Devices:** None

## Coast Guard Recruiting Service Ribbon

The Coast Guard Recruiting Service Ribbon was established on November 2, 1995 by the Commandant of the Coast Guard and made retroactive to Recruiting tours performed subsequent to January 1, 1980. It is awarded for two consecutive duty tours in Coast Guard Recruiting offices. The ribbon is worn after the Coast Guard Basic Training Honor Graduate Ribbon and before the Armed Forces Reserve Medal. Each additional successful two-year tour of duty is signified by a bronze star worn on the ribbon.

**Service:** Coast Guard
**Instituted:** 1995
**Criteria:** Successful completion of 3 consecutive years of recruiting duty.
**Devices:**  (67)  (86)

## Army Sea Duty Ribbon

The Army Sea Duty Ribbon is awarded to those members of the Active United States Army, United States Army Reserve and Army National Guard for completion of sea duty on class A or B United States Army vessels. To be awarded the ribbon, active duty members must complete two years of cumulative sea duty aboard class A or B vessels. For members for the Army Reserve, and National Guard, soldiers must have two credible years in a U.S. Army watercraft unit. In addition to being assigned to a qualifying unit, reserve component soldiers must spend at least 25 days during each of the qualifying years underway, along with two annual training exercises on a class A or B vessel. A ninety day deployment on board a class A or B vessel also qualifies. Additional awards of the Army Sea Duty Ribbon are denoted by bronze and silver stars while the tenth and final award is indicated by a five-sixteenth inch diameter gold star.

**Service:** Army
**Instituted:** 2006
**Criteria:** Completion of two (2) years of cumulative sea duty aboard Class A or B vessels.
**Devices:**  (67)  (86)  (100)

# Armed Forces Reserve Medal

Authorized in 1950 for 10 years of honorable and satisfactory service within a 12 year period as a member of one or more of the Reserve Components of the Armed Forces of the United States.

An executive order of Aug. 8, 1996 authorized the award of a bronze letter "M" mobilization device to U.S. reserve component members who were called to active-duty service in support of designated operations on or after August 1, 1990 (the M device was not authorized for any operations prior to August 1, 1990 although it had been previously proposed). Units called up in support of Operations Desert Storm/Desert Shield were the first units to be authorized the "M" device. If an "M" is authorized, the medal is awarded even though service might be less than 10 years. Previous to this change, only bronze hourglasses were awarded at each successive 10 year point (first hourglass at the 20 year point).

The front of the medal depicts a flaming torch placed vertically between a crossed bugle and powder horn; thirteen stars and thirteen rays surround the design. The front of the medal is the same for all services; only the reverse design is different (see designs below). Bronze numerals beginning with "2" are worn to the right of the

**Service:** All Services
**Instituted:** 1950
**Dates:** 1949 to Present
**Criteria:** 10 years of honorable service in any reserve component of the United States Armed Forces Reserve or award of "M" device.
**Devices:**

 (8a)  (33)  (16)

bronze "M" on the ribbon bar and below the "M" on the medal, indicating the total number of times the individual was mobilized. Bronze, silver and gold hourglasses are awarded for 10, 20 and 30 years service, respectively.

## The medal reverses are as follows:

**Army** has a Minuteman in front of a circle with 13 stars representing the original colonies.

**Navy** has a sailing ship with an anchor on its front with an eagle with wings spread superimposed upon it.

**Marine Corps** has the USMC emblem, eagle, globe and anchor.

**Air Force** has an eagle with wings spread in front of a circle with clouds and includes the inscription, "ARMED FORCES RESERVE."

**Coast Guard** has the Coast Guard emblem, crossed anchor with the Coast Guard shield in the center.

**National Guard** has the National Guard insignia on the reverse, an eagle with crossed fasces in its center.

## Army N.C.O. Professional Development Ribbon

The Non-Commissioned Officer Professional Development Ribbon was established by the Secretary of the Army on April 10, 1981 and is awarded to members of the U.S. Army, Army National Guard and Army Reserve who successfully complete designated NCO professional development courses. To indicate completion of specific levels of subsequent courses, a bronze numeral is affixed to the center of the ribbon.

The basic ribbon itself represents the Primary Level, the numeral "2" indicates the Basic Level course, the numeral "3" denotes the Advanced Level course and the numeral "4" indicates the Senior Level (Sergeants Major Academy) course. At one time, the numeral "5" signified completion of the Sergeants Major Academy but this was later rescinded.

**Service:** Army
**Instituted:** 1981
**Criteria:** Successful completion of designated NCO professional development courses.
**Devices:**  (37)

## Army Service Ribbon

The Army Service ribbon was established on April 10, 1981 by the Secretary of the Army and is awarded to members of the Army, Army Reserve and Army National Guard for successful completion of initial-entry training. It may also be awarded retroactively to those personnel who completed the required training before August 1, 1981. Officers will be awarded this ribbon upon successful completion of their basic/orientation or higher level course.

Enlisted soldiers will be awarded the ribbon upon successful completion of their initial MOS-producing course. Officer or Enlisted personnel assigned to a specialty, special skill identifier or MOS based on civilian or other service acquired skills, will be awarded the ribbon upon honorable completion of four months active service. Since only one award is authorized, no devices are worn with this ribbon.

**Service:** Army
**Instituted:** 1981
**Criteria:** Successful completion of initial entry training.
**Devices:** None

## Army Overseas Service Ribbon

The Army Overseas Service Ribbon was established by the Secretary of the Army on April 10, 1981. Effective August 1, 1981, the Army Overseas Service Ribbon is awarded to all members of the Active Army, Army National Guard and Army Reserve in an active Reserve status for successful completion of overseas tours if the tour is not recognized by the award of another service or campaign medal.

The ribbon may be awarded retroactively to personnel who were credited with a normal overseas tour completion before August 1, 1981, provided they had an Active Army status on or after August 1, 1981.

**Service:** Army
**Instituted:** 1981
**Criteria:** Successful completion of normal overseas tours not recognized by any other service award.
**Devices:**  (35)

Subsequent tours will be indicated by the use of numerals with the basic ribbon representing the first tour, the bronze numeral "2" denoting the second tour, the numeral "3" the third, etc.

Medals of America 213

## Army Reserve Components Overseas Training Ribbon

The Reserve Components Overseas Training Ribbon was established on July 11, 1984 by the Secretary of the Army and is awarded to members of the Army Reserves or Army National Guard for successful completion of annual training or active duty for training for a period of not less than ten consecutive duty days on foreign soil (outside the 50 states, District of Columbia, and U.S. possessions and territories), in the performance of duties in conjunction with Active Army, Joint Services, or Allied Forces. The ribbon may be awarded retroactively to personnel who successfully completed annual training or active duty for training on foreign soil in a Reserve status prior to July 11, 1984, provided they had an active status in the Reserve Components on or after July 11, 1984. Bronze numerals are used to denote second and subsequent awards.

**Service:** Army
**Instituted:** 1984
**Criteria:** Successful completion of annual training or active duty training for 10 consecutive duty days on foreign soil.
**Devices:** 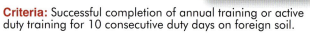 **3** (35)

## Naval Reserve Medal (Obsolete)

This medal was authorized on September 12, 1938, and awarded to officers and enlisted men of the Naval Reserve who had completed ten years of satisfactory federal service in the U.S. Naval Reserve. Eligibility ceased during a time of war or national emergency if called to active duty. After the establishment of the Armed Forces Reserve Medal in 1950, a Naval Reservist who was eligible for the Naval Reserve Medal and the Armed Forces Reserve Medal could elect which award he was to receive. The Naval Reserve Medal was terminated on September 12, 1958 and now only the Armed Forces Reserve Medal is awarded. The obverse of the Naval Reserve Medal shows an eagle in an attitude of defiance, facing left, with wings raised. The eagle is perched on an anchor, flukes down to the left. The reverse of the medal is flat, with the inscription, "UNITED STATES NAVAL RESERVE" encircling the outer edge. At the bottom is a large star and the words, "FAITHFUL SERVICE" centered in two lines. A bronze star was authorized for each additional ten years of qualifying service. However there is little likelihood that a device was ever earned since a potential recipient would have to spend the total life span of the medal (twenty years) in the Naval Reserve during both World War II and the Korean Conflict.

**Service:** Navy
**Instituted:** 1938
**Dates:** 1938-58
**Criteria:** 10 years of honorable service in the U.S. Naval Reserve.
**Devices:**  (67)

**Notes:** Replaced by the Armed Forces Reserve Medal. Some earlier versions had deep red ("plum") ribbon.

## Marine Corps Reserve Ribbon (Obsolete)

The Marine Corps Reserve Ribbon was authorized by the Secretary of the Navy on 17 December 1945 and awarded to members of the Marine Corps Reserve for ten years of honorable service. On 18 December 1965, it was superseded by the Armed Forces Reserve Medal. Service counted in completing the required time for the Selected Marine Corps Reserve Medal or the Armed Forces Reserve Medal was not eligible for this award. A Marine Reservist who was eligible for these three awards could elect which one he or she would receive.

The ribbon is gold with a thin stripe of red at each edge. The Marine Corps Reserve Ribbon is worn after the Armed Forces Reserve Medal and before any foreign awards. A three-sixteenth inch bronze star was authorized for a second, ten-year period of Marine Corps Reserve service. However, the award of a bronze star was highly unlikely since the total life span of the ribbon was exactly twenty years.

**Service:** Marine Corps
**Institute:** 1945
**Criteria:** Successful completion of 10 years of honorable service in any class of the Marine Corps Reserve.
**Devices:**  (67)

## Air Force N.C.O. Professional Military Education Graduate Ribbon

The Air Force Non-Commissioned Officer Professional Military Education (PME) Graduate Ribbon was authorized by the Secretary of the Air Force on August 28, 1962 and is awarded to graduates of all Air Force-certified NCO PME schools, i.e., NCO Preparatory Course, Airman Leadership School, NCO Leadership School, NCO Academy and SRNCO Academy. Graduation from each successive level of PME entitles the member to wear an oak leaf cluster on the ribbon. The ribbon is not, however, awarded to members who only complete the correspondence courses or similar training conducted by other military services except for completion of the U.S. Army Sergeant Major Academy or the Navy Senior Enlisted Academy. This award also has the dubious distinction of bearing the longest name in United States award history.

**Service:** Air Force
**Institute:** 1962
**Criteria:** Successful completion of a certified NCO professional military education school.
**Devices:** (43) (50)

## Air Force Basic Military Training (BMT) Honor Graduate Ribbon

The Basic Military Training Honor Graduate Ribbon was authorized by the Chief of Staff, U.S. Air Force on April 3, 1976, and is awarded to honor graduates of basic military training who, after July 29, 1976, have demonstrated excellence in all phases of academic and military training. It is limited to the top 10 percent of the training flight. The USAF BMT Honor Graduate Ribbon was designed by the Institute of Heraldry and is awarded to basic training graduates only. The ribbon has a wide center stripe of ultramarine blue flanked with equal stripes of yellow, brittany blue and white on either side. Since this is a "one-time only" award, no devices are authorized.

**Service:** Air Force
**Institute:** 1976
**Criteria:** Demonstration of excellence in all academic and military training phases of basic Air Force entry training.
**Devices:** None

## Small Arms Expert Marksmanship Ribbon

Authorized on August 28, 1962. Awarded to Air Force personnel who, after Jan. 1, 1963, qualify as Expert with either the M16 rifle or issue handgun on the Air Force qualification course or on a prescribed course or who completes the Combat Rifle Program. The ribbon is only awarded once regardless of how many times an individual qualifies as "Expert." A bronze star device is added (only once) if the recipient meets the award criteria with both the rifle and handgun.

**Service:** Air Force
**Instituted:** 1962
**Criteria:** Qualification as expert with either the M-16 rifle or standard Air Force issue handgun.
**Devices:** ★ (71)

## Air Force Training Ribbon

The Air Force Training Ribbon was authorized on October 12, 1980 and awarded to Air Force members who complete an Air Force accession training program after August 14, 1974 such as Basic Military Training (BMT), Officer Training School (OTS), Reserve Officer Training Corps (ROTC), USAF Academy, Medical Services, Judge Advocate, Chaplain orientation etc. Also authorized for Guard and Reserve members who complete the appropriate training program. If a member completes two accession training programs, such as BMT and OTS, a bronze oak leaf cluster is worn on the ribbon. The award is retroactive for those personnel on active duty as of the authorization date.

**Service:** Air Force
**Institute:** 1980
**Criteria:** Successful completion of an Air Force accession training program.
**Devices:** (43) (50)

# Award of Foreign Military Decorations

Authorized foreign decorations for wear by United States Armed Forces are military decorations (as opposed to service medals) which have been approved for wear by the Department of Defense but whose awarding authority is a foreign government. French British, Italy and other Allies decorations were presented to U.S. service members extensively during World War I and World War II. In World War I and II the French and Belgium Croix de Guerre were the most commonly awarded decorations to United States service members of all ranks.

Republic of Vietnam military awards (South Vietnam decorations) were first awarded to United States service members beginning around 1964. The Vietnamese Gallantry Cross and the Vietnamese Civil Actions Medal were awarded to many U.S. servicemen for heroism and meritorious service.

Foreign campaign (service) medals and Unit Awards have also been awarded U.S. military Personel. Those that were commonly awarded to U.S. military personnel are covered in the following pages.

While each service has its own order of precedence, these general rules typically apply to all services when wearing foreign awards::

U.S. military personal decorations
U.S. military unit awards
U.S. non-military personal decorations (in order of receipt; if from the same service, check the order of precedence shown on pages 104-112).
U.S. non-military unit awards
U.S. military campaign and service medals
U.S. military service and training awards (ribbon-only awards)
U.S. Merchant Marine awards and non-military service awards
Foreign military personal decorations
Foreign military unit awards
International decorations & service medals ( United Nations, NATO, etc.)
Foreign military service awards
Marksmanship awards (Air Force, Navy & Coast Guard)
State awards of the National Guard (Army & Air Force only)

**Croix de Guerre**
**Country:** France
**Instituted:** 1915 (1939- 1945 version shown)
**Criteria:** Individual feats of arms as recognized by mention in dispatches.
**Devices:**

**Notes:** *The ribbon for the Croix de Guerre awarded during WW I is green.*

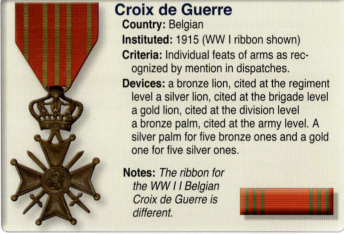

**Croix de Guerre**
**Country:** Belgian
**Instituted:** 1915 (WW I ribbon shown)
**Criteria:** Individual feats of arms as recognized by mention in dispatches.
**Devices:** a bronze lion, cited at the regiment level a silver lion, cited at the brigade level a gold lion, cited at the division level a bronze palm, cited at the army level. A silver palm for five bronze ones and a gold one for five silver ones.

**Notes:** *The ribbon for the WW I I Belgian Croix de Guerre is different.*

### Republic of Vietnam Gallantry Cross
**Country:** Republic of Vietnam
**Instituted:** 1950
**Criteria:** Deeds of valor and acts of courage/heroism while fighting the enemy.
**Devices:**

- (palm) (55)
- (bronze star) (105)
- (silver star) (106)
- (gold star) (107)

### Republic of Vietnam Armed Forces Honor Medal
**Country:** Republic of Vietnam
**Instituted:** 1953
**Criteria:** For outstanding contributions to the training and development of RVN Armed Forces.
**Devices:** None

**Notes:** 1st Class for officers is shown; the 2nd Class medal is in silver and ribbon does not have the yellow edge stripes.

### Republic of Vietnam Staff Service Medal
**Country:** Republic of Vietnam
**Instituted:** 1964
**Criteria:** Awarded for staff service to the Armed Forces evidencing outstanding initiative and devotion to duty.

**Notes:** Occasionally called Staff Service Honor Medal. First class has green edge, 2d class for enlisted has blue ribbon edge.

First Class

Second Class

### Republic of Vietnam Technical Service
**Country:** Republic of Vietnam
**Instituted:** 1964
**Criteria:** Awarded to military servicemen and civilians working as military technicians who have shown outstanding professional capacity, initiative, and devotion to duty.

**Notes:** Second Class medal ribbon awarded to NCOs and enlisted men does not have 2 center red stripes. Occasionally called Technical Services Honor Medal.

First Class

### Republic of Vietnam Training Medal
**Country:** Republic of Vietnam
**Instituted:** 1964
**Criteria:** Awarded to instructors and cadres at military schools and training centers and civilians and foreigners who contribute significantly to training.

**Notes:** First Class medal is awarded to officers and is occasionally referred to as the Training Service Honor Medal. Second Class medal ribbon awarded to NCOs and enlisted men does not have 2 center pink stripes.

### Republic of Vietnam Civil Actions Medal
**Country:** Republic of Vietnam
**Instituted:** 1964
**Criteria:** For outstanding achievements in the field of civic actions.
**Devices:** None

**Notes:** 1st Class for officers is shown; the 2nd Class ribbon has no center red stripes. Also awarded as a unit award. Sometimes called Civic Actions Honor Medal.

Medals of America 217

# Commonly Awarded Foreign Unit Awards

## Philippine Republic Presidential Unit Citation

**Service:** All Services
**Instituted:** 1948
**Criteria:** Awarded to units of the U.S. Armed Forces for service in the war against Japan and/or for 1970 and 1972 disaster relief.
**Devices:**  (80) (except Army)

The Philippine Republic Presidential Unit Citation was awarded to U.S. Armed Forces personnel for services resulting in the liberation of the Philippines during World War II. The award was made in the name of the President of the Republic of the Philippines. It was also awarded to U.S. Forces who participated in disaster relief operations in 1970 and 1972. The ribbon has three equal stripes of blue, white and red enclosed in a rectangular gold frame with laurel leaves identical to U.S. unit awards. A three-sixteenth inch bronze star denotes receipt of an additional award.

## Korean Republic Presidential Unit Citation

**Service:** All Services
**Instituted:** 1951
**Criteria:** Awarded to certain units of the U.S. Armed Forces for services rendered during the Korean War.
**Devices:** None

Awarded by the Republic of Korea for service in a unit cited in the name of the President of the Republic of Korea for outstanding performance in action. The Republic of Korea Presidential Unit Citation was awarded to units of the United Nations Command for service in Korea during the Korean Conflict from 1950 to 1954. The ribbon is white bordered with a wide green stripe and thin stripes of white, red, white, red, white and green. In the center is an ancient oriental symbol called a Taeguk (the top half is red and the bottom half is blue). The ribbon is enclosed in a rectangular gold frame with laurel leaves identical to U.S. unit awards. No devices are authorized.

## Republic of Vietnam Presidential Unit Citation

**Service:** Army/Navy/Marine Corps/Coast Guard
**Instituted:** 1954
**Criteria:** Awarded to certain units of the U.S. Armed Forces for humanitarian service in the evacuation of civilians from North and Central Vietnam.
**Devices:** None

Awarded by the Republic of Vietnam for service in a unit cited in the name of the President of the Republic of Vietnam for outstanding performance in action. The Republic of Vietnam Presidential Unit Citation referred to as the "Friendship Ribbon" and was awarded to members of the United States Military Assistance Advisory Group in Indochina for services rendered during August and September 1954. The ribbon is yellow with three narrow red stripes in the center. The ribbon is enclosed in a rectangular gold frame with laurel leaves identical to U.S. unit awards. No devices are authorized.

## Republic of Vietnam Gallantry Cross Unit Citation

**Service:** All Services
**Instituted:** 1966
**Criteria:** Awarded to certain units of the U.S. Armed Forces for valorous combat achievement during the Vietnam War, 1 March 1961 to 28 March 1974.
**Devices:**  (55)  (105)  (106)  (107)

The Republic of Vietnam Gallantry Cross Unit Citation was established on August 15, 1950 and awarded by the Republic of Vietnam to units of the U.S. Armed Forces in recognition of valorous achievement in combat during the Vietnam War. The Republic of Vietnam Gallantry Cross Unit Citation ribbon is red with a very wide yellow center stripe which has eight very thin double red stripes. The ribbon bar is enclosed in a gold frame with laurel leaves identical to U.S. unit awards.

## Republic of Vietnam Civil Actions Unit Citation

**Service:** All Services
**Instituted:** 1966
**Criteria:** Awarded to certain units of the U.S. Armed Forces for meritorious service during the Vietnam War, 1 March 1961 to 28 March 1974.
**Devices:**  (54)

Awarded by the Republic of Vietnam to units in recognition of meritorious civil action service. The Republic of Vietnam Civil Actions Unit Citation was widely bestowed on American forces in Vietnam and recognizes outstanding achievements made by units in the field of civil affairs. The Republic of Vietnam Civil Actions Unit Citation ribbon is dark green with a very thin double red center stripe narrow red stripes near the edges. The ribbon is enclosed in a rectangular one-sixteenth inch gold frame with laurel leaves identical to U.S. unit awards and is awarded with a bronze laurel leaf palm attachment.

# World War II Philippine Military Medals

The Philippine Defense Medal was authorized to any WW II veteran of either the Philippine military or an allied armed force, to recognize the initial resistance against Japanese invasion between 8 December 1941 and 15 June 1942. The award was first created in December 1944, and was issued as the Philippine Defense Ribbon. A full-sized medal was authorized and added in July, 1945.

The Philippine Liberation Medal was established by the Commonwealth Army of the Philippines on 20 December 1944, and first issued as a Ribbon. The medal was presented to Philippine Commonwealth and allied forces, who participated in the liberation of the Philippine Islands between t 17 October 1944, and 2 September 1945. A full-sized medal was authorized and added on 22 July 1945 and authorized by the United States in 1948.

To be authorized the Philippine Liberation Medal, a service member must have participated in at least one of the following actions:

- Participation in the initial landing operation of Leyte and adjoining islands from 17 October to 20 October 1944.

- Participation in any engagement against hostile Japanese forces on Leyte and adjoining islands during the Philippine Liberation Campaign of 17 October 1944, to 2 September 1945.

- Participation in any engagement against hostile Japanese forces during the Philippine Liberation Campaign of 17 October 1944, to 2 September 1945.

- Served in the Philippine Islands or on ships in Philippine waters for not less than 30 days during the period.

- World War II veterans awarded the medal for participation in any of the above-mentioned operations are authorized a bronze 3/16" service star to the Philippine Liberation

The Philippine Independence Medal was established by the Philippine Army 3 July 1946 as the Philippine Independence Ribbon. The medal was added in 1968. The medal's criteria effectively awarded the medal to anyone who had participated in both the initial resistance against Japanese invasion and also in the campaigns to liberate the Philippines from Japanese occupation in 1945. The medal was also authorized for award to the United States personnel in the Philippines up to 1948.

### Philippine Defense Medal
**Country:** Republic of the Philippines
**Instituted:** 1945 (Army: 1948)
**Criteria:** Service in defense of the Philippines between 8 December 1941 and 15 June 1942.
**Devices:**

### Philippine Liberation Medal
**Country:** Republic of the Philippines
**Instituted:** 1945 (Army: 1948)
**Criteria:** Service in the liberation of the Philippines between 17 October 1944 and 3 September 1945.
**Devices:**

### Philippine Independence Medal
**Country:** Republic of the Philippines
**Instituted:** 1946 (Army: 1948)
**Criteria:** Receipt of both the Philippine Defense and Liberation Medals/Ribbons. Originally presented to those present for duty in the Philippines on 4 July 1946.
**Devices:** None

# United Nations Military Medals

Originally, U.S. military personnel serving with United Nations Missions were permitted to wear only two UN medals, the United Nations Korean Service Medal and the United Nations Medal (Shown to the right). However, changes in Department of Defense policy in 1996 authorized the wear of the ribbons of 11 missions on the U.S. military uniform.

In 2011 sixteen more missions were added to the list, which, along with the United Nations Special Service Medal, brought the total to 28. However, only one ribbon (or medal) may be worn on the U.S. military uniform and awards for any subsequent missions are denoted by the three-sixteenth inch bronze stars.

### United Nations Service Medal (Korea)
**Service:** All Services
**Instituted:** 1951
**Criteria:** Service on behalf of the United Nations in Korea between 27 June 1950 and 27 July 1954.
**Devices:** None
**Notes:** Above date denotes when award was authorized for wear by U.S. military personnel.

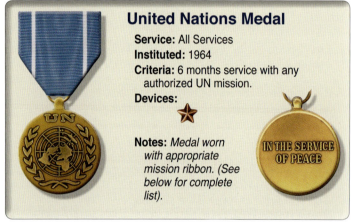

### United Nations Medal
**Service:** All Services
**Instituted:** 1964
**Criteria:** 6 months service with any authorized UN mission.
**Devices:** ★
**Notes:** Medal worn with appropriate mission ribbon. (See below for complete list).

---

**UNTSO**
United Nations Truce Supervision Organization
Country/Location: **Israel, Egypt**
Dates: **1948 - Present**

**UNMOGIP**
United Nations Military Observer Group in India/Pakistan
Country/Location: **India, Pakistan**
Dates: **1949 - Present**

**UNOGIL**
United Nations Observer Group in Lebanon
Country/Location: **Lebanon**
Dates: **1958**

**UNSF/UNTEA**
a. United Nations Security Force in West Guinea (West Irian)
Country/Location: **West New Guinea (West Irian)**
Dates: **1962 - 1963**

**UNIKOM**
United Nations Iraq/Kuwait Observation Mission
Country/Location: **Iraq/Kuwait**
Dates: **1991 - 2003**

**MINURSO**
United Nations Mission for the Referendum in Western Sahara
Country/Location: **Morocco**
Dates: **1991 to Present**

**UNAMIC**
United Nations Advance Mission in Cambodia
Country/Location: **Cambodia**
Dates: **1991 -1992**

**UNPROFOR**
United Nations Protection Force
Country/Location: **Former Yoguslavia (Bosnia, Herzegovina, Croatia, Serbia, Montenegro, Macedonia**
Dates: **1992 - 1995**

**UNTAC**
United Nations Transitional Authority in Cambodia
Country/Location: **Cambodia**
Dates: **1992 - 1993**

### ONUMOZ
United Nations Operation in Mozambique
Country/Location: **Mozambique**
Dates: **1992 - 1994**

### UNOSOM II
United Nations Operation in Somalia II
Country/Location: **Somalia**
Dates: **1993 - 1995**

### UNOMIG
United Nations Observer Mission in Georgia
Country/Location: **Georgia (Russia)**
Dates: **1993 - 2009**

### UNMIH
United Nations Mission in Haiti
Country/Location: **Haiti**
Dates: **1993 - 1996**

### UNPREDEP
United Nations Prevention Deployment Force
Country/Location: **Former Yugoslavia; Republic of Macedonia**
Dates: **1995 - 1999**

### UNTAES
United Nations Transitional Administration for Eastern Slavonia, Baranja and Western Sirmium
Country/Location: **Croatia**
Dates: **1996 - 1998**

### UNSMIH
United Nations Support Mission in Haiti
Country/Location: **Haiti**
Dates: **1996 - 1997**

### MINUGUA
United Nations Verification Mission in Guatemala
Country/Location: **Guatemala**
Dates: **1997-1997**

### UNMIK
United Nations Interim Administration Mission in Kosovo
Country/Location: **Kosovo**
Dates: **1999 - Present**

### UNTAET
United Nations Transitional Administration in East Timor
Country/Location: **Timor (New Guinea)**
Dates: **1999 - 2002**

### MONUC
United Nations Organization Mission in the Democratic Republic of the Congo
Country/Location: **Congo**
Dates: **1999 - 2010**

### UNMEE
United Nations Mission to Ethiopia and Eritrea
Country/Location: **Ethiopia, Eritrea**
Dates: **2000 - 2008**

### UNMISET
United Nations Mission of Support in East Timor
Country/Location: **Timor (New Guinea)**
Dates: **2000 - 2005**

### UNMIL
United Nations Mission in Liberia
Country/Location: **Liberia (West Africa)**
Dates: **2003 - Present**

### MINUSTAH
United Nations Stabilization Mission in Haiti
Country/Location: **Haiti**
Dates: **2004 - Present**

### UNAMID
United Nations / African Union Hybrid Operation in Darfur
Country/Location: **Darfur (East Africa)**
Dates: **2007 - Present**

### MINURCAT
United Nations Mission in the Central African Republic and Chad
Country/Location: **Central African Republic, Chad (Central Africa)**
Dates: **2007 - 2010**

### MONUSCO
United Nations Organization Stabilization Mission in the Democratic Republic of the Congo
Country/Location: **Congo**
Dates: **2010 - Present**

 **United Nations Special Service Medal UNSSM**

**Background:** Established in 1994 by the Secretary General of the United Nations, the UNSSM is awarded to military and civilian personnel service in capacities other than established peace-keeping missions or those permanently assigned to UN Headquarters. The UNSSM may be awarded to eligible personnel service for a minimum of ninety (90) consecutive days under the control of the UN in operations or offices for which no other United Nations award is authorized. Posthumous awards may be granted to personnel otherwise eligible for the medal who died while serving under the United Nations before completing the required 90 days of service.

**Clasps:** Clasps engraved with the name of the country or United Nations organization (e.g.: UNHCR, UNSCOM, UNAMI, etc.) may be added to the medal suspension ribbon and ribbon bar.

# NATO Medals

Awarded to U.S. military personnel for service under the NATO command and in direct support of NATO operations. Recipients may qualify for such NATO operations as:
(1) Former Yugoslavia: 30 days service inside or 90 days outside the former Republic of Yugoslavia after July 1, 1992 to a date to be determined.
(2) Kosovo: 30 continuous/accumulated days in or around the former Yugoslavian province of Kosovo from October 13, 1998 to a date to be determined.

Multiple rotations or tours in either operational area will only qualify for a single award of that medal.

The NATO Medal, like the United Nations Medal, has a common planchet/pendant but comes with unique ribbons for each operation. As in the case of the United Nations, U.S. Service personnel who qualify for both NATO Medals will wear the first medal/ribbon awarded and a bronze service star on the ribbon bar and suspension ribbon to denote the second award. As before however, the two medal clasps which may accompany the medal. i.e., "FORMER YUGOSLAVIA and KOSOVO" may not be worn on the U.S. military uniform.

The medal is a bronze disk featuring the NATO symbol in the center surrounded by olive branches around the periphery. The reverse contains the inscription, "NORTH ATLANTIC TREATY ORGANIZATION" in English around the top edge and the same wording in French along the lower edge. A horizontal olive branch separates the central area into two areas. Atop this, set in three lines, is the inscription, "IN SERVICE OF PEACE AND FREEDOM" in English. The same text in French on four lines is inscribed in the lower half.

In November, 2002, the NATO Military Committee issued a new NATO Medal Policy in which two classes of service awards will now be issued, namely "Article 5" and "Non-Article 5". The reference is to Article 5 of the original NATO Charter Treaty in which the member nations agreed that an armed attack against any one of them in Europe or North America shall be considered an attack against them all and if such an armed attack occurs, each of them will take such action, including the use of armed force, to restore and maintain the security of the North Atlantic area. Non-Article 5 operations are those conducted as a peace support or crisis operation authorized by the North Atlantic Council.

To date, two Article 5 Medals have been issued by NATO, the first being for Operation "Eagle Assist". Following the 9-11 attacks, NATO Early Warning (NAEW&C) aircraft were deployed from October 12, 2001 to May 16, 2002, to monitor the airspace over the United States to protect against further airborne attack by terrorists.

The second award, is awarded to personnel who took part in Operation "Active Endeavor", the deployment of a NATO Standing Naval Force to patrol the Eastern Mediterranean against hostile forces. That effort began on October 26, 2001 and will be terminated at a date to be announced in the future. In addition, two Non-Article 5 NATO have been authorized for U.S. military personnel. The qualification period for

### NATO Medal
**Service:** All Services
**Instituted:** 1992
**Criteria:** 30 days service in or 90 days outside the former Republic of Yugoslavia and the Adriatic Sea under NATO command in direct support of NATO operations.
**Devices:** ★
**Notes:** Above date denotes when award was authorized for wear by U.S. military personnel. "Former Yugoslavia" and "Kosovo" Bars not authorized for wear by U.S. Military personnel.

### Article 5 NATO Medal
**Service:** All Services
**Instituted:** 2002
**Criteria:** 30 days service as part of Operation "Eagle Assist" (Medal 1) or Operation Active Endeavor (Medal 2).
**Devices:** ★
**Notes:** As per a memorandum issued by the Deputy Secretary of Defense dated 2 March 2006, the above medals are now authorized for wear on the uniform by U.S. military personnel.

### Non-Article 5 NATO Medal and ISAF Medal
**Service:** All Services
**Instituted:** 2002
**Criteria:** 30 days service as part of NATO operations in the Balkans (Medal 3) of Afghanistan (Medal 4).
**Devices:** ★
**Notes:** As per a memorandum issued by the Deputy Secretary of Defense dated 2 March 2006, the above medals are now authorized for wear on the uniform by U.S. military personnel.

the NATO Balkans Medal is thirty days of continuous or accumulated service from January 1, 2003 to a date to be determined. The NATO medals for Afghanistan and Iraq are also awarded for 30 days of service in country.

The medal designs are the same as all previous NATO Medals. As in the past, only one NATO Medal may be worn on the uniform with subsequent operations and/or tours indicated by bronze stars affixed to the center of the ribbon bar or suspension ribbons. Also as before, the mission bars depicted above may not be worn on the U.S. military uniform.

### The NATO Meritorious Service Medal

The NATO Meritorious Service Medal

**The NATO Meritorious Service Medal** was established in 2003 for military and civilian personnel commended for providing exceptional or remarkable service to NATO. The Medal is the personal Award of The Secretary General of NATO, who signs each citation. Generally fewer than 50 medals are awarded each year and it is the only significant award for individual effort on the NATO staff. It can be awarded to both Military and Civilian staff. The criteria for the award reflects: the performance of acts of courage in difficult or dangerous circumstances; showing exceptional leadership or personal example; making an outstanding individual contribution to a NATO sponsored program or activity; or enduring particular hardship or deprivation in the interest of NATO.

The ribbon and medal fabric is NATO Blue with white edges, with silver and gold threads centered on the white. The medal disc is of silver color, occasional you will see copies being sold with the regular brass medallion. The NATO Meritorious Service Medal is now authorized for wear on U.S. Military uniforms.

## Multinational Force & Observers Medal

The international peacekeeping force known as The Multinational Force and Observers (MFO) was established following the ratification of the Camp David Accords and the 1979 peace treaty between Israel and Egypt. Its sole purpose was to monitor the withdrawal of Israeli forces from the occupied portions of the Sinai Peninsula and the return of that territory to the sovereignty of Egypt.

The MFO Medal was established by the Director General on March 24, 1982 to recognize those personnel who served at least 90 days with the Multinational Force and Observers after August 3,1981 (the requirement was changed to 170 days after March 15, 1985). Periods of service on behalf of the MFO outside the Sinai are also counted towards medal eligibility.

The medal is a bronze disk depicting a stylized dove of peace surrounded by olive branches in its center. Around the edge of the medallion are the raised inscriptions, "MULTINATIONAL FORCE" at the top and, "& OBSERVERS" on the lower half. The reverse is plain with the inscription, "UNITED IN SERVICE FOR PEACE" set on 5 lines (all inscriptions are in English).

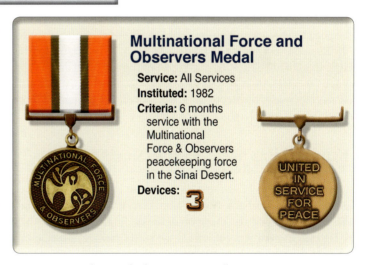

**Multinational Force and Observers Medal**
Service: All Services
Instituted: 1982
Criteria: 6 months service with the Multinational Force & Observers peacekeeping force in the Sinai Desert.
Devices: 3

## Inter-American Defense Board Medal

The medal and ribbon were authorized on December 11, 1945 by the Inter-American Defense Board, (IADB) and were approved by the U.S. Department of Defense for wear by U.S. military personnel on May 12, 1981. The IADB Medal is classified as a foreign service award and is awarded for permanent wear to military personnel who have served on the Inter-American Defense Board for at least one year, either as chairman of the board, delegates, advisors, officers of the staff, as officers of the secretariat or officers of the Inter-American Defense College. The medal is a golden-bronze circular disk with a representation of the globe of the world in the center depicting the Western Hemisphere. Around the periphery of the globe are the arrayed the flags of the member nations of the IADB. The reverse of the medal is plain. A five-sixteenth inch diameter gold star device is worn on the ribbon bar and the suspension ribbon for each five years of service to the IADB.

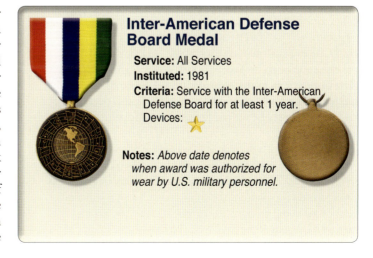

**Inter-American Defense Board Medal**
Service: All Services
Instituted: 1981
Criteria: Service with the Inter-American Defense Board for at least 1 year.
Devices: ★

Notes: Above date denotes when award was authorized for wear by U.S. military personnel.

## Republic of Vietnam Campaign Medal

The Republic of Vietnam Campaign Medal was established by the Government of the Republic of Vietnam on May 12, 1964 and authorized for award to members of the United States Armed Forces by the Department of Defense on June 20, 1966. To qualify for award, personnel must meet one of the following requirements:

(1) Have served in the Republic of Vietnam for 6 months during the period from March 1, 1961 to March 28, 1973.
(2) Have served outside the geographical limits of the Republic of Vietnam and contributed direct combat support to the Republic of Vietnam and Armed Forces for six months. Such individuals must meet the criteria established for the Armed Forces Expeditionary Medal (Vietnam) or the Vietnam Service Medal, during the period of service required to qualify for the Republic of Vietnam Campaign Medal.
(3) Have served for less than six months and have been wounded by hostile forces, captured by hostile forces, but later escaped, was rescued or released or killed in action.

Special eligibility rules were established for personnel assigned in the Republic of Vietnam on January 28, 1973. To be eligible for the medal, an individual must have served a minimum of 60 days in the Republic of Vietnam as of that date or have completed a minimum of 60 days service in the Republic of Vietnam during the period from January 28, 1973 to March 28, 1973, inclusive.

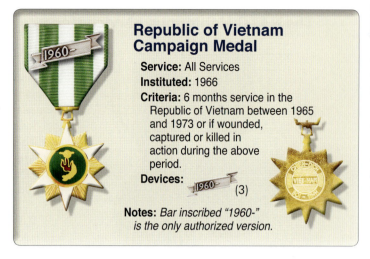

**Republic of Vietnam Campaign Medal**
Service: All Services
Instituted: 1966
Criteria: 6 months service in the Republic of Vietnam between 1965 and 1973 or if wounded, captured or killed in action during the above period.
Devices: (3)
Notes: Bar inscribed "1960-" is the only authorized version.

The Republic of Vietnam Campaign Medal is a white six-pointed star with cut lined, broad gold star points between and a central green disk with a map of Vietnam in silver surmounted with three painted flames in red, signifying the three regions of Vietnam. The reverse contains the inscription, "VIET-NAM" in a lined circle in the center with the name of the medal inscribed in Vietnamese text at the upper and lower edges separated by many short lines. The device, an integral part of the award, is a silver ribbon 28mm long on the suspension ribbon and 15mm long on the service bar inscribed, "1960-   " and was evidently intended to include a terminal date for the hostilities. Many examples of this medal are found with devices inscribed with other dates but the only version authorized for U.S. personnel is the one described.

## Kuwait Liberation Medal (Saudi Arabia)

Established in 1991 by the Government of Saudi Arabia for members of the Coalition Forces who participated in Operation DESERT STORM and the liberation of Kuwait. In the same year, the U.S. Defense Department authorized the acceptance and wearing of the Kuwait Liberation Medal by members of the Armed Forces of the United States.

To be eligible, U.S. military personnel must have served for at least one day in support of Operation DESERT STORM between January 17 and February 28, 1991 in The Persian Gulf, Red Sea, Gulf of Oman, portions of the Arabian Sea, The Gulf of Aden or the total land areas of Iraq, Kuwait, Saudi Arabia, Oman, Bahrain, Qatar and the United Arab Emirates. The recipient must have been attached to or regularly serving for one or more days with an organization participating in ground and/or shore operations, aboard a naval vessel directly supporting military operations, actually participating as a crew member in one or more aerial flights supporting military operations in the areas designated above or serving on temporary duty for 30 consecutive days during this period. That time limitation may be waived for people participating in actual combat operations.

The medal depicts the map of Kuwait in the center with a crown at its top between two encircling palm branches, all of which is fashioned in gold. Above this is a gold palm tree surmounted by two crossed swords. Surrounding the entire design is a representation of an exploding bomb in silver. The reverse is plain. The ribbon bar is issued with a replica of the palm tree with crossed swords found on the medal and is the only authorized attachment.

**Saudi Arabian Medal for the Liberation of Kuwait**
Service: All Services
Instituted: 1991
Criteria: Participation in, or support of, Operation Desert Storm. (Jan.-Feb. 1991).
Devices: (56)

# Kuwait Liberation Medal (Emirate of Kuwait)

Established in July, 1994 by the Government of Kuwait for members of the United States military who participated in Operations DESERT SHIELD and DESERT STORM. On March 16, 1995, the Secretary of Defense authorized the acceptance and wearing of the Kuwait Liberation Medal (Kuwait) by members of the Armed Forces of the United States. To be eligible, U.S. military personnel must have served in support of Operations DESERT SHIELD and DESERT STORM between August 2, 1990 and August 31, 1993, in The Arabian Gulf, Red Sea, Gulf of Oman, portions of the Arabian Sea, The Gulf of Aden or the total land areas of Iraq, Kuwait, Saudi Arabia, Oman, Bahrain, Qatar and the United Arab Emirates. The recipient must have been attached to or regularly serving for one or more days with an organization participating in ground and/or shore operations, aboard a naval vessel directly supporting military operations, actually participating as a crew member in one or more aerial flights directly supporting military operations in the areas designated above or serving on temporary duty for 30 consecutive days or 60 nonconsecutive days during this period. That time limitation may be waived for people participating in actual combat operations. The Kuwait Liberation Medal (Kuwait) follows the Kuwait Liberation Medal from the government of Saudi Arabia in the order of precedence.

The medal is a bronze disk which depicts the Kuwaiti Coat of Arms with the Arabic inscription, "1991 - Liberation Medal." The

### Kuwaiti Medal for the Liberation of Kuwait
**Service:** All Services
**Instituted:** 1995
**Criteria:** Participation in, or support of, Operations Desert Shield and/or Desert Storm (1990-93).
**Devices:** None

**Notes:** Above date denotes when award was authorized for wear by U.S. military personnel.

reverse contains a map of Kuwait with a series of rays emanating from the center out to the edge of the medal - all in bas-relief. The ribbon bar may be one of the most unusual ever displayed on the American military uniform. It consists of three equal stripes of red, white and green with a black, trapezoidal-shaped section silk-screened across the entire upper half. No attachments are authorized for the medal or ribbon.

Did You Know? The Kuwait Liberation Medal was approved by the Kuwait Council of Ministers for award in five classes, generally according to the rank of the recipient. The only version authorized U.S. service personnel is the 5th class award.

# Republic of Korea War Service Medal

The Republic of Korea War Service Medal was established in 1951 by the Government of the Republic of Korea for presentation to the foreign military personnel who served on or over the Korean Peninsula or in its territorial waters between June 27, 1950 and July 27, 1953. However, it was not approved for acceptance and wear by the U.S. until 1999. To be eligible for this award, U.S. military personnel must have been on permanent assignment or on temporary duty for 30 consecutive days or 60 non-consecutive days. The duty must have been performed within the territorial limits of Korea, in the waters immediately adjacent thereto or in aerial flight over Korea participating in actual combat operations or in support of combat operations. The 48 year interval between establishment and its formal acceptance represents the second longest period of time in U.S. history between a significant national and military conflict and the award of an appropriate medal.

The medal is a bronze disk containing a map of the Korean Peninsula at top center over a grid of the world and olive branches on either side of the design. Below the map are two crossed bullets. In the center of the ribbon and earlier medal drapes (1950's), is an ancient oriental symbol called a taeguk (the top half is red and the bottom half is blue). The reverse contains the inscription, "FOR SERVICE IN KOREA" in English embossed on two lines with two small blank plaques on which the recipient's name may be engraved.

### Republic of Korea War Service Medal
**Service:** All Services **Instituted:** 1953
**Criteria:** Service on the Korean Peninsula between 1950 and 1953
**Devices:** None

**Notes:** Above date denotes when award was authorized for wear by U.S. military personnel. Notes: Not accepted by the United States Government for wear on the military uniform until 1999. *Some original 1953 medals had a taeguk in the center of the drape like the ribbon bar.

Medals of America 225

# Marksmanship Medals

The Marksmanship Medal is a United States Navy and the U.S. Coast Guard military award and is the highest award one may receive for weapons qualification. The Marksmanship Medal is the equivalent of the U.S. Army and U.S. Marine Corps Expert Marksmanship Badge.

The Marksmanship Medal is awarded for qualifying as an expert marksman on either the Beretta M9 (Navy or Coast Guard), SIG P229 DAK (Coast Guard only), or M16 rifle. To qualify at the expert level, a superior score must be obtained on an approved weapons qualification course. The standard Navy weapons qualification course for pistol consists of several courses of fire from standing and supported kneeling positions. For the rifle, the Navy qualification course consists of firing from a sitting and prone positions.

Personnel qualifying as an expert marksman are authorized to wear the Marksmanship Medal, awarded as a separate decorations for rifle or pistol qualifications. Service members qualifying on both pistol and rifle receive both medals for wear. The Marksmanship Medal is worn as a full-sized medal on dress uniforms. On a duty uniform all qualifiers wear the award as the standard Marksmanship Ribbon. Those qualifying as an expert are authorized to wear the Expert device on the ribbon and those qualifying as a sharpshooter are authorized a "S" device.

For a decade, from 1910 to 1920, the U.S. Navy awarded a marksmanship badge, called the Navy Sharpshooter's Badge, to Sailors who qualified with the service rifle and/or service pistol. Today, Sailors are awarded marksmanship ribbons and medals to denote service weapon qualification.

PISTOL SHOT," for the service pistol. Each time a shooter requalified as expert, another Expert Qualification Clasp was hung from the badge. If no Expert Qualification Clasp was suspended from the badge, then the shooter qualified as a sharpshooter ( see example). The Qualification Year Clasp is different in design from the brooch which incorporated three ovals along its access for the placement of Year Disks. The Year Disk was made of silver and embossed with the year the shooter qualified/requalified. On the fourth requalification year, another Qualification Year Clasp was hung from the badge with a fourth Year Disk embossed with the year of requalification. There was no limit to the number of clasps that could be hung from the badge. The badge's pendant is the design basis for today's U.S. Navy marksmanship medals. The only difference between the pendant of the Navy Sharpshooter's Badge and the Navy Expert Rifleman Medal or Expert Pistol Shot Medal is the metal color (from antique bronze to gold), the deletion of the crossed rifles from behind a replica of a rifle target, and the addition of the words "EXPERT RIFLEMAN" or "EXPERT PISTOL SHOT" embossed above the rifle target.

Starting in 1920, U.S. Navy marksmanship ribbons replaced the Navy Sharpshooter's Badge. There are two types of U.S. Navy marksmanship ribbons, the U.S. Navy Rifle Marksmanship Ribbon and one for the U.S. Navy Pistol Marksmanship Ribbon. Each can be embellished with a marksmanship device to denote the shooter's qualification level. A silver "E" Device is awarded to those who qualify

The Navy Sharpshooter's Badge 1912

Expert Rifleman Medal 1941

The Navy Sharpshooter's Badge was awarded at two qualification levels, expert and sharpshooter. The Navy Sharpshooter's Badge was made of antique bronze with a rectangular brooch that had the word "SHARPSHOOTER" embossed in its center with circling serpent bookends. The badge's pendant hung from two types of clasps, an Expert Qualification Clasp and a Qualification Year Clasp. The Expert Qualification Clasp is identical in design to the brooch but with the word(s) "EXPERT," for the service rifle, or "EXPERT

as an expert (the highest qualification level) while a bronze "S" Device is awarded to those who qualify as a sharpshooter (second highest qualification). If no marksmanship device is displayed, the shooter qualified as a marksman (lowest qualification level). For an unknown period of time, a bronze "E" Device was awarded to those who initially qualified as expert; after three consecutive expert qualifications, the device turned to silver with a permanent award status. Starting in 1969, the Expert Rifleman Medal and Expert Pistol Shot

Medal were introduced and are awarded to Sailors who qualify as expert along with the appropriate U.S. Navy marksmanship ribbon with silver "E" Device.

A silver "E" Device is awarded for qualification as an expert (the highest qualification level).

A bronze "S" Device is awarded for qualification as a sharpshooter (second highest qualification).

Expert Pistol shot 1955

## Navy Expert Rifleman Medal

The Navy Expert Rifleman Medal was designed by the U.S. Mint and is awarded to members of the U.S. Navy and Naval Reserve who qualify as Expert with a rifle on a prescribed military rifle course. The medallion is a bronze disc bordered with a rope edge. The ribbon hangs from a smaller disc superimposed at the top containing the figure of an eagle clutching an anchor in its talons, taken from the seal of the U.S. Navy. The larger disc has a raised "bull's eye" (rifle target) in the center. Above the bull's eye is the raised inscription, "EXPERT RIFLEMAN" and on the lower edge, the curved inscription, "UNITED STATES NAVY." The reverse of the medallion is blank for engraving. The ribbon is navy blue with three thin light green stripes. Although originally intended as a single, one class award, the concept was extended during the Vietnam War to provide for two additional levels of achievement with the creation of the Navy Rifle Marksmanship Ribbon.

**Service:** Navy

**Criteria:** Attainment of the minimum qualifying score for the expert level during prescribed shooting exercises.

**Devices:** None

## Navy Expert Pistol Shot Medal

The Navy Expert Pistol Shot Badge was created at the same time as the Navy Expert Rifleman Badge and is awarded to Naval Personnel who qualify as experts with the pistol on a prescribed military course. The medallion is the same as the Expert Rifleman badge except for the raised inscription, "EXPERT PISTOL SHOT." The ribbon is navy blue with a narrow light green stripe at each edge. Also like its rifle counterpart, the concept was later extended to provide for two additional levels of achievement with the creation of the Navy Pistol Marksmanship Ribbon.

**Service:** Navy

**Criteria:** Attainment of the minimum qualifying score for the expert level during prescribed shooting exercises.

**Devices:** None

## Navy Rifle Marksmanship Ribbon

The Navy Rifle Marksmanship Ribbon was established by the Secretary of the Navy on October 14, 1969 to extend the range of marksmanship awards below the Expert level. To create this "ribbon-only" award, the ribbon of the Navy Expert Rifleman Medal was retained and redesignated as the Navy Rifle Marksmanship Ribbon with devices to denote the Marksman and Sharpshooter levels. To indicate the various levels, the ribbon for the Marksman level is unadorned and the Sharpshooter level uses a bronze letter "S". To reward the attainment of the Expert level, the medal is retained unadorned but a silver letter "E," is placed on the ribbon bar. The ribbon is navy blue with three thin stripes of light green. Attachment letters are affixed to the center of the ribbon. Earlier regulations provided for a bronze letter "E" to denote to first qualification at the Expert level and the silver "E" to indicate the "final" achievement of Expert status but this was soon discontinued in favor of the silver "E".

**Service:** Navy
**Criteria:** Attainment of the minimum qualifying score during prescribed shooting exercises.
**Devices:** S (20) E (12,13)

## Navy Pistol Marksmanship Ribbon

The Navy Pistol Marksmanship Ribbon was established by the Secretary of the Navy on October 14, 1969 to extend the range of marksmanship awards below the Expert level. To create this "ribbon-only" award, the ribbon of the Navy Expert Pistol Shot Medal was retained and redesignated as the Navy Pistol Marksmanship Ribbon with devices to denote the various levels. To indicate the Marksman level, the ribbon is unadorned while the Sharpshooter level uses a bronze letter "S". To reward the attainment of the Expert level, the medal is retained unadorned but a silver letter "E," is placed on the ribbon bar. The ribbon is navy blue with two thin stripes of light green. Attachment letters are affixed to the center of the ribbon. Earlier regulations provided for a bronze letter "E" to denote to first qualification at the Expert level and the silver "E" to indicate the "final" achievement of Expert status but this was soon discontinued in favor of the silver "E".

**Service:** Navy
**Criteria:** Attainment of the minimum qualifying score during prescribed shooting exercises.
**Devices:** S (20) E (12,13)

## Coast Guard Expert Rifleman Medal

The Coast Guard Expert Rifleman Medal was established to reward outstanding rifle marksmanship and to recognize the attainment of the minimum qualifying score for the Expert level during prescribed shooting exercises. The medal is a bronze pendant in the shape of a shield, the upper portion of which contains the raised inscription, "U.S. COAST GUARD EXPERT" in two lines. In the center of the medal is a pair of crossed rifles beneath which is a rifle target. The reverse is plain and is suitable for engraving the recipient's name. The ribbon is navy blue with four thin white stripes, two near the center and one each towards the edges. Although originally intended as a single, one class award, the concept was extended during the Vietnam War to provide for two additional levels of achievement with the creation of the Coast Guard Rifle Marksmanship Ribbon.

**Service:** Coast Guard
**Criteria:** Attainment of the minimum qualifying score for the expert level during prescribed shooting exercises.
**Devices:** None

## Coast Guard Expert Pistol Shot Medal

The Coast Guard Expert Pistol Shot Medal was established to reward outstanding pistol marksmanship and to recognize the attainment of the minimum qualifying score for the Expert level during prescribed shooting exercises. The medal is a bronze pendant in the shape of a shield, the upper portion of which contains the raised inscription, "U.S. COAST GUARD EXPERT" in two lines. In the center of the medal is a pair of crossed pistols beneath which is a pistol target. The reverse is plain and is suitable for engraving the recipient's name. The ribbon is navy blue with two thin white stripes, one each towards each edge. Although originally intended as a single, one class award, the concept was extended during the Vietnam War to provide for two additional levels of achievement with the creation of the Coast Guard Pistol Marksmanship Ribbon.

**Service:** Coast Guard
**Criteria:** Attainment of the minimum qualifying score for the expert level during prescribed shooting exercises.
**Devices:** None

## Coast Guard Rifle Marksmanship Ribbon

The Coast Guard Rifle Marksmanship Ribbon was established to extend the range of marksmanship awards below the Expert level. To create this "ribbon only" award, the ribbon of the Coast Guard Expert Rifleman Medal was retained and redesignated as the Coast Guard Rifle Marksmanship Ribbon with devices to denote the various levels. To indicate the Marksman level, the ribbon is unadorned while the Sharpshooter level uses a silver letter "S". For the Expert level, the medal is retained unadorned but a silver letter "E" is placed on the ribbon bar. Earlier regulations provided for a bronze letter "E" to denote to first qualification at the Expert level and the silver "E" to indicate the "final" achievement of Expert status but this was soon discontinued in favor of the silver "E". The silver and bronze M14 rifle replicas de-

**Service:** Coast Guard
**Criteria:** Attainment of the minimum qualifying score during prescribed shooting exercises.
**Devices:**

 (21)  (12,13)  (109) (59,60)

note the award of the Silver and Bronze Rifleman Excellence in Competition Badges respectively. The gold replica of a rifle target indicates the award of the Distinguished Marksman Badge. All attachments are affixed to the center of the ribbon.

## Coast Guard Pistol Marksmanship Ribbon

The Coast Guard Pistol Marksmanship Ribbon was established to extend the range of marksmanship awards below the Expert level. To create this "ribbon only" award, the ribbon of the Coast Guard Expert Pistol Shot Medal was retained and redesignated as the Coast Guard Pistol Marksmanship Ribbon with devices to denote the various levels. To indicate the Marksman level, the ribbon is unadorned while the Sharpshooter level uses a silver letter "S". For the Expert level, the medal is retained unadorned but a silver letter "E" is placed on the ribbon bar. Earlier regulations provided for a bronze letter "E" to denote to first qualification at the Expert level and the silver "E" to indicate the "final" achievement of Expert status but this was soon discon-

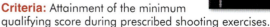

**Service:** Coast Guard
**Criteria:** Attainment of the minimum qualifying score during prescribed shooting exercises.
**Devices:**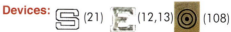

tinued in favor of the silver "E". The silver and bronze M1911A1 pistol replicas denote the award of the Silver and Bronze Pistol Shot Excellence in Competition Badges respectively. The gold replica of a pistol target indicates the award of the Distinguished Pistol Shot Badge. All attachments are affixed to the center of the ribbon.

The numbers in parentheses next to the Devices refer to the tables in "Attachments and Devices" on page 116-119.

# Bibliography

Abbott, P.E. and Tamplin, J.M.A. - *British Gallantry Awards*, 1971
Adjutant General of the Army - *American Decorations 1862-1926*, 1927
Belden, B.L. - *United States War Medals*, 1916
Borts, L.H. - *United Nations Medals and Missions*, 1998
Committee on Veterans' Affairs, U.S. Senate - *Medal of Honor Recipients 1863-1978*, 1979
Dept. of Defense Manual DOD 1348.33M - *Manual of Military Decorations & Awards*, 1996, Change 1 (2006)
Dorling, H.T. - *Ribbons and Medals*, 1983
Foster, Frank,C. - *Complete Guide to United States Army Medals, Badges and Insignia*, 2004
Foster, Frank,C. - *Marine Awards and Insignia*, 2018
Foster, Frank,C. - *Medals and Ribbons of the USAF*, 2017
Foster, Frank,C. - *Military Ribbon Guide for Army, Navy, Marines, Air Force and Coast Guard*, 2018
Foster, Frank,C. - *U. S. Marine Corps Military Ribbon & Medal Wear Guide*, 2018
Foster, Frank,C. and Borts, L.H. - *Military Medals of the United States*, 2008
Gleim, A.F. - *United States Medals of Honor 1862-1989*, 1989
Gleim, A.F. - *War Department Gallantry Citations for Pre W W I Service*, 1986
Inter-American Defense Board- *Norms for Protocol, Symbols, Insignia and Gifts*, 1984
Kerrigan, E. - *American Badges and Insignia*, 1967
Kerrigan, E. - *American Medals and Decorations*, 1990
Kerrigan, E. - *American War Medals and Decorations*, 1971
Lelle, John E. - *The Brevet Medal*, 1988
Mayo, J.H. - *Medals and Decorations of the British Army & Navy*, 1897
McDowell, C.P. - *Military and Naval Decorations of the United States*, 1984
*National Geographic Magazine*, December, 1919
National Geographic Society - *Insignia and Decorations of the U.S. Armed Forces*, 1944
Strandberg, J.E. and Bender, R.J. - *The Call to Duty*, 1994
Talley, Naomi - *Medals for Brave Men*, 1963
U.S. Air Force Instruction 36-2903 - *Dress and Personal Appearance of U.S.A.F. Personnel*, Sept, 2002
U.S. Air Force Instruction 36-2803 - *The Air Force Awards and Decorations Program*, June, 2001
U.S. Army Regulation 670 -1- *Wear and Appearance of Army Uniforms and Insignia*, 2005
U.S. Army Regulation 600-8-22- *Military Awards*, 2006
U.S. Coast Guard Instruction M1020.6F - *U.S. Coast Guard Uniform Regulations*, 2009
U.S. Coast Guard Instruction M1650.25D - *Medals and Awards Manual*, 2008
U.S. Marine Corps Order P1020.34G - *U.S. Marine Corps Uniform Regulations*, 2003
U.S. Navy Instruction SECNAVINST 1650.1H - *Navy and Marine Corps Awards Manual*, 2006
U.S. Navy Instruction SECNAVINST 15665J - *United States Navy Uniform Regulations*, 2008
U.S. Navy Manual NAVPERS 15,790 - *Decorations, Medals, Ribbons and Badges of the United States Navy, Marine Corps and Coast Guard, 1861-1948*, 1 July 1950
Vietnam Council on Foreign Relations - *Awards & Decorations of Vietnam*, 1972
Wilkins, P.A. - *The History of the Victoria Cross*, 1904
Wyllie, Col. R.E. - *Orders, Decorations and Insignia*, 1921

# Index

## A

**Actual Size Military Medal Variations 37**
  Anodized or Gold-Plated 37
  Brass Plates 37
  Bronze 37
  Enamel Hat Pins (unofficial) 37
  Enamel Lapel Pins 37
  Miniature Medals 37
  Mini Ribbons (unofficial) 37
  Regulation Ribbon Bars 37
Aerial Achievement Medal 160
Afghanistan Campaign Medal 196
Air Force Achievement Medal 165
Air Force Air and Space Campaign Medal 207
Air Force Basic Military Training (BMT) Honor Graduate Ribbon 215
Air Force Combat Action Medal 167
Air Force Commendation Medal 162
Air Force Cross 145
Air Force Expeditionary Service Ribbon 208
Air Force Gallant Unit Citation 169
Air Force Good Conduct Medal 176
Air Force Longevity Service Award Ribbon 208
Air Force Medal of Honor 134
Air Force Medals of Honor 142
  Air Force Medal of Honor 143
  Army Medal of Honor 142
Air Force Meritorious Unit Award 170
Air Force Military Training Instructor Ribbon 209
Air Force N.C.O. Professional Military Education Graduate Ribbon 215
Air Force Organizational Excellence Award 170
Air Force Outstanding Unit Award 170
Air Force Overseas Ribbon (Long Tour) 208
Air Force Overseas Ribbon (Short Tour) 208
Air Force Presidential Unit Citation 168
Air Force Recognition Ribbon 181
Air Force Recruiter Ribbon 209
Air Force Training Ribbon 215
Airman's Medal 154
Air Medal 159
Air Reserve Forces Meritorious Service Medal 179
Ameica's first military medal 12
American Campaign Medal 184
American Defense Service Medal 183
Andre Medal 18
Antarctica Service Medal 192
Anthony Wayne medal 14
Arctic Service Medal 192
Armed Forces Expeditionary Medal 193
Armed Forces Reserve Medal 212
Armed Forces Service Medal 202
Army Achievement Medal 164
Army and Navy Civil War Campaign Medals 22
Army Commendation Medal 161
Army Distinguished Service Cross First Version 28
Army Good Conduct Medal 174
Army Medal of Honor 9, 134
Army Medals of Honor 138
Army Meritorious Unit Commendation 169
Army N.C.O. Professional Development Ribbon 213
Army Occupation Medal 30
Army of Cuban Occupation Medal (Army) 127
Army of Cuban Pacification Medal (Army) 127
Army of Occupation Medal 188
Army of Occupation of Germany Medal (Army) 130
Army of Occupation of Puerto Rico Medal (Army) 127
Army Overseas Service Ribbon 213
Army Presidential Unit Citation 167
Army Reserve Components Achievement Medal 177
Army Reserve Components Overseas Training Ribbon 214
Army Sea Duty Ribbon 211
Army Service Ribbon 213
Army Superior Unit Award 171
Army Valorous Unit Award 169
Asiatic-Pacific Campaign Medal 184, 185
Aztec Club Medal 21
Aztec Club of 1847 24

## B

Badge of Military Merit 19
Battle of Culloden medal 8
Battle of Dunbar medal 8
Battle of Eutaw Springs medal 17
Battle of Flamborough Head 15
Battle of Paulus Hook 15
Benjamin Franklin's Victory Medal 17
Borts, Lawrence 2
Brig. Gen. Morgan gold medal 16
Bronze Star Medal 156

## C

Capt. John Paul Jones gold medal  15
Certificate of Merit Medal (Army)  27
China Campaign Medal (Army)  127
China Relief Expedition Medal (Navy)  127
China Service Medal  182
Civil War Campaign Medal (Army)  125
Civil War Medals of Honor  22
Civil War Service Medal (Navy)  125
Coast Guard Achievement Medal  166
Coast Guard Basic Training Honor Graduate Ribbon  211
Coast Guard Bicentennial Unit Commendation  172
Coast Guard Combat Action Ribbon  167
Coast Guard Commandant's Letter of Commendation Ribbon  166
Coast Guard Commendation Medal  163
Coast Guard Cross  146
Coast Guard Enlisted Person of the Year Ribbon  180
Coast Guard "E" Ribbon  172
Coast Guard Expert Pistol Shot Medal  229
Coast Guard Expert Rifleman Medal  228
Coast Guard Good Conduct Medal  177
Coast Guard Medal  154
Coast Guard Meritorious Team Commendation  172
Coast Guard Meritorious Unit Commendation  171
Coast Guard Overseas Service Ribbon  210
Coast Guard Pistol Marksmanship Ribbon  229
Coast Guard Presidential Unit Citation  168
Coast Guard Recruiting Service Ribbon  211
Coast Guard Reserve Good Conduct Medal  179
Coast Guard Restricted Duty Ribbon  210
Coast Guard Rifle Marksmanship Ribbon  229
Coast Guard Sea Service Ribbon  210
Coast Guard Special Operations Service Ribbon  210
Coast Guard Unit Commendation  171
Colonel De Fleury's silver medal  14
Combat Readiness Medal  173
**Commonly Awarded Foreign Unit Awards 218**
  Korean Republic Presidential Unit Citation  218
  Philippine Republic Presidential Unit Citation  218
  Republic of Vietnam Civil Actions Unit Citation  218
  Republic of Vietnam Gallantry Cross Unit Citation  218
  Republic of Vietnam Presidential Unit Citation  218
Confederate Medals  23
Congressional Gold medal 1847  21
Congressional medal  8
Cuban Occupation Medal Army  25
Cuban Pacification Medal (Navy)  128

## D

Defense Distinguished Service Medal  146
Defense Meritorious Service Medal  158
Defense Superior Service Medal  150
Department of Homeland Security Distinguished Service Medal (Coast Guard)  148
Department of Transportation Outstanding Unit Award  171
**Display Case  81**
  Engraved brass plate  81
  Golbal War on Terror Service Medal  81
  Good Conduct Medal Marine  81
  Iraq Service Medal  81
  Marine Corps medallion  81
  Marine Insignia  81
  Name plates  81
  Personal Decoration  81
  Ribbon rack  81
Distinguished Flying Cross  152
Distinguished Service Cross  144
Distinguished Service Cross, First Version 1918  144
Distinguished Service Medal (Air Force)  148
Distinguished Service Medal (Army)  147
Distinguished Service Medal (Coast Guard)  149
Distinguished Service Medal (Navy)  147
Dominican Campaign (Navy)  128

## E

**Early United States Military Medals  124**
  Army Certificate of Merit  124
  Army Medal of Honor  124
  Badge of Military Merit  124
  Fidelity Medallion  124
  Good Conduct Badge  124
  Marine Corps Brevet Medal  124
  Navy Medal of Valor  124

## F

**Foreign Military Decorations  216, 217**
  Croix de Guerre  216
  Republic of Vietnam Armed Forces Honor Medal  217
  Republic of Vietnam Civil Actions Medal  217
  Republic of Vietnam Gallantry Cross  217
  Republic of Vietnam Staff Service Medal  217
  Republic of Vietnam Technical Service  217
  Republic of Vietnam Training Medal  217
French Medal of Constantine  8

## G

General Gates' Gold Medal  13
General Society of the War of 1812  24
**Global War on Terrorism and Liberation of Afghanistan and Iraq (2001 to Present)  35**
  Afghanistan Campaign Medal  35
  Global War on Terrorism Expeditionary Medal  35
  Global War on Terrorism Service Medal  35
  Iraq Campaign Medal  35
Global War on Terrorism Expeditionary Medal  200
Global War on Terrorism Service Medal  201
Gold and Silver Palmetto Regt. Medals  21
Gold Lifesaving Medal  155
Grand Army of the Republic Society medal  24
Grand Army of the Republic Society Medal  24
**Gulf War (1991-1995)  34**
  Kuwait Medal for the Liberation of Kuwait  34
  National Defense Service Medal  34
  Saudi Arabian Medal for the Liberation of Kuwait  34
  Southwest Asia Service Medal  34

## H

Haitian Campaign Medal (Navy)  128
Humanitarian Service Medal  203

## I

Indian Campaign Medal  23
Indian Campaign Medal (Army)  126
Inter-American Defense Board Medal  223
Inherent Resolve Campaign Medal  199
Iraq Campaign Medal  198

## J

Joint Meritorious Unit Award  168
Joint Service Achievement Medal  163
Joint Service Commendation Medal  161

## K

**Korea (1950-1954)  32**
  Korea Defense Service Medal  32
  Korean Presidential Unit Citation  32
  National Defense Service Medal  32
  ROK War Service Medal  32
  UN Korean Service Medal  32
  US Korean Service Medal  32
Korea Defense Service Medal  202
**Korean Campaign Medals 1950-1954  46**
  Good Conduct Medals  46
  National Defense Service  46
  ROK War Service  46
  UN - Korean Service  46
  US - Korea Defense  46
  US - Korean Service  46
Korean Service Medal  191
Kosovo Campaign Medal  196
Kuwait Liberation Medal  226
Kuwait Liberation Medal (Emirate of Kuwait)  225
Kuwait Liberation Medal (Saudi Arabia)  225

## L

Legion of Merit  151
Legion of Merit for Foreign Military Personnel  151
Lt. Colonel Washington silver medal  16

## M

Major John Stewart's Congressional silver medal  14
Manila Bay ("Dewey") Medal  25
Manila Bay ("Dewey") Medal (Navy)  126
Marine Corps Drill Instructor Ribbon  206
Marine Corps Expeditionary Medal  182
Marine Corps Good Conduct Medal  176
Marine Corps Recruiting Ribbon  206
Marine Corps Reserve Ribbon (Obsolete)  214
Marine Security Guard Ribbon  206
Medal for Humane Action  190
**Medal of Honor  135, 137**
  Army Medal of Honor (1862-1896)  138
  Army Medal of Honor (1896-1904)  138
  Army Medal of Honor (1904-1944)  138
Meritorious Service Medal  158
Mexican Border Service Medal (Army)  128
Mexican Service Medal, 1914  26
Mexican Service Medal (Army)  128
Mexican Service Medal (Navy)  128
Military Order of the Dragon 1900  24
Military Order of the Loyal Legion  24
Military Society Medals 1865  24
Multinational Force & Observers Medal  223

## N

National Defense Service Medal  190
**NATO Medals  222**
  Article 5 NATO Medal  222
  NATO Medal  222
  Non-Article 5 NATO Medal and ISAF Medal  222
**NATO Medals (1998 to Present)  34**
  Former Yugoslavia  34
  NATO Article 5 Medal  34
  NATO ISAF Medal  34
  NATO Medal (Kosovo)  34
  NATO Non Article 5 Medal  34
Naval Reserve Medal (Obsolete)  214
Naval Reserve Meritorious Service Medal  178

Naval Reserve Sea Service Ribbon  205
Navy and Marine Corps Achievement Medal  164
Navy and Marine Corps Commendation Medal  162
Navy and Marine Corps Medal  153
Navy and Marine Corps Overseas Service Ribbon  205
Navy Arctic Service Ribbon  204
Navy Ceremonial Guard Ribbon  206
Navy Combat Action Ribbon  166
Navy Cross  28, 145
Navy "E" Ribbon  172
Navy Expeditionary Medal  181
Navy Expert Pistol Shot Medal  227
Navy Expert Rifleman Medal  227
Navy Fleet Marine Force Ribbon  180
Navy Good Conduct Badge of 1869  23
Navy Good Conduct Medal  175
Navy, Marine Corps and Coast Guard Medal of Honor  134
**Navy, Marine Corps and Coast Guard Medals of Honor  140, 141**
   Marine Corps Brevet Medal (1921)  140
   Navy Medal of Honor  141
   Navy Medal of Honor (1861)  140
   Navy Medal of Honor (1913-1917)  140
   Navy Medal of Honor (1917-1942)  140
Navy Medal of Honor  9
Navy Meritorious Unit Commendation  170
Navy Occupation Service Medal  189
Navy Pistol Marksmanship Ribbon  228
Navy Presidential Unit Citation  168
Navy Recruiting Service Ribbon  205
Navy Recruit Training Service Ribbon  205
Navy Rifle Marksmanship Ribbon  228
Navy Sea Service Deployment Ribbon  204
Navy Unit Commendation  169
NC-4 Medal (Navy)  130
Nicaraguan Campaign (Navy)  128

**O**
Order of Saint Louis  8
Order of the Cincinnati  19
Outstanding Airman of the Year Ribbon  180
Outstanding Volunteer Service Medal  204

**P**
Philippine Campaign Medal (Army)  127
Philippine Campaign Medal (Navy)  127
Philippine Congressional Medal (Army)  127
Prisoner of War Medal  173
Purple Heart  157
Purple Heart Medal of 1932  19

**R**
Republic of Korea War Service Medal  225
Republic of Vietnam Campaign Medal  224
Reserve Special Commendation Ribbon (Obsolete)  175

**S**
Selected Marine Corps Reserve Medal  178
Silver Lifesaving Medal  160
Silver Star  150
Small Arms Expert Marksmanship Ribbon  215
Society of the Cincinnatus  24
Soldier's Medal  153
**Southwest Asia, Bosnia/Kosovo, Afghanistan & Iraq Campaign Medals  49**
   Afghanistan Campaign  49
   Good Conduct Medals  49

   Inherent Resolve Campaign  49
   Iraq Campaign  49
   Kosovo Campaign Medal  49
   Kuwait Liberation of Kuwait  49
   National Defense Service Medal  49
   NATO Bosnia Medal  49
   NATO Kosovo Medal  49
   Saudi Arabia Liberation of Kuwait  49
   Southwest Asia Service  49
   War on Terrorism Expeditionary  49
   War on Terrorism Service  49
Southwest Asia Service Medal  195
Spanish Campaign Medal, 1898  26
Spanish Campaign Medal (Army)  126
Spanish Campaign Medal Army  25
Spanish Campaign Medal (Navy)  126
Spanish Campaign Medal Navy, Marines  25
Spanish War Service Medal (Army)  126
Spanish War Service Medal Army  25
Specially Meritorious Medal (Navy)  126
Stonewall Jackson Medal  23

**T**
Texas Cavalry Congressional Medal (Army)  130
Transportation 9-11 Medal  165
Transportation 9-11 Ribbon  209
Transportation Distinguished Service Medal (Department of Transportation)  149
**Types of Military Medals, Ribbons and Devices  36**
   Army Presidential Unit Citation 1942  36
   Army Service Ribbon 1981  36
   Decoration  36
   Navy "E" Ribbon 1976  36
   Navy Presidential Unit Citation 1942  36
   Ribbon and Medal Devices/Attachments  36
   Ribbon Bar with Appropriate Attachments  36
   Service Medal  36

**U**
**United Nations Military Medals  220**
   United Nations Medal  220
   United Nations Service Medal (Korea)  220
**United States Merchant Marine Medals  93**
   Atlantic War Zone Medal  93
   Distinguished Service Medal  93
   Gallant Ship Citation ribbon  93
   Korean Service Medal  93
   Mariners Medal  93
   Mediterranean Middle East War Zone Medal  93
   Merchant Achievement Medal  93
   Merchant Marine Combat Bar  93
   Merchant Marine Defense Medal  93
   Merchant Marine Expeditionary Award  93
   Meritorious Service Medal  93
   Pacific War Zone Medal  93
   Prisoner of War Medal  93
   Soviet Commendation Medal  93
   Victory Medal  93
   Vietnam service Medal  93
U.S. Antarctic Expedition Medal  187
U.S. Marine Corps Display Case  74
U.S. Marines in World War II Pacific Service  75
**USMC Display Case  76**
   Afghanistan and the War on Terror  79
   Afghanistan Service  79, 80
   Cold War Service  76
   Desert Storm  78
   Desert Storm Liberation of Kuwait  78
   Korean Service  76
   Liberation of Iraq  79, 80

   Regular Service  78
   USMC Korean Service  76
   Vietnam Service  77

**V**
Victory Medal of Independence,  9
**Vietnam (1961-1973)  33**
   Armed Forces Expeditionary Medal  33
   Armed Forces Honor Medal  33
   Civil Actions Medal (Foreign Decoration)  33
   National Defense Service Medal  33
   RVN Campaign Medal  33
   RVN Gallantry Cross Unit Citation  33
   U.S. Vietnam Service Medal  33
   Vietnamese Cross of Gallantry (for valor)  33
**Vietnam Campaign Medals 1965-1973  47**
   Good Conduct Medals  47
   National Defense Service Medal  47
   RVN Gallantry Cross Unit Citation  47
   U.S. Vietnam Service Medal  47
   Vietnam Campaign Medal  47
Vietnam Service Medal  194

**W**
West Indies Campaign Medal (Navy)  126
West IndiesCampaign Medal Navy and Marines  25
West Indies Naval Campaign ("Sampson") Medal (Navy)  126
West Indies Naval Campaign (Sampson) Medal (Navy)  25
Women's Army Corps Service Medal  183
WW I, Greenville, S.C. Commemorative  29
**World War II (1941-1945)  30**
   American Campaign Medal  30
   American Defense Service Medal  30
   Army Occupation Medal  30
   Asiatic-Pacific Campaign Medal  30
   European African Middle Eastern Campaign Medal  30
   Navy Occupation Service Medal  30
   Philippine Defense Medal  30
   Philippine Independence Medal  30
   Philippine Liberation Medal  30
   Prisoner of War Medal  30
   Women's Army Corps Medal  30
   WW II Victory Medal  30
**World War II Campaign Medals  44**
   American Campaign Medal  44
   American Defense Service Medal  44
   Asiatic Pacific Campaign  44
   Europe-African-Middle Eastern Campaign  44
   Good Conduct Medals  44
   Philippine Defense Medal  44
   Philippine Liberation Medal  44
   Victory medal  44
   Womens Army Corps Medal  44
   WW II Occupation Medal, Army & Navy  44
**World War II Philippine Military Medals  219**
   Philippine Defense Medal  219
   Philippine Independence Medal  219
   Philippine Liberation Medal  219
World War II Victory Medal  187
World War I Victory Medal  129
World War I Victory Medal with Campaign Clasps  28

**Y**
Yangtze Service Medal (Navy)  130